The Women of Katrina

The Women of Katrina

How Gender, Race, and Class Matter in an American Disaster

EDITED BY EMMANUEL DAVID
AND ELAINE ENARSON

Vanderbilt University Press ■ Nashville

© 2012 by Vanderbilt University Press
Nashville, Tennessee 37235
All rights reserved
First printing 2012

This book is printed on acid-free paper.
Manufactured in the United States of America

Library of Congress Cataloging-in-Publication Data

The women of Katrina : how gender, race, and class matter in
an American disaster / edited by Emmanuel David and Elaine
Enarson.
p. cm.
Includes bibliographical references and index.
ISBN 978-0-8265-1798-2 (cloth edition : alk. paper)
ISBN 978-0-8265-1799-9 (pbk. edition : alk. paper)
1. Hurricane Katrina, 2005—Social aspects. 2. Disasters—Social
aspects. 3. Women—United States—Social conditions. 4. Sexism—
United States. 5. Racism—United States. 6. Social stratification—
United States. I. David, Emmanuel. II. Enarson, Elaine Pitt, 1949–
HV6362005.G85 W66 2011
976′.044—dc22
2011009306

We dedicate this book to the women of the Gulf Coast.
All proceeds will be donated to the Ms. Foundation
for Women in recognition of their grassroots organizing
and continuing efforts to foster women's disaster resilience
in the region.

Contents

Foreword

William A. Anderson

The social science disaster research field is nearly one hundred years old. Samuel Prince's study of the 1917 Halifax, Nova Scotia, ship explosion when he was a sociology graduate student at Columbia University is widely recognized as the first empirical study of a disaster in North America. Since that pioneering study, American social scientists have been in the forefront of disaster research, focusing primarily, though certainly not exclusively, on hazards and disasters in the United States. Knowledge gained through this research has provided needed insights on many aspects of disasters and a basis for science-grounded decisions and actions by policy makers and practitioners such as emergency managers (NRC 2006). Major contributions from social scientists around the world have also drawn attention to the role that gender plays in disasters and how such risks are related to development.

During the years between the Halifax disaster and Hurricane Katrina, which struck the U.S. Gulf Coast region in August 2005, the disaster research field has evolved in terms of the relative prominence of topics on the research agenda and the nature of the scholarly community conducting the research. For example, researchers have broadened the fairly narrowly focused research agenda of the early years to one that now includes the five core topics of what is generally recognized as the disaster cycle: hazard vulnerability, hazard mitigation, disaster preparedness, emergency response, and disaster recovery (NRC 2006). This expansion can be attributed in part to the growing multidisciplinary character of the research community, which now includes not only sociologists and geographers, as in the early days of the field, but also political scientists, economists, anthropologists, and researchers in public administration, public health, and planning, who have brought in a variety of perspectives.

Another factor that has contributed to an expansion in core subject areas is the more recent tendency of researchers to cross disciplinary boundaries in the pursuit of knowledge, which has been facilitated by the movement toward group and team research. Perhaps this is most exemplified by the various social science disaster research centers that have emerged since the pioneering days of the field, such as the Disaster Research Center at the University of Delaware, the Natural Hazards Center at the University of Colorado, and the Hazard Reduction and Recovery Center at Texas A&M University.

In all fields of science, gaps in the research agenda must be apparent before researchers systematically pursue the understudied but critical areas revealed. The social science disaster research field is no exception. Thus while significant advances were being made in understanding such topics as mitigation, preparedness, response, and recovery in the middle years of disaster research, it became apparent more recently that some factors essential to understanding such phenomena were being overlooked or inadequately considered, including those related to disaster politics and conflicts, and to social disparities involving gender, race, ethnicity, and age. Fortunately, U.S. researchers have been helped in understanding the relevance of such factors by the research carried out in countries with more devastating disasters and fewer resources to cope with them.

While the U.S. disaster research community has been slow at times to expand and refocus its agenda in promising new directions, important changes have come about, starting with research carried out by a new generation of social scientists in the 1980s and 1990s, often armed with financial support from U.S. agencies, especially the National Science Foundation. For example, after earthquakes and hurricanes struck communities from California to Florida during this period, fresh insights began emerging on the role that politics and race play in disasters in the United States.

Also about this time, more women were entering the disaster research field than ever before, often after receiving advanced degrees from universities with major research programs in the field. From among such women emerged a network of scholars with the capacity to vigorously champion and pursue gender studies and communicate the results of their research to end users. As noted in the introduction and elsewhere in this book, as a result of women researchers working alone and especially collaborating on teams with other women as well as men, vital knowledge on gender and disaster has emerged in recent years, increasing our understanding of what makes women vulnerable to disasters and what women do throughout the disaster cycle to reduce their own vulnerability and that of their families, neighborhoods, and communities. Thus, the place of gender studies on the disaster research agenda now seems less tenuous than in the past.

In contrast to most U.S. disasters previously studied by U.S. investigators, because of its scale Hurricane Katrina has been characterized as a catastrophe (Quarantelli 2006). Thus it has provided an unusual opportunity for U.S. social science disaster researchers to test the knowledge accumulated from studying numerous smaller events over many decades and to gain new insights on community resilience in the face of more extreme events.

Katrina has indeed been a watershed event for the study and analysis of the implications of race, class, and poverty for disaster consequences, perhaps solidifying the place of these topics on the social science disaster research agenda as never before. Many social science researchers, both those established in and those new to the field of disaster research, as well as other scholars, have analyzed the racial and class implications of Katrina, especially focusing on outcomes in the black community (Anderson 2008).

With its novel mix of narratives, research reports, and expert commentaries, *The Women of Katrina: How Gender, Race, and Class Matter in an American Disaster* makes a very important contribution to the literature on gender and disaster. But it does much more. It offers a crucial message and challenge to the social science disaster research community.

There will be ongoing research on Katrina for many years, particularly on recovery matters, and *The Women of Katrina* is an important reminder that research related to gender should be a vital part of the mix. This book arose out of the strong conviction that compared to the wealth of studies of race and class, insufficient research on gender has been forthcoming and published on Katrina, especially given its historic nature. Thus it is an important critique of the social science disaster research field.

While a strong case is made that gender has been understudied in the case of Katrina, the collection of papers in this book clearly demonstrates the relevance of this area of research if we are to achieve a deeper understanding of the impacts of disasters on all segments of society. *The Women of Katrina* calls for increasing the salience of gender issues on the social science disaster research agenda. This can promote timely and rigorous research that advances theory and provides a scientific basis for sound policy and practice related to both the vulnerability of women and their capacity to further community resilience.

In my opinion, in spite of the periodic lapses of attention, the study of gender in the social science disaster research field has a bright future. This seems particularly true when champions such as the editors and contributors to *The Women of Katrina* remind us to refocus our attention whenever we seem to stray away from this critical area of research.

———

William A. Anderson recently retired as director of the Disasters Roundtable at the National Academy of Sciences' National Research Council. He was field director at Ohio State University's Disaster Research Center and later a professor of sociology at Arizona State University. Outside academia, Anderson worked at the National Science Foundation for more than twenty years, including as head of the Hazard Mitigation Section, and was a senior advisor in the Disaster Management Facility at the World Bank.

REFERENCES

Anderson, W. (2008). Mobilization of the Black community following Hurricane Katrina: From disaster assistance to advocacy of social change and equity. *International Journal of Mass Emergencies and Disasters, 26*(3), 198–218.

NRC (National Research Council). (2006). *Facing hazards and disasters: Understanding human dimensions.* Washington, DC: National Academies Press.

Quarantelli, E. (2006, June 11). Catastrophes are different from disasters: Some implications for crisis planning and managing drawn from Hurricane Katrina. Retrieved from *understandingkatrina.ssrc.org.*

Preface

We watched the Katrina catastrophe unfold from many miles away—both in Colorado, both in our own homes, both as gender sociologists. For fifteen years, Elaine Enarson had been thinking and writing about gender relations and the social construction of disasters after losing her home to Hurricane Andrew. In the wake of Hurricanes Katrina and Rita, she was flying to Sri Lanka as a consultant on gender-responsive programming with a UN agency working on recovery from the 2004 Indian Ocean tsunami. She soon returned to write "Women and Girls Last? Averting the Second Post-Katrina Disaster" and to pack for a new teaching job in Canada, where she and her students followed these events closely. Emmanuel David was a graduate student at the University of Colorado at Boulder, after having attended Loyola University New Orleans some years before. After the storm, his friends in New Orleans were scattered across the country, and several displaced students from universities in the flooded city enrolled in a course he was teaching in the Women and Gender Studies program. With no experience in disaster sociology but strong ties to New Orleans, he soon took the first steps toward the research that would become his doctoral dissertation, focusing on elite women's political mobilization in the Gulf Coast recovery.

From these vantage points, we were certain that such a book was needed, but grappled with how to pursue the project while respecting those in and around the affected areas. We faced the common challenges of researchers who are at once insiders and outsiders, with multiple and fluid connections to a space and time of crisis. Like other feminist researchers and disaster scholars, we also faced dilemmas of accountability, representation, and difference. In undertaking this Katrina project, we aimed to include as wide a range of voices and perspectives as possible. In the end, what we gathered here reflects the period in which editors and writers found one another. We strongly encourage and support the new work still emerging in this area, knowing it will help fill the evident gaps and omissions of the volume.

This was a collective venture spanning several years, so we welcome the opportunity to thank those who were involved in the project along the way. It is a privilege to acknowledge the work of Laura Dooris, a mixed media artist based in Tampa. The image on the cover, *Overwhelmed*, is part of a larger Katrina series and was inspired by her personal experiences while a resident of New Orleans in August 2005. She is pleased to donate the rights to reproduce the cover art in honor of those affected by Hurricane Katrina. More of her work can be seen at *www.lauramae.com*.

We are also grateful for the assistance of colleagues who generously shared their ideas about publishing, editing, and Katrina scholarship, and for the helpful suggestions from those who so carefully reviewed the book. Michael Ames, director of Vanderbilt University Press, saw the project's potential and offered us valuable guidance and encouragement throughout the entire process, as did Ed Huddleston, the managing editor, and Susan Havlish, the marketing manager. It is also a pleasure to thank Bill Anderson for writing the Foreword. His life work demonstrates what engaged scholarship for social change can look like, and we are pleased that he reflected on gender and disaster recovery here. The Department of Sociology at Villanova University and the Women and Gender Studies Program at the University of Colorado at Boulder offered Emmanuel a supportive environment for the project, as did Elaine's intellectual circle of friends and family for her.

Finally, we owe a great debt to those who shared scarce time and energy with researchers so that their stories could be told, and to local scholars and activists who made time to write even as their own futures were uncertain. We gratefully acknowledge each of our contributors for their fine work and sustained efforts, and express our indebtedness to the community of Katrina researchers and activists whose work informs our own. We dedicate *The Women of Katrina* to those whose lives were cut short or imperiled and hope the book helps move the nation toward a more just and disaster-resilient future.

Introduction

Elaine Enarson and Emmanuel David

With the shearing away of facades and fences, disasters illuminate the status quo and exacerbate social inequalities in everyday life. But whose experiences do they reveal, and whose do they neglect? Soon after Hurricane Katrina made landfall on the Gulf Coast on August 29, 2005, think tank and government reports, Senate committee testimonials, preliminary papers, and books circulated in an effort to understand the catastrophe. Most authors were quick to observe racial, ethnic, and socioeconomic class disparities in the devastated region (e.g., Sherman and Shapiro 2005) and, to a lesser extent, inequalities that arose from ability or age.

Hurricane Katrina made landfall on a highly gendered terrain along the Gulf Coast: images flashed around the world of pregnant women in sweltering shelters, anguished mothers searching for their children, and exhausted older women wading through filthy waters. Despite the undeniable presence of gender in these images, the dominant Katrina story that emerged did not see gender and instead emphasized the intersecting inequalities of race and class. When gender did get media coverage, it was often from pundits on the political right who were quick to blame unmarried women of color for their own suffering (Bonavoglia 2005; Ransby 2006). This pattern was not limited to mass media. Most policy and academic reports, too, overlooked census data on women's pre-Katrina vulnerability. Few offered much, if any, sex-specific data to enable gender-based analysis by others after the storm. Even the sternest critics of government ineptitude failed to reflect on the social facts of women's pre-storm oppression and their struggles for survival in the aftermath (e.g., see Waugh 2006).

Gender-blind Katrina analysis reigned, with books written authoritatively on race or class as if gender were irrelevant or secondary to either (e.g., see Dyson 2006; Hartman and Squires 2006; Mann 2006; Potter 2007). At the level of practice and policy, neither sex-disaggregated data nor the ethnographic studies of gender in prior disasters informed those in positions to intervene in response to the Katrina catastrophe or to guide community recovery. Sadly, feminist scholarship also went untapped, despite the many points of intersection between disaster studies and feminist theory (Enarson and Phillips 2008). It is difficult not to conclude that women were poorly served by research and analysis that once again neglected their issues, actions, and values (Eisenstein 2005; Enarson and Morrow 1998; Phillips and Morrow 2008).

Breaking the Gender Silence

Some observers did, indeed, protest the glaring gender disparities in the immediate aftermath of the storm and subsequent flooding (e.g., Eisenstein 2005; INCITE! 2005), and we include some of their early critiques in this volume. But more empirical data were needed to shed light on the complexities of women's experiences along the Gulf Coast. A beacon of light came from the Institute for Women's Policy Research, which took the lead shortly after the storm by producing a series of quantitative and qualitative reports that soon circulated widely (Gault et al. 2005; Jones-DeWeever 2008; Jones-DeWeever and Hartmann 2006; Williams et al. 2006). This work highlighted the extensive poverty among women and people of color along the Gulf Coast, women's labor force participation before and after the hurricane, and women's increased vulnerability, but also the conditions that served to strengthen women's leadership during this time (see also Vail 2006).

Additionally, the *NWSA Journal* published a special issue on gender, Katrina, and the politics of displacement (Boisseau et al. 2008). The volume included research on African American women survivors (Murakami-Ramalho and Duroroye 2008) and their networks in evacuating from Katrina (Litt 2008), battering and the context of safety (Jenkins and Phillips 2008a), strategies used by privileged women to promote recovery (David 2008), racialized patriarchal practices in disaster response (Luft 2008), and parenting of displaced children (Peek and Fothergill 2008). Soon after, the Newcomb College Center for Research on Women at Tulane University released a comprehensive policy report on the status of women in post-Katrina New Orleans. Contributors framed women's experiences theoretically (Laska et al. 2008) and explored the neglected topics of sexualities, domestic violence, women's employment status and earnings, health care, and housing (D'Ooge 2008; Greeley and Planned Parenthood 2008; Jenkins and Phillips 2008b; Luft and Griffin 2008; Mock 2008; Overstreet and Burch 2008; Willinger 2008a, 2008b; Willinger and Gerson 2008).

Occasional research on gender and Katrina has appeared in edited collections and specialized journals (e.g., Shenk and Covan 2010; Stockemer 2006; Tyler 2007) exploring such subjects as reproductive health and violence (e.g., Bergin 2008; Brown, Jenkins, and Wachtendorf 2010; Buttell and Carney 2009; Callaghan et al. 2007; Kissinger et al. 2007; Larrance, Anastario, and Lawry 2007; Thornton and Voigt 2007); parenting (Tobin-Gurley, Peek, and Loomis 2010); family life and senior women (e.g., Gullette 2006; Haney, Elliott, and Fussell 2007; Roberto et al. 2010); and women's collective post-Katrina action (David 2008, 2010a, 2010b; Pyles and Lewis 2007; Tyler 2007). Some academics still caught up in the storm wrote compelling accounts of how scholarly and personal life were interwoven during this period (see Batlan 2008; Belkhir and Charlemaine 2007; Hidalgo and Barber 2007), and the film *Still Waiting: Life After Katrina* profiled the experiences of one extended African American family (Browne and Martin 2007). Recent work also examines U.S. women's ethnically diverse disaster experiences (e.g., Davis and Land 2007; Redwood 2009; and see Laditka, Murray, and Laditka 2010). Such works, long overdue, add to the ever-growing gender and disaster archive in the United States.

Foundational Research on Women and Disaster in the United States

This volume is grounded in social scientific studies of disaster, a field that arose in sociology and remains strongly imbued with the sociological imagination. Gender and development theory jump-started the gendering of this subfield globally, arising concurrently with more radical perspectives on disaster that emphasized the political-economic processes that shape inequalities in disasters. The egregious loss of human life, especially among girls and women, makes structural gender analysis more salient in developing nations, where women are also more actively organized to reduce the risk of disaster (e.g., see Enarson and Chakrabarti 2009; Neumayer and Plümper 2007; Yonder, Ackar, and Gopalan 2005).

Gender goes unexamined theoretically by lead American disaster scholars in flagship collections such as *What Is a Disaster?* (Perry and Quarantelli 2005; Quarantelli 1998). Empirically, few case studies examined women or gender until after Hurricane Andrew made landfall in Miami in 1992 (Alway, Belgrave, and Smith 1998; Enarson and Morrow 1998; Morrow and Enarson 1996; but see Phillips's influential analysis of gender in emergency response to the Loma Prieta earthquake, 1993). Even monographs about families and disasters (Bolin 1982) or ethnic minorities in disasters (Perry and Mushkatel 1986) included no gender perspective. Development issues strongly related to gender relations in crisis are also overlooked in American disaster research (Bolin, Jackson, and Christ 1998; and see Enarson and Meyreles 2004, for an international review). For the most part, when study populations or samples used in disaster research are disproportionately male or female, the implications of these asymmetries are not explored, and overly general categories such as "first responder" and "parent" are used in ways that mask gender, age, and other salient lines of difference.

As Kathleen Tierney observes in this volume, the field was stubbornly gender blind in the United States until the popularization of the social vulnerability approach (principally developed by Blaikie et al. 1994; and Wisner et al. 2004; and see Anderson 2000; Cutter 1995; Cutter, Tiefenbacher, and Soleci 1992; Peacock, Morrow, and Gladwin 1997; and Phillips et al. 2009). This perspective opened a window to gender and other power structures in the social construction of risk and its uneven distribution. Sociologist Kai Erickson (1976) is a welcome exception, relating both women's and men's experiences to gender and culture in the Appalachian communities devastated by a massive dam failure, yet most work in this area implicitly accepts a male perspective but without critical analysis of men and masculinity. The work of Paul Slovic (1999) and others who take an interest in the gender dimensions of risk perception and communication has also advanced the field.

While gender analysis is not yet well integrated in national policy or the practice of disaster risk management, there are grounds for optimism. In addition to the new work in this book, more scholars are examining gender, disasters, and disaster risk management in the United States (for overviews, see Enarson 1998, 2009; Enarson, Fothergill, and Peek 2006; Fothergill 1998; and see Houghton 2010; Phillips and Morrow 2008). Women's health care and safety concerns come in for more critical examination (Brown, Jenkins, and Wachtendorf 2010; Houghton et al. 2010; Richter and Flowers 2010). More field-based practice guides and more teaching resources are also available (e.g., through the Gender and Disaster Sourcebook at *www.gdnonline .org/sourcebook*; and see the U.S.-based Gender and Disaster Resilience Alliance at *www.usgdra.org*). Networks developed by and for women in emergency management are also gaining momentum.

The experiences of women in the 2005 Gulf Coast hurricanes are linked, of course, to those of the men in their lives. Intriguing analysis of men and masculinity in disaster contexts is emerging in recent writing about natural disasters (see Klinenberg 2002; Luft 2008; Scanlon 1999; Tierney and Bevc 2007) and other catastrophic events in U.S. history, such as the *Exxon Valdez* oil spill (e.g., Larabee 2000), the explosion of the space shuttle *Challenger* (e.g., Maier 1997), and the sinking of the *Titanic* (e.g., Biel 2001). Knowing that the gendered terrain of disaster can empower men and yet jeopardize their health and safety (e.g., see Bourque et al. 2006), we anticipate and welcome further theoretical and empirical work by and about men and masculinities.

Guide to Readers

This collection brings a gender lens to bear on one specific (long-lasting) event, making Hurricane Katrina a focusing event for disaster and gender scholarship. The book is organized in five parts, framed in Part I, "In Protest," by period pieces written shortly after Hurricane Katrina that strongly conveyed women's voices of uncertainty and resistance. In Part II, "Women on the Front Lines: Testimonials," firsthand accounts portray the hardships endured by women during and after the crisis. Writing in a different voice, researchers from across the disciplines then present empirical data on two intertwined subjects. Part III, "In Deep Waters: Displacement, Loss, and Care," examines structural patterns of inequality that affected women and their families and shaped their responses. The research collected in Part IV, "Against the Tide: Resisting, Reclaiming, and Reimagining," documents women's personal and collective efforts to redefine this event and reshape their place and future. These accounts are all critical to understanding the social history of our post-Katrina nation and women's own histories of crisis and resilience. Two concluding chapters in Part V, "Gender in Disaster Theory, Practice, and Research," draw out the implications of the collection for gender-responsive disaster practice and policy and the future development of the field.

Elaine Enarson is an independent scholar based in Lyons, Colorado, with a focus on gender and disaster risk reduction in her consulting, research, and advocacy. She offers distance education courses on gender, social vulnerability, and disaster management.

Emmanuel David is an assistant professor in the Department of Sociology and Criminal Justice at Villanova University.

REFERENCES

Alway, J., Belgrave, L. L., and Smith, K. (1998). Back to normal: Gender and disaster. *Symbolic Interaction, 21*(2), 175–195.

Anastario, M., Larrance, R., and Lawry, L. (2008). Using mental health indicators to identify postdisaster gender-based violence among women displaced by Hurricane Katrina. *Journal of Women's Health, 17*(9), 437–444.

Anderson, W. (2000). Women and children in disasters. In A. Kreimer and M. Arnold (Eds.), *Managing disaster risk in emerging economies* (pp. 85–90). Washington, DC: World Bank.

Batlan, F. (2008). Weathering the storm together (torn apart by race, gender, and class). *NWSA Journal, 20*(3), 163–184.

Belkhir, J. A., and Charlemaine, C. (2007). Race, gender, and class lessons from Hurricane Katrina. *Race, Gender, and Class, 14*(1), 120–152.

Bergin, K. A. (2008). Witness: The racialized gender implications of Katrina. In M. Marable and K. Clarke (Eds.), *Seeking higher ground: The Hurricane Katrina crisis, race, and public policy reader* (pp. 173–190). New York: Palgrave Macmillan.

Biel, S. (2001). "Unknown and unsung": Feminist, African American, and radical responses to the *Titanic* disaster. In S. Biel (Ed.), *American disasters* (pp. 305–338). New York: New York University Press.

Blaikie, P., Cannon, T., Davis, I., and Wisner, B. (1994). *At risk: Natural hazards, people's vulnerability, and disasters.* New York: Routledge.

Boisseau, T. J., Feltey, K., Flynn, K., Gelfand, L., and Triece, M. (2008). New Orleans: A special issue on the gender politics of place and displacement. *NWSA Journal, 20*(3), vii–xvii.

Bolin, R. (1982). *Long-term family recovery from natural disaster.* Boulder: Institute of Behavioral Science, University of Colorado.

Bolin, R., Jackson, M., and Crist, A. (1998). Gender inequality, vulnerability, and disaster: Issues in theory and research. In E. Enarson and B. H. Morrow (Eds.), *The gendered terrain of disaster* (pp. 27–44). Westport, CT: Greenwood.

Bonavoglia, A. (2005). Hurricane pundits blow hot air on single mothers. Women's Enews. Retrieved from *www.womensenews.org/article.cfm?aid=2449.*

Bourque, L., Siegel, J., Kano, M., and Wood, M. (2006). Weathering the storm: The impact of hurricanes on physical and mental health. In W. Waugh (Ed.), *Shelter from the storm: Repairing the National Emergency Management System after Hurricane Katrina* (pp. 129–151). Newbury Park, CA: Sage.

Brown, B., Jenkins, P., and Wachtendorf, T. (2010). Shelter in the storm: A battered women's shelter and catastrophe. *International Journal of Mass Emergencies and Disasters, 28*(2), 226–245.

Browne, K., and Martin, G. (2007). *Still Waiting: Life after Katrina.* Available through Colorado State University, *www.stillwaiting.colostate.edu/index.html.*

Buttell, F., and Carney, M. (2009). Examining the impact of Hurricane Katrina on police responses to domestic violence. *Traumatology, 15*(2), 6–9.

Callaghan, W., Rasmujssen, S., Jamieson, D., Ventura, S., Farr, S., Sutton, P., Mathews, T., Hamilton, B., Shealy, K., Brantley, D., and Posner, S. (2007). Health concerns of women and infants in times of natural disasters: Lessons learned from Hurricane Katrina. *Maternal and Child Health Journal, 11*(4), 307–311.

Cutter, S. (1995). The forgotten casualties: Women, children, and environmental change. *Global Environmental Change, 5*(3), 181–194.

Cutter. S., Tiefenbacher, J., and Soleci, W. (1992). Engendered fears: Femininity and technological risk perception. *Industrial Crisis Quarterly, 6*, 5–22.

David, E. (2008). Cultural trauma, memory, and gendered collective action: The case of *Women of the Storm* following Hurricane Katrina. *NWSA Journal, 20*(3), 138–162.

————. (2010a). Redistribution of responsibility: The gendered division of labor and politics of a post-disaster clean-up project. In K. A. Bates and R. S. Swan (Eds.), *Through the eye of Katrina: Social justice in the United States* (pp. 391–411). 2nd ed. Durham, NC: Carolina Academic Press.

————. (2010b). "Studying up" on women and disaster: An elite sustained women's group following Hurricane Katrina. *International Journal of Mass Emergencies and Disasters, 28*(2), 246–269.

Davis, O. A., and Land, M. (2007). Southern women survivors speak about Hurricane Katrina, the children, and what needs to happen next. *Race, Gender, and Class, 14*(1), 69–86.

D'Ooge, C. (2008). Queer Katrina: Gender and sexual orientation matters in the aftermath of disaster. In B. Willinger (Ed.), *Katrina and the women of New Orleans* (pp. 22–23). Newcomb College Center for Research on Women. New Orleans: Tulane University.

Dyson, M. (2006). *Come hell or high water: Hurricane Katrina and the color of disaster.* New York: Basic Books.

Eisenstein, Z. (2005). Katrina and her gendering of class and race. Retrieved from *www.awid.org/eng/Issues-and-Analysis/Library/Katrina-and-her-Gendering-of-Class-and-Race.*

Enarson, E. (1998). Through women's eyes: A gendered research agenda for disaster social science. *Disasters, 22*(2), 157–173.

————. (2009). Gender. In B. Phillips, A. Fothergill, D. Thomas, and L. Blynn-Pike (Eds.), *Social vulnerability to disasters.* New York: Taylor and Francis.

Enarson, E., and Chakrabarti, P. G. D. (Eds.). (2009). *Women, gender, and disaster: Global issues and initiatives.* Delhi: Sage.

Enarson, E., Fothergill, A., and Peek, L. (2006). Gender and disaster: Foundations and possibilities. In H. Rodriguez, E. L. Quarantelli, and R. Dynes (Eds.), *Handbook of disaster research* (pp. 130–146). New York: Springer.

Enarson, E., and Meyreles, L. (2004). International perspectives on gender and disaster: Differences and possibilities. *International Journal of Sociology and Social and Policy, 14*(10), 49–92.

Enarson, E., and Morrow, B. H. (Eds.). (1998). *The gendered terrain of disaster: Through women's eyes.* Westport, CT: Greenwood.

Enarson, E., and Phillips, B. (2008). Invitation to a new feminist disaster sociology: Integrating feminist theory and methods. In B. Phillips and B. H. Morrow (Eds.), *Women and disasters: From theory to practice* (pp. 41–74). Philadelphia: Xlibris.

Erikson, K. (1976). *Everything in its path: Destruction of community in the Buffalo Creek Flood.* New York: Simon and Schuster.

Fothergill, A. (1998). The neglect of gender in disaster work: An overview of the literature. In E. Enarson and B. H. Morrow (Eds.), *The gendered terrain of disaster* (pp. 11–26). Westport, CT: Greenwood.

————. (2004). *Heads above water: Gender, class, and family in the Grand Forks Flood.* Albany: State University of New York Press.

Gault, B., Hartmann, H., Jones-DeWeever, A., Werschkul, M., and Williams, E. (2005). *The women of New Orleans and the Gulf Coast: Multiple disadvantages and key assets for recovery.* Part 1: *Poverty, race, gender, and class.* Washington, DC: Institute for Women's Policy Research. Retrieved from *www.iwpr.org/pdf/D464.pdf.*

Greeley, M., and Planned Parenthood of Louisiana and the Mississippi Delta. (2008). Sexual health of young women. In B. Willinger (Ed.), *Katrina and the women of New Orleans* (pp. 70–72). Newcomb College Center for Research on Women. New Orleans: Tulane University.

Gullette, M. (2006). Katrina and the politics of later life. In C. Hartman and G. Squires (Eds.),

There is no such thing as a natural disaster: Race, class, and Hurricane Katrina (pp. 102–120). New York: Routledge.

Haney, T., Elliott, J. R., and Fussell, E. (2007). Families and hurricane response: Evacuation, separation, and the emotional toll of Hurricane Katrina. In D. Brunsma, D. Overfelt, and J. S. Picou (Eds.), *The sociology of Katrina: Perspectives on a modern catastrophe* (pp. 71–90). New York: Rowman and Littlefield.

Hartman, C., and Squires, G. (Eds.). (2006). *There is no such thing as a natural disaster: Race, class, and Hurricane Katrina.* New York: Routledge.

Hidalgo, D., and Barber, K. (Eds.). (2007). *Narrating the storm: Sociological stories of Hurricane Katrina.* Boca Raton, FL: Cambridge Scholars Press.

Houghton, R. (Ed.) (2010). Gender and disasters. Special issue of the *International Journal of Mass Emergencies and Disasters*, 28(2).

Houghton, R., Wilson, T., Smith, W., and Johnston, D. (2010). "If there was a dire emergency, we never would have been able to get in there": Domestic violence reporting and disasters. *International Journal of Mass Emergencies and Disasters*, 28(2), 270–293.

INCITE! Women of Color Against Violence. (2005, September 11). INCITE! Statement on Hurricane Katrina. Retrieved from *www.incite-national.org/index.php?s=90.*

Jenkins, P., and Phillips, B. (2008a). Battered women, catastrophe, and the context of safety after Hurricane Katrina. *NWSA Journal*, 20(3), 49–68.

———. (2008b). Domestic violence and disaster. In B. Willinger (Ed.), *Katrina and the women of New Orleans* (pp. 65–69). Newcomb College Center for Research on Women. New Orleans: Tulane University.

Jones-DeWeever, A. (2008). *Women in the wake of the storm: Examining the post-Katrina realities of the women of New Orleans and the Gulf Coast.* Washington, DC: Institute for Women's Policy Research. Retrieved from *www.iwpr.org/pdf/D481.pdf.*

Jones-DeWeever, A., and Hartmann, H. (2006). Abandoned before the storms: The glaring disaster of gender, race, and class disparities in the Gulf. In C. Hartman and G. D. Squires (Eds.), *There is no such thing as a natural disaster* (pp. 85–101). New York: Routledge.

Kissinger, P., Schmidt, N., Sanders, C., and Liddon, N. (2007). The effect of the Hurricane Katrina disaster on sexual behavior and access to reproductive care for young women in New Orleans. *Sexually Transmitted Diseases*, 34(11), 883–886.

Klinenberg, E. (2002). *Heat wave: A social autopsy of disaster in Chicago.* Chicago: University of Chicago Press.

Laditka, S. B., Murray, L., and Laditka, J. N. (2010). In the eye of the storm: Resilience and vulnerability among African American women in the wake of Hurricane Katrina. *Health Care for Women International*, 31(11), 1013–1027.

Larabee, A. (2000). *Decade of disaster.* Urbana: University of Illinois Press.

Larrance, R., Anastario, M., and Lawry, L. (2007). Health status among internally displaced persons in Louisiana and Mississippi travel trailer parks. *Annals of Emergency Medicine*, 49(5), 590–601.

Laska, S., Morrow, B. H., Willinger, B., and Mock, N. (2008). Gender and disasters: Theoretical considerations. In B. Willinger (Ed.), *Katrina and the women of New Orleans* (pp. 11–20). Newcomb College Center for Research on Women. New Orleans: Tulane University.

Litt, J. (2008). Getting out or staying put: An African American women's network in evacuation from Katrina. *NWSA Journal*, 20(3), 32–48.

Luft, R. (2008). Looking for common ground: Relief work in post-Katrina New Orleans as an American parable of race and gender violence. *NWSA Journal*, 20(3), 5–31.

Luft, R., and Griffin, S. (2008). A status report on housing in New Orleans after Katrina: An intersectional analysis. In B. Willinger (Ed.), *Katrina and the Women of New Orleans* (pp. 50–53). Newcomb College Center for Research on Women. New Orleans: Tulane University.

Maier, M. (1997). Gender equity, organizational transformation, and *Challenger*. *Journal of Business Ethics, 16*(9), 943–962.

Mann, E. (2006). *Katrina's legacy: White racism and black reconstruction in New Orleans and the Gulf Coast*. Los Angeles: Frontline Press.

Mayer, V., Willinger, B., Jenkins, P., Tucker, S., Dietzel, S., Moore, P. W., Hemenway, B. J., Kiles, C., Bryan, V. H., and Reineman, J. (2008). Losing ground but finding high road: Teaching women's studies in post-Katrina New Orleans. *NWSA Journal, 20*(3), 185–192.

Mock, N. (2008). Health and health care. In B. Willinger (Ed.), *Katrina and the women of New Orleans* (pp. 54–58). Newcomb College Center for Research on Women. New Orleans: Tulane University.

Morrow, B. H., and Enarson, E. (Eds.). (1996). Hurricane Andrew through women's eyes: Issues and recommendations. *International Journal of Mass Emergencies and Disasters, 14*(1), 1–22.

Morrow, B. H., and Phillips, B. (Eds.). (1999). Special issue on women and disasters. *International Journal of Mass Emergencies and Disasters, 17*(1).

Murakami-Ramalho, E., and Duroroye, B. A. (2008). Looking back to move forward: Katrina's Black women survivors speak. *NWSA Journal, 20*(3), 115–137.

Neumayer, E., and Plümper, T. (2007). The gendered nature of natural disasters: The impact of catastrophic events on the gender gap in life expectancy, 1981–2002. *Annals of the Association of American Geographers, 97*(3), 551–566.

Overstreet, S., and Burch, B. (2008). Mental health status of women and children following Hurricane Katrina. In B. Willinger (Ed.), *Katrina and the women of New Orleans* (pp. 59–65). Newcomb College Center for Research on Women. New Orleans: Tulane University.

Peacock, W., Morrow, B. H., and Gladwin, H. (Eds.). (1997). *Hurricane Andrew: Ethnicity, gender, and the sociology of disasters*. New York: Routledge.

Peek, L., and Fothergill, A. (2008). Displacement, gender, and the challenges of parenting after Hurricane Katrina. *NWSA Journal, 20*(3), 69–105.

Perry, R., and Mushkatel, A. H. (1986) *Minority citizens in disaster*. Athens: University of Georgia Press.

Perry, R., and Quarantelli, E. L. (Eds.). (2005). *What is a disaster? New answers to old questions*. Philadelphia: Xlibris.

Phillips, B. (1993). Gender as a variable in emergency response. In B. Bolin (Ed.), *The Loma Prieta earthquake* (pp. 83–90). Boulder: Institute for Behavioral Science, University of Colorado.

Phillips, B., and Morrow, B. H. (Eds.). (2008). *Women and disasters: From theory to practice*. Philadelphia: Xlibris.

Phillips, B., Thomas, D., Fothergill, A., and Blinn-Pike, L. (Eds.). (2009). *Social vulnerability to disasters*. Boca Raton, FL: Taylor and Francis, CRC Press.

Potter, H. (Ed.). (2007). *Racing the storm: Racial implications and lessons learned from Hurricane Katrina*. New York: Lexington Press.

Pyles, L., and Lewis, J. (2007). Women of the storm: Advocacy and organizing in post-Katrina New Orleans. *Affilia, 22*(4), 385–389.

Quarantelli, E. L. (Ed.). (1998). *What is a disaster? Perspectives on the question*. New York: Routledge.

Ransby, B. (2006). Katrina, Black women, and the deadly discourse on Black poverty in America. *Du Bois Review: Social Science Research on Race, 3*(1), 215–222.

Redwood, L. (2009). Storm fallout: The post-Katrina rise in immigrant women farmworkers in the Southeast and the response of legal advocates. Paper presented at the annual meeting of the NWSA, Sheraton Hotel Atlanta, Atlanta, GA, November 12.

Richter, R., and Flowers, T. (2010). Gender-aware disaster care: Issues and interventions in supplies, services, triage, and treatment. *International Journal of Mass Emergencies and Disasters, 28*(2), 207–225.

Roberto, K., Henderson, T., Kamo, Y., and McCann, B. (2010). Challenge to older women's sense of self in the aftermath of Hurricane Katrina. *Health Care for Women International, 31*(11), 981–996.

Ross, L. (2005, October 10). A feminist perspective on Katrina. *Z-Net: The spirit of resistance lives.* Retrieved from *www.zmag.org/znet/viewArticlePrint/5233.*

Scanlon, J. (1999). Myths of male and military superiority: Fictional accounts of the 1917 Halifax explosion. *English Studies in Canada, 24,* 1001–1025.

Seager, J. (2005). Noticing gender (or not) in disasters. *Social Policy, 36*(2), 29–30.

Shenk, D., and Covan, E. K. (Eds.). (2010). Special issue. *Health Care for Women International 31*(11).

Sherman, A., and Shapiro, I. (2005). Essential facts about the victims of Hurricane Katrina. Center on Budget and Policy Priorities. Retrieved from *www.brookings.edu/metro/ katrina-reading-room.aspx#facts.*

Slovic, P. (1999.). Trust, emotion, sex, politics, and science: Surveying the risk-assessment battlefield. *Risk Analysis, 19*(4), 689–701.

Stockemer, D. (2006). Gender inequalities and Hurricane Katrina. *International Journal of Diversity, 6*(1), 137–142.

Thornton, W. E., and Voigt, L. (2007). Disaster rape: Vulnerability of women to sexual assaults during Hurricane Katrina. *Journal of Public Management and Social Policy, 13*(2), 23–49.

Tierney, K., and Bevc, C. (2007). Disaster as war: Militarism and the social construction of disaster in New Orleans. In D. L. Brunsma, D. Overfelt, and J. S. Picou (Eds.), *The sociology of Katrina: Perspectives on a modern catastrophe* (pp. 35–49). Lanham, MD: Rowman and Littlefield.

Tobin-Gurley, J., Peek, L., and Loomis, J. (2010). Displaced single mothers in the aftermath of Hurricane Katrina: Resource needs and resource acquisition. *International Journal of Mass Emergencies and Disasters, 28*(2), 170–206.

Tyler, P. (2007). The post-Katrina, semiseparate world of gender politics. *Journal of American History, 94,* 780–788.

Vail, S. (2006). *The calm in the storm: Women leaders in Gulf Coast recovery.* San Francisco: Women's Funding Network and New York: Ms. Foundation for Women. Retrieved from *www.wfnet.org/documents/publications/katrina_report_082706.pdf.*

Waugh, W. (Ed.). (2006). *Shelter from the storm: Repairing the national emergency management system after Hurricane Katrina.* New York: Sage.

Williams, E., Sorokina, O., Jones-DeWeever, A., and Hartmann, H. (2006). *The women of New Orleans and the Gulf Coast: Multiple disadvantages and key assets for recovery.* Part 2: *Gender, race, and class in the labor market.* Washington, DC: Institute for Women's Policy Research. Retrieved from *www.iwpr.org/pdf/D465.pdf.*

Willinger, B. (2008a). The effects of Katrina on the employment and earnings of New Orleans women. In B. Willinger (Ed.), *Katrina and the women of New Orleans* (pp. 32–49). Newcomb College Center for Research on Women. New Orleans: Tulane University.

———. (2008b). The power to influence. In B. Willinger (Ed.), *Katrina and the women of New Orleans* (pp. 73–75). Newcomb College Center for Research on Women. New Orleans: Tulane University.

Willinger, B., and Gerson, J. (2008). Demographic and socioeconomic change in relation to gender and Katrina. In B. Willinger (Ed.), *Katrina and the women of New Orleans* (pp. 25–31). Newcomb College Center for Research on Women. New Orleans: Tulane University.

Wisner, B., Blaikie, P., Cannon, T., and Davis, I. (2004). *At risk: Natural hazards, people's vulnerability, and disasters.* 2nd ed. London: Routledge.

Yonder, A., Ackar, S., and Gopalan, P. (2005). Women's participation in disaster relief and recovery. SEEDS, pamphlet no. 22. Retrieved from *www.popcouncil.org/pdfs/seeds/Seeds22.pdf.*

The Women of Katrina

PART I

In Protest

The selections in this section of the book offer an important corrective to the history of Hurricane Katrina. As we put this collection together, we wanted to show that it did not take years or even months for the issue of gender to be raised and that gender was not simply an afterthought included in the rewriting of the Katrina narrative. Hence, we open the book with a series of documents that protested the overwhelming gender disparities in the wake of the storm, some written in the days and weeks after Katrina's landfall while hundreds of thousands of Gulf Coast residents were still scattered across the United States and much of New Orleans remained under water following breaches to the city's levee system. We include these pieces verbatim, as they were produced at the height of the crisis.

Originally published in print and electronic media outlets, these protest pieces voiced concerns about not only women's well-being in the crisis but also the ideologies and structures that gave rise to gender injustices in the first place. The critics convey rage and frustration, anger and sadness, but also trust in the agency of women. With no end to the human suffering in sight, these feminist critics spoke out about the lack of attention to gender in the disaster response, and drew attention to the immediate material conditions on the ground for women and their families. While these primary sources, as historical documents in themselves, convey the sense of extreme uncertainty following the catastrophe, they also situate the plight of those left behind in relation to a host of complex and far-reaching social issues. Inequalities in crisis, the statements argue, reflect the current social order that gave rise not to a natural disaster, but to an entirely social and human-made disaster.

These voices were subsequently overshadowed by dominant discourses that privileged an analysis of race and class relations over gender relations, as if any one were more important than another. In contrast, these early protest pieces consistently addressed the intersections of race, class, and gender, and to some degree sexuality, and contextualized these compounding factors within preexisting social structures. The feminist critiques presented here are characterized by their differences as well, some calling for more liberal reform of emergency management and disaster response, others emphasizing more radical positions and anticapitalist, antiracist, and anti-imperialist sentiments. Importantly, too, the material conditions along the Gulf Coast were situated in relation to a nation at war, a rising tide of conservatism, and a highly masculinized and militarized response to the crisis. These early statements envisioned radically different responses that might have been possible in times of crisis, and by extension, they present visions of a radically different, and better, society.

CHAPTER I

INCITE! Statement on Hurricane Katrina

Dear INCITE! Friends and Supporters:

INCITE! Women of Color Against Violence is stunned by the catastrophe and tragic loss in the wake of Hurricane Katrina. In New Orleans and in many other communities along the Gulf, people are experiencing unimaginable devastating conditions. We are especially alarmed for the people who have the fewest resources, who were unable to evacuate New Orleans because of poverty, who were—and in some cases still are—trapped without food, water, and medical attention. Because of racism and classism, these people are also overwhelmingly folks of color, and because of sexism, they are overwhelmingly women of color—low income and poor women, single mothers, pregnant women, women with disabilities, older women and women who are caregivers to family and community members who were unable to leave the city. Women living at the intersections of systems of oppression are paying the price for militarism, the abandonment of their communities, and ongoing racial and gender disparities in employment, income, and access to resources and supports.

As you know, the Historic Treme Community in New Orleans recently hosted INCITE!'s Color of Violence III conference this past March. Treme is the first free community established by black people in the United States and is currently home to hundreds of black women and their families, many of whom are poor. We are deeply hurting for the families and communities that graciously hosted us and who are now facing profoundly tragic circumstances.

We have heard word from most of the sistas who are part of the New Orleans INCITE! chapter, many of whom were able to evacuate. We also received word that one of the COV 3 volunteers had a mother and sister trapped on the 8th floor of New Orleans City Hall at some point—we sincerely hope that they have reached relative safety at this time. An early letter from Shana Griffin, member of the New Orleans INCITE! chapter and the national INCITE! steering committee, is below. Our hearts and prayers go out to them and we want to provide them with as much support and as many resources as we can so that they can mourn this horrible loss, reconnect with those that are missing, and, eventually, rebuild the rich and vital communities that have been devastated. Our thoughts and prayers are also with INCITE! chapters, members, COV III participants and supporters in other areas affected by the hurricane in the Gulf States.

Many of you have thoughtfully written and asked how you can help. At this time, we are asking for donations from our supporters so that we can send money to our New Orleans chapter members who will use it to help people who need it most. We have not given up on our sisters and brothers in New Orleans and other places that have been hit. We are dedicated to pooling our resources and using those resources to continue to organize plans for survival, safety, and justice in New Orleans. [. . .]

That said, we'd like to take this opportunity to express our deep outrage at the federal government's shamefully slow and pathetic response to this disaster. It is clear that the lack of rapid and effective response is based on a racist assessment of the value of the 150,000 mostly black and poor people—a disproportionate number of whom are women—left behind in New Orleans. Further, INCITE! lays the blame of this disaster squarely at the feet of the U.S. government and particularly with George W. Bush for the following reasons:

1. Global Warming

The Bush Administration's willful denial of the existence of global warming has kept this country from taking seriously global warming's dangerous consequences, one of which is an increase in the severity of hurricanes. Hurricane Katrina, for example, began as a relatively small hurricane off south Florida, but it was intensified to a level five hurricane—the highest level a hurricane can reach—because of the unusually blistering sea surface temperatures in the Gulf of Mexico caused in large part by global warming. (Ross Gelbspan, *The Boston Globe*, 8/30/05) However, the Bush Administration, leveraged by the coal and oil industries, relegated global warming to a myth rather than the emergency environmental crisis that it is. Because the impact of Hurricane Katrina had an exceedingly disproportionate impact of devastation on people of color, Bush's failure at addressing global warming is a catastrophic example of environmental racism.

2. War on Iraq and Tax Cuts for the Wealthy

Bush's illegal, imperialist, and racist war on and occupation of Iraq—ironically, to enable consumption of more oil, aggravating global warming—as well as tax cuts to wealthy Americans, directly pulled resources away from levee construction and emergency management in New Orleans, as well as from programs and entitlements which could have provided much needed support to poor people and communities in New Orleans. In 2003, as hurricane activity in the area increased and the levees continued to subside, federal funding was specifically redirected away from addressing these problems because of spending pressures of the war on Iraq. In early 2004, as the cost of the war on Iraq soared, President Bush proposed spending less than 20 percent of what was needed for Lake Pontchartrain, according to a Feb. 16, 2004, article in *New Orleans CityBusiness*. At least nine articles in the *Times-Picayune* from 2004 and 2005 specifically cite the cost of the war on Iraq as a reason for the lack of hurricane- and flood-control dollars. (Will Bunch, *Editor and Publisher*, 8/30/05) The lack of resources to prepare for a disaster like Hurricane Katrina is a tragic example of how imperialism not only devastates communities of color abroad, but also communities of color here at home.

This criminal neglect on the part of the government is responsible for thousands more deaths—deaths that could have been prevented with adequate funding.

3. State-Sponsored Violence

It is unconscionable that, while thousands of people are suffering from horrible and deadly circumstances, the media continues to harp on the so-called "looting" in New Orleans. The constant media coverage of so-called "criminal behavior" instead of the outrageous and criminal lack of response from the federal government is racist and disgraceful.

Though we are also very distressed about reports of violence—including sexual and physical violence against women and children—in the area caused largely by widespread chaos and desperation, we condemn the current mass militarization of the area. There have been numerous accounts of vicious police brutality experienced by men and women who have survived untold horrors only to be subjected to abuse by the law enforcement officials sent to "save" them. Thousands of soldiers from the U.S. Marines and Army are currently in New Orleans to enforce evacuation orders and bring about "law and order." In response to violence in the area, Louisiana governor Kathleen Blanco shockingly remarked, "I have one message for these hoodlums. These troops know how to shoot and kill, and they are more than willing to do so if necessary." Besides the fact that it is against the law for federal troops to engage in domestic law enforcement, a militarized response is another piece of a racist pattern of de-humanizing poor people of color. Instead of seeing poor black people driven desperate by the appallingly weak and unacceptably slow response of the federal government, the media and the government frame these primary victims as criminals or blame them for bringing the circumstances on themselves by "disobeying" mandatory evacuation orders when they had no means to comply.

We demand that there be no further criminalization of survivors of the hurricane as rescue, recovery, and rebuilding efforts go forward. We are particularly concerned about the creation of temporary accommodations—expected to serve as "home" to evacuees for up to six months—which are akin to detention facilities, surrounded by barbed wire, in isolated parts of Utah, Oklahoma, and other areas, which inhabitants will be prohibited from leaving without a "pass" and in which they will be housed in gender segregated housing and prohibited from preparing their own meals. The prison-like conditions of such facilities have been justified by the soldiers guarding them as follows: "Do you know what kind of people we have coming here?"

We are also concerned about the adequate provision of medication, supplies, and child care to women with disabilities, HIV/AIDS, as well as mothers and elderly women. We are calling for support for survivor-led, women of color–driven formations within evacuation facilities and for their demands. We are also calling for support of women's individual and collective efforts to ensure their safety from physical and sexual violence within evacuation facilities while submitting that the existence of such violence is no justification for violent repression of evacuee communities.

We call for support and safety for lesbian, gay, bisexual, and transgender survivors of the hurricane, and for respect for the integrity of their families and of their needs in evacuation facilities. We are also deeply concerned for immigrant and particularly undocumented women, who fear seeking assistance for fear of adverse immigration consequences and deportation. We call for efforts to connect incarcerated women, men, and children with their families, many of whom do not know the location of those dear to them, and for authorities to ensure conditions of confinement that meet international human rights standards. We are asking for charges against those who took food, water, and supplies in an effort to survive to be immediately dropped. Finally, we are calling for support of domestic violence survivors who were displaced from shelters, support systems, and places of safety by the storm and may be at greater risk of violence from their abusers under current circumstances.

We demand an organized, rapid, and just response to save the survivors of Hurricane Katrina. We demand a comprehensive plan that is respectful of the value of the people who have been abandoned and responsive to their actual needs for survival and safety. We want immediate action operating from a vision of justice and hope.

We have pulled together a number of analyses of Hurricane Katrina and its aftermath, information about critical organizing and mobilization of poor people and people of color, letters from sistas from INCITE!, and other ways to help. Please contact us if you have questions, concerns, or resources. Our website is *incite-national.org* and our blog is *inciteblog.wordpress.org*.

> In Solidarity,
> INCITE! Women of Color Against Violence

———

INCITE! Women of Color Against Violence works with groups of women of color and their communities to develop political projects addressing multiple forms of violence experienced by women of color. Currently INCITE! collective members across the United States work on such issues as police violence, reproductive justice, and media justice.

A version of this chapter was originally published on the website of INCITE! Women of Color Against Violence (*www.incite-national.org/index.php?s=90*) on September 11, 2005.

CHAPTER 2

Noticing Gender (or Not) in Disasters

Joni Seager

As I write this in September 2005, it is one week after Hurricane Katrina precipitated what may well be the greatest disaster in modern United States history. Since the hurricane's landfall, media outlets in the United States have been providing on-the-scene nonstop coverage of the unfolding disaster. It was this media presence as much as anything else that prodded the U.S. federal government out of its stupor in the week after the hurricane's landfall. The in-your-face coverage of the accelerating calamity and the irrepressible outrage of on-the-scene reporters—usually so detached and calm—finally pricked the national conscience, and the federal machinery of disaster relief slipped into gear, albeit dollars short and days late. The pictures from New Orleans of old people dehydrating and dying on curbs, of bodies floating past storefronts, of families sleeping under highways on beds of garbage and sewage, and of thousands of people sheltering amidst squalor and sewage will haunt U.S. disaster planning, and perhaps U.S. electoral politics, for years to come.

The intense coverage also, remarkably, provoked a national discussion about race, class, and privilege. By about the third day, reporters (mostly white) started to say out loud how noticeable it was that the people trapped in the disaster in New Orleans were mostly, undeniably, black. In the tone of this discovery there is something of the quality of Captain Renault in Casablanca who was "shocked, shocked" to find gambling in his fine establishment; in point of fact, it would have been extremely difficult to *not* notice that the dead, the dying, and the desperate on the streets of New Orleans were African American. Nonetheless this enlightened "noticing" by the media produced a moment of genuine inquiry as mainstream reporters and analysts started asking tough, targeted questions about why this disaster fell so hard on one side of the race line. African Americans make up about 68 percent of the population of New Orleans (U.S. Census Bureau 2004); it is clear that they represent a considerably larger proportion than this of survivors. This is a race gap that warrants the outrage and attention it has received.

And yet there is another equally important and starkly apparent social dimension to the hurricane disaster that media coverage has put in front of our eyes but that has yet to be "noticed": this disaster fell hard on one side of the gender line too. Most of the survivors trapped in the dying city are women. Women with children, women on their own, elderly women in wheelchairs, women everywhere. Women account for 54 percent of the population of New Orleans, so the gender gap amongst victims is even more dramatic than the race gap (U.S. Census Bureau 2004). The two gaps need not compete for our attention; they are linked. The surviving victims of this hurricane are mostly African American women, and no doubt the ranks of the dead will be also.

The gender gap is no surprise, or shouldn't be. Disaster is seldom gender neutral. In the 1995 Kobe (Japan) earthquake, one and a half times more women died than men; in the 1991 floods in Bangladesh, five times as many women as men died; in the Southeast Asia 2004 tsunami, death rates for women across the region averaged three to four times that of men (UNEP 2005). The gender, class, and race dimension of each disaster needs particular explanation. Feminists working in relief agencies and the UN, for example, identified several factors that explain the gender skew in the 2004 tsunami deaths (Oxfam International 2005): sex differences in physical strength that make a difference when clinging to life might mean clinging to a tree or climbing to safety; prevailing ideologies of femininity that influence the extent to which women are encouraged to or allowed to develop physical strength and capacity, and that mean, among other things, that women and girls are not taught to swim; the different social roles and locations (metaphorical and literal locations) that men and women occupy, particularly with regards to responsibility for children. In a fast-moving storm surge, children slow things down. Mothers who stop to find and gather up children lose valuable time, and with children in their arms they can't swim, climb, or hang on.

Experience from these and other crisis zones around the world allows us to start to explain the gendered nature of the New Orleans disaster. The biology and ideology of physical strength may turn out to play as much a role in the gender-skewed survival rates in this hurricane as they did in the tsunami. Additionally we know that the poverty that leaves people more vulnerable to disaster amplifies gender as surely as it does race. Indeed, everywhere in the world women are the poorest of the poor. In New Orleans, a city with a poverty rate higher than the national average, 15 percent of all families live below the official poverty line; 41 percent of female-headed households with children fall below this line (U.S. Census Bureau 2004). People in poverty are the least likely to have access to good information ahead of disaster, the least likely to have a place they can go to and stay for days or weeks, and the least likely to have the means to leave. In the days ahead of the storm a lot of people did get out of New Orleans, almost all of them by car. Poverty combines with race and ideologies about gender to produce a metric of deep disadvantage in terms of mobility: even in a country as awash in cars as the United States, women are less likely to have a car or driver's license than their male counterparts. Of all Americans, it is poor African American women who are the least likely of all to have a car or access to one.

International disaster and refugee agencies have been profoundly influenced by feminist insights into the importance of the gender dynamics of disaster. From Oxfam to the UN High Commission on Refugees, experts now routinely incorporate the understanding that disasters magnify gender disadvantage, that women and their children have specific post-disaster recovery needs, and that preparations for gender-specific emergency intervention and recovery are integral to disaster planning. This knowledge appears to have entirely bypassed American commentators, planners and media.

The "not-noticing" of the gendered dimensions of this disaster by the American media and by the panoply of experts who interpreted the disaster to the public through the media is alarming and warrants attention in itself. Feminist theorists have long pointed to the public invisibility of women, especially women of racial minorities, and the New Orleans case study provides a dramatic example of the "unremarkability" of racialized minority women in the gaze of a predominantly male and white media. In the real world of an unfolding disaster, this comes at a price. For example, the lack of curiosity about the rapes in the midst of the New Orleans disaster is just one particularly disturbing aspect of this willful ignorance. Rapes have been reported by dozens of survivors and mentioned as a subtext in several news stories, but always in passing and with no follow-through: to date, there have been no attempts to verify the dozens of reports, no interviews with police officials about the magnitude of rape, no curiosity about the construction of masculinity that contemplates rape in conditions of such extreme human suffering, no disaster experts assuring us that rape-support teams are included in the rescue teams, no discussion about the medical and psychological resources that women will need who have survived unimaginable tragedy and stress and have then also been raped. And, of course, in the climate of conservative triumphalism in the United States, there will be no public discussion and almost certainly no provision by the government of the reproductive services, including abortion, that should be made available to women who have been raped.

American media commentators and politicians insist on referring to this as a natural disaster. There's a certain comfort and perhaps political cover in that designation, but experts eschew this term. The hurricane came ashore, but from then on it's been a human disaster all the way. The gendered character of this disaster, and the willful silence about it, is also more artifice than nature. An Oxfam report on the Asian tsunami reminds us that "disasters, however 'natural,' are profoundly discriminatory. Wherever they hit, pre-existing structures and social conditions determine that some members of the community will be less affected while others will pay a higher price. Among the differences that determine how people are affected by such disasters is that of gender" (Oxfam 2005, 1). At some point in the New Orleans disaster, this will be officially "noticed" but the costs of not paying attention to the gendered divide earlier in the disaster will be high for the women whose needs have gone unnoticed and unaddressed.

Joni Seager is chair of global studies at Bentley University. She is the author of the widely reprinted *Penguin Atlas of Women in the World*, the 1994 classic *Earth Follies: Coming to Feminist Terms with the Global Environmental Crisis*, and numerous other publications in feminist geography.

A version of this chapter was originally published as an Op-Ed in the *Chicago Tribune*, September 14, 2005.

REFERENCES

Oxfam International. (2005, March). The tsunami's impact on women. *Oxfam Briefing Note*.
UNEP (United Nations Environment Programme). (2005). Feature Focus: Gender, Poverty and Environment. *GEO Yearbook 2004/5*. Nairobi: UNEP.
U.S. Census Bureau. (2004). *American Community Survey*. Washington, DC: Government Printing Office.

CHAPTER 3

Women and Girls Last?

Averting the Second Post-Katrina Disaster

Elaine Enarson

The fault lines of American society, as much as the failings of its infrastructure, are shamefully on display in the aftermath of Hurricane Katrina. Race, class, age, and disability are now at the heart of the public debate about vulnerability, preparedness, and emergency response, but this is also a story, as yet untold, about women and men (Enarson and Morrow 1998).

It was low-income African American women, many single mothers among them, whose pleas for food and water were broadcast around the world from the Super-dome; women more than men who were evacuated from nursing homes; and women more than men whose escape of sorts was made with infants, children, and elders in tow. Now we see on nightly TV the faces of exhausted women standing in seemingly endless lines seeking help of any kind. In the long run, as we have learned from studies of past disasters, women will be at the heart of this great city's rebirth, and the emotional center of gravity for their families on the long road to the "new normal." They will stitch the commemorative quilts, organize community festivals and hurricane anniversary events, support their schools and faith-based organizations and relief agencies, and compose and sing many of the Katrina songs to come (Enarson 2001). Though not this simple, it is often said that men rebuild buildings while women re-weave the social fabric of community life (Cox 1998).

We are transfixed now by images of needy women and strong men (a few with female partners) wearing badges, carrying weapons, and riding in armored vehicles, and will soon be treated to endless photos of hardworking men hauling garbage, replacing roofs, making speeches and decisions. Behind the scenes (taking nothing away from others), women labor, too. In the dreary months ahead, after the nation's attention wanes, the burdens on women will be exceptional and exceptionally invisible. Imagine cleaning just one flooded room, helping just one toddler or teen to sleep well again, restoring the sense of security to a widowed mother's life. The basic domestic chores of "homemaking" gain new significance and are vastly more difficult in a FEMA trailer, a friend's apartment, or the basement of a church—and parents will call upon daughters more than sons for help. Nothing will change in a hurry as women pack and unpack, moving from place to place across the nation with distracted partners, bewildered children, pets, and whatever possessions remain or are gathered piecemeal. The demands on the women who take them in and make them at home are incalculable, and displaced families will stay longer than anyone now imagines. Women across the nation are also the lifeblood of voluntary organizations of all descriptions now being pulled inexorably into relief work. They will continue to do this work when the funds dry up and women (and to a lesser extent men) marginalized by race and class fall through the (gaping) cracks of the relief system. Long after we think Katrina over and done with, women whose jobs and professions in teaching, health care, mental health, crisis work, and community advocacy bring them into direct contact with affected families will feel the stress of "first responders" whose work never ends (Enarson 2000b).

These factors help explain why women more often than men report symptoms of post-traumatic stress following disasters (e.g., see Ollenburger and Tobin 1998). Their hidden emotional work with toddlers, teens, partners, parents, friends, and colleagues passing through difficult times takes a toll but is irreplaceable. Many will struggle to break through the stony silence of the men in their lives. Especially when so much is out of their control in Katrina's aftermath, men without jobs and those unable to save family members and other victims may feel unmasked and unmanly. Already we have learned of the suicides of police officers and other men in New Orleans. Some men will cope through drugs, alcohol, physical aggression, or all three, hurting themselves and putting the women and girls around them at risk. We can count on increased reports of violence against women, as this is so common in U.S. and international disasters (Enarson 1999a; Fothergill 2004; Palinkas et al. 1993). Press accounts from the grotesque world of the Superdome—a woman held at gunpoint, another woman raped and then a young girl—suggest this already but the real worry is later. Women and children displaced once already by their partner's violence into a shelter closed by Katrina will struggle to find their way, and crisis workers struggle to locate them. Some will be forced back into violent relationships through lack of housing and support. When rebuilding is in full swing and the cities and towns of the Gulf Coast flood with outsiders coming to help (or to profit), tent cities will spring up to house them and these will not be safe spaces for girls and women—any more than are the secluded homes of professional men whose businesses were destroyed. Double shifts and long commutes will be the norm after Katrina as women and men work hard to get back on their feet. In their mothers' absence, teenaged girls and their younger sisters are all the more vulnerable to sexual assaults by men known and unknown to them. Both girls and boys are at increased risk of abuse and neglect at the hands of their mothers in the difficult days ahead.

Most public housing residents, residents of mobile homes, renters, and those lacking insurance are women—often women heading households on their own income alone—but rehousing them is not a priority in our owner-focused and single-family home rebuilding plans (Enarson 1999b). The poorest of the poor before Katrina, socially marginalized women of color, will be the last to escape the confines of FEMA tent cities and other encampments (Enarson and Morrow 1997; Morrow 1997; Morrow and Enarson 1996). The finely balanced networks of support poor women develop to survive in our economy, piecing together cash from odd jobs, boyfriends, government, family, and kin, were ripped apart by this storm. Low-wage women employed at the lowest rungs of the tourist industry and as beauticians, child-care workers, home health aides, servers, and temporary office workers will not be helped back on their feet by economic recovery plans geared to major employers in the formal sector. The wives and daughters of oystermen, shrimp farmers, and oil riggers will need skills training, income supplement, child-care assistance, transportation, and economic development plans targeting women as earners as well as caregivers. Indirect losses can be anticipated, too, for domestic workers whose employers lost their homes to floodwaters and small businesswomen who struggled to keep their businesses going in the best of times. Communitywide economic recovery is impossible without the female labor force, but barriers of all kinds arise in rebuilding child-care systems, especially the family-based care upon which most American infants and youngsters depend (Enarson 2000a). Without functioning households and the social infrastructure of transit systems, schools, stores, health clinics, and child care, women's return to employment is delayed. Women supporting households single-handedly are, of course, most at risk. And will the short-term emergency relief work now being proposed reach women and men equally? Will "youth employment" recovery projects work as well for teenaged girls as for their brothers? Will steps be taken to counter pressure to employ women in "women's jobs" in government-subsidized economic relief programs?

What can be done to change this bleak scenario? How can we act now on the lessons learned about women, men, and gender in disaster recovery? If we are to craft a strategy that takes not just some but all people toward a fundamentally stronger and more just future, the national debates about reconstruction and rehabilitation now beginning must fully engage women as well as men. In the many drawers of unused plans and unlearned lessons, policy makers will find planning tools for gender-sensitive emergency response and recovery—but will they use them? Are gender-specific data being collected now so that we might evaluate and monitor budgets, programs, and plans for possible gender bias over time?

Gender-fair emergency relief is essential, and steps can be taken now to make girls and women safer, ensure that mental health services reach men effectively, promote women's economic recovery, provide respite care and support for long-term caregivers—the list goes on. But we have learned that the most urgent need of all is for those most affected to reclaim their sense of place, some degree of control and autonomy, and the certain knowledge that their views count too in the reimagining of the future. Will women's voices be heard in the independent commission likely to be appointed to review the national response to Hurricane Katrina? Will community recovery meetings be held at times convenient to those with children and in places safe for women? Will specialists on family life, women's issues, the gender concern of boys and men in crisis, poverty, race and gender, and women's environmental knowledge and activism be consulted? Measures are needed now to ensure women's representation on all public bodies making recommendations and decisions about the use of private and public relief monies. Those women most hard-hit by Katrina must take the lead and men—and other women—must learn to listen (Enarson 2004; UNDAW 2001; Yonder, Ackar, and Gopalan 2005). Women must be heard speaking out (and disagreeing) as elected officials, technical experts, community advocates, health and human service professionals, faith-based leaders, tenant association members, workers and employers, environmental justice activists, daughters, mothers, and grandmothers. The losses of grassroots organizations knowledgeable about women at risk must be made good and their capacities developed and supported. Following hurricane Andrew, the broad-based women's coalition Women Will Rebuild Miami (born the day funds were directed toward the Chamber of Commerce and away from child care) struggled for months, and unsuccessfully, to earmark just 10 percent of relief funds for girls and women (Enarson and Morrow 1998). This second disaster can be averted along the Gulf Coast.

The hurricane so gratuitously described as "flirtatious" in a recent news weekly is, in fact, a highly gendered social event. Katrina did not disrupt a social order in which women and men were equally vulnerable any more than it hit suburbanites with cars and the central city poor the same. To advocate for gender equality in reconstruction is not to press a political agenda (though there is one to advance) or deny our common humanity in crisis, but to serve both the women and the men of the Gulf Coast. This is what the future must look like, or all the talk about "building back better" to increase resilience to future disasters is just talk, and the next hurricane will find the poor poorer and women less able than today to anticipate, prepare for, survive, cope with, and recover from the next storm. This is not the hallmark of a great city or a great nation.

Elaine Enarson is an independent scholar based in Lyons, Colorado, with a focus on gender and disaster risk reduction in her consulting, research, and advocacy. She offers distance education courses on gender, social vulnerability, and disaster management.

This chapter was originally published in abbreviated form as an Op-Ed in the *Denver Post*, September 25, 2005. Revised with references for the Social Science Research Council's *Understanding Katrina: Perspectives from the Social Sciences* website, *understandingkatrina.ssrc.org/*.

REFERENCES

Cox, H. (1998). Women in bushfire territory. In E. Enarson and B. H. Morrow (Eds.), *The gendered terrain of disaster: Through women's eyes* (pp. 133–142). Westport, CT: Greenwood.

Enarson, E. (1999a). Violence against women in disasters: A study of domestic violence programs in the U.S. and Canada. *Violence against Women, 5*(7), 742–768.

————. (1999b). Women and housing issues in two U.S. disasters. *International Journal of Mass Emergencies and Disasters, 17*(1), 39–63.

————. (2000a). *A gender analysis of work and employment issues in natural disasters.* International Labour Organization InFocus Programme on Crisis and Reconstruction. Retrieved from *www.ilo.org/public/english/employment/recon/crisis/gender.htm*.

————. (2000b). "We will make meaning out of this": Women's cultural responses to the Red River Valley flood. *International Journal of Mass Emergencies and Disasters, 18*(1), 39–62.

————. (2001). What women do: Gendered labor in the Red River Valley flood. *Environmental Hazards, 3*(1), 1–18.

————. (2004). *Making risky environments safer: Women building sustainable and disaster-resilient communities.* UN Division for the Advancement of Women, Women 2000 series. Retrieved from *www.un.org/womenwatch/daw/public/w2000.html*.

Enarson, E., and Morrow, B. H. (1997). The gendered perspective: The voices of women. In W. Peacock, B. H. Morrow, and H. Gladwin (Eds.), *Hurricane Andrew: Ethnicity, gender, and the sociology of disasters* (pp. 114–140). New York: Routledge.

———. (Eds.). (1998). *The gendered terrain of disaster: Through women's eyes.* Westport, CT: Greenwood.

———. (1998). Women Will Rebuild Miami: A case study of feminist response to disaster. In E. Enarson and B. H. Morrow (Eds.), *The gendered terrain of disaster: Through women's eyes* (pp. 185–200). Westport, CT: Greenwood.

Fothergill, A. (1999). An exploratory study of woman battering in the Grand Forks flood disaster. *International Journal of Mass Emergencies and Disasters, 17*(1), 79–98.

———. (2004). *Heads above water: Gender, class, and family in the Grand Forks flood.* Albany: State University of New York Press.

Morrow, B. H. (1997). Stretching the bonds: The families of Andrew. In W. Peacock, B. H. Morrow, and H. Gladwin (Eds.), *Hurricane Andrew: Ethnicity, gender, and the sociology of disasters* (pp. 141–170). New York: Routledge.

Morrow, B. H., and Enarson, E. (1996). Hurricane Andrew through women's eyes: Issues and recommendations. *International Journal of Mass Emergencies and Disasters, 14*(1), 1–22.

Ollenburger, J., and Tobin, G. (1998). Women and postdisaster stress. In E. Enarson and B. H. Morrow (Eds.), *The gendered terrain of disaster: Through women's eyes* (pp. 95–108). Westport, CT: Greenwood.

Palinkas, L., Downs, M., Petterson, J., and Russell, J. (1993). Social, cultural, and psychological impacts of the *Exxon Valdez* oil spill. *Human Organization, 52*(1), 1–13.

UNDAW (UN Division for the Advancement of Women). (2001). "Environmental Management and the Mitigation of Natural Disasters: A Gender Perspective." Report of the Expert Group Meeting, Ankara, Turkey, November 6–9. Retrieved from *www.un.org/womenwatch/daw/csw/env_manage/documents/EGM-Turkey-final-report.pdf.*

Yonder, A., Ackar, S., and Gopalan, P. (2005). Women's participation in disaster relief and recovery. SEEDS. Pamphlet no. 22. Retrieved from *www.disasterwatch.net/Brief/Seeds2005final.pdf.*

CHAPTER 4

A Feminist Perspective on Katrina

Loretta J. Ross

A tragedy like Katrina in August 2005, which devastated the Gulf Coast and flooded New Orleans, compelled feminists to examine the impact of the storm and the response to it on women and children. As a Southern feminist, I knew that the Deep South has some of the highest poverty in America, affecting all races of people. Through a Katrina lens, the world witnessed that great dirty secret that is America's shame. Black and brown people drowning in filthy floodwaters exposed the reality that this country did not protect the human rights of its own citizens in this disaster.

Poverty in America is not only racialized but also gendered. The aftermath of Katrina, when examined through a gender lens, identified the myriad of violations experienced by women, especially women of color. A disaster like Katrina was a violation against the entire community, but when threats to women's lives were not recognized, and steps are not taken to ensure that they are, women became doubly victimized—by the disaster and by the response to it.

I wrote this article a few days after the flood because I lost a family member in New Orleans, an eighty-year-old relative in the Ninth Ward who was eventually found by cadaver dogs three months after we began searching for her. She was disabled and could not escape by herself; she had drowned in her bedroom. The flood kept our family from rescuing her. Although her son-in-law was a New Orleans sheriff, he could not get to her house or command a thorough search for her. We received a false report that she had been evacuated, and wasted months looking for her around the country. Most of my other family escaped, especially those who lived on the West Bank. But my family lost a life, several homes, and many livelihoods because of that storm and the miserable response to it. My grief and anger began on August 29 and have not subsided even as I update this article four years later.

The political became personal. The company of my sisters in struggle helped me survive those anxious days. Right after Katrina hit, I was privileged to attend a meeting September 10–14, 2005, on "Women's Global Strategies for the 21st Century" at Sarah Lawrence College organized by the Women of Color Resource Center, the Global Fund for Women, and the Center for Women's Global Leadership. This conference brought together one hundred women from around the world to have a global dialogue on critical issues facing women leaders. The workshop on militarization and occupation helped me understand some of the issues we faced here in the Deep South as we struggled to rebuild our lives after Katrina.

From a feminist perspective, there are certain predictions we made concerning what happened to some women and children based on our collective experiences in helping women and children survive trauma. We knew that women and children were more vulnerable. We knew that racist and sexist responders, commentators, and pundits would blame the victims of the disaster. We knew that violence against women would increase while services for women would decrease. And finally, we knew that the recovery from Katrina would not only fail to prioritize the needs of women and children, but would neglect to include women's concerns in the reconstruction of a city reconfigured for elite developers, not poor women and children.

Vulnerability of Women and Children

The hurricane and the subsequent flooding exposed the special vulnerability of women, children, the elderly, and the disabled by revealing the harsh intersection of life expectancy, race, class, gender, and ability. Many people could not escape not only because of poverty, but because they were not physically able to punch through rooftops, endure intense heat and dehydration, perch on top of buildings, or climb trees to survive. Horror stories of people abandoned to drown in nursing homes and hospitals emphasized that any disaster preparedness planning must take into account those unable to evacuate themselves.

Instead, many in the mainstream media and government sources chose to blame the victims as if these vulnerable people simply made bad choices, ignoring the context in which these "choices" were made. Right-wing pundits—such as those at the Heritage Foundation—quickly said that the tragedy was the fault of single mothers who were not married so that their husbands could lift them out of poverty! The prejudiced powerful did not speak about the intentional chaos in people's lives created by constantly scrambling for survival while living in poverty or with disabilities that leave many women feeling simply overwhelmed by life itself. Feminists had to respond to this sexist and racist folderol of victim blaming.

We also predicted that women's issues would not be seen as "important" during the crisis, as we were advised that larger issues like maintaining law and order and securing the affected areas were of higher priority. There was a risk of too much focus on the disaster crisis, shifting dollars from previous unmet needs, and forgetting older crises around the world and in our country. For example, Mississippi already had only one abortion provider before the storm. Women traveled to Louisiana or Alabama for services. What did an already underserved region do to help women receive reproductive health care?

While the news media focused on the black/white conflicts during the crisis, little or no mention was made of the Native American, Asian American, or Latino communities also devastated by the storm. Erasing these communities from the public's consciousness became another form of structural violence.

Redefining Military Occupation

We witnessed a very authoritarian militarization of New Orleans during the crisis as police and the military were given permission to forcibly evict survivors, arrest or shoot lawbreakers, and impose martial law on the city. No one in authority questioned whether it is ethical to give orders to shoot flood survivors, even if they are supposedly looting. Alternative media reports revealed that many of the alleged "looters" were actually heroes trying to find food to feed their families by securing food and relief supplies from stores whose inventories would have been lost to the flood anyway. The concentration camp–like conditions of the Superdome and Convention Center provided no privacy for women, no safety for children, and, for days after the tragedy, no basic needs like food, water, and sanitation. Notably, while the police and military were protecting the property rights of business owners, they somehow neglected to protect the lives of women and children jammed into the Superdome and the Convention Center. Women, children, the sick, and the elderly died waiting for help.

One of the ways in which the occupation was achieved was by controlling terminology through language coups. Did you notice that some news media reported that white people "find" food while black people "loot"? Control of communications became control of self-validation as the prejudices of the powerful constructed meanings that rendered any countervailing notion ineffective.

We may never learn the full extent of the human rights violations during this crisis. There were reports of massive arrests, police brutality, and even deaths at the hands of the police and military during the crisis, yet these reports were not featured in the mainstream news, just over alternative sources such as the Internet. There were also stories of people being shot by authorities in the Louisiana Superdome. One brief report on CNN told the story about the Gretna Police Department blockading a bridge by firing over the heads of black people attempting to flee the flooded city to this predominantly white suburb west of New Orleans. The Gretna police even confiscated food and water from women and children on the bridge at gunpoint, claiming they did not want their town "turned into another Superdome," an ominous racist reference to the fact that most of the people were African American. The normal brutality with which cops usually treat poor black people lends considerable credence to these reports of injustice, particularly if the police are operating in situations with little likelihood of formal investigations into their actions because they are "justified" by the crisis. "They came to help" language thwarted a thorough examination of the negative effects of the occupation and may forever obstruct any notion of accountability.

Unfortunately, actions like these denigrated the undoubtedly heroic actions of many people in law enforcement and the military as they risked their lives in contaminated water to rescue survivors. But as feminists, we did not confuse individual compassion with structural injustice. Katrina poignantly proved that both can exist in the same place at the same time.

What we need are expanded definitions and understanding of what is meant by military occupation. Occupation is about space, land, and resources. There is little consciousness in the minds of the American public that we live in occupied land or that we are occupiers. I don't believe the term only applies to Palestine, Afghanistan, or Iraq. Communities of color, particularly Indigenous Nations, have always experienced law enforcement and the military as occupiers, but the Katrina crisis exposed how we must expand the concept of military occupation way beyond the narrow and limited definitions of the United Nations. We must examine military occupations not only during war but also during disasters and the impact on vulnerable people.

There is a porous membrane between occupation and war, as the Iraq invasion proved. It was as if these occupying armies read their orders from the same script. The residents of the affluent parts of New Orleans hired their own private security firms to "protect" themselves against the flood survivors. Our definition of occupation must be widened to include not only agents of the state such as the police and the military, but also transnational corporations, some of whom also operated their own private armies. We redefined occupation as a violent means to maintain order and confiscate our land. The land loss from Katrina must be calculated and compensated in order to begin the process of justice. We must connect militarism with occupation and reveal who controls the resources and who benefits from the process of occupation. These are all expressions of the same phenomenon.

Economic and Environmental Impact

Ironically, the occupation of New Orleans and the occupation of Iraq shared one major obvious commonality. Both were greased by oil—its production and its shipping. It is no coincidence that a port through which much of America's oil flows was quickly militarized while hundreds of people died in flooded houses. Offshore platforms in the Gulf were responsible for about 30 percent of U.S. crude-oil production and states along the Gulf Coast were home to half of the nation's refining capacity. The same company in Iraq—Halliburton—received major contracts to help in the rebuilding of New Orleans.

What was particularly telling about the Gulf Coast crisis was that the owners of casinos and Walmarts were apparently able to return to their businesses much more quickly than others to repair storm damages long before federal assistance arrived to reduce the needless loss of lives. They were the first businesses to offer jobs to the massive numbers of people forced into unemployment because of the storm. More than 400,000 jobs were lost in the disaster. Workers were not in any position to challenge their labor practices and impact on communities, as they are the only employers available. Walmart already discriminates against the women it presently employs. President Bush relaxed the minimum wage laws for companies hired to rebuild the Gulf Coast, and women made even less money, below the paltry $5.15/hour federal minimum wage of 2005.

The impact of the storm and subsequent flooding on women was studied by the Institute for Women's Policy Research (IWPR), which reported that 3,000 licensed Gulf Coast child-care facilities were damaged or destroyed and only 10 percent received federal assistance to reopen. Charity Hospital, Louisiana's biggest hospital for the poor and mentally ill, was closed after Hurricane Katrina and has yet to be reopened.

Approximately 142,000 units of affordable housing were damaged or lost as a result of the storm; nearly four-fifths (79 percent) were affordable to low-income housing, according to IWPR. Because of the housing shortage, many women shared accommodations with extended family members, friends, and—in some cases—with known batterers and rapists in order to have a home.

Of course there were damaging environmental impacts because of Katrina. Or more properly, damaging the environment through global warming and criminally ineffective levee construction and maintenance precipitated the disastrous flooding of New Orleans. The effects of the storm on injuries, environmental exposures, and infectious diseases have been reported by the Katrina Environmental Research and Restoration Network and Advocates for Environmental Human Rights, among others. Exposure to environmental contaminants, psychological stress, and the lack of adequate health care during the disaster had serious consequences for women and children, particularly pregnant women. Studies have revealed an increase in problem pregnancies, low birth weights, spontaneous abortions, and untreated chronic diseases such as diabetes and high blood pressure in the wake of the storm.

Despite our worst fears as feminists, what we did not anticipate were the attacks on housing, health care, education, and municipal services for poor people after Katrina. We did not imagine that the local, state, and federal governments would collude to actively eliminate affordable housing in New Orleans. We did not predict that restoration of health care services and educational institutions like schools would be a low priority for those with the responsibility for protecting the human rights of the people of New Orleans. Katrina became a hideous example of how a storm and the response to it violate the human rights of vulnerable women and children.

Gender-Based Violence

Often poor women and children were the first ones forced into prostitution to survive. There was an increase in the demand for prostitution created by the massive military and police presence in the affected states, similar to the rise in prostitution that already surrounds our military bases around the world. Women are not "opportunities to relieve stress," as many soldiers are encouraged to believe. Because of the limited real choices women face, there was a rise in the prostitution and trafficking of women and children. There was also a rise in the exploitation and sexual abuse of displaced children. Increases in the abuse of women and children meant rises in other things like unwanted pregnancies, sexually transmitted diseases, and HIV/AIDS. We expected these things because they occur to women and children even without the desperation and vulnerability created by such a national disaster.

We received reports of the rapes and murders of women and children among the survivors herded together in the Superdome and New Orleans Convention Center under inhumane conditions. We do not know whether or not media racism exaggerated these reports, but we already know that some men do not know how to cope with a lack of control over their lives and they often express their frustration by abusing and violating women and children. Domestic violence and sexual assault increased because women are more vulnerable and more men will become violent as the occupation and displacement continues. This culture of violence breeds more violence against women. This happens every day anyway and a tragedy like Katrina exacerbates these dangerous tendencies, especially in a situation lacking any social control and order.

Because women's social networks and battered women's services were disrupted by the hurricane, many women found it harder to escape domestic violence. They were more vulnerable because of economic insecurity and the lack of affordable housing, meaning that they were often forced to continue living with their abusers. Researchers studying violence against women report that in post-Katrina New Orleans, programs increasingly found themselves helping the predisaster populations, but also middle-class women, immigrants, and others who had not previously sought shelter care, according to Pam Jenkins and Brenda Phillips, who studied the conditions battered women faced after the disaster.

Violations of International Human Rights Standards

We also witnessed the incredible violations of the human rights of the Katrina survivors. Not only was their right to survive threatened by the painfully slow response of local, state, and federal governments, but also their right to stay united as families, their right to adequate and safe shelter, their right to social services, their right to accurate information, and their right to health care and freedom from violence. All of these are human rights violations but the one that brings the Middle East most forcefully to mind is the violation of the right to return to one's home. For those of us with short-term memories, keep in mind that the Supreme Court ruled in 2005 that governments have expanded powers of eminent domain that were used to prevent some survivors from ever returning to their communities as land was turned over to corporate developers. New limits on the protections of bankruptcy laws caused further harm to Katrina's survivors.

The concept of peace and security was dreadfully misused during this crisis to impose a police state. The United Nations urged societies a decade ago to reexamine what is meant by security, beyond law enforcement, the military, and the state. The 1994 Human Development Report by the United Nations introduced a new people-centered concept for human security: "Human security means . . . safety from constant threats of hunger, disease, crime and repression. It also means protection from sudden and hurtful disruptions in the pattern of daily lives, whether in our homes, our jobs, in communities, or in our environment." Activists in the United States, especially after 9/11, requested a reconsideration of security that included the protection of human rights and civil liberties, the meeting of people's basic human needs, and the use of peace processes and UN mechanisms that can avoid war and prevent human rights violations by the state, individuals, and corporations.

The reality is that women live in a borderland of insecurity all the time, yet the needs of women were invisible during discussions on security preoccupied with criminals and terrorists. Poverty, hunger, and deprivation of human rights are the real threats to security because security is determined by the extent to which people have their basic needs met and can live in freedom and safety, not by the number of armed occupiers in their communities. A militarized community does not feel safer, just more policed, so that what is allowed, what is accepted, and whose needs are met are decided by those outside the community.

Our people from New Orleans who fled the flood were called "evacuees" by the media and the government, a term that has no legal basis in international law. They are, in fact, internally displaced persons, a status that affords them legal rights and protections. The U.S. government was very careful not to use this term to describe the people from New Orleans and the rest of the Gulf Coast because it would trigger obligations defined by human rights treaties to meet the needs of our people.

The U.S. government is always careful not to use language that requires it to protect people's human rights, especially in applying human rights standards to the United States to question its own behavior and responsibilities.

For example, the U.S. government was resistant to using the word "genocide" at the 2001 World Conference Against Racism to describe the theft of Indigenous lands and the enslavement of Africans. John Bolton, the former U.S. ambassador to the United Nations appointed by President Bush, was busily trying to undermine antipoverty goals at the UN Millennium Summit in 2005, instead of focusing on eradicating poverty, improving education, and empowering women. The U.S. government's assault on the human rights framework is unending, and we must not let them get away with it. We must respond by ensuring that the Katrina survivors learn about their human rights and the obligations they are due from our government.

Speaking of racism, it was blatant racism that stopped the distribution of the $2000 debit cards to the survivors. Right-wing critics halted FEMA's distribution of this immediate cash relief by falsely claiming that the mostly black poor people were irresponsible and likely to cheat the system. Instead, the government switched to a bank account deposit system, ignoring the fact that many poor people did not have bank accounts or could not access them because of the disaster. Many did not have the identity documents required to use standard banking procedures. Some survivors who received the cards before they were discontinued reported that they received much less than $2000; some received only $200. What agency did a race, gender, and class analysis of who received what relief?

Despite the magnitude of the catastrophe, it is amazing that the authorities found the time to harass undocumented immigrant women and men in the affected region. Reports of people targeted by immigration officials surfaced, and many people were afraid to seek help for fear that their suffering would be exploited as an opportunity to forcibly deport them. Those without Social Security numbers were denied emergency assistance by some agencies and harassed by law enforcement.

Another underreported story is what happened to the survivors in some of the cities to which they escaped. Because of antipoor ordinances in cities like San Antonio and Atlanta, some survivors were quickly arrested for panhandling and jaywalking in cities they perceived as refuges. Some were concentrated into hastily erected camps resembling detention centers, isolating them from the communities that purportedly welcomed them. There was an increase in the criminalization of the poor leading to a surge in growth for the prison industrial complex.

Development for Whom? Using a Gender Lens to Rebuild

There is a difference in how women see what ought to happen and how men see what should be done. It was important during this crisis to listen to the women of the Gulf Coast and incorporate their perspectives on what should be done to help people recover from this disaster.

We can learn a lot from our sisters around the globe who have endured terrible tsunamis and callousness from military occupiers and humanitarian agencies. Women from the Gulf Coast contacted our sisters from Asia who survived the December 2004 tsunami or women from the Middle East who have lived for years under military occupations. They offered valuable lessons about empowering women during national crises. They were the experts we needed, not the men with guns pointed at us as we sought food and shelter. Katrina became a moment for global solidarity, even if the Bush administration was too arrogant to accept help from people in countries they don't respect.

This was not only a teachable moment for America but an opportunity for learning as well. Katrina provided an opportunity to have serious discussions about the lack of human rights protections in this country by asking the question, "Why were we so vulnerable?" Even many government officials had to admit that the unjust war against Iraq decimated our country's ability to respond to this crisis in a timely and effective manner. This was a chance to connect issues of poverty, war, occupation, racism, homophobia, militarism, and sexism, and make the distinction between natural disasters and man-made ones.

Women's voices were lifted to evaluate the role of humanitarian agencies that responded to the crisis. There were many agencies and groups profiting from our suffering while ignoring our local women's organizations and our capacity for making decisions about what we need. In fact, some of these humanitarian agencies actually facilitated the occupation of our communities by turning over lists of undocumented people to the authorities, not recognizing the family rights of same-sex couples, or participating in redevelopment strategies that ignore the needs and perspectives of women.

To counter this, women seized our power and made our concerns known in the media, to government agencies, and to the humanitarian organizations. There are human rights standards that humanitarian agencies should follow and most require that women's perspectives are respected and incorporated. Women's organizations worked together, giving space to the creativity, energy, and brains of young women. Leadership by the Women's Health and Justice Initiative, a project of Incite! Women of Color Against Violence, brought women leaders and concerns to the decision-making tables. Their contact info is *www.whji.org/home.html.*

Women must ask critical questions during this crisis. Who are the groups benefiting from the disaster and who are the groups hurting or excluded? We must work together to address our collective trauma, fear, and anxiety so that we can reduce its multigenerational impact. We have the right to quality schools for our children, jobs that pay living wages, communities free of environmental toxins, and opportunities to develop our full human potential. We have the right to reclaim our land, rebuild our homes, and restore our communities.

Under the classic style of economic development of poor areas of America, communities are destroyed, people are forcibly relocated, and transnational corporations are invited to redevelop the seized lands. They called this urban renewal in the 1950s and 1960s. The 1970s brought us spatial deconcentration. In the 1980s and 1990s, it was called gentrification. Now it is called security.

It may take many years to rebuild the Gulf Coast, particularly the city of New Orleans, and right now we need to demand that the services to which we are entitled—that are our human rights—are delivered with respect, efficiency, and dignity. Our sisters from other countries advise us that disasters can wipe out the past and create an opportunity to better include people to reshape the future. We can use this moment to force bureaucracies to become more flexible, like changing normal admissions procedures to get our kids back in schools or demanding that quality public housing be provided instead of permanent refugee camps. We need schools, voter registration, immigrant services, driver's licenses, housing, medical care, and public assistance put on the fast track, not bottlenecked services mired down in the typical bureaucratic snarls that characterize government assistance programs.

We need to demand economic redevelopment strategies that center our needs, not those of casino owners, in the picture. It will be mighty tempting to use this as an opportunity to not rebuild our communities in New Orleans or the rest of the Gulf Coast. New Orleans is particularly at risk of becoming a tourist mecca with a French Quarter, plantation mansions, and endless casinos where the only jobs available to people of color will be low-paying ones supporting the tourist and oil industries. We have to claim our human right to sustainable development and insist on the enforcement of economic and social rights in redevelopment strategies.

Because many people lost their identities during the disaster, we can learn from our sisters in South Africa and Palestine who lost their identities when their countries were occupied. They took advantage of the chaos to create their own identities, determine their own facts, and promote community-based definitions of identity. They registered their own people as aid recipients and issued numbers and identity cards to help people have access to services. We have to define citizenship from our own point of view to challenge the powers that are taking over our communities and committing human rights abuses. People who are in occupied territories lose faith in the benefits of citizenship and in legal rights that are frequently denied. This is where international human rights laws become important. Claiming identities as internally displaced persons forces our governments to not define us as charity cases, but as citizens with rights that must be respected and protected.

Loretta J. Ross is a doctoral student in women's studies at Emory University. She earned an honorary doctorate of civil law from Arcadia University. Cofounder and the national coordinator of the SisterSong Women of Color Reproductive Health Collective, she was one of the first African American women to direct a rape crisis center and writes extensively on the history of African American women and reproductive justice.

This chapter was originally published in the SisterSong publication *Collective Voices* 1(3), 2005. Minor revisions by the author, August 2009.

PART II

Women on the Front Lines

Testimonials

In the first section of this book, we presented feminist voices of protest and dissent that aimed to bring nationwide attention to the gender inequalities of Hurricane Katrina. But how did women caught up in the storm make sense of the tragic events that would forever change their lives? The second section of this anthology includes personal narratives from women who directly experienced the catastrophe as survivors, volunteers, and participants in the early stages of recovery efforts. We include firsthand accounts of women who themselves were stranded in horrific and unbearable conditions, of those who cared for others in volunteer roles in overcrowded shelters and in hospitals without power, and of those whose labor in the community recovery helped shape the postdisaster landscape. Some wondered if they and those around them would survive the rising floodwaters, while others who worked with evacuees wondered if they had done enough to help. In these entries we see women's innovation and cooperation in the midst of disorder, at times in direct confrontation with armed men hooked on power and masculine authority. Their accounts document how women, as active and resourceful agents of change, struggled to cope with the hardships encountered throughout the crisis and the immediate aftermath.

Many of these entries were first penned in letters and diaries while women lived through the storm and provided critical physical and psychological care for others. In this sense, the words are unique in that they were not written for this collection or for the eyes of the general public, at least at first, but instead were privately recorded as a way to make sense of the events. In some cases, these recordings were made in real time as journal entries or as desperate attempts to communicate the conditions to others as a plea for help. Advocacy organizations, too, sought to document the different perspectives, for example, in the stories of women laborers and community organizers, whose voices are included here. Taken together, these accounts begin to convey the diversity and complexity of women's ideas and experiences, though of course, these tell only one part of the Katrina story. Including these first-person accounts adds a different voice and compelling context to the empirical studies that follow.

CHAPTER 5

Surviving Hurricane Katrina

Mary Gehman

Tuesday, August 30

A restroom call woke me at 3 a.m.: I was catapulted into one of the worst days of my life. Had I known what was to come, I very probably would not have gotten out of bed. The dogs greeted me with canine expectation, seeming a bit less nervous than before. I remembered the rising water downstairs and grabbed the flashlight, shining it down the winding stairwell. Water had risen to cover the second step—I knew if I didn't go down there immediately and collect everything I could of fresh water, food, and other items, we would be doomed.

The water, as I eased into it from the slick hardwood stairs, came up above my knees to mid-thigh, well over two feet deep. The flashlight flickered in the thick, humid darkness. Why hadn't I bothered to put new batteries into it? I scolded myself and went back upstairs to get a lit candle and set it on the stairs as a reference point. This was not the time for panic. The floorboards were slippery, coated I assumed by a film of oil and filth. I was barefoot in order to feel my way better and maintain a grip. Already the floorboards were beginning to warp, and the linoleum on the kitchen floor was soggy under my feet.

What to grab from the mess downstairs? Systematically I reached for the most practical first: five one-gallon jugs of fresh water I had set aside, packaged snacks, some canned goods, several apples left on the kitchen table. The refrigerator would be hard to open due to the water so I could only speculate what was left to rot inside it. Ice cubes from the top freezer unit were dumped into a cooler floating near the stove. I added a half-eaten carton of ice cream and a plastic bag of frozen blueberries on top of the ice. Who knew how many days I'd be holed up with eating as my only diversion? The dog food came next with a box of dog biscuits and more newspaper.

It soon became obvious that I'd tire too fast making the trip each time into the upstairs rooms, so I began setting things on the steps, beginning with the top one first. Later I could fetch items from there as needed or as the water kept rising. Twice in my haste I took a nasty spill on the slippery steps, once nearly dropping my key ring into the murky water. I hit my tailbone and elbow and already felt bruises forming. I couldn't afford to break a leg or arm! Some things would have to stay downstairs for lack of space to store them upstairs or lack of time and energy to carry them up. The flashlight kept flickering with its mean threat to quit on me. Somehow I hadn't figured it would take this much time, planning, and energy to complete such a simple task.

It was nearly 5 a.m. as I finished bringing up as many items as I could from downstairs. The shelves of books would have to stay put, as would my grandson's toys. The water had come up over three feet, just even with the top of the dining room table. After washing my feet and legs from the clean water in the bathtub, I remembered that my camera had been forgotten in the top drawer of the French antique hutch and waded back down into the water to retrieve it, taking a few shots from various angles of the side entrance foyer of my furniture standing stoically in the dark, sparkling water. My eyes were blurred by obstinate tears—I could not believe I had lived to see such a scene. Already I was beginning to disassociate myself from the comfortable house and life I had held so dear and worked relentlessly to maintain. It was still all salvageable if the water went down in a day or two, but I had no assurance it would.

Upstairs I untied the tall cypress shutters and walked out on to the balcony. A silent watery sunrise greeted me. All around the buildings swam in a lake of dark, foreboding water. It had not yet begun to reek of raw sewage and flotsam but that was obviously coming as the day heated up. Voices wafted across the water from around street corners in eerie displacement. Someone was yelling for Dana and someone, presumably Dana, was calling back from a distance. A motorboat churned past out on Tulane Avenue. The dogs wanted to come out on the balcony and it occurred to me that if I led them to the far corner where the railing went along the side to the end of the house, they'd relieve themselves. I was right—they were immediately calmer. Too bad I hadn't thought of that the night before.

Saving Ms. Jane from Drowning

Helicopters criss-crossed the skies directly overhead. Between their noisy flights a woman's voice was audible to me on the balcony from several houses down in the alley. It startled me to realize that Ms. Jane was still in her house, barely visible as she stood in the front doorway in water up to her midriff. Why hadn't she left when the water started coming in? There was no access to the attic of her one-story house, and had there been, she was not strong enough to ax her way through the roof. "I've been standing here for hours, calling for help," she sniffled. "My legs are tired. I have to sit down." Immediately I called to a man standing eye level to me on the second story of a covered parking garage of the office building across the alley to help rescue my neighbor (also my tenant). A mini–police center had been set up there. He said he had heard her there and was already trying to get a boat to stop for her. Thank goodness the generator of that ten-floor-tall building had run out of fuel and shut off; otherwise we couldn't have heard a thing.

For the next two hours I was out on the balcony assuring Ms. Jane that help was on the way if she could just hold on a little longer. She could swim, she said, but we couldn't figure out to what she should swim and whether or not, given her age and heavy smoking, she'd make it. Then what? Several times boats filled with passengers passed by out on the avenue and promised to come back but we waited without much hope. I tied a white t-shirt to a long stick and waved it from the balcony, hoping to catch the eye of a helicopter pilot but to no avail. The water must have stopped rising because Ms. Jane was not sinking farther. I wracked my brains thinking of a way to get to her. She could stay with me upstairs if only I could get her over the balcony railing. There was no way she could get in downstairs.

Just as I was starting to feel hysterical, like a mirage, an inflatable dinghy from the sheriff's office rounded the corner of Tulane and headed down the alley. A lot more people in the office building had gotten in on the yelling for a boat and they steered the rescuers to Ms. Jane, who nearly collapsed as she was pulled like a sack of potatoes over the side of the dinghy. We all clapped and hooted as the boat took off. I have no idea as I write this what happened next for Ms. Jane nor if I will ever see her again. I do know that the immense panic and sadness one feels in the face of helplessness, topped for me by equally immense relief to see my neighbor rescued, were emotions tumbling around inside me much like clothes inside an electric dryer. Like those clothes at last dry, I felt warm and cleansed in spite of the uncertainty of what lay ahead.

For an hour or two Tuesday afternoon I listened to the wind-up radio and tried to figure out what to do next. I wanted to stay on with the dogs, to stick it out until the water receded. We had enough food and water, and if pushed to do so, I could always go downstairs for more. There was no more running water but we'd make do with what we had. The prospect of being the only person on the block, and a lone woman at that, bothered me a bit, given the reports of looting, potshots at police, a general sense of lawlessness. At night it was pitch black, and even the dogs would be useless in facing down a determined intruder, especially if he or they had guns.

The commentators on WWL radio kept saying the water was still rising in some parts of town, the levee break could not be repaired for days, maybe weeks, and that anyone who had remained in N.O. should get out. How was not quite clear. The Superdome was full and there were people standing on overpasses in various places. As I lay on the bed in the quiet heat with no fan to cool me as usual and listened to repeated pleas by city officials to evacuate, I thought about how there was no way to let my family know I was O.K. They must be wondering about me by now. I also heard another wood-cracking sound like I had heard during the storm, then another coming from a new line opening up in the plaster on the far wall of my bedroom. It dawned on me that the water downstairs could be putting extra stress on the structure of the house, and I had visions of the upper floor collapsing onto the first on top of me in the middle of the night. This was not at all what I had imagined toughing it out to be!

Mary Gehman is a researcher, writer, and publisher specializing in Louisiana topics, specifically Louisiana women, Creoles, and the River Road. She is the owner of the publishing company Margaret Media, Inc. A longtime New Orleans resident, she lost her home to Katrina and now lives upriver in Donaldsonville, Louisiana.

This chapter was reprinted with permission from the diary of Mary Gehman, recorded September through October 2005, *www.margaretmedia.com/Surviving_Katrina.pdf.*

CHAPTER 6

We Cannot Forget Them

Annette Marquis

September 18: Success Stories

When seventy-six-year-old Gilda arrived at the shelter she quickly won everyone's heart. Rather than evacuate New Orleans with various members of her family who were heading in different directions out of the city, she chose to drive a sixty-year-old, mentally challenged friend of hers to Mississippi where this woman's relatives lived. Just outside Hattiesburg, her car broke down. The car had to be left and Gilda and her friend were given a ride to the shelter to sit out the storm. For the next three weeks, Gilda searched for her daughter, her niece, anyone who could take her in. She posted her information on the Internet, she was interviewed by the newspaper, she spoke with the radio and the TV news. Her health deteriorated and she spent time in the hospital before returning to the shelter to wait for some information about her family.

One day last week, when she returned to the shelter after a doctor's visit, she found that her friend had left the shelter without her. Now utterly alone, she tried hard not to despair but despair was clearly setting in. She was angry, hurt, and terrified of never finding her family. But even then, she had a good word for anyone who would listen; she helped the woman in the cot next to hers find clothes that would fit her; and she hugged anyone who needed a hug.

Then, just two days ago, she received a call at the shelter. Her niece found her listed on the Internet and immediately called her. Yesterday, her niece came to get her and took her home with her. I can't think about Gilda without tears coming to my eyes. What an amazing spirit she is! God clearly lives in her soul.

Although not quite as dramatic as Gilda's story, Mary's story touched me in a different way. With no home of her own, Mary worked as a live-in caregiver to an elderly woman. The house where she was living was destroyed and the person she was caring for moved in with relatives. Like countless others, suddenly Mary had no place to live, no job, and no hope of getting a FEMA trailer. She thought she could get another live-in job but with no phone where potential employers could call her, the prospects didn't look good. She was becoming more and more depressed by the day. After we talked on Friday, I was pretty convinced she would be one of the long-term victims of Katrina with little chance of recovery. Then on Saturday, a woman stopped by the shelter. Mary happened to overhear her tell the Red Cross worker at the registration desk that she lives alone in a four-bedroom house just down the road from the shelter and wondered if anyone there wanted to come live with her. Mary jumped at the chance and now has a nice place to live, a new friend, and renewed hope. She hugged me when she left and thanked me for the time I had spent with her. She walked out the door of the shelter with a smile on her face.

September 25: My Eyes Are Tired

A member of the Gulf Coast UU Fellowship told a story at this Sunday's service of being out with her grandson one day last week. "Grandma," he said, "can we go home now? My eyes are tired." Like so many others, he was tired of seeing debris and devastation, tired of downed trees, blocked roads, and damaged buildings, and what another member described as "seeing people's lives thrown out on the curb." . . . I must admit, my eyes, too, have grown tired—tired of seeing people in despair and recognizing that there is only so much that outsiders can do. We can give emotional support, we can offer money, we can even provide physical resources, but in the end, it is up to the residents to rebuild their communities, to restore balance, to regain control, to reestablish routines, to renew their compassion, and to recreate places to rest their eyes. What those of us on the outside have to recognize, however, is that this region is a long way from rebuilding and an even longer way from routine.

October 6: The Story That Broke My Heart

As I returned to my home in Michigan, I realized that I saved the hardest stories until I had time to process them, to cry about them, to feel some distance from them. The hardest stories were those that touched my heart in some way that I have not let it be touched in recent memory. They dug deep, like a rabbit burrowing into the earth to build a strong, safe home to protect her from the harsh Michigan winter. They clung to me, invading my soul and demanding to be let in. These are the stories of trust, of pain, of love, of helplessness, of hope.

It was Friday night at the Hattiesburg shelter. I had been working there for three nights now and was pretty familiar with the people there and with what to expect. My crisis intervention training has taught me to never be surprised, to expect the unexpected, to be ready for anything. I thought I was. And then at about 7 p.m. I overheard a woman at the front reception desk tell the Red Cross worker that she needed help. She had driven from St. Bernard Parish with several others because they had heard that they could get help from the Red Cross in Hattiesburg. They had lost everything in the storm, were staying with family and friends, and had been unable to get any help in the area they were in. They needed food and clothing for their children. Was there any help available here? The response she received was not what she wanted to hear. She was told she had to register with the Red Cross the next morning and then she'd be given a time to come back for assistance. The woman started crying and said, "Can't anybody help us?"

When it was clear she was not going to get any help there, I asked her to step outside so I could talk with her. Two other women followed her. "Are they with you?" I asked. "Yes, and so are these other people," she said, pointing to a group of others standing outside. "We caravanned here because we have to find some help." I asked them all to pull up chairs so we could talk. Nine people gathered around. Five women and four men of varying ages. "Are you all related?" I asked. "No," was the response. "We just found ourselves in the same situation. We all have children and we all are desperate for help," an older man replied.

As they told their stories, I learned that these nine people were all heads of households. They all had children but no place to call home. The only help they had received so far was from a church that brought a few meals into the neighborhood where they were staying. Their welcomes were wearing out with the families that took them in. They came to Hattiesburg out of pure desperation because they heard this was where the Red Cross had set up their offices. They figured if they couldn't get help here, they couldn't get help anywhere. Looking into their eyes was like looking into a deep well where you could only imagine how far down the bottom was.

I asked if they had eaten today. "No," was the universal reply. The timing was good because the late dinner was about to be served at the shelter and they were welcome to eat there. I also asked if they would each write down their names, their children's names, their ages, and where they were staying. Each person took the notebook and in turn, wrote down their family information. When they handed the notebook back to me, I took a sharp intake of air as I reviewed the list: Robert, age 10, Robin, 11, Regina, 12, Devonta, 7, BruShawn, 10 months, Johnita, 4 months, two sets of twins: Jessica and Joshua, age 1 and Brittney and Daniela, 6 months, and the list went on— 34 children, 4 adults, plus the 9 adults who were sitting in front of me, 47 people ranging in age from 4 months to an aging grandmother who felt so much desperation that she rode with them 125 miles to try to find help for her family. I knew we had to do something.

While they were devouring their dinners, I called Rev. Jacqueline Luck, the minister I was working with, and asked for her thoughts. She said she would call the member of the Ellisville church, Peggy Owens-Mansfield, who was the Red Cross director in Laurel (see an article about Peggy on the *UU World* website: "Mississippi Red Cross leader inspired by Universalist Clara Barton"), thirty-three miles up the road, and see what she suggested. Within minutes Jacqueline called back. "If they get to the fairgrounds in Laurel at seven o'clock tomorrow morning, they can apply for and get a check from the Red Cross. They will need identification and Social Security numbers of their family members. Do they have that?" Yes, they had brought whatever they could find. Because they would not be able to cash the checks until Monday, Jacqueline said she would drive in to meet them and to give them cash to hold them over. When Jacqueline arrived, we gave each family $40 out of a private $1000 donation Jacqueline had received. Not a lot of money but enough to buy food to get them through the weekend.

We discussed staying the night in the shelter and then leaving early in the morning. But after much discussion, they decided to head up to Laurel and sleep in their cars so they would be first in line. One woman was especially concerned about leaving her babies overnight with the family they were staying with. She was afraid they would kick them out. But after reaching them by phone, she agreed to the plan to spend the night in Laurel.

Before they left, I invited them all back to the clothing distribution room in the shelter to pick up some things they needed. Each person searched for clothing and supplies to help their families, who had nothing. They picked up jeans, diapers, a housecoat, t-shirts, a pair of shoes. Enough to get by till something else comes along.

After expressing their gratitude for our help, they were on their way. As the cars pulled out of the shelter's parking lot, Jacqueline and I both questioned whether we had helped enough, whether what we did made a difference, and, we're both sad to say, whether we had been scammed. What I know is that the eyes of these people came back to life as their stomachs were filled. I know that their bodies relaxed, they became more talkative, and they became more trusting as a bit of hope was restored. I can't know more than that. Helping strangers is always a risk but in this case, I can't help but believe the risk was well worth it. What we knew was that forty-seven people had food in their stomachs that weekend. Forty-seven people had a few clothes on their backs. Forty-seven people had hope that the generosity of others would pull them through this tragedy.

October 10: We Cannot Forget Them

This is the final entry to my diary and I must admit that I am hesitant to write it. I'm hesitant because I am so afraid that we will move on to another story, another tragedy, another priority. There are certainly enough to choose from: the earthquake in Asia, mudslides in Central America, fires in California. But the people who were affected by Katrina cannot move on. They cannot move on until they have a place to live, a job to earn an income, schools to send their children to, stores to buy groceries from. And this will not happen if we move on to another crisis, if we forget that as we go about our "normal" routines, hundreds of thousands of people are struggling to find new routines, a new way to be in the world, a new way to survive.

Annette Marquis resides in Charlotte, North Carolina, and serves as district executive in the Southeast United States for the Unitarian Universalist Association of Congregations. She has extensive experience in crisis intervention, mental health, and trauma support services, and strives to use her writing to help others see the world through different eyes.

This chapter was excerpted with permission from the journal of Annette Marquis, Unitarian Universalist Association News and Events, Fall 2005, *archive.uua.org/ news/2005/050831_katrina/diary.html.*

CHAPTER 7

"Help!" a Little Girl Cries

Women and Children in Catastrophic Times

Denny Taylor

In the middle of the chaos children are crying. It's five weeks since Katrina and my second emergency response to the hurricane. Some of the children have no expression on their faces; others look anxious and afraid. A few are playing. One little girl sits on the edge of a cot and silently screams. She mouths, "Help!" over and over. "Help! Help!" I stop and ask the little girl if she is okay. She looks at me and nods. The pain in her eyes is distressing to see and I want to sit with her, but I am in a hurry. It's late. There is another emergency—a woman is seriously ill. I leave the little girl to get medical help and when I return I can't find her.

When the levees broke the day after Katrina, the River Center Shelter in Baton Rouge filled up. The first time I was there was ten days after the storm. I visited the shelter as soon as I got off the plane and managed to return several times between my visits to schools to provide first-response support for principals, school counselors, and teachers. At the time there were 4,500 people in the shelter—poor families with young children, older adults who were sick and frail, and many men and women with physical disabilities or needing mental health services.

Watching as the scene played out in television news coverage there was a terrible tension, hopelessness and helplessness, guilt and culpability. Talking heads blamed the evacuees for not leaving. They said they should have got out. They should have left before it was too late. But nagging at all of us was the knowledge that we didn't rescue them. We knew we left them without food or water or medical help. We waited until it was too late.

"Nothing never came," a man says, when I stop and speak with him.

"I lost everything," a woman from the Ninth Ward says, when I sit with her. "I'm just trying to survive." She tells me her name is Sherry. I ask if she would tell me her age. "I'm seventy-nine," she says. "Seventy-nine and I lived in the Ninth Ward all my life."

"They say they're giving trailers," another woman says.

"We really need a place to stay," a man says, who is there with his wife and eight children. "I've always worked and supported my kids, but they want to bus us out of town. What do we do when we get to another state? You've got a bus ride, but then what? My kids will be on the streets."

"We need help now," a grandmother in a wheelchair cries. "Now!" Her grand-daughter is also in a wheelchair.

The shelter is filled with cots, air beds, piles of bedding, clothes in plastic bags, paper bags, bottles, cardboard boxes. People are walking, standing, sitting up, lying down, hidden under grey blankets, curled and out straight, wracked, boots on, socks off, nodding, smiling, vacant, staring, shocked and startled, hands moving quickly, rocking back and forth, in wheelchairs holding their heads, ashen, sick with fevers, flushed, coughing, struggling to catch their breath. I spend my time in the shelter talking with people, making note of emergency supplies—items that we forget are needed, like adult incontinent garments, lotion—and take them in when I next visit.

Mostly I just listen. Taking the time to listen is an important response when catastrophic events take place, and as an ethnographer I have spent a lifetime listening to people talk about what has happened to them. So I walk cot to cot, introduce myself, sit down if invited, and sometimes hold hands as I talk with them and hear their stories if they tell them. However, I do not ask what happened to them during the storm. Psychiatric research cautions against such direct questioning.

Four weeks later, I am back in the shelter. I find Suzie and her sisters, Diane and Marianne, whom I met during my first visit. Their house was in New Orleans Parish in the section known as Lakeview. "Ground Zero," her sister, Marianne, called it. Suzy has Crohn's and is a double amputee. Just after the hurricane I sat with them in the shelter and they showed me pictures in the photograph album they had managed to save. They showed me pictures of Suzy when she was a young girl, standing, laughing, and later when her legs had been amputated still smiling with her arms around a valentine pillow. They show me pictures of their mother, who died when Suzy was a child, and their father, whose house they had lived in all their lives.

"Two years ago Daddy died," Marianne tells me. "Then our little dog died and it snowed at Christmas in New Orleans." She turned a page in the album. "I take a picture of this tree every year. I love this tree. Now it's gone. There is nothing left. It's all gone."

I find Diane sitting on her own. She tells me that Suzy is ill and that Marianne has gone with her to the women's room. There's an awkward moment when she confides that they need undergarments for Suzy and she tells me what to get. We talk for a while. Diane says they have been unable to get medical help for Suzy, and that they have been unable to find a place to live. She says Suzy is spending hours in the bathroom and might not be back for a long time. I suggest that I visit with other people while I wait. It was during this time that I met Gent'il, whom you will meet soon, but first I am going to write about what happened to Suzy.

When I return, Suzy is sitting in her wheelchair. Her face is ashen and she looks so malnourished I'm visibly shaken by the amount of weight she has lost in the last four weeks. Diane and Marianne are looking at me. They are both haggard and there are dark circles beneath their eyes.

"She's had to take her legs off," Diane tells me. "She has lesions on her stumps and they are bleeding."

"They're bleeding a lot," Suzy says. "They keep bleeding."

Marianne and Dianne tell me that Suzy has not been seen by a doctor, and they recount all their efforts to get medical assistance for Suzy. They talk about trying to get food that she could eat. Every day they continue to struggle to take care of Suzy, as well as try to find a place to live. There are piles of newspapers in which they have been searching for accommodation. I have written about getting assistance for Suzy and will not recount the struggle to get medical assistance for her, except to state that what happened to her and to her sisters is an indication of the inadequacy of the first-response models that framed life in the River Center Shelter. The lack of support *and* the ineffectual establishment of inappropriate rules and regulations reduced the opportunities of the three sisters to take care of each other and find a place to live. They were made dependent and then given nothing to depend on. It is not an exaggeration for me to write that it was the grit and determination of Diane and Marianne that was keeping Suzy alive.

From a research perspective other questions arise. Equally important are the insights their story and the one that follows provide into the difficult decisions that first responders have to make when disasters occur. There were many others in the shelter who desperately needed assistance. Taking a different approach to emergency intervention than the approach that had become institutionalized in the shelter, I helped Suzy get the medical care she needed, made arrangements for her to be provided with a special diet, and left with the promise that a special-needs trailer at a nearby hospital would be obtained for her and her sisters. But there were others whom I would have helped if Suzy's situation had not been so dire.

While I wait to say hello to her, I visit with other people still living in the shelter. A woman tells me her daughter is having contractions, but she says she is taking care of her. I ask her daughter if I can visit and she invites me to sit down. She explains that she is trying not to have her baby.

"Your baby is due?" I ask.

"Yes," Gent'il says. She is lying on a cot and her three-year-old daughter, Shanuja, is standing by her.

"How long have you been in the River Center Shelter?"

"Since August 31."

"That's a long time! How are you feeling?"

"Okay now," Gent'il says, as she slowly sits up. "Sometimes I have my pains. Yes, I am feeling pains. I'm having contractions."

Gent'il says she has been told that preparations have been made to transfer her to the nearest hospital as soon as she is ready to go. She says that in the meantime her mother is trying to take care of her. She says she has not told anyone that she is having contractions. She explains that she is trying *not* to have her baby because she doesn't have a place to live.

"They told us that they got trailers," Gent'il says. "But they have to send them back. So we might be here 'til the first of next month."

"The first of November?" I ask. "That's another month."

"I can't be here until November," Gent'il says, "because I need to have my baby. I don't want to come back in here. It's a place you don't want to be. I don't want to come back and I don't want to go to another shelter." She talks about going to the hospital. "We'll *all* go," she says, looking determined as she explains. "As long as I *get in* the hospital and they give me a place, I'll bring my mother and daughter. Once they give me one, I'll take everybody with me."

"If you wanted someone to know something about being here with your daughter, what would you want them to know?"

"It's *not* a good place to be, *especially* with a child," Gent'il says. "You don't know who has the cold or sickness. My daughter got sick. She got a fever for five days. I gave her some medicine. Don't know the name right now but it fights infections and makes her feel better. It keeps her well."

"Have you been sick?"

Gent'il nods. "When I go outside, it clears up and I feel better, but when I come back inside, it's messed up and I feel sick."

"Is there anything you need that I can bring you?"

"Not offhand," Gent'il smiles, as she shakes her head. "Just a place to live."

Gent'il is incapacitated by the inadequacy of the support she is receiving. The difficulties the people in the shelter experienced with the emergency relief are deeply rooted in our enculturation into "blaming the victim." We ascribe to individuals in-adequacies and deficiencies that are socially constructed and deeply embedded in the organizational structures that adversely affect people's lives—especially the lives of their children.

We do not know what effect the uncertainty of Gent'il's life in the aftermath of the storm will have on the child she is carrying, but we do know that the health and well-being of mothers affects their unborn children. Similarly we do not know what the possible life consequences will be for Shanuja, but we do know that the physical, cognitive, social, and emotional development of even the youngest of children can be adversely affected.

At the River Center Shelter Gent'il lies still. Her mother is watching Shanuja. She says that when the time comes they are ready to go and that the Red Cross vol-unteers have made arrangements for Gent'il to be taken to the hospital. She smiles and says that she and Shanuja will go with her, adding that Gent'il will not go with-out them. Reluctantly I say goodbye and tell them I hope they have a place to live soon. I return to the sisters and it is then that I learn how sick Suzy has become. The rest of my time in the shelter that evening is spent trying to get medical help for Suzy.

Writing now about the struggle to help Suzy reminds me again of the little girl silently shouting, "Help!" and I relive the scene. I bend down and speak to her. She is sitting on a cot and the cots on either side are empty. There are no adults in her immediate vicinity. I ask her if she is okay, knowing that she is not. I wonder if she is reliving what happened to her during the hurricane, but I do not know. She stops shouting for help but the look on her face is far away. I want to sit with her, hold her hand, and be there for her, but I stand up and tell her I'll come back. She looks at me as if she doesn't expect to see me again. It hurts to write this.

The shelter is closing for the night and I have been told I have to leave. I hurry on to the medical unit on the other side of the shelter to get help for Suzy. The unit is closed but I refuse to go. A Red Cross volunteer promises me that Suzy will receive the medical assistance that she needs. Notes are made so actions can be taken.

I hurry back to find the little girl, but I can't find her. A woman is lying on the cot next to the one on which the little girl had been sitting. The woman says she hasn't seen her. She says no one was on the cot when she came back to her own, and that there aren't any children on the cots near her. I look around. There are adults ar-ranging bedding ready for the night, sitting talking, lying down, but no children. I cannot find her. I hurry on to let the three sisters know that Suzy will receive the help she needs.

Later, I am allowed back into the shelter with undergarments for Suzy if I promise to "be quick." In haste I try to find the little girl, but now the cots are just a mass of grey blankets. Again, I wonder what happened to her. I know exactly where she is in the pages of my notebook, in which file in my computer, but I have worked with so many children since then that I am not sure I would recognize her if I met her again. Paradoxically, I can't see her face, but I can see her open mouth and hear her silent scream. I imagine her as everybody's child. Each time I research the statistics on children when catastrophic events take place, or read the psychiatric research on children and mass trauma, she is there. In between the words, behind the photographs, she is the nameless, faceless child who represents the millions of children who live in areas of armed conflict, natural disasters, extreme poverty, and public health emergencies around the world.

I do know what happened to Suzy. I was able to follow up and visit her and her two sisters when they eventually found a house to rent in Baton Rouge. But I have no idea what happened to Gent'il and her baby, or to Shanuja and her grandmother. Thinking of them makes me question whether I could have done more to help them. I tell my students that if we do research in the real world we have to get comfortable being uncomfortable—and I am uncomfortable. But if I was not? If we are not? What would that say about us? Our humanity? Our capacity for empathy?

Taking responsibility and acting in the world in the hope of making a difference means more than responding to a catastrophe, whatever the magnitude. Each disaster has its own signature. Catastrophic events and acts of mass violence create complexly interrelated cultural, historical, ethnic, racial, religious, political, and national ways of being that are constitutive of the individual and collective identities of the people whose lives are affected—especially the lives of women and children.

Denny Taylor is a professor of literacy studies at Hofstra University, where she is also founder and director of the International Center for Everybody's Child. She is the author of nine books, and her postdoctoral studies include socio- and psycholinguistics and, for the past ten years, psychiatric research on children and mass trauma.

CHAPTER 8

Unexpected Necessities

Inside Charity Hospital

Ruth Berggren

The skyscraper housing the oldest continuously operating hospital in the country, New Orleans's Charity Hospital, was erected in 1936, to replace a centuries-old complex that had grown rapidly to keep pace with the health needs of impoverished southern Louisiana. In August 2005, shattered windows notwithstanding, this twentieth-century Charity endured Hurricane Katrina's winds and survived. On Sunday, August 28, I was assigned as teaching physician for the infectious diseases unit on the ninth floor of the hospital. There were eighteen patients in the unit, of whom four had active tuberculosis and thirteen had opportunistic infections related to HIV infection and AIDS. We also had a boarder from surgery with a complicated gunshot wound and vascular access problems.

After the hurricane hit, I discovered that medical care in such situations becomes a matter of first aid and survival. We had no laboratory tests, no radiology services, no ability to confer with specialists, and poor communication. The medical decisions I faced were fairly simple: if possible, patients who had been receiving intravenous medication were switched to oral medication, and central venous catheters were removed to prevent bloodstream infections. We monitored vital signs and the blood glucose levels of patients with diabetes. We continued to dispense medications and used clinical diagnostic skills to make therapeutic decisions. I did perform a lumbar puncture Tuesday morning after the power went out to manage increased intracranial pressure in my patient with cryptococcal meningitis.

What became most important in this crisis, however, had little to do with medical management and much to do with personal preparedness, professionalism, and ethics. Survival, functioning, and sanity, for both patients and care providers, depended critically on a number of unexpected necessities, ranging from simple commodities to principles and codes of behavior. My list of ten of these necessities begins with the seemingly trivial and progresses to those that became the most critical as the crisis deepened from Sunday through Friday.

Shoes. Sunday morning, I drove home to collect my husband and our twelve-year-old son. As our son climbed into the car with pillows and a cartoon book, it never occurred to me to look at his feet. Days later, I learned that he and several other preadolescent children of physicians had left their homes with nothing but socks on their feet. Perhaps the child development experts could enlighten us about this phenomenon.

For me, running shoes were perfect for the countless trips up and down nine flights of stairs after the power went down. People with bad shoes have a much more difficult time climbing in and out of rescue boats after a flood.

NSAIDs. For lack of brewed coffee or cold Cokes after Monday, we all had severe caffeine-withdrawal headaches. The large bottle of generic nonsteroidal anti-inflammatory pills that I had brought made me popular throughout the hospital and allowed me to take care of my coworkers.

Underwear and a fanny pack. As the days passed without running water, each of us wanted more clean underwear. The extreme heat didn't help, and it made it impossible to wear the traditional white coat with pockets. Wearing shorts and sleeveless shirts, we found that fanny packs were ideal for keeping track of messages, prescription pads, pens, and flashlights.

Flashlights and D batteries. The flashlight I had brought with me burned out after four days, and I had to beg, borrow, or steal illumination thereafter. I needed a flashlight even during daylight hours to navigate the dark halls and stairwells. The emergency lanterns distributed from the emergency department on Wednesday night could have lit an entire nursing station, but for one problem: each required eight size-D batteries, and there were none to be found.

Toilets. The toilets filled up by Tuesday morning, and the "portapotty" placed at the end of a long hallway became equally unpleasant several days later. There was no water to wash our hands, and we worried about the bacteria we were spreading. Clostridium difficile had been rampant on the ward before the storm; by Wednesday, everyone had diarrhea, and I put most patients on metronidazole, suspecting an outbreak.

A night nurse wearied of our complaints and stayed up during the day shift to create two restrooms. In the room where a nonambulatory patient had been evacuated, the toilet was still pristine; she scoured it with bleach and designated it for urine only. In the adjacent room, she set up a bedpan on a chair protected by an absorbent disposable pad. She placed a roll of large biohazard bags nearby and taught us to insert the bedpan into a biohazard bag when we needed to relieve ourselves, to invert the bag over the bedpan afterwards, and to knot it and drop it into a covered biohazard waste bin. Such innovations kept us human.

Shift work and adequate sleep. The nurses, experts at the concept of shift work, adhered to a disciplined schedule. They started at 7 a.m., ended at 7 p.m., gave report, and went to sleep. The night nurses did the same from 7 p.m. to 7 a.m. They maintained their ability to communicate coherently and to dispense kindness and caring to those who were suffering. In contrast, the doctors were terrible about sleep. Except in the emergency department, there was no clear delineation of shift work. After forty-eight hours, a dedicated and respected colleague was already displaying word-finding difficulty, and the problem continued to worsen. We are biologic creatures, and there is just one way for us to recharge our cognitive functions. If we don't discipline ourselves to do this, we compound the danger with our incoherence.

Morale-boosting activities. The hospital organized daily prayer services with a chaplain and several gospel singers. I attended one service with the mother of my patient who desperately needed evacuation for dialysis. I saw blacks and whites, young and old, patients and providers, rich and poor holding hands and praying for deliverance. I will never be able to sing "We Shall Overcome" quite the same way again.

At the suggestion of our nursing codirector, we made a banner from sheets—"9 West has a big heart, Katrina can't tear us apart"—and hung it out the fire escape. In twenty-four hours, fifteen more banners followed on other units. One night, we hosted a flashlight-illuminated talent show, to which we invited everyone—including the patients with tuberculosis, who donned N95 masks.

The strength of initiative to make your rescue needs known. It was painful to watch helicopters ceaselessly evacuating insured patients from the roof of nearby Tulane Hospital while our 250 patients were evacuated by twos or threes in boats said to lead to buses that sometimes did not appear. These halting efforts were interrupted for hours by gunfire. No National Guard was in evidence, other than as intermittent rescue personnel. Even colleagues at the neighboring Veterans Affairs hospital were unaware of the desperate conditions at Charity. Because our unit had a functioning telephone line and I had friends with media connections, I was able to communicate our situation to television and radio reporters. I received calls offering helicopters and one from CNN medical correspondent Sanjay Gupta. When I sought clearance for him from hospital officials, they gruffly asserted: "He can film whatever he wants; the media is our rescue plan now." When television cameras were pointed at us, the help came faster and more effectively.

Self-possession in the face of desperate armed men. We had a patient from Orleans Parish Prison on our ward, with newly diagnosed HIV infection, pancolitis, and bloody diarrhea. He was initially shackled to the bed and had armed guards, but soon the two guards dwindled to one and the shackles were removed without explanation. When the remaining guard began to disappear for hours at a time, I objected—and had words with him, though he was sweaty, disgruntled, and armed. The chief of security had to come mediate.

I was never afraid of wind, water, fire, hunger, or disease. My moments of fear came when I was confronted by agitated, fearful human beings bearing firearms. My husband was exposed to sniper fire twice while helping to evacuate the emergency-room dock. People with guns shut down an entire hospital evacuation for many hours. The real Katrina disaster was not created by the elements but by a society whose fabric had been torn asunder by inequality, lack of education, and the inexplicable conviction that we should all have access to weapons that kill.

A team. The most critical necessity is a team of professionals who care about their patients and one another. All eighteen members of our team (black, white, rich, poor, gay, or straight) had chosen to care for the disenfranchised, the tuberculous, and the HIV-infected. We might not have been able to control what was happening to us, but we could control how we treated one another. I repeatedly declined the option of fleeing to the Tulane helipad across the street, where my son waited with another family. Our group received an offer of special rescue, which we did not accept until each and every one of our patients had been evacuated.

In the end, we were kicked off the ward by armed men and shouted at by people herding us with bullhorns as they shoved bound, violent psychiatric patients past us on gurneys in the dark, fetid hallway, nearly knocking us to the ground. We were foisted onto boats by rough game wardens oblivious to our requests to travel together. After leaping into the swamp boats, we were rushed by armed guards to an empty helicopter pad, where we missed our would-be rescuers by minutes. We were then herded onto buses and repeatedly confronted by police, who insisted that we were not allowed at the airport. After several frantic cell-phone calls, our mostly intact group was directed to an unsecured hangar on the airfield to wait. Through the night, lying on the tarmac by the airstrip, I reflected on the reasons for our survival.

Ruth Berggren joined the faculty at University of Texas Health Science Center San Antonio in 2006. Formerly associate professor of medicine and an infectious disease specialist at New Orleans's Charity Hospital and Tulane Medical Center, she remained at Charity for six days and nights after Katrina struck, working with medical staff to care for critically ill, abandoned patients.

This chapter was originally published in the *New England Journal of Medicine*, October 13, 2005, pp. 1550–1553. © 2005 by the New England Journal of Medicine. Reprinted by permission.

CHAPTER 9

"We Like to Think Houma Women Are Very Strong"

Brenda Dardar Robichaux, Ms. Foundation for Women Profile

Brenda's Story

"Up the bayou, down the bayou, across the bayou," replaces north, south, east, and west, where Brenda Dardar Robichaux grew up in Southeast Louisiana. Just forty-six miles from New Orleans, her hometown of Golden Meadow and its surrounding environs have been home to the United Houma Nation for generations.

Robichaux's father was an oyster and shrimp fisherman; her grandfather, a "traiteur," or healer. Her father's education ended in the seventh grade, because that was as far as Native Americans were allowed to go—hers was the first generation to integrate regular public schools and then to graduate from high school. Robichaux's mother served on the tribal council of this matriarchal tribe—the foundation, perhaps, for Robichaux's own tireless service to the United Houma Nation. Professionally, she works for the school board, helping them meet the academic and cultural needs of Native students. But her nonpaying job is as Principal Chief of the United Houma Nation.

"I remember growing up and thinking, I'm never getting involved in tribal politics," Robichaux says. "And then I ran for Principal Chief and won with 74 percent of the vote. Four years later, I ran unopposed and won. It is a labor of love." This devotion to her people was what inspired her to start the United Houma Nation Relief Fund in the wake of Katrina, which is helping thousands of tribe members return home and rebuild.

The United Houma Nation—whose 18,000 members make it the largest tribe in the State of Louisiana—live at what was to become the intersection of Hurricanes Katrina and Rita. First, Katrina devastated the tribe's small settlements in lower Plaquemines, lower St. Bernard, and lower Jefferson Parishes, leaving 1,000 members homeless, their homes completely destroyed by wind and water. Then, as the tribe marshaled their resources to help Katrina victims, Hurricane Rita pushed a massive storm surge into the bayous farther west of New Orleans. [. . .]

Keeping Generations Close to Their Land and History

When Katrina hit, Robichaux and her husband were on the Rosebud Sioux Reservation in South Dakota attending a tribal conference. By the time they returned to

Louisiana, people were already stranded at the airport. Robichaux quickly mobilized the resources of the tribe. They began searching for the members and addressing basic needs.

To help smooth this process, Robichaux's husband cleared out his grandfather's general store—which had been closed for fifty years. The once empty store, with its tin roof and faded American flags painted on the shutters, soon began to overflow with donated clothes, food, water, cleaning supplies, and plastic containers, and Robichaux created a system for disseminating and tracking the goods. "The attitude in the store was comforting," she says. "People only took what they needed—that's the spirit in our people." The story of Robichaux's good works was picked up by both Native radio and the mainstream press, and as a result, people from other tribes, from churches, and from across the United States responded. With their help, the United Houma Nation Relief Fund would eventually provide assistance to some 8,000 Houma families.

Immediately after the storms hit, however, the situation was particularly dire. The National Congress of the American Indian rented a plane to fly a few local leaders over Plaquemines Parish, and what they saw was near total devastation. "We became physically ill when we saw our community in this parish," Robichaux remembers. "The village of thirty families had nothing left—people's homes looked like they never existed; their homes were simply gone. They are all fishermen, and their boats were ashore, somewhere inland."

During those early days, Robichaux traveled down the bayou in her husband's truck; when they reached a point where water still covered the road, they got into pirogues (dugout canoes made from cypress) and brought people food and water that way. One day at 11:30 they got a call informing them that people had to leave the local shelter by noon. The tribe members were in total despair: kids were crying and no one knew where to go. People saw everything they owned on the side of the highways. Black, sludge swamp mud was everywhere, in homes and schools, and few people had insurance. Robichaux had never seen her people depressed in this way. "We like to think Houma women are very strong—they feel they must be the strong ones. I had to tell people that they had the right to feel bad." For months afterwards Brenda would sit on her porch with her face in her hands and cry, wondering, "How much can people endure?"

Yet it was in individuals that she found hope, Robichaux says. "The overwhelming response from all walks of life was astounding. People from across the country came to volunteer." Robichaux paired the volunteers with tribal members (to ensure that the tribal members they were serving would be comfortable), and sent them out to locate people and then deliver supplies. At the same time, the EAGLES— Emergency Air and Good List Evacuation Services—arrived with tribal doctors to administer flu and tetanus shots at the shelters and outside the general store. Tribal and nontribal members received shots; so many people turned up that the police had to be called to direct traffic.

Robichaux opened her home to these volunteers, some of whom slept on her front lawn in tents. Every night she cooked. "I learned how to cook big pots of lots of things that weren't expensive. And, at dinner, I learned about the volunteers' days. They were my eyes and ears in the community." Robichaux is clear that the presence of the volunteers made all the difference in the world: "They were a blessing. Even now I can still feel their presence, their energy. At night we held workshops on tribal history, basket weaving, so they could go back and educate people about the Houma."

Robichaux's greatest challenge, however, came from the federal government, which she believed should have come to their aid. The tribe is fighting for federal recognition status through the Bureau of Indian Affairs. To compound their pending status, no one could get through to FEMA or the Red Cross. "They were incompetent and ineffective," Robichaux comments. "I don't know where we would be without the volunteers. Our people have language barriers and education barriers; 47 percent of the adult population has less than a high school education."

Still, Robichaux is happy to describe the efforts that did make a difference, including those of a group of schoolchildren in California: "They had a 'break the rule day' [where] the kids could wear hats, temporary tattoos and break other rules, all for a dollar. We donated that money to a local school." Also, there has been help from the Native American community: the leader of the American Indian Movement made a detour from the "Sacred Run," which traditionally goes from Oklahoma to Washington, DC, stopping in Golden Meadow, where the tribal center is, to help raise awareness of the tribe and their traditions.

Though mindful of the many ways in which the generosity of others has made life better in the months since Katrina, Robichaux remains focused on her overall goal: to bring her people home. "I don't want it to be under my watch that we lose our community," she says. The communities that lost their homes have already begun to establish that community once again, in side-by-side FEMA trailers. And at one point after the storms, thirty-two tribal members shared a three-bathroom house. "Our people live all together—we have a strong sense of community," Robichaux says. "People just want to go home. It is not just land—we have lived here for generations. It is a community."

Life after Katrina: The Challenges One Year Later

Robichaux's home is now part office for the United Houma Nation Relief Fund. A bookshelf displays the traditions of her tribe: woven baskets, dolls, turtles, and alligators crafted from the Spanish moss that hangs from the oak trees. She and her staff are still caring for people's basic needs, but they will soon transform the general store from relief center to museum. It will honor their heritage and provide the tribe with a library and gift shop.

At the same time that they move ahead, Robichaux continues to search for displaced tribe members and to helping them resettle once they are found. A recent *New Orleans Times-Picayune* profile of her work helped her find another twenty members who were evacuated to Texas; now reconnected, she will work to bring them home. She finds that one year later, people are still sleeping on their floors when staff from the United Houma Nation Relief Fund arrives to distribute furniture. Robichaux relates, "The tears are always here. I'm seeing so much suffering, so much need, yet it is the strong spirit of the people that inspires me. I don't know how I would react [if I had lost everything]. We have made progress. The strength of our people is to say,

'We can overcome this and rebuild.'" Following in the footsteps of the strong Houma women before her Robichaux credits her ability to keep moving forward to her matrilineal heritage. She says: "Our women have been leaders. If not for being a strong Houma woman, I would not be where I am today. They've had to be strong and I've had to be strong."

Of her childhood, she remembers that "when I was a kid in school it was the civil rights movement, and I was in the first class to integrate. The other kids teased me; there was lots of name-calling. My mom would have to defend me." Now Robichaux's challenge is as a mother of a nine-year-old girl: to keep her safe and to raise her to be a strong Houma woman. "We've all adapted," Robichaux remarks. "It has been a family effort."

Home Is about Her Heritage and Her Community

Robichaux reflects on how her sense of home has changed since the hurricanes: "Oh yes, I get caught up in that materialistic world. [But] all it takes is one trip down the bayou," where her tribe members' homes were destroyed, to remind her how little "things" matter.

According to Robichaux, the storms affected just about everything. "Life as we knew it changed," she says. From Katrina until May, she and her family had people camped out in their home—and then, in the middle of it all, both of her parents were diagnosed with cancer. (Though as she recalls it, her father the fisherman "was more worried about missing shrimping" than he was about his diagnosis.)

Robichaux is very conscious of taking care of "her elders"—that is, all the elders. By her own admission, her greatest pleasure and connection to home and community came from fixing up Miss Marie Dean's home. This ninety-year-old tribe elder lost everything in the storm. She speaks only French and has been a resident artist at the Smithsonian. While volunteers cleaned her home, Miss Marie made moss dolls and baskets. In the end she said: "I raised my six kids here and my home has never been so pretty." Robichaux attended to every detail as though it was her own home.

She also notes that people who have left their homes ungutted for months are now beginning to go back to look for things. She says she appreciates deeply how the volunteers have taken great care to find and clean the remnants of her people's lives— the photos, the altars, the shelf someone's father carved—all to preserve community.

Brenda Dardar Robichaux was elected chairwoman of the 16,000-member Houma Nation and in 2002 attained the position of principal chief. Following hurricanes Katrina and Rita, she started the United Houma Nation Relief Fund helping thousands of tribal members to return.

This chapter is reprinted with permission from a Ms. Foundation report originally published December 15, 2006. *ms.foundation.org/our_work/broad-change-areas/ building-democracy/katrina-womens-response-fund/katrina-grantee-stories/ brenda-dardar-robichaux.*

CHAPTER 10

Coastal Women for Change

Biloxi, Mississippi

Sharon Hanshaw, Ms. Foundation for Women Profile

Sharon Hanshaw was out of town when Hurricane Katrina hit her lifelong home of Biloxi, Mississippi. She returned to face the total destruction of East Biloxi. She had lost both her home and the beauty salon she owned for twenty-one years. Hanshaw retrieved one antique table and photographs. The photos took sixteen hours to clean, but she wanted them, "to remember that she had a life."

After the first storm, Hanshaw ended up in Houston with her sister. Then when Rita hit, they were on the road for twenty-three hours, trying to leave town. Hanshaw soon returned to the Gulf Coast, where she spent five months moving between her children's homes until she received a FEMA trailer. Women of all ages, ranging from eighteen to eighty-two, and many nationalities began meeting nearby to talk about survival after the storm and what was happening to the community. Her car gone, Hanshaw hitchhiked to the meetings. She found that just talking made a difference for everyone, saying, "The women were broken down, they lost family members. The meetings helped people understand that everyone was going through the same thing."

Launching Coastal Women for Change:
Giving a Voice to East Biloxi Women

At the same time that the women needed to tell their stories to get beyond their personal experiences, Hanshaw became increasingly concerned as she watched developers and casino owners dominate Biloxi's recovery planning. "We have no houses, but we have casinos," Hanshaw observes. There were no organized community groups in Biloxi. Hanshaw helped start Coastal Women for Change (CWC) in January 2006 to give women a voice for their concerns about the direction and future of their community.

Initially, Hanshaw volunteered to be the secretary. Seeing her relentless spirit and tireless initiative, they asked her to serve as the executive director. In May 2006 Hanshaw began her second career. Not far from her office is a street named after her father, a revered minister who was active in the civil rights movement. Perhaps she is now following in his footsteps. Hanshaw says, "It became obvious that the poor people were the only group that was not organized and our needs were so great but we did not have a voice."

47

The group's first event was a community forum with the mayor, city council, and other elected officials. With the help of professional facilitators, two hundred people faced the mayor and asked him to explain what he was doing about their community's needs. "Many of us felt we had no input in the process. We realized that after giving our ideas related to the recovery of East Biloxi, our ideas were heard and acted upon if we had an organized effort," explains Hanshaw. Next, CWC members asked for seats on the mayor's planning commission. They were given five seats, on the subcommittees for finance, education, transportation, land use, and affordable housing. In July, Coastal Women for Change partnered with the NAACP to hold a Women of Color forum, "Assuming Leadership in the Aftermath of Katrina," identifying issues for a legislative housing agenda. CWC then collected 950 signatures on a fair-housing petition and presented them to elected officials.

When Moore Community House asked CWC to conduct a child-care needs-assessment survey in East Biloxi that was required to renew Moore House's license, CWC found that it was an opportunity to learn more about the community's needs in general. In their door-to-door surveys, Coastal Women for Change found women desperate for child care, but also discovered incidences of robbery and abuse of elders living alone in trailers who were now fearful to come to the door. Hanshaw alerted the police to increase patrols and surveillance, and created Emergency Preparedness Kits for seniors to record their emergency contact information, evacuation options, and prescriptions.

Life after Katrina: The Challenges One Year Later

One year after the storm Hanshaw says, "We may have to march to take our town back." Her message to the "decision makers" is, "Don't leave us out; let us be involved. Don't act like we don't exist." She is keenly aware that "we are on casino row—we're in the way." More and more lots are being bulldozed, some without people having a chance to go through their homes to try to find some remnant of their lives. Many people are still away and can't return. The city is silent and vacant.

The people who have returned to Biloxi are losing significant amounts of money to price gouging and fraud. Contractors are overcharging by twenty and thirty thousand dollars. Rents have doubled, "which makes you take a roommate from hell or take husbands back that you don't want," Hanshaw explains. There is no child care; mothers are nervously leaving their children with people they barely know. There have been forty-eight funerals since Katrina and the people dying are getting younger and younger. Hanshaw believes that it is partly due to the environment, that toxins are in the water, soil, and trailers.

People are depressed and desperate and crime is increasing. Hanshaw sees women becoming numb and self-medicating with alcohol and drugs. She does not judge them, but knows, "we can't be too busy for each other," so she keeps checking in on people. Hanshaw is a role model. She says, "I want the women to know that they all can make it—there's no choice, I must keep moving. I realize there will be obstacles and hardships."

One of Hanshaw's biggest challenges is one voiced repeatedly by people throughout the Gulf Coast region: people wondering why, a year later, she still isn't "over it." Her response is simple: "Just change spots, stay in my trailer for a night."

On the Difficulties of Being Seen and Heard as a Black Woman

"As black women we're catching it triple. They look over you and ignore you," says Hanshaw as she relates her recent visit to the bank. "They took several people ahead of me in line and treated me as though I was invisible. Finally a teller came over and intervened." Hanshaw's experience of "give it to the white girl first" has been the same in lines for food, FEMA trailers, and even State Farm Insurance. Hanshaw concludes, "It is 2006 and we're still in slavery."

Hanshaw finds that it is the women who are strong and dealing with life after Katrina. She notices how many men couldn't deal with it and left. "If we stop we will disintegrate—we have to keep moving—it is worse than being homeless. We're not saying take care of us, just give us a boost," Hanshaw comments. She has found that many of the young people who have come down to help aren't bound by the color line in the same way. It is they, along with her own children, the women around her, and her faith that motivates Hanshaw. "I know it is going to make a difference, if you believe, and you put God in there—we are going to succeed."

Recreating Home and Community

Hanshaw describes herself as "homeless and homelesser." She once created her sense of home by cooking and feeding people. Every Sunday was a family dinner, and it was always in her home. Now she has it at her daughter's house to try to recreate home. She longs for her own place to cook, her own gas stove top, explaining, "I made candy, homemade pralines. I sold them. It was the treat I gave people."

It is hurricane season again, and she is nervous about having her community once again scattered and once again without a plan. But this year she is taking charge. CWC has organized people to call the city and demand locations for the transit buses to evacuate people, as well as assurance that the citizens of East Biloxi will be part of any evacuation plan.

Priorities for Programs and Policies

CWC's survey tells them people want to come home, but to make this a reality their needs must first be met. Housing: There is a great need for funds for rent, and for supplies such as paint and wood. CWC has created a "Mini-Grant Home Improvement" project to increase the ability of ten low-income families to access a $500 grant for home improvement repairs. Advocacy is also needed around the Living Cities plan that aims to move public housing projects to the corners of the city. CWC will be at town meetings with Living Cities. Child care: The wait list is currently six months to a year to secure childcare (one-year-olds and older, only). Elderly support: CWC created a database and called seniors to find them, then created elderly preparedness kits for seventy-five seniors. CWC is now taking oral histories from the seniors in order to document the history of the community. Mental health: One of CWC's greatest concerns; they have sought gift cards for comforts like manicures and massages, and are seeking funding for a retreat for women to help them rejuvenate their spirits after so much trauma. Other significant challenges include the environment, insurance, transportation, and jobs.

The Ms. Foundation Helps Give Gulf Coast Women a United Voice

Prior to Katrina there was no community-based organization that advocated for lower-income people, especially women, in Biloxi. During both the relief and recovery phase, their needs were sorely neglected, first by FEMA, then by city officials. It appeared that the needs of the people did not exist, only the concerns of the developers and casinos.

Ms. funding helped start this organization in an effort to involve women from the East Biloxi community in the long-term Hurricane Katrina Recovery Effort on the local, state and national levels. CWC does this by ensuring that the community has adequate information in a timely manner and by providing input into the decision-making process.

Sharon Hanshaw is executive director of Coastal Women for Change, which began in January 2006 to help community members in Biloxi, Mississippi, to take part in long-range community planning and rebuilding after the Gulf storms. She was featured in Oxfam America's "Sister on the Planet" about women fighting climate change in their communities.

This chapter is reprinted with permission from a Ms. Foundation report originally published December 15, 2006. *ms.foundation.org/our_work/broad-change-areas/building-democracy/katrina-womens-response-fund/katrina-grantee-stories/sharon-hanshaw.*

CHAPTER II

"Estaba Reclamando Mi Sudor"

(I Was Demanding What I Had Earned with My Sweat)

"Antonia"

I've been living in New Orleans for four years. There were Latinos here before the hurricane, but not so many like now. Because of the hurricane, my husband and I went to New York. While we were in New York, a friend of mine called me from here and said, "Come back down here, there's work." We needed the work, so we came back, and I began working for a company doing clean-up work. Every day we got to work at 7 a.m. and left at 5 p.m. There was still so much water. We began cleaning—pulling out all the filthy things that were completely wet, covered in mold. They smelled awful. We pulled out all the trash from the buildings, tore down the walls with hammers, and then dragged everything outside. It wasn't easy.

We worked in different locations and I wasn't paid anything for my work. The company owners kept telling us that we were going to receive our checks—first it was Monday and then it was going to be Wednesday. We would all wait in a long line for our paychecks from 6 p.m. until midnight or 2 a.m. after working all day. There were hundreds of us waiting. Some people would be paid, but the majority were not. When my turn arrived to get my check, I'd already been working two weeks, and I was angry because I hadn't been paid. I'd been working to make enough money in order to buy food.

The owner said that my check hadn't been issued by the computer, and I would just have to wait to get it another day. I began crying in front of everyone and told the owner, "You're abusing us." There were four security guards, and the owner yelled to them, "Kick this woman out of here." I told the security guards not to touch me because I was within my rights, and I was only demanding what I had earned with my sweat.

It was Christmastime and, after not being paid, I went to New York to visit my children. I had to go there without a cent. Now, two months later, I still haven't received a single check for that work. The work was so hard and so difficult that we did. Imagine them not paying you for it!

I'm afraid that I'll be hurt by the companies again. I want to leave here because I'm really frustrated. Now, people don't trust working here because they think they're not going to be paid for their work. Really, those people abused us all. I'm planning to leave for New York. I've spent four years in New Orleans, but now I just want to leave. I don't want to be here anymore.

"Antonia" shared her story with the Immigrant Justice Project of the Southern Poverty Law Center, which spoke with over five hundred women and men who worked in New Orleans between October 2005 and February 2006. The names of the New Orleans workers featured in the SPLC project were changed to protect their identity.

This chapter is reprinted with permission from "Broken Levees, Broken Promises: New Orleans' Migrant Workers in Their Own Words," Immigrant Justice Project, Southern Poverty Law Center, August 2006. *www.splcenter.org/get-informed/publications/broken-levees-broken-promises.*

PART III

In Deep Water

Displacement, Loss, and Care

Descriptions of individual experiences of Hurricane Katrina have thus far provided vivid details of struggle and survival, but description without any elucidation of social context is insufficient for a broader understanding of this catastrophe. To avoid overemphasizing personal experiences of the event over broader social structures, we present research in Part III that links the prestorm risks that women faced in their everyday lives with the challenges they encountered in the immediacy of the storm. Shifting the level of analysis, contributing authors in this section examine how differently women were situated, sometimes with devastating consequences. When and where to evacuate? With whom? How to survive in the diaspora? How to return home? With what resources and under what conditions?

The chapters focus on women's experiences while positioning them within scholarly frameworks of disaster vulnerability and resilience. This provides a survey of the research landscape on gender and Katrina that demonstrates through empirical data the critical socioeconomic and cultural patterns that might otherwise be interpreted as simply individual circumstance. By uncovering these pre- and poststorm patterns, these chapters frame Katrina experience in more sociological terms, tracing the trends of displacement, loss, and care.

The studies illuminate just how significantly sex and gender did, indeed, set up the conditions that were so harmful to so many. Mindful, as ever, that gender alone explains neither vulnerability nor resilience, authors examine both and link gender with other social concerns that arise in all disasters such as race, class, and ability. A consistent thread running through these chapters is the fact that everyday life for many women in the affected area was difficult long before Katrina; racism, sexism, and ableism, for example, endangered them ahead of the dangerous winds and waters of the storm. Yet authors also write about how women have learned to cope, routinely adapting and striving to overcome the obstacles that thwart their goals and ambitions. Not just gender disparities but women's own strengths, indigenous knowledge, informal ties, and kinship networks factored into their evacuation and preparedness efforts and their response to the host of challenges they confronted around postdisaster housing and employment, health and well-being, parenting, and schooling in their areas of relocation and as they made their way home.

For legions of American women, living at risk is the normal state of affairs, shaping every decision made (or not) and every step taken (or not) toward self-protection and self-reliance, both before the storm and in its aftermath. These chapters make clear that realities embedded in women's daily lives set them up for difficulties long before an extreme event such as a hurricane or any other environmental, technological, or human-induced disaster strikes. Disasters will continue to unfold on this gendered terrain unless we address these issues as a matter of urgency for all people.

CHAPTER 12

Setting the Stage for Disaster

Women in New Orleans before and after Katrina

Beth Willinger and Janna Knight

Sex and gender as the basis for social vulnerability have numerous elements that function to differentiate among and between women and the manner in which women might experience a disaster and the recovery process. Factors thought to place some women at greater risk than others include household composition, along with caregiving roles and responsibilities, race or ethnic identity, age, employment status, occupation, and income (Enarson, Fothergill, and Peek 2006). Thus, women considered most vulnerable are those who are members of a racial or ethnic minority and heads of household—particularly if they are caregivers, poor, and either elderly or very young. In turn, these vulnerability factors affect other life sources such as housing and transportation (Morrow 1999).

To explore the relationship between these social vulnerability factors and the recovery of New Orleans women following Hurricane Katrina, we draw on data from the U.S. Census Bureau's American Community Survey, which is based on a sample and released in the year following data collection. We compare 2005 prestorm data for Orleans Parish to 2006 and 2008 data in order to track the recovery process one year and then three years after Katrina and the levee breaks. Our use of a single data source to explore demographic, social, and economic indicators allows for valid comparisons over time and between geographies, and reduces errors associated with combining data from different sources using different methodologies.[1]

The Predisaster Vulnerability of New Orleans Women

New Orleans in 2005 was home to a sizable number of people who would be considered at high risk of experiencing the negative impacts of a disaster. Our aim is to map the vulnerability of the 233,284 women and girls who accounted for 53.4 percent of the city's population in 2005. Nearly three-fourths of that number identified as a member of a racial or ethnic minority: approximately 70 percent black/African American, 3 percent Hispanic/Latina, and 2 percent Asian. Approximately one-fourth of the female population was made up of women over sixty-five years of age (12.7 percent) and girls under ten years of age (12.8 percent) (Table 12.1; USCB 2005).

Household Composition: Family and Nonfamily Households

Nearly 41 percent of some 90,500 *family* households had a woman household head with no husband present in prestorm New Orleans. Of these, 56 percent had children under eighteen years of age, and 16 percent were headed by grandmothers. Married-couple families formed 53.4 percent of all family households, 38 percent of which had children under eighteen. This picture contrasted quite dramatically with the 2005 national average of 74.3 percent married-couple households and 18.9 percent female-headed family households of which 11 percent were headed by grandmothers (Table 12.2).

More than half (53.5 percent) of the nearly 73,000 *nonfamily* households were headed by women. Women were living alone in 86.4 percent of these households, and in more than one-third of the households (35.5 percent), the women were over sixty-five years of age. Statistics for nonfamily households in New Orleans were quite similar to the 2005 national averages. However, when the number of family and nonfamily households were combined, nearly half (46.3 percent) of all pre-Katrina New Orleans households were headed by women, compared to 30.4 percent of households nationally (see Table 12.2).

The large number of female-headed households meant that as the storm approached, almost half of all New Orleans households had but a single adult to carry out disaster preparations accomplished traditionally by two. For many women, protecting property and preparing for evacuation were further stymied by the need to protect and care for others and the responsibility of getting self and others to safety.

Caregiving

Peek and Fothergill (2008) suggest that women's caregiving responsibilities may both increase their predisaster vulnerability by reducing the caregiver's mobility to seek safety, and decrease postdisaster recovery by limiting options for employment, housing, and access to needed services. In the absence of precise measures of women's caregiving responsibilities, we considered those most in need of care: children, the elderly, and the disabled.

In pre-Katrina New Orleans, 43 percent of married-couple and female-headed family households had children under eighteen years of age; 16.8 percent of these family households had children under age six (male-householder families are excluded from analysis). Additionally, 29 percent of these family households had one or more members sixty years of age or older (USCB 2005, S1101). New Orleans also had a higher percentage of disabled residents compared to the national average (15.6 percent vs. 14.9 percent), particularly among the population sixty-five years of age and older (46.1 percent vs. 40.5 percent) and those in poverty (27.3 percent vs. 21.1 percent) (USCB 2005, S1801). Consequently, as the storm approached, the need for caregivers was great and this responsibility fell heavily on the majority of the city's women, many of whom had limited physical or financial resources.

Race and Ethnicity

The double burden of racial discrimination and gender inequity has served to limit the social and financial assets of black/African American women particularly. The above-average number of black/African American women in New Orleans, 37.2 percent of the New Orleans population (and more than two-thirds of the female population) compared to 6.5 percent of the U.S. population (and 12.8 percent of the female population nationally), suggests that a large number of New Orleans women had inadequate resources to secure their own safety and security and required additional assistance to prepare for, survive, and recover from disaster (see Table 12.1). Moreover, the intersection of race with other vulnerability characteristics, such as age and poverty, intensified the vulnerability of black/African American women.

Employment Status and the Gendered Division of Labor

In 2005, 62 percent of New Orleans women sixteen years old and older were in the labor force and were providing or helping to provide for themselves and their families. Black/African American women accounted for 36.1 percent of the New Orleans labor force and constituted the largest demographic group of workers (white women were 14.4 percent of all workers; black/African American men, 25.4 percent; and white men, 18.6 percent). Black/African American women also represented a disproportionate number of the unemployed, nearly 22 percent compared to 5 percent of white women (Table 12.3).

Women's labor force participation has been concentrated in service, sales, and office occupations, and underrepresented in the traditional male occupational categories of construction and production/transportation. In pre-Katrina New Orleans, more than half the women (51.6 percent) who worked full-time, year-round were employed in the two occupational categories of sales and service, especially in food service and secretarial positions. Fewer than 4 percent of New Orleans women were employed in construction and production/transportation (Table 12.4). Thus before Katrina, women and men followed very traditional occupational paths in the workplace, with one exception: almost 45 percent of women held positions in management, professional, and related occupations, compared to 35 percent of women nationally (see Table 12.4). However, New Orleans women in managerial and professional positions earned just 74 percent of the wages earned by men in these positions (Table 12.5).

Earnings

The South's more traditional habit of classifying jobs as male or female—both within and across occupational categories—perpetuated wage inequities between women and men. In 2005, New Orleans women earned on average $28,950, while men earned $35,470—over $6,500 more (Table 12.6). Consequently, the average income for New Orleans family households was almost twice the income of nonfamily households—$39,428, compared to $20,901—the majority of which were headed by women.

Race as well as gender has had a significant effect on wages in New Orleans.

Whereas white women earned on average 94.8 percent of white men's wages, black/ African American women earned just 79.3 percent of black/African American men's wages, and 57 percent of white men's wages. More problematic was the disparity in earnings among women. Black/African American women earned 60.1 percent of white women's wages, and Hispanics/Latinas earned just 54 percent of white women's wages (Table 12.7).

The disparity in earnings between women and men and also between white women and women of color with regard to employment, occupation, and education results from a labor force segregated by both race and gender (Gault et al. 2005; Williams et al. 2006; Willinger 2008). Black/African American women in pre-Katrina New Orleans accounted for 50 percent or more of the women employed in nine of the ten *lowest*-paying jobs, while white women predominated in five of the ten *highest*-paying jobs (Williams et al. 2006). As a result, black/African American women were overrepresented among the working poor. In 2005, more than 26 percent of New Orleans women had incomes below the poverty level; the vast majority (84.5 percent) were black/African American. This compared to the national rate of 15 percent women in poverty, of whom 24.1 percent were black/African American. Further, approximately 42 percent of all New Orleans female-headed families lived in poverty, compared to 29.4 percent nationally (Table 12.8).

Though New Orleans women were not equally vulnerable to the impact of the storm, the vast majority constituted a highly vulnerable group. Below-average incomes, high poverty rates, persistent racial inequities, and the large number of female-headed households with only a single wage earner foretold a population that would lack the physical resources and cash reserves to protect property left behind during an evacuation, acquire emergency supplies, evacuate successfully, or afford living costs while away from their residence and employment.

Transportation

Women's lower average incomes also meant that car ownership was beyond the means of a large number of women. In 2005, 26 percent of all New Orleans household units and nearly 15 percent of women workers reported they had no vehicle available, compared to 12.4 percent of New Orleans working men and just 4.3 percent of working women nationally (USCB 2005, B08201 and B08014).

The lack of transportation was a visible yet overlooked marker of the economic vulnerability of New Orleans women facing a disaster (Bullard, Johnson, and Torres 2009; Schwartz and Litman 2008). Brinkley (2006: 20) estimated that over 100,000 New Orleans residents were without transportation to evacuate, the vast majority poor and black/African American—and, we would add, women.

Housing

New Orleans has long been a city of renters, as evidenced by the large number of shotgun doubles: one side of the home for the owner; the other side rental property. In 2005, 76 percent of married-couple families owned the residence they occupied, whereas just 38 percent of women family and nonfamily householders did (USCB

2005, S1101). Of those New Orleanians renting, more than half (51.7 percent) were considered housing-cost burdened, spending more than 30 percent of their house-hold income on rent (USCB 2005). Renters often have full responsibility for protecting their rented property yet lack the rights associated with home ownership. For example, renters may lose access to their rented housing and personal property left behind in an evacuation, and then have no authority to make repairs or receive assistance for rebuilding.

Cultural Glue

The high incidence of renters should not be understood to mean that New Orleans housed a large transient population. New Orleans was and continues to be a city of distinct neighborhoods. Attachment to a specific neighborhood built and maintained by generations of the same families perpetuated a cultural allegiance and historical knowledge of place that was exceptional in the United States (Luft and Griffin 2008). Tied to one another through cultural traditions and neighborhoods, New Orleanians only reluctantly welcomed outsiders into their social networks.

This attachment to place was both a cause and an effect of low levels of outmigration. Unlike most Americans, who have family and friends located throughout the country, many New Orleanians had only other New Orleanians to rely on. In 2005, 82 percent of Louisiana's native-born population still lived in Louisiana, second only to New York (82.3 percent) in the percent of people who lived in the state in which they were born. Nationally, the average was 67.5 percent (USCB 2005). New Orleanians who could, evacuated to the homes of family or friends. For those who had no family or friends outside the city, who had never stayed in a hotel or travel lodge, and who had no money to do so, the idea of leaving was more frightening than staying.

Post-Katrina Recovery Processes

Hurricane Katrina was unique in its call for the evacuation of more than a million people, some 450,000 of whom resided in New Orleans, and over 70 percent of whose homes were lost or severely damaged by wind, water, or both. The damage to residential and commercial buildings was magnified by the slow pace of receding water and the rapid growth of mold brought about by the sweltering heat and the long delay in remediation efforts. As the mandatory evacuation stretched out for nearly a month, and the prospect dwindled of returning to a job or having adequate housing, many New Orleanians decided to remain in their city of evacuation. The decision to relocate was often supported by better employment opportunities, higher wages, and school systems that offered more opportunities for intellectual advancement and creative expression than existed in New Orleans even before the storm.

Nevertheless, based on New Orleanians' attachment to place, returning home was judged to be an important measure of the recovery process. As post-Katrina bumper stickers read: "New Orleans: Proud to Swim Home"—a play on the slogan of the Young Leadership Council's pre-Katrina campaign to promote civic pride, "New Orleans: Proud to Call It Home."

Exactly how many New Orleanians returned and how many of the current population are post-Katrina immigrants remains highly speculative (Carr 2009). One year after the storm, the New Orleans population was less than half its pre-Katrina number. By December 2008 the population of New Orleans had reached nearly 74 percent of its 2005 population (GNOCDC 2009b), and by July 2009, nearly 80 percent (USCB 2009).

Repopulation

Sex, Race, Ethnicity, and Age

One year after the storm, census data indicate that women had returned to New Orleans in greater numbers than had men, with the female population recorded at 52 percent of the pre-Katrina level and the male population at 50 percent. Visually, however, New Orleans was a "city of men" (Batlan 2008). For more than a year following the disaster, the city was populated largely by men who had returned, had migrated for construction work, or had been sent by federal agencies to police the city and to clear the debris. Some called New Orleans the new frontier; others called it a ghost town. Women and families were visually absent, hindered in their return not only by the damage or destruction to residential properties, but also by the lack of services such as child care, health care, school openings, and facilities for senior citizens.

Slowly, women and families did return. By 2008 the repopulation of New Orleans by males and females was nearly equal, at approximately 70 percent, with women again a majority (53 percent) of the city's population (see Table 12.1). However, black/African American women have been slower to return than white women or Hispanics/Latinas. In 2006, 74.4 percent of Hispanics/Latinas and 68 percent of white women had returned, while fewer than half of black/African American women had. Three years after the storm, the population of black/African American women remained down by more than a third of its pre-Katrina level, while Latinas increased slightly in number to account for about 5 percent of the female population.

Repopulation of the city among women sixty-five years of age and older has been achieved at a higher rate than among younger women. Again however, black/African American women have been among the slowest to recover, while Latinas have increased in number and as a percent of women over sixty-five years of age. Thus, contrary to social vulnerability theory, the twinning of women and age alone does not make women over sixty-five more vulnerable to the negative impact of disaster. However, the twinning of race and gender, specifically black/African American and female, does appear to have a negative impact over and above being sixty-five and female.

Loss of Life

Not all women could return. About 460 women lost their lives. However, the immediate mortality rate of Hurricane Katrina showed men to be slightly more likely to be storm victims than women. Of the 820 confirmed deaths and 135 open cases reported by the Louisiana Family Assistance Center (2006), 48 percent were female, 68 percent of whom were seventy-one years of age or over (two were over a hundred). By comparison, the mortality rate for men was spread among men forty years old and older, with 46 percent of the deaths among men seventy-one years and older. A total of thirteen children twenty years of age or younger were the victims of Katrina; two, both girls, were ten or younger. Thus a disproportionate number of storm fatalities were elderly women and men who were unable or chose not to evacuate, or who evacuated but were unable to survive the evacuation or the immediate poststorm adverse public health conditions (Jonkman et al. 2009; *Times-Picayune* 2005–2006). The relatively low loss of life among children and women under sixty-five years of age suggests that, despite the difficulties associated with evacuation, women's self-protective actions and caregiving roles reduced fatalities.

Household Composition: Family and Nonfamily Households

Data supports the hypothesis that the households most hindered in recovery are *family* households with a female householder and *nonfamily* households headed by women. Immediately following the storm and continuing for three years, female householder families were considerably less likely than married-couple families to have returned to New Orleans (–56.8 percent compared to –42.4 percent in 2008; see Table 12.2). Nonfamily households headed by women also were less likely to have returned than were married-couple families after three years (–46.2 percent compared to –42.4 percent). This was particularly the case among the subgroup of female householders who lived alone and were sixty-five years of age or older (–50.0 percent). However, as the number of married-couple households with someone over sixty years of age significantly increased between 2005 and 2008, it appears that many older women who may have lived alone before Katrina found it necessary to move in with family members (USCB 2005; USCB 2008, S1101).

Among family households, the presence of children under eighteen years of age apparently served as a major deterrent to return. In 2008, the number of married-couple family households with children under eighteen reached just half of their pre-Katrina level, while the number of women-householder families with children reached just one-third of their pre-Katrina number. Grandparent households, however, reached approximately 75 percent of their pre-Katrina number (see Table 12.2). Though not statistically significant, grandparents assumed greater responsibility for caregiving following the storm, while the number of grandmothers who had responsibility for their grandchildren increased from 73 percent in 2005 to 84 percent of all grandparent-householder families in 2008.

Women's Lives after Katrina
Caregiving and Resource Availability

The slow return of family households with children lends support to the hypothesis that women's caregiving responsibilities negatively affect their postdisaster recovery. However, in the Katrina disaster, the lack of institutional resources, not the incapacity of individuals, may have been the greater obstacle to recovery. Moreover, the prolonged process of rebuilding the city's infrastructure created additional problems for the health of caregivers.

For families with children, the process of recovery was hampered by the glacial slowness in the restoration of schools and affordable and accessible child care. One year after Katrina, only 23 percent of the pre-Katrina child-care centers were open and most were operating at lower capacity than before the storm. In 2007, 36 percent of the pre-Katrina child-care centers were open, and only 45 percent had opened by January 2008. By October 2009, 151 centers were operating, compared to 275 centers before Katrina (GNOCDC 2009a).

All but a handful of New Orleans–area public and private schools were closed August 2005 through December 2005. School buildings were severely damaged or destroyed, which, when coupled with the large number of failing schools pre-Katrina, made the immediate return of families with children difficult and highly problematic. By fall 2008, the number of schools open reached 69 percent of the pre-Katrina number (89 of 129), over half of which opened as charter schools (GNOCDC 2009c).

For those in relatively good health, being over sixty-five years old and female was not by itself a significant vulnerability factor in recovery. The same was true for those with a disability. The disabled as a percent of the population remained relatively stable at about 15–16 percent. However, from 2005 to 2007, there was a significant increase of disabled among women sixteen to sixty-four years of age or older (from 11.7 percent to 15.7 percent) (USCB 2005; USCB 2007, S1801 [2008 data unavailable]). The increase could be stress related. For those returning, the lack of facilities and social services contributed to high levels of psychological stress, which was reported to be more severe for women and girls than for men and boys. Mental health disorders were particularly acute among caregivers. Overstreet and Burch (2008) report on a study of 576 caregivers that found 46.5 percent of female caregivers experienced clinically significant psychological distress, compared to 37.5 percent of male caregivers. Stress related to parenting was one of the primary reasons given. The mental health of caregivers also was found to be a significant risk factor for psychological disorders among children (Scheeringa and Zeanah 2008). Moreover, the estimates of mental health disorders in the New Orleans area were considerably higher than those made in the wake of other U.S. disasters, and held steady or increased as far out as two years (Overstreet 2009). Chronic storm-related stress also was blamed for a threefold increase in heart attacks more than two years after Katrina. Physicians noted that those stricken were "too busy trying to put their lives back in order to pay attention to their own health" (Gautam et al. 2009).

Employment Status and the Gendered Division of Labor

Women were highly engaged in the New Orleans labor force before Katrina and have continued as a vital part of the workforce since Katrina. Although women's labor force participation dropped by 6 to 7 percent after Katrina (men's dropped just 3 percent), women continued to account for approximately half of all New Orleans workers (49.4 percent in 2008). Black/African American women continued to be the largest demographic group of workers, despite a 10 percent decline in their participation rate between 2005 and 2008. In 2008, the New Orleans labor force was made up of nearly 30 percent black/African American women, approximately 18 percent white women, 23 percent white men, and 25 percent black/African American men. However, black/African American women also continued to shoulder much of the unemployment burden with a rate of 14.9 percent in 2008, compared to just 2.4 percent for white women (see Table 12.3).

Before and after Katrina, mothers with children under eighteen years of age were more likely to work than not, but their number decreased after the storm. In 2005, approximately 77 percent of New Orleans women with children under eighteen years of age were in the labor force, their numbers dropped to 69 percent in 2006, and remained approximately the same (70 percent) in 2008 (USCB 2005; USCB 2006; USCB 2008). Rather than showing a trend among mothers to stay at home, it is likely this decrease in working mothers exposes the ongoing challenges of recovery, particularly for families with children.

The changing skills needed for a post-Katrina labor force, particularly the demand for construction workers, did not change the gendered segregation of the New Orleans labor force. The number of women holding jobs in construction never reached more than 1.5 percent of the female workforce. More than half of all women workers continued to work in sales, service, or office occupations; while fewer than 7 percent worked in the traditionally male fields of construction or production. The slight shifts that did occur—an increasing proportion of women in production and construction and decreasing percentages in managerial and professional positions—were not statistically significant. However, the decrease in both white and black/African American women's participation in management and professional occupations deserves further exploration to ascertain if the decrease was the result of storm-related barriers for women working in challenging careers, the women's choices, or discrimination (see Table 12.4).

Just as the storm failed to disrupt the sex segregation of the New Orleans labor force, so too did it fail to disrupt the pre-Katrina occupational patterns of black/African American and white women. Before Katrina, black/African American women were fairly evenly distributed among the three major occupational categories: management and professions (32 percent), service (30 percent), and sales and office (33 percent). White women were concentrated more in management and the professional positions (59 percent), with sales and office occupations a distant second (28 percent). There was no significant change in the types of jobs black/African American or white women held after Katrina, and the pattern of occupational employment was largely repeated (see Table 12.4).

The biggest change in New Orleans's post-Katrina occupational structure was the recorded entry of Latinas. One year after the storm, nearly half of the Latinas in the labor force were in sales and office occupations (47.4 percent), followed by management and professional occupations (37.4 percent). Although many Latinas entered the labor force during the period of rebuilding, they were as unlikely as other women to take up nontraditional occupations. Three years after Katrina, the labor force participation of Latinas showed less concentration in any one occupation and nearly equal participation in the three traditional occupational categories.

Earnings

An important finding of this research documents the decline in women's earnings and the nearly 20 percent increase in men's earnings in the year following the storm.

The significant increase in men's median annual earnings was largely attributable to the earnings of white men (up 46 percent), while the decrease in women's wages fell largely on black/African American women (down 14.4 percent) (see Table 12.6).

The changes observed in the earnings of women and men one year after the storm had nearly disappeared three years later. The 2008 median annual earnings of men and of women did not differ significantly from their 2005 earnings. White women and Latinas recorded an increase in earnings between 2005 and 2008, while the earnings of black/African American women remained below their pre-Katrina level. As black/African American women's earnings before Katrina were significantly below the earnings of white women and black/African American men, a decline in the earnings of black/African American women increased their burden of daily living, making recovery nearly impossible.

The drop in women's average earnings immediately following the storm coupled with the rise in men's earnings is evident in the gender wage gap (see Table 12.7). Before Katrina, women earned on average 82 percent of men's earnings. The storm widened the gap: the ratio of women's to men's earnings fell 20 percent in 2006, and women earned on average just 62 percent of men's average earnings. By 2008, white women had more than made up for the decline, earning more than white men. Hispanic/Latina women reached near equity with Hispanic/Latino men (97 percent), yet earned just 54 percent of white males' earnings. For black/African American women however, the wage gap that widened after the storm remained large. In 2008, black/African American women earned just 49 percent of white men's earnings and 77 percent of black/African American men's earnings (see Table 12.7).

The storm also exacerbated wage inequities between and among women. The gap in earnings between white women and women of color widened in 2006 and in 2008 remained significantly greater than before Katrina (see Table 12.7). Specifically, the increase in white women's earnings and the decrease in black/African American women's earnings resulted in nearly a 12 percent greater gap in wages between white and black/ African American women in 2008 than in 2005. In 2008, black women earned just 49 percent of white women's wages.

Labor shortages following the storm required employers to pay higher wages. However, the higher wages did not accrue to women workers, particularly not black/African American women. One reason may be that even in good times, men's earnings more often than women's include overtime and bonus payments. Following Katrina, it was nearly impossible for women with caregiving responsibilities to work overtime, while men may have been required to do so.

The earnings disparity between women and men following the storm can be better understood by examining earnings by occupational categories (see Table 12.5). For example, in 2005, women in managerial and professional occupations earned 74 percent of what men in those occupations made. In 2006, the earnings gap widened to 56 percent, as men's earnings increased 30.7 percent to $72,087 while women's earnings dropped slightly to $40,360, $31,727 less than men's. By 2008, women's earnings in managerial and professional occupations bettered their pre-Katrina earnings yet were $14,000 less than men's, the same disparity that had existed before Katrina.

In sales and office occupations, the favorable prestorm earnings ratio of 92 percent between women and men was shattered as men's incomes increased 34 percent to $35,550, while women's earnings increased just 8 percent to $26,449. In 2008, women's earnings in sales and office occupations fell below their 2005 earnings, while men's earnings remained 27 percent higher and the wage gap widened to 68 percent. The widening wage gap between men and women in sales and office occupations reflects the segregation within occupations. Men more often benefited from commission on the sales of autos, refrigerators, and other major appliances lost in the storm, whereas women were employed more often in housewares and clothing departments, where commissions remain an exception. The large number of women employed in sales and office occupations (30 percent), as well as in managerial and professional occupations (39 percent), resulted in income disparities and severe financial disadvantages for women. Though New Orleans workers were somewhat shielded from the national recession by massive rebuilding and consumer spending, money pouring into New Orleans for rebuilding primarily benefited white males, particularly those in management and professional occupations and sales.

Poverty

The lower wages paid to women in post-Katrina New Orleans meant that poverty continued to be a burden for large numbers of women and their families (see Table 12.8). Though the overall proportion of women and families in poverty declined after Katrina, analysts attribute the decline to the lack of services and governmental support for poor women and families struggling to return to the city, rather than to a decline in poverty among those who have returned (Williams et al. 2006). Moreover, the rates remain unacceptably high and well above the national averages.

The most significant decline in the number of women-headed families in poverty was among those with children under five years of age (see Table 12.8). Still, approximately 45 percent of female-headed family households with children were living in poverty after Katrina. Grandparent households (most of which are headed by grandmothers) became more vulnerable after the hurricane as the percentage of grandparents in poverty who had responsibility for their own grandchildren increased to 45.2 percent in 2006. By 2008, the percent of grandparent households in poverty was identical to the pre-Katrina level of approximately 25 percent.

Housing and Transportation after Katrina

HOUSING

According to FEMA (Federal Emergency Management Agency) damage records, 134,564 (71.5 percent) of New Orleans housing units were damaged or destroyed, and 56 percent of these units sustained severe or *major* damage by wind or water caused by hurricanes Katrina and Rita and the flooding that followed (HUD 2006). Contributing to the housing shortage was the demolition of four public housing complexes—some 7,000 units—in 2007, the majority of which were occupied by women householders (IWPR 2010).

The housing shortage is the major but not the sole cause of a significant increase in housing costs that affects both owners and renters. Both household and flood insurance, as well as city property taxes and utility rates increased after Katrina. Many property owners passed along these increases to renters. But many home owners had to add such tax and insurance increases to the costs of renting a temporary residence while trying to rebuild their home. Renting a home or apartment became a housing-cost burden to 65.4 percent of Orleans Parish residents who were paying 30 percent or more of their household income on rent in 2008. For many, housing became unaffordable, and the estimated homeless population of New Orleans nearly doubled, to more than 19,000 (Filosa 2010).

Few women had the professional training or the skills to rebuild their own home. However, women assumed much of the responsibility for overseeing the rebuilding of residential properties, as the large number of New Orleans female householders would predict. Several nonprofit organizations reorganized or were established after Katrina to assist owners with the rebuilding process. The disabled, seniors (mainly women), and families with children have been the major users of services provided by groups such as Catholic Charities, the St. Bernard Project, and Beacon of Hope (Laska et al. 2008; Willinger and Powell 2009).

TRANSPORTATION

The Regional Transit Authority (RTA) sustained serious damage to its infrastructure, and the rebuilding of the public system was especially slow. Five months after Katrina, 45 percent of pre-Katrina routes and 15 percent of buses were operational. More than three years after the storm, 48 percent of pre-Katrina routes and 29 percent of buses were operational (GNOCDC 2009b).

The free transportation offered by the RTA for more than a year following the storm somewhat eased complaints about the sporadic and inconsistent service. Yet according to 2008 data, little changed in terms of how many women used public transportation to get to work (7.5 percent). However, the proportion of households and of women workers reporting they were without a vehicle declined significantly from 2005. In 2008, 20.3 percent of household units (vs. 26 percent in 2005) and 9.5 women workers (vs. 15 percent) were without a vehicle. The fewer women without a vehicle after Katrina likely reflects women's need to have a car to return to the city in the first place, as well as their greater need for personal transportation once they returned (USCB 2008).

Because ACS data focus on transportation for employment purposes, it is probable that the percentage of women without a car is higher than 10 percent, as indicated by household units without a vehicle. Linking transportation with employment belies the need for transportation to accomplish a myriad of tasks required in the process of recovery. Enarson (2001), among others, discusses lack of transportation as an exclusionary practice that limits, and all but prohibits, access to employment, to medical and social services, and to participation in community-rebuilding efforts. In essence, lack of transportation isolates women from the essential work of rebuilding their communities in addition to their homes.

Conclusions and Implications

With few exceptions, the women judged most vulnerable before Katrina—those with children; black/African American women, especially those over sixty-five years of age; and the working poor—were slowed in their return to New Orleans. Three years after the storm, many families with children had not yet returned, whether the families were married couples, female-headed, or grandparents with responsibility for children. Thus, while caregiving responsibilities led to protective actions in advance of the storm to reduce fatalities among women and children, responsibility for children hampered the ability to return home.

In the midst of the unprecedented destruction caused by Hurricane Katrina, there emerged an optimism that New Orleans could rebuild to be an even greater American city, notable for its cultural richness, promotion of the arts, institutions of higher education, and quality of life of all citizens. This optimism was fueled by a renewed sense of community and by the visibility of women-led community organizing that called for reform in local and state government, education, and crime prevention. Some of these changes have been made, notably by the efforts of Citizens for 1 Greater New Orleans, which worked to reduce to one the number of tax assessors and levee boards. The much-needed transformation of the educational system appears to be making some progress, particularly because of the strong charter school movement. Despite the reforms, the K–12 education in New Orleans remains highly segregated by race, with the Orleans Parish public schools enrolling 90 percent black/African American students and private schools the preferred option among families who can afford the high tuitions (GNOCDC 2009c).

Still, rather than improving the condition of New Orleans women, Hurricane Katrina and the rebuilding of New Orleans have had the overall effect of worsening the status of women and children, particularly those who were most vulnerable before the disaster. The disaster did benefit those least vulnerable. White males in management and professional positions and in sales experienced a significant increase in earnings after Katrina.

There is little doubt that the additional responsibilities brought about by hurricane recovery for caregiving and residential living have fallen largely on women. Whether these domestic responsibilities meant women worked fewer hours or no overtime, accepted lower pay in exchange for more flexible hours, or moved to jobs with less responsibility, the result was lower wages (NOBA 2009; Willinger 2008. The added responsibilities coupled with women's lower-on-average postdisaster incomes means that women have fewer financial and physical resources to cover day-to-day necessities, let alone to prepare for another possible disaster. Many women remain without private means of transportation and will rely on the city for evacuation of themselves and their families come another hurricane. For those who held hope for a better life after Katrina, the hard reality of daily life and the continuing view of devastation contribute to ongoing psychological stress years after the storm.

This research contributes to our understanding of the ways a disaster affects women and women's recovery. Rather than disrupting long-standing inequalities marked by sex and race, Hurricane Katrina served to codify differences between women and men, and between white women and women of color. The research largely supports the hypothesis that those who are the most vulnerable before a disaster will have the most difficulty recovering from the disaster. The ability to anticipate, survive, and recover from a disaster is not universal and requires specific attention to the differences among women.

———

Beth Willinger is founding director of Tulane University's Women's Studies Program, and is a research professor and former executive director of Tulane's Newcomb College Center for Research on Women. She edited the report *Katrina and the Women of New Orleans* and conducted research leading to the establishment of the Louisiana Women's Policy and Research Commission, to which she was reappointed chair in 2009.

Janna Knight is a research assistant at the Louisiana Public Health Institute. Her research interests lie in women's social and health inequities.

TABLES

Table 12.1. Percent change in Orleans Parish female population by race and age (over 65), 2005–2008

	2005	2006	2008	% change 2005–2008
Total population	437,186	223,388	311,853	−28.7[a]
Female	233,284	120,925	164,998	−29.3[b]
% female	53.4	54.1	52.9	
Race				
White	61,374	41,872	54,049	−11.9[b]
Black/African American	162,571	74,070	104,997	−35.4[b]
Hispanic/Latina	6,809	5,064	7,118	+ 4.5
Age 65 and older				
White	12,025	9,570	10,845	−9.8[b]
Black/African American	16,746	9,773	12,118	−27.6[b]
Hispanic/Latina	1,074	808	1,252	+16.6
Total age 65 and older	29,673	19,712	23,246	−21.7[b]

Source: U.S. Census Bureau, 2005, 2006, and 2008. American Community Survey Detailed Tables for Orleans Parish: B01001, A, B, D, I, "Sex by Age." Orleans Parish is coterminous with New Orleans's city limits.
Note: Data for Asian women was available only for 2008 and was not included.
a. Estimate is controlled; a statistical test for sampling variability is not appropriate.
b. Indicates statistical significance at the 90% confidence interval.

Table 12.2. Percent change in Orleans Parish family and nonfamily households by type, 2005–2008

	2005	2006	2008	% change 2005–2008
Family households	90,461	40,134	46,740	–48.3[a]
Married couples	48,301	24,641	27,823	–42.4[a]
With children under age 18	18,528	7,332	9,353	–49.5[a]
Female householders, no husband present	36,686	12,523	15,861	–56.8[a]
With children under age 18	20,505	5,101	6,997	–65.9[a]
Grandparents responsible for grandchildren	5,816	2,024	4,393	–24.5
% grandmothers	72.8	85.0	83.9	+11.1
Nonfamily households	72,873	33,382	40,402	–44.6[a]
Female heads	39,018	17,830	20,973	–46.2[a]
Living alone	33,708	15,306	18,754	–44.4[a]
Age 65 and over	11,950	5,636	5,985	–50.0[a]

Source: U.S. Census Bureau, 2005, 2006, and 2008, American Community Survey for Orleans Parish. Tables S1102, "Grandparents"; S1101, "Households and Families"; B11010, "Nonfamily Households by Sex of Householder by Living Alone by Age of Householder"; "Selected Social Characteristics in the United States: 2005." Orleans Parish is coterminous with New Orleans's city limits.
a. Changes reported between 2005 and 2008 are outside the margin of error and judged statistically significant at the 90% confidence level.

Table 12.3. Percent change of Orleans Parish women in labor force age 16 and over by race/ethnicity, 2005–2008

	2005	2006	2008	% change 2005–2008
Total population age 16 and over	336,748	179,325	255,126	–24.2[a]
Females	184,841	98,497	137,509	–25.6[a]
% in labor force	61.9	54.1	54.7	–7.2[a]
White	53,578	37,430	48,292	–9.8
% in labor force	58.5	51.3	56.9	–1.6
% unemployed	4.8	6.8	2.4	–2.4
Black/African American	124,009	56,756	84,547	–31.8[a]
% in labor force	63.4	56.0	53.2	–10.2[a]
% unemployed	21.8	16.5	14.9	–6.9

Source: U.S. Census Bureau, American Community Survey for Orleans Parish. 2005, Table B23001, "Sex by Age by Employment Status for the Population 16 Years and Over"; 2006, 2008, Tables C23002A, B, I, "Sex by Age by Employment Status for the Population 16 Years and Over." Includes part-time and full-time workers. (Census numbers for Hispanic/Latina and Asian women were too few to be displayed.) Orleans Parish is coterminous with New Orleans's city limits.
a. Statistically significant at the 90% confidence level.

Table 12.4. Percent of Orleans Parish women in occupational categories by race/ethnicity, 2005–2008

	2005	2006	2008	% change 2005–2008
Management, professional, and related	40.5	41.6	39.0	−1.5
White	59.1	55.4	54.9	−4.2
Black/African American	31.9	25.1	27.7	−4.2
Hispanic/Latina	n/a	37.4	34.0	n/a
Service	25.0	20.1	25.0	0.0
White	11.6	14.1	15.6	+4.0
Black/African American	30.2	32.2	32.3	+2.1
Hispanic/Latina	n/a	15.2	26.3	n/a
Sales and office	31.0	30.6	29.6	−1.4
White	27.6	27.6	25.7	−1.9
Black/African American	33.3	33.2	34.1	+0.8
Hispanic/Latina	n/a	47.4	37.6	n/a
Construction, extraction, maintenance, and repair	0.2	1.3	0.7	+0.5
White	0.5	0.9	1.5	+1.0
Black/African American	0.1	1.7	0.2	+0.1
Hispanic/Latina	n/a	n/a	1.1	n/a
Production, transportation, and material-moving	3.3	5.2	5.7	+2.4
White	1.2	1.6	2.2	+1.0
Black/African American	4.5	7.8	5.6	+1.1
Hispanic/Latina	n/a	n/a	1.0	n/a

Source: U.S. Census Bureau, 2005, 2006, 2008, American Community Survey for Orleans Parish. Tables C24010A, B. "Sex by Occupation for the Civilian Employed Population 16 Years and Over." Includes part-time and full-time workers. Orleans Parish is coterminous with New Orleans's city limits.

Table 12.5. Median earnings of Orleans Parish by occupational category for full-time, year-round workers age 16 and over, by sex, 2005–2008

| | 2005 | | 2006 | | 2008 | | % change 2005–2008 | |
	Males	Females	Males	Females	Males	Females	Males	Females
Management, professional, and related	$55,134	$40,822	$72,087	$40,360	$61,654	$47,199	+11.8	+15.6
Service	24,879	17,380	27,099	16,404	19,353	19,747	−22.2[a]	+13.6
Sales and office	26,507	24,501	35,550	26,449	33,605	22,910	+26.8[a]	−6.5
Construction, extraction, maintenance, and repair	31,422	8,750[b]	32,491	40,810	33,076	30,566	−5.3	n/a[b]
Production, transportation, and material- moving	34,694	21,202	34,198	12,500	30,376	20,805	−12.4	−1.9

Source: U.S. Census Bureau, 2005, 2006, and 2008, American Community Survey for Orleans Parish. Table S2402, "Occupation by Sex and Median Earnings in the Past 12 Months (in inflation-adjusted dollars) for the Full-Time, Year-Round Civilian Employed Population 16 Years and Over." Orleans Parish is coterminous with New Orleans's city limits.

a. Statistically significant at the 90% confidence level.

b. Too few sample observations were available to compute a standard error and thus a margin of error.

Table 12.6. Median earnings of Orleans Parish full-time, year-round workers age 16 and over, by sex and race, 2005–2008

	2005	2006	% change 2005–2006	2008	% change 2005–2008
Males	$35,470	$43,745	+23.3[a]	$35,990	+1.5
White	42,192	61,619	+46.0[a]	45,577	+8.0
Black/African American	30,302	33,516	+10.6	29,291	−3.3
Hispanic/Latino	34,004	38,202	+12.3	25,384	−25.3
Females	28,950	27,042	−6.6	26,434	−8.7
White	39,988	41,374	+3.5	46,300	+15.8
Black/African American	24,037	20,572	−14.4	22,488	−6.4
Hispanic/Latina	21,582	20,492	−5.1	24,619	+14.1

Source: U.S. Census Bureau, 2005, 2006, 2008, American Community Survey for Orleans Parish. Tables B2001, 7A, B, I, "Median Earnings in the Past 12 Months (in inflation-adjusted dollars) by Sex by Work Experience in the Past 12 Months for the Population 16 Years and Over with Earnings in the Past 12 Months." Orleans Parish is coterminous with New Orleans's city limits.
a. Statistically significant at the 90% confidence level. A large margin of error in the 2008 Hispanic/Latino and Black/African American data sets accounts for nonsignificant findings despite large differences.

Table 12.7. Comparison of Orleans Parish earnings by sex and race/ethnicity, 2005–2008

	2005	2006	2008	% change 2005–2008
% of women's to men's earnings	81.6	61.8	73.4	−8.2[a]
White	94.8	67.1	102.0	+7.2
Black/African American	79.3	61.4	76.8	−2.5
Hispanic/Latino	63.5	53.6	97.0	+33.5
% of women's to women's earnings				
Black/African American to white	60.1	49.7	48.6	−11.5[a]
Hispanic/Latina to white	54.0	49.5	53.2	−0.8

Source: U.S. Census Bureau, 2005, 2006, 2008, American Community Survey for Orleans Parish. B20017, A, B, I, "Median Earnings in the Past 12 Months (in inflation-adjusted dollars) by Sex by Work Experience in the Past 12 Months for the Population 16 Years and Over with Earnings in the Past 12 Months." Orleans Parish is coterminous with New Orleans's city limits.
a. Statistically significant at the 90% confidence level. A large margin of error for the Hispanic/Latino population accounts for the nonsignificant findings.

Table 12.8. Comparison of Orleans Parish and U.S. women and families in poverty, 2005 and 2008 (in percentage)

	2005		2008	
	Orleans Parish	USA	Orleans Parish	USA
Total family households in poverty	21.8	10.2	14.9	9.7
Female householder families, no husband present	41.8	29.4	33.5	28.0
As % of total family households	40.6	18.9	33.9	18.9
With children under 18	50.6	37.7	45.3	36.3
With children under 5	64.1	47.4	45.9	44.8
Grandparents responsible for grandchildren under 18 in poverty	25.9	20.2	25.6	23.2
Females, income below poverty (last 12 months)	26.5	14.8	23.4	14.5

Source: U.S. Census Bureau, 2005 and 2008, American Community Survey for Orleans Parish and the United States. "Selected Economic Characteristics"; Tables C17001, "Poverty Status in the Past 12 Months by Sex by Age"; Tables B10059, "Poverty Status in the Past 12 Months for Grandparents Living with Own Grandchildren under 18 Years by Responsibility for Own Grandchildren." Orleans Parish is coterminous with New Orleans's city limits.

NOTE

1. Data reported are based on the 2005, 2006, and 2008 American Community Survey one-year estimates and rely on ACS definitions of subject characteristics. See U.S. Census Bureau, American Community Survey, Methodology, *www.census.gov/acs/www.methodology/methodology_main/*.

REFERENCES

Batlan, F. (2008). Weathering the storm together (torn apart by race, gender, and class). *NWSA Journal, 20*(3), 163–184.

Brinkley, D. (2006). *The great deluge: Hurricane Katrina, New Orleans, and the Mississippi Gulf-Coast.* New York: HarperCollins.

Bullard, R., Johnson, G., and Torres, A. (2009). Transportation matters: Stranded on the side of the road before and after disaster strikes. In R. Bullard and B. Wright (Eds.), *Race, place, and environmental justice after Hurricane Katrina.* Boulder, CO: Westview Press.

Carr, S. (2009). Does the post-storm loss of natives and influx of newcomers dilute the city's cultural gumbo, or season it with new flavors? The new New Orleans. *Times Picayune*, August 23. Retrieved from *www.nola.com*.

Enarson, E. (2001). What women do: Gendered labor in the Red River Valley flood. *Environmental Hazards, 3*(1), 1–18.

Enarson, E., Fothergill, A., and Peek, L. (2006). Gender and disaster: Foundations and directions. In H. Rodriquez, E. Quarantelli, and R. Dynes (Eds.), *Handbook of Disaster Research* (pp. 130–146). New York: Springer.

Filosa, G. (2010). Post-Katrina housing costs put many on the edge. *Times-Picayune*, September 14. Retrieved from *www.nola.com*.

Gault, B., Hartmann, H., Jones-DeWeever, A., Werschkul, M., and Williams, E. (2005). *The women of New Orleans and the Gulf Coast: Multiple disadvantages and key assets for recovery.* Part 1: *Poverty, race, gender, and class.* Washington, DC: Institute for Women's Policy Research. Retrieved from *www.iwpr.org*.

Gautam, S., Menache, J., Srivastav, S., Delafontaine, P., and Irimpen, A. (2009). Effect of Hurricane Katrina on the incidence of acute coronary syndrome at a primary angioplasty center in New Orleans. *Disaster Medicine and Public Health Preparedness, 3*, 144–150.

GNOCDC (Greater New Orleans Community Data Center). (2009a). Child care center environmental scanner. Retrieved from *www.gnocdc.org*.

———. (2009b). The New Orleans Index: Tracking the Recovery of New Orleans and the Metro Area. Retrieved from *www.gnocdc.org*.

———. (2009c). Public school enrollment—LA Dept. of Education. February. Retrieved from *www.gnocdc.org*.

HUD (U.S. Department of Housing and Urban Development). (2006). Current housing unit damage estimates: Hurricanes Katrina, Rita, and Wilma. February 12. Retrieved from *www.gnocdc.org*.

IWPR (Institute for Women's Policy Research). (2010). Mounting losses: Women and public housing after Hurricane Katrina. Fact Sheet. August. Retrieved from *www.iwpr.org*.

Jonkman, S. N., Maaskant, B., Boyd, E., and Levitan, M. (2009). Loss of life caused by the flooding after Hurricane Katrina: Analysis of the relationship between flood characteristics and mortality. *Risk Analysis, 29*(5), 676–698.

Laska, S., Morrow, B. H., Willinger, B., and Mock, N. (2008). Gender and disaster: Theoretical considerations. In B. Willinger (Ed.), *Katrina and the women of New Orleans* (pp. 11–21).

New Orleans: Newcomb College Center for Research on Women. Retrieved from *newcomb .tulane.edu/article/report-katrina-and-the-women-of-new-orleans?department_id=nccrow-research*.

Litt, J. (2008). Getting out or staying put: An African American women's network in evacuation from Katrina. *NWSA Journal, 20*(3), 32–48.

Louisiana Family Assistance Center. (2006). Reuniting the families of Katrina and Rita: Louisiana Family Assistance Final Report. Retrieved from *www.dhh.state.la.us/offices/?ID=303*.

Luft, R. E., and Griffin, S. (2008). A status report on housing after Katrina: An intersectional analysis. In B. Willinger (Ed.), *Katrina and the women of New Orleans* (pp. 50–53). New Orleans: Newcomb College Center for Research on Women, Tulane University.

Morrow, B. H. (1999). Identifying and mapping community vulnerability. *Disasters, 23*(1), 1–18.

Neumayer, E., and Plümper, T. (2007). The gendered nature of natural disasters: The impact of catastrophic events on the gender gap in life expectancy, 1981–2002. *Annals of the Association of American Geographers, 97*(3), 551–566.

NOBA (New Orleans Bar Association). (2009). Katrina and the women of New Orleans NOBA survey. New Orleans. Unpublished survey. Author files.

Overstreet, S. (2009). Hurricane Katrina and the women (and children) of New Orleans. Presentation to the New Orleans Bar Association, New Orleans, June 19.

Overstreet, S., and Burch, B. (2008). Mental health status of women and children following Hurricane Katrina. In B. Willinger (Ed.), *Katrina and the women of New Orleans* (pp. 59–64). Newcomb College Center for Research on Women. New Orleans: Tulane University.

Peek, L., and Fothergill, A. (2008). Displacement, gender, and the challenges of parenting after Hurricane Katrina. *NWSA Journal, 20*(3), 69–105.

Scheeringa, M. S., Zeanah, C. H. (2008). Reconsideration of harm's way: Onsets and comorbidity patterns of disorders in preschool children and their caregivers following Hurricane Katrina. *Journal of Clinical Child and Adolescent Psychology, 37*(3), 508–518.

Schwartz, M., and Litman, T. (2008). Evacuation station: The use of public transportation in emergency management planning. *ITE Journal on the Web*, January. Victoria Transport Policy Institute. Retrieved from *www.vtpi.org/evacuation.pdf*.

St. Bernard Project. (2009). Retrieved from *www.stbernardproject.org/v158*.

Times Picayune. (2005–2006). Katrina's lives lost. In memoriam. A series of profiles of those who lost their lives. Retrieved from *www.nola.com/katrina/*.

USCB (U.S. Census Bureau) American Community Survey. (2005, 2006, 2008). For Orleans Parish and the United States. Retrieved from *factfinder.census.gov/*.

Williams, E., Sorokina, O., Jones-DeWeever, A., and Hartmann, H. (2006). *The women of New Orleans and the Gulf Coast: Multiple disadvantages and key assets for recovery.* Part 2: *Gender, race, and class in the labor market.* New York: Institute for Women's Policy Research.

Willinger, B. (2008). The effects of Katrina on the employment and earnings of New Orleans women. In B. Willinger (Ed.), *Katrina and the women of New Orleans* (pp. 32–49). Newcomb College Center for Research on Women. New Orleans: Tulane University.

Willinger, B., and Powell, V. (2009). Women's leadership in post-Katrina New Orleans. Interviews and vertical files. Katrina Collection, Newcomb Archives, Newcomb College Center for Research on Women, Tulane University, New Orleans.

CHAPTER 13

Out of Sight, Out of Mind

Women's Abilities and Disabilities in Crisis

Elizabeth Davis and Kelly Rouba

Over 40 percent of those who did not evacuate during Hurricane Katrina were physically unable to leave or were caring for a person with a disability. According to Lex Frieden, director of the Independent Living Research Utilization, approximately 50 percent of the thousands of people who died as a result of Katrina were either elderly or disabled (Morin and Rein 2005). In this chapter, we allow women with disabilities to speak for themselves to help us understand this tragic outcome. These accounts were solicited by both authors as members of EAD & Associates, LLC, a consulting firm that specializes in inclusive emergency management, including the issue of disability and disaster.

Selena Buccola's Story

A quadriplegic, Selena Buccola was living in an RV on her mother's property in Bayou La Batre, Alabama, before Katrina's landfall. Her mother's home was a brick house designed in the 1950s. "It was a fairly good house. It had survived [hurricanes] Camille, and Frederic, and Ivan, and everything anybody ever threw at her."

Since the home had held up through previous storms, "we actually considered staying until Sunday morning; they said she's turning to the east and I said, 'Uh oh, Mom, I think we are getting out of here.' She said, 'I've got no place to send the dogs.' I said, 'We'll lock the dogs in the house. We are only going to be gone two or three days probably.' And she said okay."

Emergency Plans

At the time of the storm, Buccola said she had an emergency plan in place—to "stay either at the shelter or the cousin's house, like we'd done for thirty years, [and we knew to] take medical supplies, take pills, make sure your kids and the dogs and everybody is all right." Fortunately, Buccola was able to get out before it was too late. "I drive my own van. That's the only reason I got out. It's because I took my own initiative; I packed up about a week's worth of food and some clothes and blankets, pillows, things like that, and put them in my van."

Seeking Shelter

"We put the cats in one room and the dogs in the other, and we went to my cousin's house, who lived up on high ground," Buccola said. Her cousin's home was about six miles up the road. "We stayed there for the hurricane and when we got back, we couldn't get into the house because there were tree limbs down, my wheelchair ramp had pulled away from the house . . . we just couldn't get in and our insurance said don't touch anything until the assessor comes out. So the house sat for a month and a half."

With their house a shambles, Buccola decided to head to a shelter. "My mom, I couldn't see her handling that with her health," said Buccola. "I sent her to her sister's house because I thought she'd be safer there and have a little more mobility."

"I figured I'd been ten years with no health problems at all, I can handle a shelter for a few days. And a few days turned into a month." Buccola first sought shelter the day after the storm hit. "I actually tried to go to the only handicapped-accessible Red Cross station in the city. During Katrina, that was the only [shelter] and they closed a day later because . . . they had to get the kids back in school because they set it up in a high school. And there was no way I could stay and keep driving twenty miles back and forth to the house trying to take care of my animals and do whatever I had to do. . . . That's when I moved to the Bayou La Batre shelter, on that second day when they closed down the Baker facility."

Buccola was disappointed by the government's lack of concern for people with special needs. "They just did not think anything about what was happening. I mean, we had elderly people from nursing homes that didn't have decent back-up generators and they were dying left and right because of the heat. For a week after Katrina, there was triple digits in the south, 100-degree heat."

Buccola also felt that the shelters in her area were not very accessible. "They tell you everybody's got to have handicapped-accessible facilities and it doesn't work," she said, adding that she used to be a seasoned traveler and knows what needs to be done to make a room accessible. "Good Lord, you would have thought the government would have figured it out too."

Adjusting to Shelter Life

Managing activities of daily living like grooming in the confines of a shelter wasn't easy. "In the shelter, I'd take [my wheelchair] into one of the ladies' bathrooms, and I'd get them to lock the door or I'd get one of the ladies from the Red Cross to help me strip down, and I'd bathe down the best I could and wash my hair in the sink every other day. . . . I was lucky I had the leg bag and a couple extra Foleys [catheters] on hand, or I'd had been in so much trouble," she said. In Bayou La Batre, "there aren't a lot of people in wheelchairs that are independently living down here. So the four major companies sent everything they had over to Mississippi and New Orleans. And I couldn't get a hospital bed for three and a half weeks. They had to send me one from Atlanta, and it couldn't get here because of the roads being down and all the horrendous things that everybody was going through."

Buccola was having an especially tough time adapting to living in a shelter. "I didn't realize I was going to be sleeping in my wheelchair and because of that and not being able to get in and out of a cot, I stayed in my chair and wound up developing a bone infection. I fell asleep in my chair and I wasn't getting pressure release while I was asleep, obviously." Over the course of her stay, Buccola's health worsened. "I was not getting enough pressure releases. My body got worn down in a hurry because I couldn't take care of myself properly," she said. "I wound up with a major infection and almost died. . . . When Katrina hit, I was healthy as a horse. I had taken such good care of myself. I had my own exercise equipment," she said. "[My health problems] all started because of Katrina."

Those weren't her only brushes with death during the aftermath of the storm. "Before I even went in the hospital, I was running around down here and almost died of heat stroke because they didn't have enough aid stations, and I wound up having to sit for three hours with no water and no way to get water. I had to wait for a volunteer fire department that had MREs [meals ready to eat] and ice. In the south end of the county, there was only one left. The first one opened up down the road from us and they didn't have enough stuff; they closed back down in forty-five minutes."

Returning Home

The next summer, Buccola began receiving physical therapy to help her get back in shape. She was finally able to return home from the hospital at the end of July. However, Buccola was forced to live in a one-bedroom trailer given to her mother by FEMA (Federal Emergency Management Agency). She later moved into another mobile home her mother bought until they had a new home built.

After the storm, Buccola reached out to FEMA for financial assistance to help cover the damage to her RV and her mother's home. "Now, when Katrina hit, because I had no insurance, FEMA denied me everything. They said [the RV] looks good enough to live in. I was laughing because the generator was down, all the water heaters, everything electrical, and the engine won't run, so how the heck are you going to get it anywhere so you can plug it in? They don't look at things like that."

Fortunately, things were better for her mother. "Because my mother was disabled and so am I, we got one of the houses," Buccola said. "Our insurance paid for the foundation work and the federal grant paid for the house." Getting settled in their new home wasn't a quick process. "This house just got built three years after Katrina," Buccola said. And although the doors are wide enough for her wheelchair, the entryway was equipped with an electric-powered lift that is both faulty and useless during power outages.

"I've had trouble with my lift ever since I've moved into this house. I have gotten stuck in it for anywhere from fifteen minutes to five hours and nobody could get me out. I'd have to wait for somebody to rescue me. I've been begging for a ramp. The government finally released the money this year to help people that are still suffering from Katrina-related incidents, and I begged them. I'm number 94 on a list of 457, I think they said, to see if I can qualify for a ramp on the front end of the house so they can make me live up to fire code, which says that any primary residence has to have two exits out of the house for a fire. With that lift, mine is only one and I have to go through one of the most dangerous fire hazards in the house, the laundry room, to get out."

More Problems at Home

Soon after the home was built, it began deteriorating. "They are not going to fix it," Buccola said. "It's on me. I'm responsible for it. I don't know what the heck I'm going to do, and what am I supposed to do? I don't have any money. I live on $575, which is what I get out of my Social Security, and $830 out of my retirement and that's what I live on. And . . . my mom, she got $1,200 between her Social Security and her retirement from the University of South Alabama Medical School. It took every dime we had to put food on the table and pay our bills and the life insurance policy and the medical policies and coverage for the Medical Part B that she'd gotten."

Buccola said she was seeking help through Vocational Rehabilitation Services in Alabama to develop a business plan for selling homemade jewelry. "[They] helped me get a license. But two and a half months ago, I had an abscess and a UTI [urinary tract infection] that went septic in my bloodstream. I just got out of the hospital on July 30, so I haven't even had the chance to set up my business yet."

Through all this, Buccola did find one bright spot. "I got lucky. The people at the National Spinal Cord Injury Association heard what I went through with the heat stroke and all the things during and after that hurricane and how many times I came close to dying from a bone infection and then a staph infection and then another staph infection. . . . They helped me acquire some money from FEMA and they raised money for me to help transform an old handicapped school bus into a camper."

Tiara "Sunshine" King's Story

Tiara "Sunshine" King moved to New Orleans in 2004, hoping for a fresh start in life and a chance at a peaceful existence. Little did she suspect that it would be anything but peaceful. "I was injured in 2004 in Maryland—a survivor of domestic violence— and I was in a training hospital at the time," said King, who suffered an incomplete spinal cord injury after her husband shot her in her jaw and spine. At the time, King was living in a second-floor condominium, which was not handicapped accessible. "I got discharged from [the hospital] on January 5. That same day I moved to New Orleans."

When King, her parents, and her son moved to New Orleans, they stayed with one of her father's friends until they found accessible housing uptown on Burdette Street. "Of course, the house was one level. [When] we were at a friend's house, . . . [I] had to manage going up and down about seven to ten steps every day in a wheel-chair; my mom and father was carrying me up and down the steps, so that was really hard for about two months—it was a little bit longer than that. Once we got to the accessible housing, I was a lot better and I was able to get a little bit more strong and independent and all," King said.

King's father also worried about their welfare should a serious storm come their way.

"We didn't have our own vehicle, so we was pretty much in the midst of every-body else using public transportation, catching cabs, as well as using the mobility vehicle that was down there," King said. "My father, he always talked to the cab driver and was always saying, 'When the big one does come, what happens? Where do people go?' And the cab driver said, 'We'll take you wherever you want to go as long as you can pay for it.'"

Time to Go

A few days before Hurricane Katrina hit, King and her family had planned to re-turn to Maryland for a wedding. "So we were already kind of packed up around the same time period and our flight was for that Thursday and everything was canceled," she said, adding that she was confused about why people couldn't leave if the storm hadn't approached yet.

Around that time, "the mayor was saying he wanted everybody—well, it was man-datory for people to leave their homes to go to the Superdome. . . .We knew right there it would have separated the family; there was no way to find each other once we'd actually get there. So my father made some calls to his friends and found out that Louisiana State University [LSU] was transforming their gymnasium into a special needs shelter. So he called the cab driver up and we were ready to make way."

"It cost us $180 [by taxi] to go officially from New Orleans to Baton Rouge. It usually takes about an hour and thirty minutes to get there on a normal day. Well, since we left that Sunday morning, it took us twelve hours to get there. It was a peaceful twelve hours, but at the same time, for a person with paralysis, it's not as peaceful as it could be because I'm in one location and I'm in the chair."

During the ride, the family began to worry. "We've got as much stuff as we can, [but] I'm worried about whether we have enough medical supplies for me," King said. "And we really don't know how is LSU going to be set up. Are they going to have cots for us? Will I have to stay in my chair the whole time? All these things is going through our minds."

Give Me Shelter

Eventually, King and her family made it to the shelter at LSU. "Once we got there, it was really nice. They had everything organized," King said. "The only thing was, it was only for the caregivers and their patients. So Mom and I was able to stay there. They had a chapel on the campus, so they allowed my father and son—there was other family members there, too, who came with their loved ones—to stay at the cha-pel that night. However, they [eventually] had to leave with the Red Cross and they were shipped about thirty minutes away from us."

At the shelter, "they had supplies. I used a leg bag because I knew for sure I most definitely needed that for the long travel. And it kind of worked out from New Orleans to Baton Rouge. When I got there, things were getting a little backed up, so the nurse was able to help me with it. However, they had to get two guys to get the cot for me and get me down to the cot so I could change and everything and get my special needs taken care of. They did have [supplies] there, but I'm glad I had my own because some things they had was latex, and I'm allergic to latex. So by being able to have some type of supplies on hand, it also made it easier for them to know what I needed. They did have the supplies and things that you needed, and they also had built partitions around and had things around you so that when it was time for you to take care of your privacies and your special needs, you would be able to do that."

Moving On

King had been at the shelter at LSU for about three days when she was informed that she and her mother would be transferred to a shelter in Lafayette, Louisiana. The two weren't sure they wanted to go. King immediately inquired whether the shelter in Lafayette would be set up the same way and be as accommodating of her special needs. The staff said they didn't know. "I said, 'Well, can you just give us one more night, because we are trying to catch a plane out to get back to Maryland,' so they allowed us to stay. My father and my son was able to stay in contact and somebody was able to bring them back."

Eventually they all made it back to Maryland. "We stayed in hotels from September until January. The Red Cross paid for that." The Red Cross and several other organizations also tried to help King find accessible housing, but to no avail. "Anywhere they suggested wasn't accessible. When you got there, you had to go up steps to get into the leasing office," King said, adding that at one of the apartments, it was suggested she go in through the patio door. "I said, 'No, it's not safe for me to use my patio door as my front door.' People just don't understand what a person actually needs in terms of a disability or how accessible things have to be."

Eventually, King found an apartment on her own. Through the Brian Joseph McCloskey Katrina Survivors with Disabilities Fund, "The National Spinal Cord Injury Association helped me with furniture to furnish the apartment as best we could," she said. "We was able to get a sofa, things that we need, a bed, and a dresser."

Having a Plan in Place

Ever since 9/11, King has had a go bag on hand. It is filled "with medical supplies and deodorant and just little things I need to keep me up and going. My son wasn't even one years old yet and ever since then I just kept a little bag of supplies for him with his baby stuff, because I wasn't disabled at the time. But now with me going through Hurricane Katrina and the experience of 9/11, it was like, okay, whatever you do, have a little bag, even a regular book bag, with my medical supplies and a leg bag—especially a leg bag, because you can't let it go too long."

Earline Roth's Story

It was the Friday evening just before Hurricane Katrina made landfall, and Earline Roth, who has a spinal cord injury, was working with a local committee preparing for a large senior health event. "My daughter came in early Saturday morning to inform me that a storm was coming," Roth said. "She said, 'Mom, get your medicine. That's all you can take. We have to leave now.' When we left, we left with my medications but no clothes, no nothing."

For twenty-five days, Roth stayed with family and friends in a shelter in Baton Rouge. "One of our relatives worked there. He let us come there to stay," Roth said, noting that her daughter served as her caregiver. "The shelter was pretty good," Roth added. "They were very gracious to us. They had prepared meals and everything."

But her stay wasn't without problems. "Because I had a C-7 fused vertebrae and was paralyzed, I could not lie on the cot on my own," Roth said, "so I had to sit up in a wheelchair those days. It shut me down where I couldn't walk anymore." Moreover, "I had only been able to go to the bathroom to wash up and had to sit in the chair from morning until night, so I became a night person. I stayed up all night." Because she remained sedentary and her diet was altered, Roth gained a lot of weight during her stay. "I am five foot three. I weighed maybe 145 and went up to close to 170."

On the Mend

For Roth, the road to recovery hasn't been easy. "I was walking with my cane before the storm," she said. "I am still going to physical therapy to get myself able to walk again." Roth's home is also not yet back to its original state. Only recently were she and her mother able to return to their home. "I was living in an upstairs apartment. Since Katrina, I'm not able to go back upstairs."

After the storm, "I didn't know when I was going to come back to my home and what condition it was in," she said. "It needed a lot of repair. Fortunately, I lived upstairs so a lot of my stuff didn't get damaged, but the roof came off. And the wheelchair ramp came down in the hallway."

A Failed Plan

Although Roth wasn't aware a storm was coming, she had made efforts to prepare for such occasions. "I had all my gear and my meds, flashlight, and everything in the closet but because my daughter was out of town and I was by myself, I couldn't get to it," Roth said.

Her heart goes out to all those impacted by the hurricane and she feels many suffered needlessly. "I think the city wasn't prepared for this, and as a whole, they wasn't prepared for people with disabilities at all."

Cheryl Pettypool's Story

When Hurricane Katrina hit, Cheryl Pettypool was living in a nursing home in Kenner, Louisiana. "They didn't evacuate us until four days after the hurricane, so I was basically in the hurricane," said Pettypool. "We had nobody to watch us except the [nursing home's] four maintenance men."

Pettypool, who relies on a wheelchair to get around, said she was one of sixty residents left behind when staff left to join their own families before the hurricane hit. Alone in her room, she grew increasingly frightened as the storm approached. Fortunately, the maintenance men moved all the residents into the hallway for fear that windowpanes would shatter and cause harm. "If it hadn't been for those maintenance men, I probably wouldn't be here right now," Pettypool said.

For three days, the residents remained in the hallway. No one received showers, and after a few days, their only source of nourishment came from bottled water. "There was no electricity. Wednesday, we ran out of food," she said. Once the residents were rescued on Friday, they were sent by ambulance to the airport, then taken by army helicopter to a makeshift trauma center on the basketball court at LSU. Pettypool believes the American Red Cross facilitated the effort.

At the trauma center, Pettypool said, "they evaluated us and depending on what kind of condition you were in, they would leave you there or call up different nursing homes and take you there." Pettypool was ultimately transferred to another nursing home about three hours away in Lake Charles. "My family and my friends couldn't find me," she recalls. Her cousin called the nursing home in Kenner and was told Pettypool was never a resident.

To make matters worse, Hurricane Rita hit Lake Charles not long after Pettypool arrived in September. "I felt like I was a hurricane magnet," she said.

Although she misses her hometown, Pettypool plans to stay in Lake Charles because she feels the staff is caring and takes safety precautions. "As soon as I got here, they always made me feel at home," she said. "I lost everything I had at the other nursing home, which was a TV and some personal items. They called and asked me if I wanted to come home to the rest center and I said no. Why would I want to go through this again?"

However, any headway the center made stopped when Lake Charles residents were forced to evacuate for Hurricane Rita. "We didn't get much notice. We had to grab everything and just flee. It was a nightmare," Pettypool said. "Our own people became the victims."

Dinah Landry, executive director of the Council on Aging in Cameron, Louisiana, still receives requests for medical equipment from residents affected by the storm. The most requested items are shower chairs, wheelchairs, walkers, and commodes. "None of them were recovered and a lot of people couldn't evacuate with those things," she said. In the Cameron area, about 90 percent of homes were completely destroyed, Landry said. Among those affected were 1,500 elderly, 300 of whom are disabled, and about 125 disabled individuals who are not seniors. "We are trying to focus on building [them] homes. They're on the priority list."

The council has received a number of grants to provide housing, handicapped ramps, and medical equipment. "We are making a lot of progress. We are having a lot of volunteers coming in [and] we are building ramps on people's trailers," Landry noted. While they may be making progress, Landry said, they still have a long way to go before everyone can move out of temporary trailer homes. In the meantime, "Nobody is going without anything."

Diane Calmes's Story

When Katrina hit, Diane Calmes and her daughter, Callie, were living in Diamondhead, Mississippi. "My parents live around the corner," said Calmes, a paraplegic. "They're seventy-nine and eighty-two."

Hearing that a severe hurricane was headed their way, Calmes suggested they evacuate. Her parents were averse to the idea, saying they were too old to start over and weren't going to leave. Calmes couldn't get her parents to budge. "They were by God not leaving. What do you do? I know enough that if I'm on the outside, I can't come back in here to check on them." Feeling she had no choice, Calmes said, "I stayed, because I couldn't leave my momma and daddy."

Riding out the Storm

When Katrina hit, Calmes said, "we got eight foot of water in my house. We rode it out in the attic. My former husband—we had been divorced but we share a daughter—he came down to rescue us and boarded up the windows and piggybacked me up in the attic. We took in eight neighbors next door up in the attic. One was eight and a half months pregnant."

"It took like forty-five minutes from nothing in my ditch to eight foot in my house. We were vapor locked in the house. We took hinge pins and everything and you could not open the door. Luckily, the top half of my front door was glass. So David busted that out and passed the daughter through and then was passing me through when the neighbors next door came over." The water "was about knee deep to my ex-husband. It was already up to the motors in the computer head in my wheelchair, [which] was out; it was water dead. I mean the water is steady rising as we're doing this. . . . We got out that evening, by dark."

Ironically, looters helped rescue Calmes from her home. "One of them found somebody with a flat-bottomed bass boat and sent them into us to get me out. So they came and we had just bedded down. We had our animals up there with us and everything. We had bedded down for the night and somebody comes hollering, 'We are looking for the lady with the wheelchair.'" Calmes responded and agreed to board the boat. "My ex had secured my manual chair behind some stuff in the garage so it wouldn't float away, so at least I had that."

Heading for Shelter

Calmes will never forget shelter life. "People couldn't take baths because they only had bottles of water for drinking purposes. Everybody was kind of stinking after a few days of being in sewer water." At the shelter, Calmes was forced to stay in her wheelchair. "I did not get out until I left and went to my brother's. My brother came over and got me and took me to Louisiana to his place. My daughter stayed with some friends in Baton Rouge so that she could go to school. I stayed with my brother because I was just deathly ill."

While Calmes stayed with her brother, her ex-husband remained behind. "David was here in Diamondhead trying to get all the dead fish and yucky crap out of the house. And I called him and said, 'Come get me the hell out of here! I ain't riding another one.' He went to Baton Rouge, picked up Callie, went to my brother's and picked up me. We went to Vicksburg." By the time they got to Vicksburg, Mississippi, Calmes's health had gotten worse. "I got infected in the water," she said. "I had an open wound on my foot and one on my behind. So I [ended up] in the hospital in Jackson for two months on an antibiotic drip. I was quarantined for the first five weeks."

Going Home

After finally being released from the hospital, Calmes returned home to Diamond-head. "Our house was gutted. We had one air mattress and a big pile of sheetrock. David slept on the sheetrock and my daughter slept on the air mattress. And that's while I was in the hospital. When they brought me home, my momma and daddy's house only got four feet of water, so theirs was only half gutted, so we set up a bed up in their living room [for me] because I had to be sanitary. Everybody just scrubbed down this one room [with] bleach, . . . the mold and everything."

An Uphill Battle

Katrina seems to have washed away Calmes's zest for life and ruined her health. "Since the anniversary, I had a massive heart attack and a triple bypass," she said. "When I had that heart attack, they told me I had had one [previously]. 'We see scarring from you having one [already].' And I think it was like the Wednesday after the storm; I think that was the heart attack they saw the scarring from."

Calmes's ex-husband also suffered a heart attack after the storm and had a difficult time dealing with the stress caused by the catastrophic event. "[David] committed suicide," Calmes said. "He took as much as he could. He was bipolar. He finally got his act back together and he had a small heart attack and couldn't deal with it and he hung himself." Damage caused by the hurricane still weighs heavily on her. "All the joy is gone," she said. In spite of all she went through, Calmes says, "I'm not going to complain because there are still people in freaking campers four years later, so I don't really feel right complaining."

According to Calmes, FEMA had also given her a trailer that wasn't accessible. By the time officials returned a month later to put a ramp on the entrance for her, she had already given the trailer to another man in Bay St. Louis, Mississippi. Since the hurricane, Calmes has been making necessary repairs to her home—at a high price. "You're paying top dollar. You paid top damn dollar to get people in here," she said, adding that it wasn't always quality work. On the upside, Calmes did receive financial assistance from the National Spinal Cord Injury Association. "We lost 95 percent of everything," she said. "The [National] Spinal Cord [Injury Association] helped me get wheelchairs and medical supplies. I think they sent me $11,000. I had to send them a list [of what I needed]. I mean, I lost my blood pressure kit. I lost my diabetes stuff. You lose everything. You lose your toothbrush! Of course, when I evacuated I didn't have my glasses on, so I had no glasses for three months."

The Importance of Preparedness

"I was so totally prepared for the hurricane," Calmes said. Or so she thought.

"My daughter had gone to Europe the summer before with [the organization] People to People. They were required to have these one-mile distance walkie-talkies, so we had a pair of very good quality walkie-talkies. I had given one to my momma and daddy, and one to us. We knew we were going to lose electricity. We stuffed the freezer. We were boxed up with water and canned goods. I know how to do for a hurricane, but I didn't know how to do for a forty-five-foot tidal wave. I was not ready for that at all." Plus, she said, "I had a brand damn new generator. It made one pot of coffee before the water got it. That's a hurricane."

Aside from the fact that generators do not always work, Calmes learned a few other things about preparedness. "Keep an axe in your attic. I'm serious," she said. "Always have a front door with at least half glass so you can get out if you have to bust it. Mine now is solid glass. But we never dreamed we'd be vapor locked in." And for easy access, "I always keep my house insurance papers in one envelope right next to my computer," Calmes said.

If you are sheltering in place, she recommends putting important paperwork in a dry dishwasher and locking it. "It's waterproof," she said, adding that she also uses plastic storage boxes to store paperwork. "I do my own genealogy research. I lost ten years of paperwork [in Hurricane Katrina]. All my paperwork now is in plastic single file boxes with the handle on top. I have not unpacked it and I will not unpack it." Also, during severe weather, since cabinets can fall down, "breakable, precious treasures, you can put in your oven," since ovens seem to stay in place.

Since Katrina, Calmes has purchased a handheld device with a radio, a light, and a cell phone charger. "It hand cranks for the power. It was like forty dollars, but I promise you that thing is going to be worth its money when it's needed." She also keeps extra medical supplies on hand, including catheters and leg bags, and orders her supplies by the case instead of a one-month supply just so she is sure she'll have enough in an emergency.

But perhaps the most important lesson Calmes and her family learned is to evacuate when advised. "I'm never gonna stay for another one again," Calmes said. "Last year, when [Hurricane] Gustav was coming, . . . I booked to Tennessee."

This was one lesson her parents learned the hard way. On her mother's birthday, Calmes recalled, "She said, 'Baby, I am so sorry. I almost killed us all, didn't I?'" Even though Calmes has learned a lot about preparedness, she hopes that she will never see another catastrophic event like Katrina. "I could live a lifetime without another Hurricane Katrina. I wouldn't wish it on my worst enemy."

Advice to Others

The following are among the many hard-won lessons learned by the women who speak here, presented in their own words, as others so often speak for women with disabilities.

Leave Early

"Just get out of town early. Get out of town early would be best, especially if you know where [the storm is] gonna hit."

"Just make sure you don't get stuck. Don't wait around. Just go."

Have Backup Systems

"Stay prepared. You really don't know when it could happen. The most important thing is make sure you have your medications. Make sure you have pharmacies that you can reach across the state. Make sure you have all your proper papers. Also, maybe have a couple of changing clothes. If you need disposables, . . . keep a stash on hand. Make sure you have cash. The credit cards are good. I think that's important, . . . [and] make sure you have a flashlight handy. Even staying in a shelter, have a flashlight."

"Keep a manual chair in your house. If you own an electric wheelchair, keep a manual chair just for emergencies just so it's easier to get you out. Yes, it's inconvenient if somebody has to push you, but you'll survive.

"Take your meds with you. Take everything you can. Take at least three changes of clothes, if not more. Take bedpans, take diapers, take extra Foleys and catheters. If you have a bedside commode and you can take it with you, fine. But take everything you need to take care of yourself."

"There's not always a way to get in the bathroom, even in public shelters. Those bathrooms are designed for what they consider handicapped kids at high schools and stuff, and they don't build them to where you can do anything but pull straight in and try and flip yourself around, and I don't know a lot of people that can do it, especially when they're like me with a cervical injury."

"You can use air mattresses. You might have to have help getting in and out, but I'd rather do that and know I've got a cheap air mattress that I can take with me than have to go through what I went through that put me in the hospital for the better part of the year."

"If you have to rely on public transportation and you don't have those options where the cab companies will actually take you anywhere as long as you have the money, . . . have that Plan B where family members and everybody comes together and you get that car rental the week before."

Know Who Needs Assistance

"You've gotta have a regular database that says how many people in your community have a disability . . . [and a plan that] shows that you get the elderly and people with disabilities first. At least get their information down and then with the local schools and everything, they have their database and people's information is going to transfer over."

Use Your Networks

"If you can afford it, get together with some people and get on a handicapped bus and just go." Do not wait for government officials or first responders to assist you. They assume anybody able-bodied enough to get out is going to take care of their own. But what about the rest of us who can manage on our own for the most part but there's things that we need help with? In my little town, all they did was the police came around and said, 'You've got to go. You've got 'til six o'clock this evening. If you stay, we will not be responsible.'"

Overall, "I don't know how to tell anybody to get prepared other than to keep a line open to an able-bodied person aside from a government entity."

Conclusion

These portraits convey images of women as more than the sum of their disabilities—what they cannot do unassisted. They are people who reach out to others, plan ahead, and fight for what they need and want. Further, their lives revolve around particular needs for functional assistance but, like others caught up in disaster, just as much around health issues, reduced income, inadequate transportation, and family responsibilities. Women with disabilities faced inhumane shelter conditions, barriers to safe and secure rehousing, and unresponsive relief and recovery systems, just as legions of others did after Katrina. The women who spoke out here are rarely heard either in gender stories or disability stories, but the national imperative to address these safety and equity concerns begins by understanding both at once.

The stories of these women who survived Hurricane Katrina bring to life the need for research, analysis, planning, and action to protect and enhance the safety of all persons living through disasters with disabilities (Clive et al. 2009; and see Brenda Phillips in this volume). We must build on their experiences to develop policy frameworks responsive to the needs and capacities of women across ability communities, taking into account both the particular and the general issues they confront. A piecemeal approach that considers either disability or gender, or one or the other in turn, will not do, as amply demonstrated by these women's experiences. The women who speak out here demonstrate the spirit, creativity, and determination needed to join in the hard work of building disaster resilience. This begins with both hearing and listening to their hard-won lessons from Katrina and applying those to national resilience strategies based as much on the principles of disability and gender justice as on the need for efficiency and effectiveness in disaster management.

———

Elizabeth Davis is an emergency management consultant who focuses on inclusive emergency management, encompassing special needs planning, disaster human services, and related issues through her firms EAD &Associates, LLC, and the National Emergency Management Resource Center, as well as the not-for-profit she leads, Emergency Preparedness Initiative Global. She began public service with the New York City Mayor's Office for People with Disabilities; moved to the New York City Office of Emergency Management, and later became the first director of the National Organization on Disability's Emergency Preparedness Initiative.

Kelly Rouba is a former associate with EAD &Associates, an inclusive emergency management consultancy, and also serves as disaster assistance employee/access and functional needs specialist with the Department of Homeland Security out of Region II. As well, she is a published author and sits on several service-related boards.

REFERENCES

Clive, A., Davis, E., Hansen, R., and Mincin, J. (2009). Disability. In B. Phillips, D. Thomas, A. Fothergill, and L. Blinn-Pike (Eds.), *Social vulnerability to disasters* (pp. 187–215). Boca Raton, FL: CRC Press.

Morin, R., and Rein, L. (2005). Some of the uprooted won't go home again. *Washington Post.* September 16. Retrieved from *www.kff.org/newsmedia/7401.cfm.*

CHAPTER 14

Factors Influencing Evacuation Decisions among High-Risk Pregnant and Postpartum Women

Marianne E. Zotti, Van T. Tong, Lyn Kieltyka,
and Renee Brown-Bryant

It is estimated that one-quarter of New Orleans residents did not respond to mandatory evacuation orders before Hurricane Katrina because they were unable or un-
willing to leave (Kates et al. 2006). These people, who were predominantly African
American and had low incomes, and may have been aged or infirm, sought refuge
in sites such as the Superdome, convention center, hospitals, upper stories of homes,
and elevated highways before being moved to other cities. The full poststorm evacuation of New Orleans was completed about one week after Hurricane Katrina.

Although it is not known how many of those who did not respond to evacuation orders were pregnant, it is estimated that at least ten thousand pregnant women
were among the total number of displaced people from Hurricane Katrina (Buekens,
Xiong, and Harville 2006). Before the disaster, women living in the New Orleans
area were already at greater risk for poor pregnancy and infant outcomes than women
overall in the United States (Callaghan et al. 2007). Disaster effects such as poor living conditions, overcrowding, constraints on breastfeeding, and disruption of health
care can negatively affect the health of pregnant women and infants. Furthermore,
pregnancy and the postpartum period carry a high risk for depression and anxiety,
making pregnant and postpartum women, especially those of low income or education, particularly vulnerable to disaster-related psychological and physical stress
(Buekens, Xiong, and Harville 2006). Stress is a well-established risk factor for poor
birth outcomes such as preterm birth; social support, on the other hand, has been
found to have positive effects on birth weight (Hobel, Goldstein, and Barrett 2008).
Maternal stress after disaster has also been associated with negative effects on cognitive development among children (King and Laplante 2005), including intellectual
and language functioning among toddlers (Laplante et al. 2004) and cognitive and
linguistic functioning among five-year-olds (Laplante et al. 2008).

The literature is sparse about the effects of disaster on pregnancy in general
(Buekens, Xiong, and Harville 2006), with even less known about the unique needs
among high-risk pregnant and postpartum women after a disaster. Therefore, on
March 12–13, 2008, the Division of Reproductive Health of the Centers for Disease Control and Prevention (CDC) collaborated with Healthy Start New Orleans

and the Louisiana Office of Public Health to conduct focus groups among high-risk women, defined as those who were pregnant or postpartum at the time of Hurricane Katrina. The project was designed to understand the effects of this event on pregnant and postpartum women and to consider the implications for practical action such as communication strategies to reach this population.

This chapter focuses on factors that affected decisions among high-risk pregnant and postpartum women regarding when and how to evacuate surrounding the time of Hurricane Katrina, including the initial decision, decisions to move around, and decisions to return to New Orleans. Their poignant stories, told in their own words, demonstrate everyday realities and choices among this high-risk group that faces unique challenges.

Understanding Evacuation Decisions

Three conceptual frameworks were employed to collect and analyze qualitative data, including social networking, resource theory, and the determinants of health behaviors as factors that contribute to these women's experiences. Of particular interest were factors affecting evacuation decisions, and the experiences and needs of women at two points of time—during evacuation and through the journey of displacement.

Social Networks

Strong ties to extended family, friends, and community groups appear to affect evacuation (Bateman and Edwards 2002; Eisenman et al. 2007). Racial and ethnic minorities are more likely to heed warning messages with confirmation from other sources such as family and social networks (Fothergill, Maestas, and Darlington 1999). In a qualitative analysis of Hurricane Katrina evacuees, the most common theme focused on social networks: "Participants described factors influencing evacuation decisions that were complex, interacted with one another, and most importantly were influenced by extended family and other members of participants' social networks, either facilitating or inhibiting evacuation" (Eisenman et al. 2007, S113). Social networks can influence transportation, health, and shelter. Broad networks of family and friends created demands on participants and delayed evacuation among households and groups. Obligations to the family, especially to elderly family members, further inhibited evacuation. However, the structural component of perceived social support, which encompasses the size, activeness, and closeness of a network, has been found in several studies to protect victims from psychological stress and protect victims' health, mental and otherwise (Litt 2008; Norris et al. 2002). Gendered caregiving roles are reported in earlier studies of disaster evacuation, displacement, and return in the context of floods (e.g., Enarson and Scanlon 1999).

Resources

For many residents of New Orleans during Hurricane Katrina, a lack of resources delayed evacuation and limited options (Phillips and Morrow 2007). In a Texas shelter survey, the largest portion of individuals who did not leave New Orleans before the storm lacked transportation out of the city (Brodie et al. 2006). Additionally, costs of evacuation were prohibitive (Curtis, Mills, and Leitner 2007). Hurricane Katrina hit at the end of the month, when those surviving on government entitlement programs had run out of money for gas, food, hotels, and general evacuation (Phillips and Morrow 2007).

Personal and Social Factors

Personal and social factors that influenced African Americans' decisions not to evacuate during Hurricane Katrina were examined qualitatively using the Health Belief Model (Elder et al. 2007). According to this model, an individual will perform a health-related behavior if the individual perceives that his or her health is in jeopardy, the condition is potentially serious, and the benefits of the action outweigh its costs, and if a precipitating force ("cue to action") leads to action. Three determinants of health-related behaviors (we count evacuation decisions in the context of Hurricane Katrina as health-related behaviors) are: (1) perceived susceptibility, including optimism about the outcome as a result of past experience "riding out" hurricanes at home and of religious faith; (2) perceived low severity of probable impact because of inconsistent evacuation orders; and (3) barriers to action based on financial constraints and on fear because of perceived high levels of neighborhood crime. Distinct from the Health Belief Model but also relevant is the role played by the perceived indifference of emergency authorities toward low-income African Americans affected by the hurricane, a perception revealed in the Texas shelter survey (Brodie et al. 2006).

Research Design

CDC and the Louisiana Office of Public Health approved the project as public health practice. Participants received a stipend, travel reimbursement, lunch, a resource list, and access to on-site child care and to a mental health professional experienced in providing services to Hurricane Katrina survivors.

Sample Description

Potential participants in this convenience sample were identified and contacted through a local market research company and the New Orleans Healthy Start office. Criteria for inclusion were: (1) living in New Orleans at the time of Hurricane Katrina; (2) being pregnant or up to nine months postpartum at the time of the hurricane, or becoming pregnant in the three months following the hurricane; (3) living in Orleans Parish at the time of the focus groups; (4) having no postcollege education; (5) claiming an annual household income of less than $35,000; and (6) returning to New Orleans by August 29, 2006. Twenty-seven women participated.

Complete demographic information was available for twenty-five of the twenty-seven participants. All participants had at least completed high school. Most (92 percent) were African American, 80 percent were single, 52 percent were working full time, and 80 percent were current or past Healthy Start New Orleans participants. Fifty-six percent were pregnant during Hurricane Katrina, and another 16 percent became pregnant within three months after the storm. Most (79 percent) were aged nineteen to twenty-six years (n=24). In the discussion that follows, participants are described as they were at the time of Hurricane Katrina. For example, the term "pregnant woman" refers to a participant who was pregnant at the time of Hurricane Katrina, not necessarily at the time of the focus groups.

Through a semi-structured approach during each two-hour session, participants were asked to describe their experiences in evacuation, their concerns as pregnant or postpartum women, the services they had needed, and how they had received information. They were also asked for recommendations about communicating information to high-risk women in future disasters.

The information presented here is taken directly from the women's evacuation descriptions. Audio recordings with no identifying information were transcribed and cross-checked by three reviewers. Responses were coded both inductively, by determining major themes that emerged from the data and subthemes within major themes, and deductively, by identifying themes from preconceived frameworks, particularly the Health Belief Model construct. We analyzed the findings over time, classifying the sequence of events as, first, the initial evacuation from New Orleans, which occurred up to the first week after Hurricane Katrina and thus included the poststorm evacuation period; and, second, the displacement or "the journey," including mobility and events that occurred after the initial evacuation from New Orleans.

Findings

Although everyone in the sample eventually evacuated from New Orleans, women's experiences varied by whether they initially left the city before or after the hurricane. Seven of the twenty-seven pregnant or postpartum women reported that they and their families did not evacuate before the storm. While both subgroups of high-risk women were strongly affected, factors affecting their decisions and experiences differed, depending on whether they evacuated before or after the storm.

Perceived Susceptibility

Women who did not evacuate New Orleans before the storm described a lack of perceived susceptibility that affected their decision not to leave. Most women did not perceive themselves susceptible to the storm due to previous hurricane experiences. They said things like they weren't "sure the hurricane was going to happen." One woman seven-and-one-half months pregnant said she did not even consider that the hurricane was dangerous to her: "She [my girlfriend] had a big-screen TV, so when I looked, I said, 'Oh Lord, girl, that thing coming straight here, . . . watch it just blow over.'" Later she said changes in the wind influenced them to leave her friend's home and go to downtown New Orleans. They did not immediately leave the city.

Among the women who evacuated before the hurricane, one stated she left because she was afraid that she and her baby would drown. However, most women did not mention that they had perceived they might come to harm from the storm; they simply described what they and their families did to evacuate.

Social and Familial Networks

In most cases, women did not leave because their family members desired to stay. This postpartum woman explained:

> I stood [stayed] for the hurricane. Me and my family. My momma, my five sisters, and all their kids, . . . my momma ain't wanna leave. So we stood . . . there a couple of days. . . . Mom decided we was gonna leave because the water went a rising, and the toilets went a backing up. So we walked from the [name] project to the Superdome.

A woman who was pregnant but later miscarried stayed with her family, but her mother's condition influenced where they could stay:

> We didn't evacuate. I stayed in the Lower Ninth Ward. . . . My mother, she's real obese. My sister was working at a hotel, so we had got to stay [there] . . . until that Thursday. And it was flooded. . . . It was so stink throughout the whole hotel. . . . To flush the toilet, we had to walk down eight flights of stairs. . . . We had to walk up and down the stairs to dump the water . . . to flush the toilet. . . . And with my mother being real big, she can't go up and down the stairs.

Another woman who also miscarried talked about how others came to stay with her:

> I stayed in the projects. At the time, my son was four and my daughter was like six. It was me, my two kids, and my boyfriend, but his people also came by me because by me being in the project, they thought it was safer there. So everybody came by me. The water was rising. The toilet was stopped up. . . . We was running out of food, water, and all of that. . . . So I got nervous and I was like, well, I think we should leave because we have a lot of people in here, and I don't know how far the water is going to get.

After a while she, like others who did not evacuate because of family pressures, decided that the lack of sanitation and basic necessities made it impossible for anyone to stay.

The twenty women who left New Orleans before the storm also described the influence of their social networks. Family members influenced when women and their families initially evacuated, especially because these women acquiesced to maternal authority figures such as their mothers and mothers-in-law. These authority figures focused on women's safety and that of their infants, as this young mother describes:

> We was going to ride it out at first, but his momma was like, "Get in the car, you not staying here with this baby." . . . Good thing we left, though. Because . . . her roof, her ceiling in her kitchen, came down.

Another pregnant woman also mentioned her mother-in-law's influence:

> So she [husband's mother] was actually the one that got us out of the apartment. . . .
> I wasn't going to go anywhere because, again, I was pregnant, didn't have any
> money, didn't have a decent-running car. That lady sat in our driveway and would
> not move until we got in that car. So thank the Lord we did, because we lost
> everything.

Resources

Interestingly, of those who did not evacuate before the storm, none cited financial
factors that might have interfered with this decision. In contrast, women who left
before the storm spoke of lack of resources that delayed evacuation. One pregnant
woman said:

> We slept on the [Lake Pontchartrain] Causeway, and then all of a sudden the
> van won't start so we couldn't move. We stayed there for a little while, and I was
> panicking because . . . I done brought so much of milk.

Another pregnant woman spoke about both family influence and resources, reporting
that her boyfriend's mother told them that everyone needed to leave. The community
worked together to evacuate:

> She woke us up five o'clock Sunday morning crying, saying, "We got to get of here.
> We've got to get out of here." I don't have no money. We don't get paid until that
> Thursday after Katrina hit. . . . Everybody in the neighborhood got up together and
> put in some gas money. And my gas gauge wasn't working. . . . So every two hours
> we was stopping for gas.

Traumatic Events and Mental Health

Initial decisions to stay for the storm led to a series of seemingly traumatic events for
these women. Five women (four pregnant and one postpartum) reported sleeping at
least one night on a highway bridge, on the interstate, at the airport, or in the Superdome. All seven women who did not evacuate before the storm reported traumatic
events and losses during the initial evacuation. For example, the woman who stayed
to honor her mother's wishes explained how they improvised to keep children safe in
the water:

> So we walked from the [name] project to the Superdome. We had a air mattress for
> the kids. I'm short, and the water was higher than me. So I'm panicking. I don't
> want to go out there. So I had my baby. . . . She was six months, and I had a little
> niece that was like nine months. We put them two on the air mattress and the other
> kids on the air mattress. Got under a bridge where they had no water, and we set
> the air mattress down. The air mattress busted. So they had some people pushing

file cabinets. So they stopped cause the file cabinet stopped floating. So we decided to get the file cabinet and put it in the water and put all the children in there. So we put all the older kids [in the cabinets] and the two little ones in a cooler.

She further expressed difficulty in getting over these experiences: "A couple of days later, I made it to the bus. . . . After being in the water so long, I was hallucinating. I was jumping up thinking that I was still in the water. I was like that for a while." A pregnant woman spoke about her grandmother dying during the flood. Although these experiences occurred two and a half years before the taped interview, she was still emotionally unable to tell her full story:

Well, I stood for the storm. The water rose. . . . My grandma was downstairs. . . . We had to rush and get her up; . . . we stood on the second floor. My grandma passes like the third day. We had to sleep in the house with her, the dead body. Then they came and got us the next day. . . . Told us to pack a few things, and my grandpa . . . went to grabbing my grandma's stuff. They had been together like fifty-four years. . . . He went to break down crying. My grandmother laying on the floor like she sleep. It just was horrible. They rescued us. . . . Brought us to the airport. We slept out there. . . . Oh it's so much, I skipping pieces. We saw dead bodies floating in the water, all kinds of stuff. I just [*sniffles and takes a deep breath*]—it was just ridiculous. I can't talk.

A third example of mental health effects is provided by the woman quoted earlier whose boyfriend's family stayed with her. She described extending her caregiving role as she and her boyfriend assisted others before being able to escape themselves:

My boyfriend got a boat. And we were just going around picking up people, people we didn't even know. . . . I brought them back to my house, . . . so we was in the water for like a day or something, just getting people. . . . And I was trying to take as many as I can because I had the space. Some people slept downstairs, in the kitchen, upstairs, or whatever. So . . . I was like, well, I think we should leave. . . . The next morning . . . I got my kids together. . . . We were walking through . . . a good five feet of water. They had alligators in the water. I heard a girl hollering. I didn't know what she was hollering for but I started running and trying to get to . . . the bridge. . . . So we made it to the bridge, thousands of people on the bridge.

She describes her fear for their safety, inadequate facilities, and the harrowing climate as they moved inside the Superdome:

So we made it to the Superdome. . . . The smell was horrible. They had a lot of people in there setting fires. It was so bad to the part that when some people slept who was with us, they had to have a security guard—somebody up all night while the other people sleep. When he gets tired or the other person wakes up, then they would be the security guard. . . . It was bad in there. Children was getting raped. You could hear them hollering at nighttime, but you know, there was nothing nobody could do. The bathroom smelled; . . . it was bad, it was so bad.

Later, as she was "panicking" at this point, she and her daughters pushed their way onto the bus to leave New Orleans.

In contrast, women who evacuated before the storm generally did not report such horrific events. Even so, their evacuations were traumatic. The biggest worry of two women was not knowing the whereabouts of family members and wondering if they were dead. Speaking about their evacuation experience was still very difficult for several women. A postpartum woman cried while relating her story:

> They said my grandma had a heart attack when she saw the water coming up. So they was in Texas, . . . so we went to [another city in Texas]. That wasn't no better neither [*crying*]. Everybody was in the shelter looking sad. My mamma didn't want to go to sleep. It just was. . . . It was messed up.

Early evacuees still faced the challenges of travel, housing, and lack of basic necessities, all of which were especially acute for pregnant and postpartum women. The women reported many difficulties in their travels. Three stayed in hotels, and three others went to shelters. Women reported they did not stay long in either of these sites. Three others reported going to relatives' homes, where one reported forty people living together in a house; another stated that she was in a two-bedroom apartment with "twenty something" other people staying there. A postpartum woman described her helpless feelings while living in their car when her baby was sick:

> We stood in Baton Rouge for like two days, and we was like sleeping in the cars and stuff and the whole while I left my house, my baby was sick. And I really didn't know what was wrong with her. She just kept crying and throwing up all over. And it was just making me so mad because I couldn't do nothing about it.

Others described difficulties and extended travel times during evacuation. Several reported that their trips from New Orleans to places such as Baton Rouge (about 80 miles) and Houston, Texas, (about 350 miles) took eighteen to twenty hours. Additional stressful obstacles included lack of gasoline and closed gas stations, and lack of space on overfilled buses. Many pregnant and postpartum women talked about the lack of basic necessities such as electricity, water, and food as they evacuated. Women who went to Mississippi or Baton Rouge did not have electricity. One woman said: "After the storm hit, Baton Rouge was without electricity. And some things that you want to have when you have a five-month-old." Many women cited the lack of electricity as their reason for moving to another place.

Social Support

Three women reported that once they left New Orleans, individuals unexpectedly helped them. One pregnant woman said: "A lady I knew . . . had paid a deposit down on an apartment for us in Houston. And that was like before they started doing the voucher." A postpartum woman described how a security man helped them by buying "some Pampers for the baby and stuff," then took off early from work to drive them to a relative's house: "So the man drove us all the way to the other side of Houston, to they house." Another pregnant woman related being befriended by a young couple at a shelter in Baton Rouge:

> A young couple had saw us, we were sitting outside the shelter. They invited us to their home for a couple of days. . . . They drove us to Houston, where they paid for the hotel for a week or so.

Among those leaving before the storm, three women described how churches aided them. One pregnant woman talked about a church in Mississippi where the pastor "kept us there, he fed us; . . . he bought us dinner and all kind of stuff" for her entire caravan of evacuees. A postpartum woman said a church "put my whole family up in the church with them . . . for like two weeks." The third woman needed some medications while she was staying at a hotel; she went to a nearby church shelter, where these medications were provided by the pastor's wife.

The Journeys of Pregnant and Postpartum Women after Katrina

Both groups of women reported similar experiences after the initial evacuation, the starting point of a journey during which many women and their families relocated repeatedly, staying a short time at one site, then moving on. All the women described staying in from two to seven locations after leaving home; most of the twenty-seven reported that they had stayed in from three to five places before moving back to New Orleans.

Factors Affecting Mobility

Several factors affected the decisions made by this high-risk group of pregnant women and women with infants about where to go next in the wake of Hurricane Katrina. Key factors included difficulties in the new setting, organization of government benefits, and the effects of Hurricane Rita, which hit southwest Louisiana only three weeks after Hurricane Katrina.

DIFFICULTIES IN A NEW SETTING

A woman who miscarried described leaving Baton Rouge because she did not like it and going to a town in Pennsylvania. However, though a house was located for her, she felt as though she did not belong there: "And I'm not from here, I don't know nothing about here, so I need to get back . . . to Louisiana, a little closer to where I know. So I came. My momma was in Arkansas. So I went there." Another postpartum woman reported feeling unwelcome in the town where she settled:

> They had gave us apartments out there. . . . Some people were saying that we needed to go back to New Orleans, stuff like that, because they don't like New Orleans people. . . . We ain't really know what to do, because it was their city.

Though family is often a valuable resource in postdisaster relocation, a pregnant woman in our sample described not feeling welcome among her husband's family:

And we get there, . . . a two-bedroom apartment. I am the only one with children. I am pregnant. Oh Lord, my husband, I love his family cause they are always there, but you know, in-laws get on your nerves [*everyone laughing*]. . . . So they there all the time. I am pregnant, my children around. Cousin talking bout how my children doing this, doing that. So I got fed up with that [*laughs*]. . . . So we tried to find somewhere else to go.

Financial constraints were very real, and sometimes gender inequalities affect one's ability to access resources, even short-term shelter after a disaster. This postpartum woman reported having difficulty arranging a longer hotel stay until the bill was put in the name of her infant's father instead of her name:

They was saying, "Oh, y'all only can stay for one week, then y'all gotta go somewhere." It don't make no sense to a hotel, then we gotta come back. . . . Well, it was at my name, they only want to give me a week. But we put it in his [infant's father's] name, they gave a month or two.

ACCESSING GOVERNMENT BENEFITS

Government benefits also influenced evacuation decisions. A pregnant woman described the helpful way services were organized in Dallas, Texas: "They had like this big convention center or something. Yes, so we really got set up. They set up with the FEMA [Federal Emergency Management Agency]. Everything went really quickly. It was long lines and everything, but everything we needed was right there." She was still living in a FEMA trailer in New Orleans at the time of the interview. Another pregnant woman said the receipt of vouchers helped them find a larger apartment, although, as a third woman noted, they had to move when FEMA benefits stopped.

Contradictory requirements for government resources were also a deterrent in the case of one pregnant woman, a young mother. She reported that she learned while staying with other people, rather than in a shelter, that they were not eligible to get FEMA assistance:

So also at the shelter they said, "Well, . . . since you are prone to miscarry, it's better to be in your home where you're comfortable than to be out here with these people. And you're stressed about this and that and the other." Plus my other child was three and very busy. So we ended up going to stay with them. But when we tried to get the help that everybody else got, they say, "You're in a home and you're not in a shelter, so you're not eligible for help."

A SECOND STORM: HURRICANE RITA

A few women reported that Hurricane Rita affected their travel. One woman with a five-month-old recounted how they left Baton Rouge due to lack of electricity to go to Beaumont, Texas, because her husband had family there. However, due to Hurricane Rita, they had to leave Beaumont, and they relocated to Arkansas, where they stayed about two weeks. Here she explains how they decided to return to New Orleans:

Because a lot of . . . the aid . . . was running out. Because after you are in, been in a place for about two weeks and you have FEMA taking care of you, a lot of places wouldn't allow you stay so long. So our time was up in Fayetteville, and we had to make a choice to either go back to Beaumont, who was still recovering from Rita (we didn't want to go there because his family was without) or just go back to New Orleans and see what we had to deal with.

Assets and Losses during Displacement

Nearly all the women described traveling or living together in large groups, which was an asset, better than traveling alone. However, it often resulted in unique problems, as a woman with an infant explained:

> When I evacuated, it was my mother, my father, my older brother, my younger brother—who had a wife who was eight months pregnant at the time—I had a five-month-old, and my husband. And so we kinda moving around in a caravan, and every time we had to find somewhere to stay. It wasn't like finding a place for your immediate family, like for my son and my husband. It was for my mother, my father, my two brothers, his . . . expecting wife. . . . It was a lot to think about.

MATERIAL LOSSES

Most women reported losses such as homes, belongings, or both from Hurricane Katrina. For example, one pregnant woman stated that she had to replace what she had prepared for her infant: "We had lost *everything*. Brand-new school clothes, stuff for my baby that wasn't born yet. I mean everything." Another had to replace household goods that were unusable after the flood:

> And then all my kids are premature, so they was in the house for less than ten minutes and was completely sick. I was in a hospital with them, so I had to get rid of everything from curtains, to clothes, to tables, to sofas, whatever. And start all over again.

A woman who became pregnant after the storm described both the destruction in her home and a lack of community resources such as schools.

> They had done broke into a lot of houses. . . . They was writing and looting all over people houses. It just was horrible to come back to see how you left your house spotless and to come back and it's all messed up. Somebody had been living in our house. So that meant we had to get rid of all of our bedding stuff and get all new stuff. . . . In November . . . '05, I came back home. . . . My job was open. But I didn't want to go back because my children all wasn't in school. . . . They had a couple of schools open. But . . . my . . . two big children . . . couldn't go back until they opened up a high school for them.

FAMILY LOSSES

Six women reported losses, including miscarriages and deaths of family members. One pregnant woman talked about not being able to find family members, then miscarrying: "And I couldn't find a lot of my family and stuff like that. I still don't know where my daddy is to this day. I was stressed out. I had lost my baby in November."

Another pregnant woman described how her son, born when she was living away from New Orleans, became disabled at age eight months after an accident—and then her mother died:

> Two weeks later, well, my mom had cancer, but she never let us know that she had it. It was before the storm and during the storm, . . . and then my brother called me and told me my mom was sick and I didn't know. So we went back out there, I had to help take care of her. It was after my baby got out of the hospital. . . . You know he got admitted to the hospital, so he's a sick child now. And two weeks later, my mom, she got into in-home, she was in a hospital, and she got into in-home hospice. We had to take care of her for about August, September. She died in October, October 5.

A third woman also raised the issue of pregnant women caring for unwell relatives, speaking of both her mother and aunt dying: "My momma, she was real sick herself because she wasn't used to being away from home. So she was in and out of the hospital. She passed on December 19. Her twin sister, she died during the storm in Atlanta." Women did not need to have experienced the death of a relative to feel loss. A pregnant woman in our sample described how hard it still is for her because her mother and sister went to different places and did not return to New Orleans.

Conclusions and Implications

The women who participated in these focus groups very often based their decisions about when and how to evacuate on needs of their family, both immediate and extended. They acquiesced to maternal influences in deciding to leave, whether this was before or after the storm, and highlighted their responsibilities in caring for infants and family members with special needs. Due to the significance of their social networks, they also traveled after the event to connect again with family members. Pregnant and postpartum women described struggles related to lack of resources and basic necessities and the housing and transport challenges that resulted from traveling in large social networks.

Perceived susceptibility seemed less important to these women's decision making than the influences of others in their social network, especially maternal authority figures. Among women who did not evacuate before the storm, many stated that they did not perceive themselves to be susceptible, consistent with the Health Belief Model employed here. In this group of seven, none cited lack of resources as a reason for staying but emphasized instead the influence of others in their social networks and their caregiving responsibilities in these networks, which continued when they evacuated. These women experienced horrific events as they and their friends, family, and kin left their homes to seek refuge in sites such as the Superdome, convention center, and elevated highways.

Women who evacuated early also spoke rarely about perceived susceptibility but often about the strong influence of those in their social networks who encouraged them to leave before the storm. They, too, described their caregiving roles for infants, children, and adults that continued throughout the evacuation process.

Exploring these unique postdisaster needs among high-risk pregnant and post-partum women is an important first step, but further research is critical to understanding needs, roles, and responsibilities among these women. Furthermore, future studies closer in time to the disaster may illuminate factors that were not disclosed in these groups. Even so, many of the issues that these women discussed are consistent with findings in other studies among low-income people who were in shelters after Hurricane Katrina.

Although these data are from a small nonrepresentative group of New Orleans high-risk women affected by Hurricane Katrina, these findings suggest that, as public health and other agencies prepare for disaster, they need to consider the overall needs of the individual as part of a larger social network, as well as needs arising from the caregiving roles of pregnant and postpartum women. Among other suggestions, we recommend that officials may reach such high-risk women by employing multiple approaches for communicating with them about an impending disaster. These could include targeting influential community leaders trusted by high-risk pregnant and postpartum women and voluntary agencies in close touch with them.

Evacuation plans might include targeting resources to reach and move such high-risk populations, who often lack what is needed for timely evacuations. These plans could also consider what assistance is likely to be most needed by large extended families, which tend to move together when possible. This effort could enable resource sharing and enhanced social support among family members.

Finally, disaster messages created for pregnant and early postpartum women may need to acknowledge and incorporate the familial caregiver role that women in this stage of life often have. For example, following analysis of the data reported here, the CDC Division of Reproductive Health incorporated caregiving into 2008 hurricane preparedness materials for pregnant women and those with young children (see *www.cdc.gov/Features/Emergencies/Pregnancy-Infants.html* and *www.cdc.gov/reproductivehealth/emergency*). In these preparedness suggestions, there are reminders for also ensuring care for other family members. This approach, if more widely adopted in public health and emergency management materials, might be very useful for women of childbearing age, especially low-income and poorly educated pregnant and post-partum women likely to be affected by disaster.

While future disaster effects among this group of high-risk women cannot be entirely prevented, we can and should be proactive in planning to address the needs revealed as this group of women vividly shared their personal struggles during Hurricane Katrina.

Marianne E. Zotti is lead epidemiologist in the Division of Reproductive Health at the Centers for Disease Control and Prevention. Selected as a fellow in the American Academy of Nursing, she focuses on postdisaster reproductive health in the United States and internationally on international refugee reproductive health, including the development of the Reproductive Health Assessment Toolkit for Conflict-Affected Women.

Van T. Tong obtained her degree in population and family health from the Bloomberg School of Public Health at Johns Hopkins University before joining the Centers for Disease Control and Prevention as a fellow in the Public Health Prevention Service. She is an epidemiologist conducting research in reproductive health at the CDC.

Lyn Kieltyka is the lead maternal and child health epidemiologist assigned to Louisiana through a multistate cooperative agreement with the Centers for Disease Control and Prevention Applied Sciences Branch, Division of Reproductive Health. In addition to Katrina research, she actively participates in the state's Infant Mortality Reduction Initiative by providing data to help improve pregnancy outcomes.

Renee Brown-Bryant is the associate director for health communication science with the Division of Reproductive Health at the CDC, has worked with the National Center for Prevention Services program to directly fund HIV/AIDS education services through community-based organizations, and was project officer for the National Prevention Information Network.

All authors are employed by the Centers for Disease Control and Prevention, Atlanta, Georgia. Lyn Kieltyka is a CDC assignee to Louisiana Office of Public Health in New Orleans. The findings and conclusions are those of the authors and not necessarily the official position of the CDC. Correspondence to Marianne Zotti: *drhinfo@cdc.gov*.

REFERENCES

Bateman, J. M., and Edwards, B. (2002). Gender and evacuation: A closer look at why women are more likely to evacuate for hurricanes. *Natural Hazards Review, 3*(3), 107–117.

Brodie, M., Weltzien, E., Altman, D., Blendon, R. J., and Benson, J. M. (2006). Experiences of Hurricane Katrina evacuees in Houston shelters: Implications for future planning. *American Journal of Public Health, 96*(8), 1402–1408.

Buekens, P., Xiong, X., and Harville, E. (2006). Hurricanes and pregnancy. *Birth, 33*(2), 91–93.

Callaghan, W. M., Rasmussen, S. A., Jamieson, D. J., Ventura, S. J., Farr, S. L., Sutton, P. D., Mathews, T., Hamilton, B., Shealy, K., Brantley, D., and Posner, S. (2007). Health concerns of women and infants in times of natural disasters: Lessons learned from Hurricane Katrina. *Maternal and Child Health Journal, 11*(4), 307–311.

Curtis, A., Mills, J. W., and Leitner, M. (2007). Katrina and vulnerability: The geography of stress. *Journal of Health Care for the Poor and Underserved, 18*(2), 315–330.

Eisenman, D. P., Cordasco, K. M., Asch, S., Golden, J. F., and Glik, D. (2007). Disaster planning and risk communication with vulnerable communities: Lessons from Hurricane Katrina. *American Journal of Public Health, 97*, S109–S115.

Elder, K., Xirasagar, S., Miller, N., Bowen, S. A., Glover, S., and Piper, C. (2007). African Americans' decisions not to evacuate New Orleans before Hurricane Katrina: A qualitative study. *American Journal of Public Health, 97,* S124–S129.

Enarson, E., and Scanlon, J. (1999). Gender patterns in flood evacuation: A case study in Canada's Red River Valley. *Applied Behavioral Science Review, 7*(2), 103–124.

Fothergill, A., Maestas, E. G., and Darlington, J. D. (1999). Race, ethnicity, and disasters in the United States: A review of the literature. *Disasters, 23*(2), 156–173.

Hobel, C. J., Goldstein, A., and Barrett, E. S. (2008). Psychosocial stress and pregnancy outcome. *Clinical Obstetrical Gynecology, 51*(2), 333–348.

Kates, R. W., Colten, C. E., Laska, S., and Leatherman, S. P. (2006). Reconstruction of New Orleans after Hurricane Katrina: A research perspective. *Proceedings of the National Academy of Sciences USA, 103*(40), 14653–14660.

King, S., and Laplante, D. (2005). The effects of prenatal maternal stress on children's cognitive development: Project Ice Storm. *Stress, 8*(1), 35–45.

Laplante, D., Barr, R., Brunet, A., du Fort, G., Meaney, M., Saucier, J.-F., Zelazo, P., and King, S. (2004). Stress during pregnancy affects general intellectual and language functioning in human toddlers. *Pediatric Research, 56*(3), 400–410.

Laplante, D., Brunet, A., Schmitz, N., Ciampi, A., and King, S. (2008). Project Ice Storm: Prenatal maternal stress affects cognitive and linguistic functioning in 5 1/2-year-old children. *Journal of the American Academy of Child and Adolescent Psychiatry, 47*(9), 1063–1072.

Litt, J. (2008). Getting out or staying put: An African American women's network in evacuation from Katrina. *NWSA Journal, 20*(3), 32–48.

Norris, F. H., Friedman, M. J., Watson, P. J., Byrne, C. M., Diaz, E., and Kaniasty, K. (2002). 60,000 disaster victims speak. Part 1: An empirical review of the empirical literature, 1981–2001. *Psychiatry, 65*(3), 207–239.

Phillips, B. D., and Morrow, B. H. (2007). Social science research needs: Focus on vulnerable populations, forecasting, and warnings. *Natural Hazards Review, 8*(3), 61–68.

CHAPTER 15

Mothering after a Disaster

The Experiences of Black Single Mothers Displaced by Hurricane Katrina

Megan Reid

> Me and my oldest son was just talking about it. He's like, "Man, if we was at home, we wouldn't be like this." And we never did, we never had worries, . . . you know, not knowing where our next meal comes from. We didn't have this. And then we had family and friends around there too. We just been sat here in the middle of a bunch of strangers and just trying to make the best of it, and it's even harder. Oh yes, indeed. —Xia

Xia, a thirty-three-year-old black woman with four children, is also the primary care-taker of her teenage brother. Along with her husband and children, Xia was forced to evacuate New Orleans due to the flooding created by Hurricane Katrina and the ensuing breach of the levees. When they arrived in Austin, Texas, the family faced numerous problems permanently relocating to an unfamiliar city after losing everything they owned in New Orleans. Soon after Xia's arrival in Texas, her husband was incarcerated and she faced the challenges of taking care of her displaced family alone. Her children faced problems both enrolling in and fitting in at their new schools. Though they were impoverished in New Orleans, Xia felt that her family had always been able to make ends meet. This was no longer the case after their displacement.

In this chapter, I explore the experiences of black single mothers like Xia who were forced to evacuate New Orleans and relocate to Austin due to Katrina. I especially focus on their roles as caretakers. Women with dependent children are especially vulnerable to lasting challenges caused by disasters (Fothergill 1996). Katrina, unique in many ways, was also part of a larger history of gender as an organizing principle of the disaster cycle (Enarson 1998). Compared to men, women are disproportionately responsible for the care of children in everyday life (Shelton and John 1996), and caretaking is left to women in most disaster recovery situations as well. In the case of Katrina, Fothergill and Peek (2006) found that children were resilient after the storm, but that they also were vulnerable and needed assistance from their parents in recovering. Peek and Fothergill (2008) also examined parenting in the context of the longer-term Katrina recovery processes, and focused on the multiple ways parents ensured the emotional and material well-being of their children. They noted significant gender differences with regard to mothers' and fathers' child-care responsibilities. As in most non-disaster situations, mothers and other women relatives did the majority of the child-care work, and this was the case even for women who were married. This extra burden partly explains the greater difficulty women have recovering after a disaster (Enarson and Morrow 1998).

Additionally, intersecting inequalities of race, class, and gender (Collins 2000) among the population displaced by Katrina posed unique challenges with regard to disaster recovery. Women of color are more likely to be poor and to experience the negative impacts of a disaster (Enarson and Fordham 2004). Many of those who were displaced due to Katrina were poor black mothers who had few resources before Katrina hit (Jones-DeWeever and Hartmann 2006), making it especially difficult for them to be the primary caretaker of children after such a life-altering experience.

Because caretaking is a gendered activity, understanding how it operates in the context of disaster displacement is important for understanding how gender, as mediated through race and class, structures the disaster experience. Understanding the interconnectedness of the experiences of mothers and children leads to a better grasp of the relationships among gender, family, and disaster recovery. Knowing the specific problems that mothers—especially impoverished mothers of color—experience in caring for their children after a disaster can lead to policies that can help mitigate the gendered, raced, and classed differences in recovery from such events.

Methods

To investigate the long-term impact of disaster on black single mothers, I analyzed in-depth interviews with mothers who evacuated to Austin, Texas, as a result of Katrina, a component of the Services in the Aftermath of a Disaster study conducted at the University of Texas at Austin. In early September 2005, the study began in an ad hoc manner as it became apparent that the large number of people evacuating to Austin presented an opportunity to document the experience of disaster recovery. The research team, of which I was a member, conducted 139 interviews with seventy-one people over a two-year period, beginning in the days after the storm hit, and followed initial respondents over time.

For this chapter, I analyzed a subsample of these interviews: twelve black women who were either single mothers of minor children or primary caretakers of minor children, interviewed at least once four months or more from the date Katrina struck New Orleans. One of these women was married (but parenting alone after the hurricane), one was widowed, and the rest were single. I conducted a holistic assessment of their descriptions of their financial situations before and after Katrina to get a sense of their economic situations. From this assessment, I determined that all the single mothers in this subsample were low income or working class. This qualitative assessment of class status takes into account the women's lived experiences of class as expressed through their narratives.

Displaced Mothers and Their Children: Challenges and Resources

Mothers displaced by Katrina had to work hard to provide stability for their children and to help them recover. They felt anxiety and fear about fulfilling their children's basic needs for education and food. The problems their adult children faced were also of concern to them, though many depended on these children to help them through difficult times. In the following sections, I address three central issues mothers faced in regard to their relationship with their children: addressing their children's problems in school, ameliorating their children's food insecurity, and drawing support from their relationships with their adult children.

School

Katrina hit just as the 2005 school year was beginning, creating an uncertain situation for parents of school-aged children. Peek and Fothergill (2008) found that relocated mothers had primary responsibility for finding and enrolling their children in new schools, and emphasized the importance of having their children settled for the school year. Likewise, one of the first tasks mothers in this study faced once they realized they would be displaced for a long time was enrolling their children in Austin schools. Most of them encountered at least minor problems. Several mothers faced bureaucratic obstacles when enrolling their children and behavioral problems stemming from their children's difficulties fitting in at their new schools.

Overcoming Bureaucratic Obstacles

In order to enroll children in U.S. public schools, a parent or guardian must present up-to-date immunization records for their child (Orenstein and Hinmen 1999). If the records cannot be produced, children must get immunizations again. Some mothers found this requirement to be a serious roadblock in finding stable schooling for their children, as they, like many Katrina survivors, were not able to bring records and legal documents with them as they evacuated.

Xia, quoted earlier, had a challenging time obtaining and presenting proper immunization records for each of her children. She was able to contact her former landlord, who found one of her son's records and faxed them to her. She also obtained the records for her youngest daughter and took them to the school, where they made a copy that they later said they never received. When the school asked her for the records again, she did not know where she had put them and was told her that her daughter would not be allowed back at school until she presented the records or had her re-immunized.

Xia was also the primary caretaker of her seventeen-year-old brother, whose immunization records she did not have "because he's been backwards and forwards, with different people taking care of him." She took him to a local clinic for revaccination, where she learned he could not receive all the vaccines at once. After the first series of shots, she ran into problems when the Medicaid number she tried to use to pay for the visit and shots was denied. She learned through a social worker that she needed to pick up a new Medicaid card; unlike in Louisiana, she could not get it by mail in Texas.

As Xia explained:

> They want every child to just retake all these shots, and at teenage age, even the big kids, it's seventeen [shots] for my teenagers, for my other boys it's . . . like fifteen shots for a nine- and ten-year-old to take. And they can't give them to them at one time, so I mean in the process of days for them taking these shots it's still days they can't go to school, because they have to have all the shots in order to go to school.

Xia was worried that she would face legal action for the missed days of school. Finally, she was able to get all the shots for the children from a mobile vaccination service, which she chased around the city:

> I have a list . . . of where they had these van services. And it was just getting ridiculous because a lot of the places, some of the places they had the vans go to, they wouldn't go. So when I finally caught up with them yesterday, they were supposed to be there at one o'clock. We sat down until a quarter to two, so I tried to go to another clinic, the van had just left that clinic, so I returned . . . and went back to [the first apartment complex], and they finally was there.

Not all mothers had this much trouble providing documentation to their children's schools, but many had problems finding the paperwork they needed. Jeri, a widowed fifty-six-year-old black woman who is the primary caretaker of her godson, described her uncertainty and worry. Her godson had been diagnosed with ADHD in New Orleans, but Jeri was unable to provide any school records, including disability documentation, to his new school. In an interview almost two months into the school year, Jeri said: "I don't know what I'm going to do about the school situation because I can't get his school records. . . . I don't know what is going to happen because they want certain things and I don't have them right now." She told us that the administration had scheduled a meeting to discuss this lack of documentation with her. She worried that her godson might get kicked out of school if she could not provide the records.

That lack of documentation was such a struggle for some Katrina survivors speaks to the mismatch between some school policies and the realities of displaced disaster survivors. When disaster survivors' city has been largely destroyed, schools need a policy that exempts them from ordinary requirements. There should be additional understanding and support for impoverished children, whose families may have an especially difficult time both getting to places that their children can receive vaccinations or educational testing and paying for these services. It was up to the mothers to meet the requirements of the school and in some cases this required a significant time commitment and caused stress.

The issue of documentation is not unique to disaster victims. Many poor women struggle in ordinary times to provide documentation for themselves and their families as they navigate institutions such as schools and public assistance programs (Edin and Lein 1997; Hays 2003). While middle-class mothers also face challenges with respect to vaccinations and documentation, poor mothers confront additional barriers. They must find time and transportation in the context of inflexible work schedules and limited transportation opportunities. They must also find a way to pay for costly vaccinations; even in the best-case scenario, they must navigate the time-consuming and confusing requirements of Medicaid or other assistance programs before receiving services. Mothers in this study with school-aged children had to overcome many obstacles to getting their children's records, medical or otherwise, in order to meet the documentation requirements.

Addressing Children's Social Struggles

In addition to the bureaucratic struggles of enrolling their children in school, mothers also had to address the numerous challenges and problems their children faced once they were attending school in Austin. Research has shown that some Katrina survivor students faced hostile teachers and students and overcrowded classes in new cities (Picou and Marshall 2007). Though children ostensibly faced these challenges on their own, either the child or school personnel often asked parents to intervene.

Louise, a single forty-five-year-old black woman with three children, was very upset by the problems her children experienced at school, which she believed were due to their status as Katrina survivors. She felt that her children and other survivors at the school were singled out by the administration, sometimes receiving "special treatment" such as ice cream parties just for children from New Orleans and not requiring them to take the Texas standardized tests. Though it is likely that the school administration was trying to help the displaced students, Louise felt that the school's efforts made things worse by creating a separation between groups of students. The school was almost entirely composed of students of color (AISD 2009), but she felt other children were discriminating against her children because they were Katrina survivors. She says that they were "stereotyping children by children being Katrina storm victims" and felt the school was "pushing [her] children far away from these [Austin] children." She wanted to tell them that "if you want to make this our home, bring everybody together."

Louise reported that her sixteen-year-old son experienced continued harassment at school and twice got "jumped on," or beat up, by a group of boys. When asked if she thought her son was being picked on because he was from New Orleans, she replied, "Yes, and I think it's the way he's dressed." She explained that teenage boys in New Orleans dressed differently than boys in Austin. She felt the other children might have been jealous of her son's clothes and harassed him because of it. However, she explained that she tried "to make sure that he have everything he wants so he won't have to go out there and sell no drugs, steal, or nothing like that." Louise said she knew many other mothers who also had problems with their children being harassed and feeling alienated, which she attributed to resentment on the part of Austin children for the treatment the survivor children were receiving. She worked hard to try to ensure that her children were well taken care of and could avoid harassment.

Louise also reported that her children were getting in trouble for things they had not been in trouble for before. For example, her son and daughter both were punished for cutting class and smoking marijuana, problems she said they never had in New

Orleans. Cynthia, a forty-year-old black mother of one child and guardian of her brother, reported a similar "jumping" incident that involved her high school daughter. In addition to this attack, her daughter experienced sexual harassment by a member of the school administration. These struggles led to Cynthia's decision to withdraw her daughter from the school and enroll her in a charter school for at-risk youth.

Enrolling their children in an alternative or charter school was a common experience for mothers of teenagers. Some mothers who did not face obstacles in enrolling their children in school later faced the challenge of finding a new, more suitable school and enrolling their children there. Many respondents' high schoolers had trouble adjusting to a new school and ended up going to alternative schools to get their degree or GED. This was the result of both academic and social issues. In fact, of the seven mothers with teenagers, five eventually enrolled their children in alternative schools after they had struggled in other Austin schools.

Many mothers also experienced legal problems related to school and their teenage children. In addition to Louise's son, who was arrested for skipping school and smoking marijuana, Xia's fifteen-year-old son was arrested twice in Austin and had a hearing scheduled to decide whether he would be allowed back at school. He had been in some trouble in New Orleans, but his problems became much worse when he arrived in Austin, Xia said. She "thinks it is just [rebellion against] what he been through." To make matters worse, a warrant was put out for Xia's arrest because her son had missed so many days of school. Many of those absences were the result of his incarceration, but Xia needed to provide documentation of his incarceration to lift the warrant. Likewise, Alisha, a twenty-three-year-old black woman with three children and custody of four of her sisters, described her fourteen-year-old sister as a "troublemaker" who had often cut class since coming to Austin: "This is why I keep going to court," Alisha said. Several mothers had to pay fees or go to court to deal with their children's problems in school.

Children and teenagers face unique challenges coping after a disaster (Fothergill and Peek 2006), and this may be especially true for the children of mothers in this study. Research on the impact of the September 11 disaster on New York City families found that living in a low-income household and living in a single-parent household both correlated with increased behavioral problems among children after the disaster (Stuber et al. 2005). In the case of Katrina, students displaced within Louisiana exhibited common signs of trauma, such as fighting and violating school rules (Pane et al. 2006), and parents of adolescent students displaced to Colorado reported that their children exhibited negative changes in behavior and emotional states (Reich and Wadsworth 2008). Though the 9/11 attacks were significantly different from Hurricane Katrina, Mercuri and Angelique (2004) found that the psychological outcomes for children exposed to life-threatening events were consistent regardless of cause, and often resulted in behavioral problems.

If it is true that children in low-income and single-parent families are more likely to manifest behavioral problems after a disaster, then low-income single mothers face a unique and especially difficult obstacle in helping their children resettle and recover with regard to schooling and thus education. Mothers may have to address the fallout from this initial challenge long after the disaster has occurred, as children with behavioral problems and children who switch schools frequently have poorer educational outcomes than children who do not (Havenman and Wolfe 1995; McLeod and Kaiser 2004). The majority of the mothers in this study said that their children did exhibit new or increased behavioral problems, which suggests they will have to continue to address school-related problems on behalf of their children.

Food Insecurity

A lack of food security, defined in simple terms as access to and sustainability of a secure and sufficient food supply (Maxwell 1996), was a significant problem for many displaced Katrina survivors (Pyles, Kulkarni, and Lein 2008). In a new city, with scant knowledge of transportation and social services and few if any personal financial resources, mothers in this study were especially concerned about having a stable supply of food for their children. Though most of these women had been impoverished in New Orleans, food insecurity was a new experience. Not being able to provide for their children caused significant stress for mothers.

Some of the main problems they faced were bureaucratic roadblocks to securing food stamps. Many became ineligible for food stamps when a temporary Katrina food-stamp program ended six months after the storm. At the time survivors arrived in Texas, the state was switching its food-stamp program over from a paper system to an electronic one, which caused additional delays and processing problems (Pyles et al. 2008). Jeri explained that she received food stamps for three months after Katrina but was told she was no longer eligible once that program expired. When asked if she felt that she could meet all her food needs, she said: "No, . . . this is the truth: I spend three hundred dollars a month just on food, and I've been trying to help my grandchildren, their mother in Baton Rouge, and then I've been trying to help my son in Shreveport." In addition to providing food for her young child, Jeri was concerned about helping out her older children and her grandchildren, who were also facing food insecurity because of their displacement.

Several mothers told us they could get by without much food, but they wanted to be sure that their kids had enough. Tiffany, for example, was able to get food stamps but did not think that they provided enough food for everyone. She reported that she was "fine, but the kids have to eat, so I take the [food-stamp] card and go get them something to eat, little snacks or whatever, but other than that, as long as I have water, I be fine." Cynthia expressed a similar sentiment: "I don't know what it is to be hungry; I'm learning now." She said that she "will be full as long as [my] kids are not hungry. They be eating a lot of cereals and Hot Pockets, and all that. That's not food, you know, but I can only buy what I can afford. I don't want to resort to crime or stealing things . . . but it's just not right." Upset that she could not feed her children what she considered to be real meals, Cynthia implied that she eats last and only if there is enough food for her children.

The stress and work of feeding one's family most often fall to mothers, even in two-parent families (DeVault 1994), and is especially difficult for poor single mothers, as illustrated here. In their experience of long-term displacement as a result of Katrina, these mothers found themselves with fewer financial and social resources than they had relied on in Louisiana and with little knowledge about how to navigate the assistance systems in Austin.

These experiences are similar to those of poor single mothers in everyday situations. While most of the food issues these mothers faced can be either directly or indirectly attributed to their displacement, it is not uncommon for single black mothers in the United States to face food insecurity. In 2002, 32 percent of families headed by a single mother and 22 percent of black households experienced food insecurity (Nord, Andrews, and Carlston 2003). Some poor mothers in the United States skip meals or eat less to be sure their children get enough to eat (DeVault 1994), strategies also mentioned here. Similarly, McIntyre and colleagues (2003) found that single mothers in Canada compromise their food intake in order to give their children an adequate diet, and Maxwell (1996) found that "maternal buffering"—mothers reducing their food intake to ensure that their children get enough to eat—is a coping strategy among food-insecure mothers in Uganda. This behavior points to the interconnectedness of the challenges children face and the challenges their mothers face in situations of food insecurity. In a disaster, the gendered practice of sacrificing one's well-being for the health of children may have especially negative consequences for mothers.

Adult Children

Some of the mothers in this study described an interdependent relationship with their adult children when discussing how they dealt with displacement problems. It was apparent that mothers' roles as caretakers did not end when their children turned eighteen or moved out of their house. In many poor communities, such as those many displaced Katrina survivors came from, families are very close-knit and depend on each other for survival (Edin and Lein 1997). The single mothers in this study knew that their older children depended on them and that they depended on these older children for emotional and sometimes material support.

For example, Jeri used to live close to her adult children and was anxiously waiting for her family to come back together:

> I just hate to see everyone kind of scattered at this point. But we was, you know, my daughter was like ten or fifteen minutes away. My son, like ten or fifteen, you know, but you did get to communicate or you did get to see [them], you know. I just want the people I worry about more to be closer.

For Jeri, having her adult children closer to her would alleviate some of her worry about them. As mentioned, she was also helping these children with food costs, which made it harder for her to make ends meet. Tiffany reported a similar sentiment here earlier. These mothers continued to worry about and provide help to their children even when their children were grown up, far away, or both.

Some mothers depended on their adult children for support before displacement and were having difficulties securing child care or transportation without this help. Twenty-one-year-old Tiffany reported that her mother, Louise, was often sick when they lived in New Orleans and that she helped take care of her younger siblings. Though they both came to Austin after the storm, they moved into different apartment complexes. Louise's health problems made it difficult for her to walk up the hilly street to her daughter's complex as often as she would like. She told us that, in

New Orleans, she had lived "not too far from or with" Tiffany since she had been born and wished they could live the same way in Austin. When asked who she turns to when she needs emotional support or financial assistance, Louise replied: "Tiffany."

Samantha, a thirty-nine-year-old black woman, faced an investigation by a child welfare agency and depended on her twenty-three-year-old daughter to take care of her younger children. When she received a call from her lawyer asking if she would feel better if her daughters were placed with their sister as opposed to foster parents, she reported that she emphatically responded in the affirmative. Though she was very unhappy without her children, she expressed relief that they were with their sister and not a stranger. In this case, Samantha depended on her adult daughter to do the child-care work that she was unable to do.

In New Orleans, Susan and her seventeen-year-old son lived in a different neighborhood than her twenty-three-year-old daughter. When they arrived in Austin, a church gave Susan and her son a house to live in for six months. After that, she planned to apply for FEMA (Federal Emergency Management Agency) housing assistance until she could find a job. However, she explained, in order to get the assistance, one had to have a lease, but in order to have a lease, most landlords wanted proof that the tenant would be getting a FEMA voucher. Because of this in this catch-22, she was forced to move in with her daughter, who obtained housing assistance through the transfer of a New Orleans–based housing voucher.

The experiences these mothers had with their adult children demonstrate the interdependent nature of these relationships, especially after a displacement. Though mothers described worrying about and providing for both their adult sons and daughters, their adult daughters provided reciprocal support when they needed it. This finding is consistent with a body of work that finds that women are more likely than men to maintain closer ties to their parents and children (Fingerman 2001) and to play the role of "kinkeeper" by facilitating the continuation of parent-child relationships (Lye 1996). These relationships have been found to be important to the survival of impoverished women (Edin and Lein 1997). This support may be especially salient in the aftermath of a disaster, when resources are in short supply but urgently needed. A closer look at this topic through the intersecting lenses of race, class, and gender is warranted.

Theoretical Insights and Policy Implications

Two primary insights on the relationship between gender and disaster emerge from the experiences of mothers in this study. The first concerns how gender structures disasters, in many ways similar to the ways in which gender structures everyday life. Many of the biggest challenges in the aftermath of a disaster occur in arenas that women are responsible for in everyday life. These include taking care of children who have been through a traumatic event, addressing children's social and behavioral problems, providing food for families, and keeping extended families and social networks together. Thus there is disproportionate strain on women after a disaster, as they must continue this care work under adverse conditions. This is especially the case for low-income single mothers, who are likely to be left with even fewer material and social resources after a displacement.

The parenting challenges outlined in this chapter speak to how gender structures not only the experience of disaster and displacement, but also everyday life for poor and working-class black single mothers. Taking the experiences of these mothers as an extreme case study, it is evident that low-income single mothers will go to great lengths to ensure that their children have a good education and adequate food supply. This research illustrates how, in doing so, mothers may put themselves at risk for both mental and physical health problems caused by stress, lack of proper nutrition, or both.

Relatedly, the second insight concerns the connection between children's and mother's experiences of disaster. Since parenting is a gendered activity, largely done by women regardless of their relationship status, the connection between children's and women's experiences of disaster must be examined as mutually constitutive. Fothergill and Peek (2006) address this important topic by highlighting Anderson's (2005) claim that disaster researchers who focus on gender should extend their analysis to include children. This study demonstrates how single mothers' abilities to recover and resettle after a disaster are contingent on their children's abilities to cope and recover. When children experience problems in school and food insecurity, mothers experience worry, stress, and, in some cases, inadequate nutrition.

This connection is not limited to the relationships women have with their younger children. The mothers in this study demonstrate the interdependence of their and their adult children's experiences after Katrina. Children depended on mothers, and mothers depended on their children. Future research should explore this issue further in the disaster context, and particularly seek to understand whether a mother's having young children mediates the type of relationship she has with her adult children. All the mothers in this subsample had young children, but there are many mothers and fathers who have only adult children. Subsequent work should focus on potential differences between these two family forms, and the specific ways mothers and their adult children depend on each other in the face of displacement.

In addition to the important theoretical insights that can be gleaned from the experiences of the mothers in this study, practical suggestions for improving policy also emerge from their experiences. The problems these mothers faced were due to a combination of predisaster inequalities (Cutter, Boruff, and Shirley 2003; Morrow 1999), the devastation of Hurricane Katrina, and disaster relief policies that failed to take into account the unique needs of displaced poor families. There is a need for policies that place children's safety and stability at the forefront, as emphasized by the experiences of the mothers in this study.

Mothers faced many challenges helping their children settle in a new city following displacement. Many of these problems can be attributed to the policies and practices of various institutions, such as schools and social service programs, in the receiving city. It would be impossible to pinpoint one organization or policy that exacerbated these mothers' challenges, which makes it difficult to succinctly recommend one policy change that is likely to significantly improve the circumstances poor mothers face after a disaster. However, the experiences of the women interviewed for this project suggest several crucial areas that must be addressed in order to help impoverished children and families recover after displacement due to disaster.

The problems mothers had with school documentation illustrate the need for a uniform policy that ensures quick and stable school enrollment for children displaced by disaster. Documentation requirements could be waived for an extended period of time, or schools could move to electronic scholastic records that would make it easier for children in both disaster and non-disaster situations to switch schools. In addition, schools might develop a set of guidelines for how to successfully integrate new and potentially traumatized students into the social environment. Many of the mothers in this study reported that their children were teased or victimized because of their status as Katrina survivors. Though teasing is an extremely common part of children's experiences in school (Macklem 2003), a concerted effort to ensure harmony between established and displaced students by fostering an understanding about what a disaster is and how it affects people could mitigate stereotypes local students may have and help ease the tensions that affect both children and their parents. With better planning and policies, schools could be a source of support rather than additional strain.

An overarching issue that exacerbated all the problems discussed in this chapter was the lack of understanding about and accommodations for the nonnuclear structure of most of the families in this study. Some of the documentation problems with schools were the result of mothers not having paperwork for the children in their custody, as Xia's immunization struggle exemplifies. Similarly, evacuation and post-evacuation housing policies left many families separated and living in new and different arrangements because the policies failed to recognize the importance of extended families to this population. This failure contributed to problems with food insecurity, as many families who previously were able to get by through sharing resources when necessary found themselves unable to do this once separated. If policies recognized that the people most negatively affected by disasters tend to depend heavily on both nuclear and extended family, a strategy of relocating families in ways that they could continue to help each other could be employed.

Post-disaster housing policies must take the needs and wants of disaster survivors into consideration. While the first priority should be to provide stable and adequate housing, policy makers must realize that housing policy goes far beyond finding a place with enough bedrooms. Placing someone in "housing" also means placing someone in a school district, a neighborhood, a location in the public transportation system, a job market, and oftentimes a social network. All these aspects of housing are important determinants of how quickly and fully displaced people can recover from a disaster. For those with few resources and multiple challenges after disaster displacement, such as single mothers, easy access to transportation, jobs, social services, and social support networks are crucial for successful recovery. Future disaster planning should consider the larger and long-term impact of post-disaster relocation and housing policies to give the displaced the ability to adjust to and resettle in their new city.

Megan Reid is a project director at the Institute for Special Populations Research at the National Development and Research Institutes, Inc. She earned her MA and PhD in sociology from the University of Texas at Austin. Her dissertation focused on race, gender, class, and post–Hurricane Katrina housing issues. She received several fellowships for this work, including the PERISHIP Fellowship in Hazards, Risk, and Disasters, and has published related work in *Sociology Compass* and the *Journal of Family Issues*.

REFERENCES

Anderson, W. A. (2005). Bringing children into focus on the social science disaster research agenda. *International Journal of Mass Emergencies and Disasters, 23*(3), 159–175.

AISD (Austin Independent School District). (2009). LBJ High School campus report card 2008–2009. Retrieved from *www.austinisd.org/schools/docs/ratings_2007_2008_AISD/227901014.pdf.*

Collins, P. H. (2000). *Black feminist thought: Knowledge, consciousness, and the politics of empowerment.* 2nd ed. New York: Routledge.

Cutter, S. L., Boruff, B. J., and Shirley, W. L. (2003). Social vulnerability to environmental hazards. *Social Science Quarterly, 84*(2): 242–261.

DeVault, M. (1994). *Feeding the family: The social organization of caring as gendered work.* Chicago: University of Chicago Press.

Edin, K., and Lein, L. (1997). *Making ends meet: How single mothers survive welfare and low-wage work.* New York: Russell Sage Foundation.

Enarson, E. (1998) Through women's eyes: A gendered research agenda for disaster social science. *Disasters, 22*(2), 157–173.

Enarson, E., and Fordham, M. (2004). Lines that divide, ties that bind: Race, class, and gender in women's flood recovery in the U.S. and U.K. *Australian Journal of Emergency Management, 15*(4), 43–52.

Enarson, E., and Morrow, B. H. (1998). *The gendered terrain of disaster: Through women's eyes.* Westport, CT: Praeger.

Fingerman, K. L. (2001). *Aging mothers and their adult daughters: A study in mixed emotions.* New York: Springer.

Fothergill, A. (1996). Gender, risk, and disaster. *International Journal of Mass Emergencies and Disasters, 14*(1), 33–56.

Fothergill, A., and Peek, L. (2006). Surviving catastrophe: A study of children in Hurricane Katrina. In *Learning from catastrophe: Response research in the wake of Hurricane Katrina.* Special publication no. 40. Boulder: Natural Hazards Center, University of Colorado.

Havenman, R., and Wolfe, B. (1995). The determinants of children's attainments: A review of methods and findings. *Journal of Economic Literature, 33*, 1829–78.

Hays, S. (2003). *Flat broke with children: Women in the age of welfare reform.* New York: Oxford University Press.

Jones-DeWeever, A. A., and Hartmann, H. (2006). Abandoned before the storms: The glaring disaster of gender, race, and class disparities in the Gulf. In C. Hartman and G. D. Squires (Eds.), *There is no such thing as a natural disaster: Race, class, and Hurricane Katrina* (pp. 85–102). New York: Routledge.

Lye, K. L. (1996). Adult child-parent relationships. *Annual Review of Sociology, 22*, 79–102.

Macklem, G. L. (2003). *Bullying and teasing: Social power in children's groups.* New York: Kluwer Academic.

Maxwell, D. G. (1996). Measuring food insecurity: The frequency and severity of "coping strategies." *Food Policy, 21*(3), 291–303.

McIntyre, N., Glanville, N. T., Raine, K. D., Dayle, J. B., Anderson, B., and Battaglia, N. (2003). Do low-income lone mothers compromise their nutrition to feed their children? *Canadian Medical Association Journal, 168*(6), 686–691.

McLeod, J. D., and Kaiser, K. (2004). Childhood emotional and behavioral problems and educational attainment. *American Sociological Review, 69*(5), 636–658.

Mercuri, A., and Angelique, H. L. (2004). Children's responses to natural, technological, and na-tech disasters. *Community Mental Health Journal, 40*(2), 167–175.

Morrow, B. H. (1999). Identifying and mapping community vulnerability. *Disasters, 23*(1), 1–8.

Nord, M., Andrews, M., and Carlson, S. (2003). Household food security in the United States, 2002. *Food Assistance and Nutrition Research Report Number 35*. Washington, DC: U.S. Department of Agriculture.

Orenstein, W. A., and Hinmen, A. R. (1999). The immunization system in the United States: The role of school immunization laws. *Vaccine, 17*(S3), S19–S24.

Pane, J. F., McCaffrey, D. F., Tharp-Taylor, S., Asmus, G. J., and Stokes, B. R. (2006). *Student displacement in Louisiana after the hurricanes of 2005: The experiences of public schools and their students*. Arlington, VA: Rand Corporation.

Peek, L., and Fothergill, A. (2008). Displacement, gender, and the challenges of parenting after Hurricane Katrina. *National Women's Study Association Journal, 20*(3), 69–105.

Picou, J. S., and Marshall, B. K. (2007). Social impacts of Hurricane Katrina on displaced K-12 students and educational institutions in coastal Alabama counties: Some preliminary observations. *Sociological Spectrum, 27*, 767–80.

Pyles, L., Kulkarni, S., and Lein, L. (2008). Economic survival strategies and food insecurity: The case of Hurricane Katrina in New Orleans. *Journal of Social Service Research, 34*(3), 43–53.

Reich, J. A., and Wadsworth, M. (2008). Out of the floodwaters, but not yet on dry ground: Experiences of displacement and adjustment in adolescents and their parents following Hurricane Katrina. *Children, Youth, and Environments, 18*(1), 354–370.

Shelton, B. A., and John, D. (1996). The division of household labor. *Annual Review of Sociology, 22*, 299–322.

Stuber, J., Galea, S., Pfefferbaum, B., Vandivere, S., Moore, K., and Fairbrother, G. (2005). Behavior problems in New York City's children after the September 11, 2001, terrorist attacks. *American Journal of Orthopsychiatry, 75*(2), 190–200.

CHAPTER 16

State Policy and Disaster Assistance

Listening to Women

Susan Sterett

Public assistance in the United States has often tracked people as "deserving" or not, with the undeserving poor most often a focus of scrutiny concerning their individual characteristics and personal choices (e.g., Hancock 2005). American disaster relief has been treated as wholly separate from assistance to the poor, and in justifications in American public policy those who have suffered through disaster have seemed more deserving than people who have long been poor, and therefore the subjects of suspicion concerning what they deserve (Landis 1999). African American women especially have been envisioned as passive and undeserving recipients of benefits (Hancock 2005), despite a long history of acting to protect family as best women can (Stack 1997) and a history of making collective claims against welfare officials (Kornbluh 2007).

Women as targets of assistance have received attention as mothers, and sometimes as widows of working men, and sometimes as workers in their own right (Orloff 1994; Skocpol 1992). The National Welfare Rights Organization in the 1960s argued for the right to motherhood for poor women, criticizing punitive policies that made it difficult to raise children, work, and live. That organization faded in the face of hostile public policy that demonized welfare queens (Hancock 2005; Kornbluh 2007). Since then, poor women have often acted as clients of policy outside of collective claims.

Social welfare scholarship has since explained barriers limiting women's ability to make collective claims or develop a shared sense of citizenship. Even within limits, women do strive to make state rules work in their lives (e.g., Gilliom 2001; Soss 2000), though the displaced women of Katrina were in no position to make claims collectively. Not only did so many have caretaking responsibilities, making it difficult to leave home; they were accessing a new program that changed frequently and mysteriously.

To explore women's experiences with policy further, I turn now to the stories of three women displaced to Denver. Each story tells of women's engagement with the law, both through the decisions that brought people to Denver via government planes, and through accessing state housing assistance. Both policies were enabled through the Stafford Act, the statute that is central to disaster assistance in the United States. However, taking women's experiences rather than the statute as the center of analysis allows one to understand how people see legal obligations and resources alongside what family can offer and demand. Even though people find themselves tangled in law and situated in new places by law, the law may not be the center of their concerns or considerations in deciding where and how to live. In engaging law from the point of view of the experience of law's subjects, this analysis does not take law to be a fixed object, which it can seem when the Stafford Act is at the center of analysis. Rather, law can be an uncertain subject of reinterpretation.[1]

Displacement and Assistance

Commentators immediately after Katrina argued that the storm would lead to a commitment to address long-term poverty in the United States (Bobo 2006; Frymer, Strolovitch, and Warren 2006). It did not, though many community groups and advocates came together to rebuild community connections and improve conditions in New Orleans (e.g., David 2010; Kromm and Sturgis 2008). Many who had fled did not return to New Orleans; the city has remained smaller than it was before the storm, and working to rebuild a city in which one does not live is difficult to do. Concern for the city focused on concern for place; the people who were not in Houston or New Orleans itself rapidly became less visible, including women evacuated to cities that were not the recipients of most evacuees, including Denver.

In the immediate aftermath of the storm, Colorado agreed to accept evacuees. Colorado's governor was friendly with both the Texas governor and President George W. Bush, and Colorado received a federal emergency declaration as a result. This then allowed federal planes filled with evacuees to fly to Buckley Air Force Base, and from there they were taken to a rehabilitated dormitory. For the governors and their advisors and for the presidency, flying people to Colorado made good political sense, and it was a decision they could make rapidly. Those flown out via federal planes were not told where they were going, and no plans were in place to take people where they might have family or friends. Other people arrived in Denver on their own. Some were invited to stay by relatives and friends. Others came in order to avoid Houston and Atlanta, which they suspected were too crowded to welcome more evacuees.

Under the Stafford Act, disasters allow money to flow from the federal government to reimburse costs incurred by states. Assistance offered under the Stafford Act paid rent for many displaced persons, although the act itself was soon a site of contest in poststorm lawsuits (Sterett 2009). First, people received emergency rental assistance in a lump sum; later, they received individual rental assistance, eventually promised in three-month increments when people could demonstrate they could not return to New Orleans and could not pay rent through some other means. Because of ongoing policy changes, FEMA (Federal Emergency Management Agency) would threaten to cut off the rental assistance program and then extend it. Caseworkers and recipients reported that they experienced the threats and extensions as confusing and exhausting.

International concerns also shaped what displaced persons received and advocacy around the rights of displaced persons. In December 2005, the United Methodist Committee on Relief received a grant from international donations earmarked for Katrina relief, which then paid for casework in cities with displaced people. Later, advocacy organizations referred to the UN Guidelines for Internally Displaced People dated from 1998, and the violation of those guidelines by ordinary practices after Katrina (Kromm and Sturgis 2008). International law and guidelines are the language of cosmopolitan advocates, but seldom of the people who experience conditions that are the subject of international agreements (Merry 2005). Although some people landed in Denver via federal plane without consenting beforehand—a violation of UN Guidelines—people who received assistance did not mention that violation as one of their concerns. The problem of the storm, and how badly they were treated, was from their point of view an American one, not international. Others did not expect to be able to consent to policy, so while they might have been shocked to land in Denver, they did not complain about an inability to consent.

Once people were out of their homes, the federal government paid emergency housing assistance after Katrina for people who had lost housing after the storm and who had left home. It paid rent for a longer period than in any other disaster, but always with an uncertain end and shifting requirements. People who had qualified were gradually excluded, but the program itself did not end until after the Obama administration took office. As it did in many cities across the nation, FEMA paid the rent for the apartments evacuees had in Denver. First, FEMA paid rent as emergency assistance, cutting checks for $2,358, an average of three months of the nationwide average of fair market rent. Weeks after cutting the checks, FEMA sent out notices explaining that the money could be used only for rent. FEMA transitioned people to individual assistance, under which FEMA continued to pay rents but required that recipients requalify every three months. Individual assistance was capped at $26,200, which was intended to cover all documented property losses.

This broad outline does not explain how people understood the money they had received. Understanding how state assistance works often proceeds from the point of view of the policy makers, not of the recipients. Yet, in disaster assistance as well as other programs, without taking account of how those who are the targets of policy experience assistance, we can readily misunderstand the mixture of disaster assistance, family help, and ongoing government programs and, for some, work, that people relied upon to live in a new city. We see the trade-offs and problems that people encounter in trying to make their lives work, especially in the unfamiliar places in which people displaced by disaster find themselves. This alternative approach to policy accords participants respect (Soss 2000), taking people's real-life problems as the central concern (Shapiro 2005).

Research Design and Context

A research team explored the delivery of assistance to Katrina evacuees based in Denver through interviews the first year after the hurricane. We conducted interviews with ninety-one adults in two waves as part of a research project co-led by social science faculty members at the University of Denver. The interview teams included the three faculty members who had designed the research project; most interviews were conducted by young white women in teams of two, often led by a graduate student in psychology. Undergraduate students were also trained and assisted in interviews. Most interviews occurred in interviewees' homes; each lasted between one and three hours, and was taped and transcribed. We asked open-ended questions that elicited stories of life before the hurricane, evacuation, how people came to Denver, and how people accessed government resources. After transcription, we coded the interviews thematically for information concerning where people had lived before the storm, how they had organized their households, how they understood home, how they had evacuated, and how they had accessed assistance.

Displaced people who are not in camps have no single place to congregate, so we could not go to one place such as a government assistance office to recruit people to talk to, unlike other projects concerned with people who receive state assistance payments (e.g., Sarat 1991; Soss 2000). We volunteered at a warehouse where goods were distributed to evacuees, where we made flyers available concerning the project. We attended meetings of the local long-term recovery committee, where we asked representatives of nongovernmental organizations, volunteer caseworkers, and state services representatives to distribute our flyers inviting participation in the project. Interviewees were also recruited through a newsletter that a church put out for evacuees, by word of mouth, and through caseworkers and volunteers who worked with evacuees. Evacuees were paid for each interview.

The first wave of interviews began in November 2005, about two months after evacuees had arrived in Denver, ending in March 2006; the second wave of interviews was conducted six months later. The research team also spent time in community meetings of caseworkers, tracked e-mail Listservs, a wiki page concerning housing assistance, and the policy decisions otherwise available concerning housing assistance by the federal government.

Of the ninety-one people we interviewed, 56 percent were women and 44 percent were men. Sixty-two percent were African American. The modal age range for African American interviewees was between forty and fifty; for white interviewees, between twenty and thirty. Most interviewees had rented homes in New Orleans in the private rental market. Some had lived in public housing, while others lived in homes their families had long owned. Of the white interviewees, one held a mortgage; African American respondents who did not rent either in the private market or in public housing reported either homelessness or living in family-owned homes.

Of the women, about half were African American, with a modal age range between forty-one and fifty; the modal age range for white women was between twenty-one and thirty. That meant the African American women were more likely to have grown children and were likely to find it more difficult to resettle and find work, since being older is a barrier to employment.

Before the storm, women had worked in casinos, in restaurants, and for the federal government. Many had children, and older women had grown children upon whom some could rely. Others had teens and younger children, and they worried about children who were having a hard time settling into school (Reich and Wadsworth 2008). About 30 percent of the people we spoke to reported receiving federal disability benefits. Because we were unlikely to interview the people who would find it most challenging to participate in a long interview, we believe our sample underrepresented evacuees to Denver who received federal disability assistance. In New Orleans, 23.6 percent of all residents from twenty-one to sixty-four years old had disabilities (Fussell 2006).

Government assistance after Katrina shares some characteristics with other bureaucratic social welfare systems such as Temporary Assistance to Needy Families: it required that people develop a plan to get off the assistance. In other ways it was wholly unlike any other program: it paid assistance longer than other disaster relief had and it was not tied to work or contributions, as other programs in the United States are. Exploring policy processes that are not well defined requires tracing the process of implementation; tracing that process from the point of view of recipients can discover strengths in people and confusion in policy not clear in following the policy makers, such as FEMA.

Making It Work for Women, Making It Work in Denver

Many people we interviewed remained away from home longer than had survivors of other disasters in the United States, and many had been poor before Katrina. Middle-class women may find it humiliating to accept public relief, as Alice Fothergill found after the 1997 Grand Forks, North Dakota, flood (Fothergill 2004). Government assistance was not new to many of the women displaced after Katrina, who had combined government assistance with help from family and friends before the storm. Displacement changed the help people offered and received; adults needed help from parents or from adult children that they had not had to rely upon before, they lost help they had had in their neighborhoods, and they could find caretaking obligations more intense without their family or neighborhood stores nearby. Disaster assistance did not replace wages; it paid for housing. Finding work was also important for the many people who could not move back to New Orleans quickly and did not have another sufficient source of income. Yet few displaced women found employment quickly after they fled New Orleans (Zottarelli 2008). When finding work was difficult in an unfamiliar city with unreliable public transportation, the requirement that one use assistance only for housing payments was confusing. People might need it for living expenses, or might wish to pay back family who had loaned money. For people who had experienced government assistance before, and had other sources of humiliation such as not being able to work or having to rely for help on family members when they had not, simply receiving help was not humiliating in the same way that Alice Fothergill found. The uncertainty, the restrictions, and the problems with family could be greater sources of sorrow than needing to accept assistance.

The next section tells stories of two women we spoke to in Denver. They are of different ages, with different work histories, family obligations, routes to Denver, and experience with assistance. Each woman had assistance based on being the victim of a hurricane, and each told us of what she had done to be a responsible family member and citizen. Each found that working with the rules of assistance could contradict her own understanding of how to be responsible to family.

Family Stories: Sarah and Emily

Sarah welcomed us into the new apartment she was sharing with her sister. She had come to Denver via the federal government, which airlifted the two women straight from Sarah's apartment to the airport in New Orleans. Sarah and Emily had not self-evacuated in New Orleans when the mandatory evacuation order came because they had been through hurricanes before and it was difficult to leave with Emily's disabilities. Sarah explained to us that she had prepared for the hurricane; she couldn't understand what those who had not were thinking. She filled every imaginable container with drinking water and laid in food in coolers, knowing the electricity would go out. For Sarah, preparing for disaster required planning to help her neighbors with food and water. Because Emily was disabled and the two women did not have a car, they could not leave New Orleans before the storm, and they believed they could ride it out. After the storm and the flood hit, Sarah used her cache of supplies to cook for neighbors in the apartment building, relying on other residents to distribute food by walking along rooftops to avoid the floodwaters.

The airport was in a horrible state when they got there, and Sarah wanted to get out as quickly as possible. She and her sister soon were put on a federal military plane to leave New Orleans because she and twenty-four people from neighboring apartments claimed to be a family: "When they came to get Barbara, Barbara started hollerin', 'You gotta get the rest of my family! You gotta get the rest of my family!' At the airport they was tryin' to keep families as well together as they could. And she started pointin' out, 'That's my family. That's my family. That's my family. That's my family.' And so that's how we got pulled so quickly." Claiming to be family was a good way to get out of a miserable situation. They could not choose where they were going; they knew only what they were escaping.

Sarah thought they were going to Texas; they were not told their destination until they were landing in Denver. They were welcomed by state workers and volunteers and taken to a former college dormitory that had been rehabilitated quickly over Labor Day weekend to receive Hurricane Katrina evacuees. Under the promise of emergency assistance from the federal government, the state worked to place people quickly in apartments. When we met Sarah and her sister Emily in November 2005, they were in a new apartment building. Because developers and the City of Denver had followed principles of new urbanism, residents could depend less than others must on cars or Denver public transportation, which can be difficult to use in a sprawling city where services are often not close to where people live. A public library and a grocery store were within a short walk, as were shops and cafes surrounding the grocery store. The grocery store did not have the food that tasted like home to Sarah: no pickled pig meat or pickled okra. She told us she could not imagine how we cooked.

Sarah was fifty years old, African American, and a lifelong resident of New Orleans, where she had adult children and a sister and brother-in-law nearby. She had lived in Section 8 housing there and worked in the casinos. Her disabled sister, Emily, who was close to Sarah's age, lived nearby in her own apartment. Emily had a seizure disorder and her immediate family and neighborhood had been crucial to her living in her own apartment in New Orleans. Both had been in the neighborhood long enough that Sarah could count on help with her sister from relatives and close neighbors. In her old neighborhood, Sarah kept to herself as much as she could because of drug dealing and other criminal activity she didn't like. Still, it was her neighborhood and one that allowed her to care for her sister with the help of others yet live apart from her. Emily collected federal disability benefits, and the cost of living in New Orleans was low, making it possible to live independently so long as others would periodically check in and shop for her. These federal benefits, not targeted particularly to disaster-affected people, followed her to Denver.

Sarah was much more isolated in Denver than she had been in New Orleans. She had to stay home and care for her sister. She appreciated her proximity to the grocery store and library and she appreciated the volunteers who would come and collect her and her sister to attend church. She was certainly pleased with the new furniture she had received courtesy of FEMA and a local minister, who had negotiated donations with suppliers. The money she had received, which had not first been clearly marked for rent, allowed her to pay off old debts. She also could make donations to others in a holiday toy drive; she could contribute to the world during disaster and while displaced even while policy treated her as a victim (Fothergill 2004). For her, Christmas had to include toys for children, and she had to contribute for the children who did not have enough.

Emily's federal disability benefits were essential, as neither sister could work. Emily had not worked in New Orleans, unlike others with whom we spoke who reported receiving federal disability payments while engaging in off-the-books casual employment. Federal disability distributes benefits categorically; one can or cannot work, and mixing benefits with work is penalized. Getting by combining disability benefits with unreported work was such an ordinary way to make ends meet that it was described in Tom Piazza's *City of Refuge* (2008), one of the first novels about leaving New Orleans after Hurricane Katrina. The most likely work for Sarah was in the casinos, many miles outside Denver, difficult to access without a car, and with a different feel from those in Louisiana. In any event, she couldn't leave her sister alone without any regular help.

For Sarah and Emily, federal assistance before and after disaster, disability, and responsibility for family all intersected to produce their lives in Denver, where they could get by but found themselves isolated, certain they would need to be closer to family (and away from Denver but not in New Orleans) when the housing assistance stopped.

Family Stories: Jane

At twenty years old, Jane saw much greater hope than Sarah did. Also African American, she fled to her hometown, Denver, with her husband and young child after Hurricane Katrina, retracing the route she had taken when she had left Denver for New Orleans to attend college. Unlike Sarah and Emily, she was not a longtime resident of New Orleans. She missed New Orleans, but life in Denver was familiar. Although she found her extended family members emotional, dramatic, and difficult to deal with, they were also helpful, the people in town Sarah and Emily lacked. She had not landed in Denver by federal plane, with no explanation of where she was going, and she saw her resettlement in the area more as a choice than Sarah did. She was immediately responsible for her husband, her child, and her baby on the way; luckily, her husband had found work at a retail store. She did not work and didn't plan to, since her young children would need her care. Jane's in-laws in New Orleans had suffered tremendous damage and had their own concerns, so moving to Denver increased rather than decreased the number of family members Jane could rely upon. Yet she did not have an easy relationship with her father, so help came at a price: "Sometimes it's drama, . . . so that made it complicated moving here." Indeed, by the second time we spoke with her, her father was asking her to use FEMA funds to repay a loan he had made to her earlier, and Jane was worried about the legality of this and about how to continue working on her college degree.

Tangled in the Rules

Even in the face of "enormous oppression," black women have acted in "pursuit of self-empowerment and structural transformation" (Hancock 2008, 23). Like those who cleaned New Orleans after the flood (David 2010), the family work Katrina evacuees did was a form of community work done by women to reduce the problems they faced in making a life for themselves far from home. In Sarah's case, even in the worst of circumstances—fleeing home without a say concerning where she landed, moving from employed to unemployed, becoming a full-time caretaker for a disabled sister—she could show us what she had done to make her life work better. She reflected upon what she could do next; moving back to New Orleans was unlikely and staying in Denver difficult. Perhaps she could find family to live with elsewhere.

Her story and Jane's allow analysis of the experience of public policy, and of trying to make the rules work. Individual assistance payments, for example, do not encourage women to rely upon each other as friends or sisters, absent specific legal arrangements, though many women do. When women did try to share government resources, they ran the risk of an investigation for defrauding the government. For example, Sarah explained to us that she wanted to pass on her Section 8 housing in New Orleans to a sister who remained in the area and could use it. The housing authority explained that it was not her property to pass on; claiming Section 8 would require claiming that she lived in New Orleans. She could not claim to be living there when she also claimed assistance based on being displaced to Denver. If she did, she would be guilty of fraud. Yet to Sarah mind, she had lived in Section 8 housing for so long, and she had helped family with it, so she could not see why she couldn't when she was far away.

Displaced persons could lose their rental assistance for any number of reasons: because the federal government requested documentation that someone had lost housing in New Orleans and a person could not provide it, or because she had reached the cap in assistance, or because she could not document that she had spent the rental assistance money on rent, or because FEMA had decided she did not need the money anymore (for a detailed overview of the housing assistance policy for displaced people, see Sterett 2009). Spending the money on something other than rent could make one subject to recoupment later. But for many people, the rental assistance money was "new" money, much needed by caregivers to pay off bills or meet immediate family needs. Both Sarah and Jane explained that they had used some of the money to pay bills from before the hurricane, or to buy their children shoes. Jane could not understand how FEMA could provide rental housing assistance, on the one hand, but not help with other immediate needs evacuees had, and she could not understand why the federal government would cut off her housing assistance when all she had done was take care of her family's needs. Creativity in working with the rules was either difficult, as it would be for Section 8, or a problem, as paying down bills would be. The primacy of responsibility for family that Sarah and Jane assumed got caught in the individuation central to U.S. social policy.

Housing assistance from the federal government allowed Sarah and Emily and Jane to live outside New Orleans, supplemented in Emily's case by federal disability benefits. Finding a job would not have been easy for Sarah, and she was not certain her job in New Orleans would be available again soon. Without federal disability payments, she and Emily would probably have had to move in with family who lived in neither New Orleans nor Denver. Family obligations changed after Katrina, and family made living away from New Orleans complicated, if necessary.

Federal housing assistance made it possible for people to delay their return to New Orleans, but we know little about how family, rental assistance, or both actually factored into the calculations of displaced people about relocation or return. Survey data have not addressed these family obligations, or women's concerns about children's health care, both crucial infrastructure. Sarah, for instance, could not move back to New Orleans without family to help her with Emily, and Jane worried about health care in New Orleans for her young children. Another woman in the study explained that her grandmother had evacuated for Katrina and she simply did not believe her grandmother was capable of another move. Because the granddaughter took responsibility for her grandmother, she could not see how she could move back to New Orleans either, whether or not others in the family wanted to.

Both Sarah and Jane spoke of family and individual assistance from the federal government as influencing their decisions about where to move, though in different directions. Sarah saw returning as unlikely: New Orleans was a "Polaroid picture in reverse," she had heard, and she needed medical care for Emily:

> I'm not going back home now. I'm not going back until they tell me I can go back, that things are a little bit better, there are more hospitals open, in case I need to bring her. Because right now, there's only two. There's one in Jefferson [Parish] and they just opened one up in Orleans [Parish].

Sarah and Emily both had FEMA numbers and both were eligible for assistance, since they had lived in separate residences in New Orleans. If they were now one household after displacement, though, they were eligible for FEMA assistance for only one household. Further, while Sarah believed that her Section 8 voucher should be transferable to someone who needed and could use it in New Orleans during her absence, it was not. She wanted to put her name on a subsidized residence in New Orleans to give her sister and brother-in-law a home, but she learned that this would subject her to fraud charges so long as she lived in Denver.

Jane also did not want to return to New Orleans; she could imagine making a life in Denver, particularly with the help of her family. If Sarah's concern was for her sister, Jane worried about which resettlement location would be best for her children and her husband. The schools were better in Denver, and she and her husband had wanted to move sometime anyway. She could go to college there, and her husband had already found a job. She worried that her husband dreamt of help in New Orleans that just was not there: "He had this idea in his head that if he was living near his parents . . . everything would be all right. I guess it is understandable. They helped him before so it sounds like he is putting his faith in them and it's like, okay, they are struggling too."

When we spoke to Jane for the second time, she was worried that she would be losing housing assistance from FEMA and indeed that she and her husband might eventually be in trouble for fraud, as they had used some rental assistance money to pay off other bills. Again she expressed frustration that FEMA funds could not be used for assistance with other needs. Like Sarah and many others we spoke to, Jane saw the first check from FEMA as found money that could be used wherever her family most needed it: "I mean you have other expenses and you've got all this money sitting in here and you need to pay something." The restriction was puzzling to Jane; she needed living expenses, her husband's job did not pay well, and paying down debt ought to have been an allowable use of rental assistance after the hurricane. The money should have been to help people rebuild their lives, but the model of temporary displacement central to disaster recovery in the United States did not allow rebuilding.

Neither Sarah nor Jane could imagine how the posthurricane policy could make life work well for them. FEMA's rental assistance would end one day and Section 8 housing could be extremely difficult to find, especially for women looking for a place to share with family or close enough to family to be able to turn to them for help. (Although cities may put disaster victims at the top of their Section 8 waiting lists, they need not.) At the second interview, Jane saw her family's lives as better in Denver, but she believed they might well be moving back to New Orleans. Her husband wanted to move back and she was worried about how unhappy he was. When we searched for Sarah and Emily for the second round of interviews, they were gone.

The responsibilities of family help account for why women are stretched so thin, and family is also a strength—for example, Jane's reliance on her father or Sarah's reliance on competent adults near her in New Orleans. Listening to Sarah and Jane also illuminates the interplay of race, gender, and disability as these intersect with government policy, family, and place. Jane's and Sarah's stories may not be typical (any more than any single story is) of women displaced from their homes by Hurricane Katrina, but tracking their stories opens up questions about how citizens mix forms of state assistance and family support.

Conclusion

Disasters disrupt routine, making systems transparent that had previously left no trace because they were seen as a natural and ordinary part of existence, as Bruno Latour has argued (2005). When relocation is required, it is all the more difficult for women to accomplish the "hidden work" that stretches essential state benefits. Relatives who shared housing or helped with disabled family members are no longer around. Low-wage work is no longer available, and under-the-table work that requires connections and referrals in a neighborhood is gone. First-person accounts illuminate the awareness of rights people believe they have, such as Sarah's belief that she ought to be able to pass on her Section 8 housing voucher. Stories like hers also illuminate the blurred jumble of policy that can make legal rules incomprehensible:

why should such responsible behaviors as paying for family necessities, or paying back a loan, constitute fraud?

By approaching policy from the perspective of the displaced, we gain a richer understanding of the strengths people bring to bear, and of where people might need more help. Were we to approach disaster social policy this way, policy could be constructed around what would best allow them to move toward recovery from crisis and rebuild their lives in their own way.

Susan Sterett is professor of political science at the University of Denver. She has written on social welfare and on immigration from sociolegal perspectives; her books include *Creating Constitutionalism?* (1997) and *Public Pensions: Gender and Civic Service in the States, 1850s–1937* (2003). The research for this article received support from NSF CMMI-0555117.

NOTE

1.   For an extended discussion of perspectives in law and society, which does take on law from the point of view of its subjects, see Ewick and Silbey 1998, 33–56.

REFERENCES

Bobo, L. (2006). Katrina: Masking race, poverty, and politics in the 21st century. *Du Bois Review: Social Science Research on Race, 3*(1), 1–6.

Burkhauser, R., and Daly, M. (2009). *The declining work and welfare of people with disabilities: What went wrong and a strategy for change.* Washington, DC: American Enterprise Institute Press.

David, E. (2010). Redistribution of responsibility: The gendered division of labor and politics of a post-disaster clean-up project. In K. A. Bates and R. S. Swan (Eds.), *Through the eye of Katrina: Social justice in the United States* (pp. 391–411). Durham, NC: Carolina Academic Press.

Edin, K., and Lein, L. (1997). *Making ends meet: How single mothers survive welfare and low-wage work.* New York: Russell Sage.

Ewick, P., and S. Silbey. (1998). *The common place of law: Stories from everyday life.* Chicago: University of Chicago Press.

Fothergill, A. (2004). *Heads above water.* Albany: State University of New York Press.

Frymer, P., Strolovitch, D., and Warren, D. (2006). New Orleans is not the exception: Re-politicizing the study of racial inequality. *Du Bois Review: Social Science Research on Race, 3*(1), 37–57.

Fussell, E. (2006). Leaving New Orleans: Social stratification, networks, and hurricane evacuation. Retrieved from *understandingkatrina.ssrc.org/Fussell.*

Gilliom, J. (2001). *Overseers of the poor: Surveillance, resistance, and the limits of privacy.* Chicago: University of Chicago Press.

Hancock, A. (2005). When multiplication doesn't equal quick addition: Examining intersectionality as a research paradigm. *Perspectives on Politics, 6*(1), 63–79.

———. (2008). Intersectionality, multiple messages, and complex causality: Commentary on *Black Sexual Politics* by Patricia Hill Collins. *Studies in Gender and Sexuality, 9,* 14–31.

Kornbluh, F. (2007). *The battle for welfare rights: Politics and poverty in modern America.* Philadelphia: University of Pennsylvania Press.

Kromm, C., and Sturgis, S. (2008). *Hurricane Katrina and the Guiding Principles on Internal Displacement: Global human rights perspective on a national disaster.* Washington, DC: Brookings Institution.

Landis, M. (1999). Fate, responsibility, and "natural" disaster relief: Narrating the American welfare state. *Law and Society Review, 33*(2), 257–318.

Latour, B. (2005). *Reassembling the social.* New York: Oxford University Press.

Merry, S. (2005). *Human rights and gender violence.* Princeton, NJ: Princeton University Press.

Orloff, A. S. (1994). *The politics of pensions.* Madison: University of Wisconsin Press.

Piazza, T. (2008). *City of refuge.* New York: Harper.

Reich, J. A., and Wadsworth, M. (2008). Out of the floodwaters, but not yet on dry ground: Experience of displacement and adjustment in adolescents and their parents following Hurricane Katrina. *Children, Youth and Environments,* 18(1), 354–370.

Sarat, A. (1991). "The law is all over": Power, resistance, and the legal consciousness of the welfare poor. *Yale Journal of Law and the Humanities, 2*(2), 343–380.

Shapiro, I. (2005). *The flight from reality in the human sciences.* Princeton, NJ: Princeton University Press.

Skocpol, T. (1992). *Protecting soldiers and mothers.* Cambridge, MA: Harvard University Press.

Soss, J. (2000). *Unwanted claims: The politics of participation in the U.S. welfare system.* Ann Arbor: University of Michigan Press.

Stack, C. (1997). *All our kin: Strategies for survival in a Black community.* New York: Basic Books.

Sterett, S. M. (2009). New Orleans everywhere: Bureaucratic accountability and housing policy after Katrina. In A. Sarat and J. Lezaun (Eds.), *Catastrophe: Law, politics, and the humanitarian impulse* (pp. 83–115). Boston: University of Massachusetts Press.

Zottarelli, L. (2008). Post-hurricane Katrina employment recovery: The interaction of race and place. *Social Science Quarterly, 89*(3), 592–607.

CHAPTER 17

The Katrina Difference

African American Women's Networks
and Poverty in New Orleans after Katrina

Jacquelyn Litt, Althea Skinner, and Kelley Robinson

Hurricane Katrina revealed what impoverished African American women in New Orleans already understood: the United States experience is not monolithic but varies according to class, race, and gender. The population we report on in this chapter—low-income African American women who fled the city because of Katrina—were at an economic disadvantage in New Orleans long before the flooding devastated their city and stole their homes. A quick overview of the status of black women before the storm signals the hardship: in 2002 women earned on average 76 percent of men's wages nationally but only 68.5 percent of men's wages in Louisiana. White women's earnings were 37 percent higher than their black counterparts'. Female-headed households accounted for 56 percent of New Orleans's families with children, compared to 25 percent nationally. One-quarter (24.9 percent) of Lower Ninth Ward houses, primarily African American, were female headed with children under eighteen. Forty percent of female-headed households lived below the poverty line citywide (Gault et al. 2005; Jones-DeWeever and Hartmann 2006).

This social geography meant that when the storm hit, it had a tremendous and disproportionate impact on the low-income black population. The flooding was most severe in areas where individuals were least prepared to respond in terms of insurance, disaster planning, or emergency supplies (Pastor et al. 2006). They had few resources for evacuating (Haney, Elliott, and Fussell 2007) and have had the hardest time recovering after the catastrophe (Pastor et al. 2006; Williams et al. 2006). Hurricane Katrina was a social event embedded in preexisting social inequalities. Indeed, gender, race, and socioeconomic status are among the characteristics most predictive of vulnerability to natural disasters, along with the more predictable geographic attributes such as low sea level and coastal erosion (Cutter et al. 2006).

African American Women, Vulnerability, and Network Resources

Yet as this study makes clear, women's care work has played a significant role in Katrina recovery. It is often in their capacities as mothers that women act as agents in their own and their families' and communities' recovery (Enarson 2001; Fothergill 2004; Fothergill and Peek 2006; Morrow 1997). At the same time, we argue that a largely neglected but critical dimension of women's survival—their kin-network relationships and labor—has had a significant impact on post-Katrina recovery, as this chapter shows.

African American grandmothers and mothers have been recognized as maintaining vital kin networks through their carework in households and communities (Collins 1990; Hill 1999; Litt 1999; Stack 1974). Indeed, women's outreach has long been understood as a bulwark against the ravages of poverty. Quantitative studies published primarily in the 1990s show the deleterious effects of economic changes on African American kin exchange (Eggebeen 1992; Eggebeen and Hogan 1990; Roschelle 1997). The explanation for these changes lies in ways the economy, internal migration, and labor force trends have affected African American family life, and thus networks of exchange. In particular, the flight of middle-class communities from urban centers left a dearth of resources in these areas and significantly reduced the resources available to network members. Further, federal policy has weakened unions, reduced welfare benefits, and withdrawn funding for poor urban centers. The deindustrialization of the urban economy has pulled more women into lower-paying service jobs, also changing household life. Women are charged with accommodating these diminishing resources as part of their care work responsibilities.

This is not to suggest that women in households easily absorb weaknesses and new policies in the social environment. González de la Rocha asserts that in Latin America, resource exchange among the poor who are suffering from the economic and social dislocation wrought by structural adjustment policies is no longer sufficient to stabilize poor urban households. She documents a trend from the "resources of poverty to the poverty of resources" that has eroded the previous survival model of families and households (2001, 72). It is that same deterioration that we see in some women's networks in New Orleans.

Research Design

The women we interviewed spoke longingly about the kin relationships that had surrounded them before Katrina. They described exchange relationships that included sharing food, transportation, child care, households, money, job information, and other kinds of mutual support. These were ongoing, routine, and normative dimensions of their lives before Katrina and were central to kin and household survival. We ask in this chapter how women's care work differs from this pre-Katrina context and how women's networks, in which their care work is embedded, vary in their capacity to promote disaster recovery.

This chapter explores two networks as they respond to the experience of living in New Orleans after Katrina. In using the network as the unit of analysis, we offer a rare look into how women's labor in networks manages resource flow in and out among kin after the disaster. As we describe, the decline in resources for women in managing their households and networks in New Orleans presents conditions that may well challenge, if not destroy, their traditional practices of kin exchange. We also show strategies that women have adopted to successfully buffer the new deprivations in the city. Some networks, we discovered, were better able than others to maintain their cohesion and exchange of resources, and to acquire a variety of resources upon which they can depend. Our two case studies exemplify both kinds of networks.

The material in this chapter is drawn from interviews with sixty-three evacuees from New Orleans, approximately half of whom now reside in Houston and the other half in New Orleans. We interviewed members of a large extended kin network, all originating in New Orleans and now spread between the two cities. Our connections to the women were made by our key respondent, Wendy, whom the lead author has known since Wendy and Rona (discussed later) evacuated to Columbia, Missouri, in 2005. Two graduate students and the lead author conducted all the interviews. Respondents were interviewed in private households for forty-five to ninety minutes in the spring of 2009. We used a standard protocol that examined evacuation and resettlement experiences, women's use of network relationships for resources, and the significance of women's networks in their present-day location. Those participating received a fifty-dollar gift card to Walmart. Interviews were transcribed and coded using computer software, with coding by at least two individuals for inter-rater reliability.

New Poverty in New Orleans after Katrina

The respondents in this study—African American low-income women who have returned to the New Orleans since Katrina—almost uniformly told us that life was harder, more vulnerable, and less stable than before the storm. Undoubtedly, the relative lack of infrastructure in post-Katrina New Orleans compared to the city before the storm makes it harder to get by. Five years on, these women and thousands like them still struggle to secure housing and basic services. The face of the city has changed, mostly in ways that have made it harder for individuals with low incomes and few resources to survive. After Katrina, New Orleans is smaller, richer, whiter, and older and is populated by a more educated workforce, with fewer renters and fewer children. The planning district incorporating the Lower Ninth has only 19 percent of its 2005 residents back. The decline in the percentage of black residents who have returned to the city (57 percent) is higher than for whites (36 percent). The official Hispanic population has increased by at least 1 percent. The increase in homeowners and college-educated residents alongside the decrease in residents without a high school degree suggests what might be the permanent out-migration of people with fewer resources (Frey, Singer, and Park 2007). Indeed, poor residents dropped by 6 percent, with 83 percent of single mothers unable to return to New Orleans as of 2007 (Jones-DeWeever 2007; Liu and Plyer 2009). Indeed, Groen and Polivka (2008b) find that nonmarried African Americans with low education levels are least likely to return to New Orleans compared to others.

African American residents with low incomes who have come home returned to a city where it is considerably more difficult to establish a comfortable life, including caring for loved ones. In part because there are fewer properties to go around (six thousand vacant and sixty-five thousand blighted properties still plague the city), rents have increased 46 percent since the storm. The Housing Authority of New Orleans only exacerbated the housing crisis by demolishing four of New Orleans's ten public housing developments—claiming that they were damaged beyond repair, but also in order to replace them with more desirable mixed-income housing lucrative for investors. New Orleans's homeless population doubled to twelve thousand individuals between 2005 and 2008 (Liu and Plyer 2009). Public institutions providing services in the urban core have largely not recovered, leaving the city's poor residents with less public infrastructure to rely on. The city's only public hospital that attended those without insurance has been closed since the storm. Moreover, as of June 2009, barely half the local licensed child-care centers had reopened, limiting essential services for some workers. As of February 2009, 88 public schools, including charters, operated in New Orleans, compared to 126 in 2005. By July 2008, barely one in five public buses was running even half the routes it ran before the storm. This transportation issue, alongside the loss in the storm of many individually owned vehicles, forms a significant barrier for return, employment, and successful resettlement among the working poor (Liu and Plyer 2009).

To understand the distinctive nature of post-Katrina poverty and the way individuals live and survive within it also requires investigation into women's work within their families. Their labor can expose much about a community's vulnerability, as well as its strategies for survival. We demonstrate that the plunge in public resources in New Orleans after Katrina and the threatened network exchange capacity creates a dual burden for women and families, and that together these dynamics make post-Katrina poverty distinctive. We also distinguish between two types of networks in terms of their access to resources: flat networks with thin and homogenous resources, and heterogeneous networks in which resources come into the network in diverse ways and from diverse sources.

Women's Networks in Disaster: Two Case Studies

What has been the experience of poverty and survival for women who have returned to this unique context? Have networks frayed to such an extent that they are not viable as a collective resource, or have women been able to recreate them to withstand the new challenges of living in a deteriorated city? We attempt to answer these questions through a close analysis of how two women's networks functioned in marshalling resources in present-day New Orleans. With this analysis we argue that post-Katrina poverty is distinctive, compared to pre-Katrina poverty, but that women do not experience it monolithically; important variations exist that impact how women's networks respond and function.

Rona's Flat Network

Rona's network is made up of her husband and four children. Her mother is deceased, and while Rona has some relationship to all of her siblings, as we shall see, few are part of her daily routines and networks. The exceptions are her brothers Kendall (who lives with her) and Tom (described later in Karen's network), who told us that he distanced himself from Rona because of her drinking.

Before Katrina, Rona lived in a rented house in the Seventh Ward of New Orleans with her children and husband. She was employed as a housekeeping supervisor and had a second job at a janitor maintenance company. Her husband, Derk, was working at a car shop, a job he got through one of Rona's brothers. At the time of evacuation, Rona and Derk, the children, and her father-in-law joined a caravan of more than twenty-five individuals who traveled to Baton Rouge to the home of Brownie, the mother of Rona's best friend, Wendy. They stayed for six weeks with fifty-three others in the house. Wendy and Rona then moved their families to Columbia, Missouri, where an old family (New Orleanian) friend lived, where they stayed until August 2006. Both Wendy and Rona returned to Baton Rouge, and shortly thereafter, Rona took her family back to New Orleans. Since returning to Louisiana in the summer of 2006, Rona has moved at least three times looking for a better place for her children to live. After only three months in her Ninth Ward home, she and her children rarely left the house for fear of violent crimes and theft.

At the time of our interview, Rona was unemployed, living in a barely restored area of East New Orleans to which many other poor, black families have returned. She lives with her brother Kendall, husband Derk, her four children, and Derk's cousin in a run-down row house, one of the few inhabited on the block. Rona was extremely upset when describing her current situation; her mental state and physical appearance had deteriorated significantly since the lead author met her in the fall of 2005 in Missouri. She described feeling hopeless and depressed, and repeatedly said that she wants to leave New Orleans, as "there is nothing out there." One of her sons asked the lead author whether he could return with her to Missouri. Rona was terribly distraught over the lack of good school programs and opportunities for her children. Her rent is $850 a month, for which she receives no housing support from state or federal programs. Although she received a Section 8 housing voucher while living in Missouri, she could not get the benefit transferred back to Louisiana, for reasons she does not understand. Utility costs are also very high, largely because of the added "fuel adjustment" charges to residents of New Orleans to rebuild the energy infrastructure. She is not satisfied with her housing or its cost: "Look at the house here. You know, but you have to find something to live in."

It is not surprising that Rona's situation is so desperate. In addition to living in an underserved area of the city, her network exhibits qualities of flatness; that is, there is a relative homogeneity in the resources available for the network's use. When asked, for example, whether household members helped with expenses, Rona said:

> No, because they don't have no jobs. . . . The living is hard out here. I mean, they could go to like the temp service, but you've got to get up at four o'clock in the morning and you've got to walk there because we don't really have buses that run that early in the morning.

Aside from transportation problems, Rona repeated what we heard multiple times: previous informal networks through which many people acquired jobs could not be rebuilt after Katrina. "If you don't know nobody, you can't get on." Later in the interview she says of her husband's difficulty in securing employment: "No. He's not working. He was working for my brother, but he didn't want to pay so he stopped working." As it turns out, Rona's brother also lost his job at the car shop because the owner had to cut down on employees.

It has also been uncharacteristically challenging for Rona's brother Kendall to find regular employment. Before Katrina, he repaired sprinkler systems and, during displacement, he had so many options that he had to turn down work. Kendall returned home in 2007 to open a car mechanics shop with his brother but found he was locked out of employment networks. Kendall explains these in racial terms:

> It's a dog-eat-dog world in these streets. . . . You circled up down here now. . . . You've got to stick together. . . . Put it like this: before Katrina, it was . . . New Orleans for the blacks. Blacks still owned businesses. . . . Now, it's Arabs, . . . and if you're not click-clack with nobody . . . and you're not helping nobody out, . . . it's hard; . . . you barely making it, you know?

Like "Arabs," "Mexicans" figured largely in respondents' narratives as representing threatening newcomers to the city, changing the city's familiarity and workforce patterns (see Litt, forthcoming). Kendall's statement illustrates the power of network insiders and outsiders, and his new perspective of being outside decent job connections.

Rona's closest and constant companion before and immediately after the storm was Wendy, who now lives in Baton Rouge, not around the corner in New Orleans as before the storm. This is a significant loss to Rona's resources and her well-being. With Wendy no longer her daily companion, Rona is happy when her friend comes to visit:

> Wendy comes down here [to New Orleans]. She'll sleep the whole weekend there, her weekend off. And that would be the happiest days, when me and her together. That's my happier days with Wendy. Yeah. And she be like, "Girl, come with me to Baton Rouge." I be like, "No, I don't want to put no burden on, you know, nobody. I don't want to stress you and your husband and your family out. I'll just stay home." But it's horrible out here.

Rona also identified Miss Brownie, Wendy's mother, as someone she can rely on. She had dinner with Brownie and Wendy virtually every night in pre-Katrina New Orleans, but Brownie is no longer a feature of Rona's everyday life because she now lives in Baton Rouge:

> Like if I have problem right now. Like if I was losing my house or my life go, I mean, she'll send for me. She's like a mama, like. As my mama gone. But she just picked up that stuff for me. You know, she's been like that since even before the hurricane. She's been like that since me and Wendy was growing up. She's been like that. Give anybody. Big heart.

Aside from those in her household, Rona has four women cousins who regularly visit her house, a companionship she finds somewhat satisfying, but she also states they overstay their welcome at times. Our research team interviewed the cousins and found all but one was destitute, absolutely without resources, despite having promised to help Rona if she returned to New Orleans. As Rona explains it:

> You know, when I was in Columbia, they was like, "Oh, come back home. We miss you. We're going to help you when you fall short or this and that." [I] get down here. It's no help. Like I was telling my husband, "When I came down here, I gave

cars away and all that. Now I don't have a car." I can't get nobody to bring me here or there. Me and my children, we do want to go somewhere, we walking.

When asked why this happened, she said:

I don't know. I mean. It's tight now. . . . I guess they have problems, too. I don't know. What if I had known they weren't going [to give], I would have stayed where I was. Like saying, "Oh, I miss you. Oh, come down here. We're going to do." Started off like that. No, it wasn't like that.

Rona came home with expectations of assistance that she did not receive, and she actually gave away the few material assets she had—two cars. Now her employment and shopping options are extremely limited. She has to pay someone to take her shopping and, with the lack of public transportation in her area, has very limited employment options. Rona explained: "It's hard, . . . because we don't have no vehicle. . . . You're stuck, . . . catch the bus or pay somebody gas to bring you home. And they charge you an arm and a leg, . . . sometimes thirty dollars, forty dollars [because] Walmart [where she likes to shop] is uptown. It's way up there."

If, as we contend, it is collaboration of resources among network members that provides the safety net for security, then we can see what makes Rona so especially vulnerable. We already know that she cannot rely on her cousins or most of her siblings. She mentions Wendy and Brownie as emergency backups, but she is not in a position day to day to undertake exchange and sharing. Nor does she have access to good public resources that could considerably relieve the severe shortage of informal, kin resources.

Karen's Heterogeneous Network

Karen's network is entirely different from Rona's. First, as a woman in her sixties, she is a generation older and completely immersed in the lives of her children and grandchildren. She is interconnected on a daily basis with a broad, diverse network, the same people she lived near and depended upon before the storm and during evacuation. Unlike Rona, the material investments Karen and her network members made both before and during evacuation, the continued shared resources, and the collective return to their old area in New Orleans have resulted in a more secure and stable environment. Karen currently lives with and takes care of one of her son's children and also cares for a girl from Child Protective Services. She receives disability support due to her bronchitis and asthma. They reside in the home she has owned in New Orleans East since 1972, which is fully paid off. She continues to pay for homeowner's insurance, and her children renovated the house after Katrina. This is where she raised her two sons and three daughters, many of whom lived along her street in 2005 with their own children. When Katrina hit, Karen was living among these family members, as well as housing and caring for seven grandchildren. Karen's daughter Karalyn also lived in the Ninth Ward, though further west, sharing an apartment with her husband (Rona's brother), Tom, and their four children, the oldest of whom was eighteen.

Karen asserted, and her son corroborated, that the decision to evacuate was hers, knowing that her entire network would go with her. "Well, me and him [her son]. We make the decision, you know, like to go. Like if I would have stayed, wasn't nobody going to go. And if I go, everybody going." While they traveled together to Mississippi, they were split up for various reasons. Karen's entire network was not able to travel in her caravan, resulting in the family being spread across two states. When FEMA (Federal Emergency Management Agency) attempted to send Karen to Oklahoma, even farther from her kin, she resisted. By virtue of their commitment to stay together, the family set up what they referred to as a "tent city" in Mississippi and created a home for their dispersed family members. The tents were set up in a row so they could walk between tents without going outside. Though they applied for one, no FEMA trailer came in the two years they lived in tents. FEMA's standard $2000 household reimbursement provided Karen the funds to buy an old trailer for power and to outfit their tents.

Yet in New Orleans, utility and insurance payments are very high and so are food costs. Karen sometimes drives two hours one way to buy food. "I go get twenty-five pounds of sugar at Winn Dixie [in New Orleans] is $12-something. I go to Mississippi, I only pay $9.99. . . . Now I pay $38 to fill my tank up. I can go there and back. And when I come back, the van will be full of food." She then supplements these trips: "I go to the food bank. She [Karalyn] gives me stuff, too, from her food bank. All of them give me stuff. People just give me stuff. At school like when they have a party, I get all the leftover food because I'm the grandma with the most kids." By cobbling together food from many sources, Karen ensures there is enough to go around for all: "If I have a little meat, I can take that and make a meal and find something to go with it. I feed everybody around here. I cook two pounds of beans. Two pounds of spaghettis. Ten pounds of chicken. And you know, anybody want to eat, they can eat." The close proximity of the family on the street also means that they can share resources like clothing, tools, and child care. Furthermore, with a close kin network of exchange, skills are bartered, such as child care and home repair.

Divergent Networks and Women's Poverty in New Orleans

Karen's kin network had a collective resource base—both in the period of dislocation in Mississippi and upon their return. They were able to pool resources to rent the land and create the "tent city." They were also able to send kin back and forth to renovate the house, which resulted in a restored home in precisely the area they had loved and left. Karen describes the present-day neighborhood this way: "We still together, like go around the corner. We're within walking distance. And she [Karalyn] was the only one that live farther away. She about to move out here. 'Cause like right now. This whole area is family." Indeed, at the time of the 2009 interview, Karalyn had just signed her lease for a duplex a street away.

Further, Karen's networks have been able to benefit from investments that pay back. She had to sue their homeowner's insurance company for assistance with reconstruction costs but did get more funds. She invested some of her FEMA funds in fixing up the house, another investment with long-term payoff. Karen's daughter, Karalyn, also has stable housing, yet another resource for the entire network.

In stark contrast, Rona initially evacuated to Missouri, where she had access to housing support, and then used FEMA money to furnish a house there, settled her children in school, and developed new networks of support, all with her friend Wendy. But she returned, with no disaster relief available, without a renovated home, with no access to housing assistance, and with kin who actually depleted her resources.

The resources coming into Karen's network were much more heterogeneous then Rona's. First, the fact that Karen owned her house meant that it served as a kind of nerve center and physical resource for the network, and provided safety and stability for the extended family. Second, the neighborhood was not described as overly dangerous; pressure to stay inside and protect children from the street did not appear as abiding a concern as it did for Rona. Children, grandchildren, friends, and siblings gathered at Karen's constantly. Third, Karen's network was full of other resources. Her daughter Karalyn works for six dollars an hour. Karalyn also receives a disability check and rental assistance. Her husband, Tom, also works and together they have a car. Interestingly, although Tom is Rona's brother, he does not share any of his income with her. Also, while Karalyn used to see Rona pretty regularly before the storm, things are different now: "[They used to be] around the corner. When they were staying around the corner, I used to go visit Rona there. . . . She moved, so I don't really go too much. I stay here all day." In this, Rona lost regular access to yet another close network member (like Wendy and Miss Brownie) who actually does have resources. Finally, Karen felt a much greater sense of efficacy and control in and through her network, clearly valuing her own contribution to its well-being. While Rona also contributed to her network's survival, she did not exhibit the same sense of accomplishment or control but felt dependent on her husband, who had refused to leave New Orleans. She felt it was necessary to take others in but was offered little help to get what she needed and wanted.

Both Rona and Karen attempted, as much as possible, to organize their lives in ways that could maintain their immersion in kin exchange networks. Yet there is no doubt that Rona's daily kinship exchange no longer satisfies her needs or those of her household or extended kin. Her network consists of individuals who not only have little access to resources but also lack a diversity of skills, connections, and networks. There is little variation in the ways that network members reach beyond the household to resources outside it. In the end, it is primarily through SSI insurance that Rona receives any financial resources. Furthermore, all the investments that Rona made in her pre-Katrina rental apartment in New Orleans, in her temporary home in Columbia, and in the multiple homes she has lived in since her return to New Orleans have been left behind. The jobs, the household necessities, the neighborhood contacts, the job connections, and so on are not sustained as she continues to move, allowing virtually no accumulation of material or social goods. Rona was at the limits of what she could give, both emotionally and materially. In fact, after the study was concluded, Rona and Wendy called us to say that Rona and her family had moved in with Wendy in Baton Rouge.

Karen's network, by contrast, has very successfully managed to create a diverse array of resources available for kin consumption and exchange—largely by staying together and maintaining some continuity of place. Housing vouchers, jobs, neighbors' food assistance, SSI, and so on point to a richness of resources and a variety of sources from which to get them. These network members are not reliant on only one or two sources of support, nor are they reliant on only one or two individuals. Karen's network has been able to benefit from the investments it has made. Karen lost all her possessions in the storm, but she owned her house, had flood insurance, and benefited from FEMA's Road Home money.

Karen's and Rona's networks had radically different capacities to absorb the devastated public services in the city. Despite their differences, without these women—the strategies they create and the norms they set for an ethos of collectivity—networks could not have functioned as resource-sharing mechanisms at all.

More research is needed to determine the driving forces that set these networks onto different pathways in recovery. We suggest three areas for more investigation. First, *capitalization and decapitalization*. One of the consequences of the displacement and ongoing crisis for evacuee families is the loss of material goods, that is, the inability to benefit from prior investments. Thus, homeownership before the disaster as well as the capacity to rebuild (which for many low-income individuals has not been possible) may provide a level of material stability that distinguishes network capacity and reinforces that capacity for postevent resilience. Second, *life-cycle stage*. Karen's children were older and capable of contributing to the family's resource base. While Karen cared for her grandchildren, her own children were caring for her and providing material for exchange for the larger network. In this way, responsibility for network resources was itself dispersed. Rona's children, by contrast, were school age. They did not provide resources, nor could they be left unattended. Thus Rona has intensive mothering responsibility as well as a lack of resources to call on. Third, *job opportunities for men*. An unanticipated finding in the research was the deterioration in men's networks of job support. For both women and men, jobs were obtained through network ties. Many of our respondents worked in places with kin. Yet adult men, particularly in Rona's but also in other networks, reported that the dispersal led to the disintegration of their job exchange networks. This was distinctly gendered; we saw little evidence that job connections were destroyed in women's networks, although this might be because women tend to work in large-scale institutions (such as fast food or hotels) and men in small businesses.

Conclusion

The data presented here suggest that African American women created the conditions for collectivizing resources, for maintaining connections among kin members, and for steering their families toward a better future. We identified two networks with vastly different capacities for responding to postdisaster conditions. The doubly cruel problem of poverty in New Orleans is the simultaneous destruction of public provision and the fragility of social networks' resilience.

These findings have policy implications. If the daily lives of women and their networks, families, and neighborhoods were considered, planners could manage resources in a way that leverages the strength of networks, rather than impedes them. With more understanding of why and how some networks rather than others maintain their capacity, support could be provided to buttress all families. Creating housing options, like Karen's, that place kin back near each other in a safe, affordable, and stable environment will go a long way toward rebuilding lives. At the same time, helping to recreate kin networks will do little if the necessary building blocks of the public sector—hospitals, transportation, jobs—are not available. Thus planning for future disasters—and trying to improve the current tragedy in New Orleans—demands policy that *simultaneously* builds infrastructure and supports women in creating network strength.

Jacquelyn Litt is dean of Douglass Residential College and Campus and professor of women's and gender studies at Rutgers University, New Brunswick, New Jersey. She is writing a book, *Women of Katrina: Crossing Borders, Weaving Networks, and Taking Care,* that documents the strategies of survival women applied to disaster recovery in the Katrina diaspora. Her primary research has been on motherhood, care work, and inequality.

Althea Skinner is a graduate student in international development at American University focusing on the ecological and human sustainability of development interventions in Latin America and Sub-Saharan Africa. As an undergraduate at Rice University, she founded and directed the university's gay, lesbian, and allied resource center and later interned in The Hague at the International Criminal Tribunal for the Former Yugoslavia.

Kelley Robinson studies women's and gender issues at the University of Missouri–Columbia and is a regional organizer in the Government Affairs Department at Planned Parenthood of the Heartland in Des Moines, Iowa. She has been organizing and pursuing social justice initiatives throughout her career, with special attention to issues of hate, bias, and gender-based violence.

REFERENCES

Collins, P. H. (1990). *Black feminist thought: Knowledge, consciousness, and the politics of empowerment.* Cambridge, MA: Unwin Hyman.

Cutter, S., Emrich, C., Mitchell, J., Boruff, B., Gall, M., Schmidtlein, M., Burton, C., and Melton, G. (2006). The long road home: Race, class, and recovery from Hurricane Katrina. *Environment, 48*(2), 8–20.

Eggebeen, D. (1992). Family structure and intergenerational exchanges. *Research on Aging, 14,* 427–447.

Eggebeen, D., and Hogan, D. (1990). Giving between generations in American families. *Human Nature, 1,* 211–232.

Enarson, E. (2001). What women do: Gendered labor in the Red River Valley flood. *Environmental Hazards, 3,* 1–18.

Fothergill, A. (2004). *Heads above water: Gender, class, and family in the Grand Forks flood.* Albany: State University of New York Press.

Fothergill, A., and Peek, L. (2006). Surviving catastrophe: A study of children in Hurricane Katrina. In *Learning from catastrophe: Quick response research in the wake of Hurricane Katrina* (pp. 97–129). Boulder: Natural Hazards Center, University of Colorado.

Frey, W., Singer, A. and Park, D. (2007). *Resettling New Orleans: The first full picture from the Census.* Brookings Institution Metropolitan Policy Program, 1–28. Washington, DC: Brookings Institution.

Gault, B., Hartmann, H., Jones-DeWeever, A., Werschkul, M., and Williams, E. (2005). *The women of New Orleans and the Gulf Coast: Multiple disadvantages and key assets for recovery.* Part 1: *Poverty, race, gender, and class.* Washington, DC: Institute for Women's Policy Research.

González de la Rocha, M. (2001). From the resources of poverty to the poverty of resources? The economic crisis, social polarization, and class struggle, part 2. *Latin American Perspectives, 28*(4), 72–100.

Groen, J., and Polivka, A. (2008a). The effect of Hurricane Katrina on the labor market outcomes of evacuees. Office of Employment and Unemployment Statistics, U.S. Department of Labor. Working paper 415. Washington, DC: U.S. Department of Labor.

———. (2008b). Hurricane Katrina evacuees: Who they are, where they are, and how they are faring. *Monthly Labor Review.* Division of Employment Research, Office of Employment and Unemployment Statistics, Bureau of Labor Statistics, 32–51. Washington, DC: U.S. Bureau of Labor Statistics city, publisher?}

Haney, T., Elliott, J., and Fussell, E. (2007). Families and hurricane response: Evacuation, separation, and the emotional toll of Hurricane Katrina. In D. L. Brunsma, D. Overfelt, and J. S. Picou (Eds.), *The sociology of Katrina* (pp. 71–90). Lanham, MD: Rowman and Littlefield.

Hill, S. (1999). *African-American children: Socialization and development in families.* Thousand Oaks, CA: Sage.

Jones-DeWeever, A. (2007). Women in the wake of the storm: Examining the post-Katrina realities of the women of New Orleans and the Gulf Coast. Washington, DC: Institute for Women's Policy Research.

Jones-DeWeever, A., and Hartmann, H. (2006). Abandoned before the storms: The glaring disaster of gender, race, and class disparities in the Gulf. In C. Hartman and G. D. Squires (Eds.), *There is no such thing as a natural disaster: Race, class, and Hurricane Katrina* (pp.185–101). New York: Routledge:

Litt, J. (1999). Managing the street, isolating the household: African American mothers respond to neighborhood deterioration. *Race, Gender, and Class, 6*(3), 90–108.

———. (2008). Getting out or staying put: An African American women's network in evacuation from Katrina. *NWSA Journal, 20*(3), 32–48.

———. (In preparation). *Women of Katrina: Crossing borders, weaving networks, taking care.* Austin: University of Texas Press.

Liu, A., and Plyer, A. (2009). *The New Orleans index: Tracking recovery of New Orleans and the metro area.* New Orleans: Brookings Institution Metropolitan Policy Program and Greater New Orleans Community Data Center.

Morrow, B. H. (1997). Stretching the bonds: The families of Andrew. In G. Peacock, B. H. Morrow, and H. Gladwin (Eds.), *Hurricane Andrew: Ethnicity, gender, and the sociology of disasters* (pp. 141–170). New York: Routledge.

Pastor, M., Bullard, R., Boyce, J., Fothergill, A., Morello-Frosch, R., and Wright, B. (2006). *In the wake of the storm: Environment, disaster, and race after Katrina.* New York: Russell Sage Foundation.

Roschelle, A. R. (1997). *No more kin: Exploring race, class, and gender in family networks.* Thousand Oaks, CA: Sage.

Stack, C. (1974). *All our kin: Strategies for survival in the Black community.* New York: Harper and Row.

Williams, E., Sorokina, O., Jones-DeWeever, A., and Hartmann, H. (2006). *The women of New Orleans and the Gulf Coast: Multiple disadvantages and key assets for recovery.* Part 2: *Gender, race, and class in the labor market.* Washington, DC: Institute for Women's Policy Research.

CHAPTER 18

Doubly Displaced

Women, Public Housing, and Spatial Access after Katrina

Jane M. Henrici, Allison Suppan Helmuth, and Angela Carlberg

The Institute for Women's Policy Research (IWPR) has been producing reports on the women along the Gulf Coast since the devastation that followed Hurricanes Katrina and Rita in 2005 (Gault et al. 2005; Jones-DeWeever 2008; Jones-DeWeever and Hartmann 2007; Williams et al. 2006). Other researchers have noted that planners and policy makers sometimes find opportunity within disaster (Button and Oliver-Smith 2008; Gunewardena 2008; Klein 2007; Lubiano 2008; Reed Jr. 2008; Schuller 2008); we recognize that researchers also might do so. One of the objectives of our research is to use this advantage to contribute to policy and planning that responds to the needs of women and vulnerable populations while respecting individual and community agency in spite of the classic dilemma of representation. Those who contribute to our study tell us that they interrupt their days to talk with us, even though telling their stories can be disturbing and draining, partly so their experiences may inspire improvements in policy and planning. A former New Orleans public housing tenant telephoned to update us on her situation in Houston as we wrote this chapter: "You have got to tell somebody. . . . I just think that people ought to know what's happening. You still have folks like myself that are stuck in limbo."

We base this chapter on findings from our ongoing interviews with women living in New Orleans, Baton Rouge, and Houston, all of whom resided in one of four New Orleans public housing developments when Katrina struck. Due to the gendered, racialized, and classed character that we and other researchers have found to be part of disasters and of displacement of any sort, we argue that the women and families in this study are among the most vulnerable of all of Katrina's victims. We anticipated their facing high levels of continued and compounded difficulties with very low levels of support, and have been interested at where this configuration has been most apparent. We have also learned much that we did not expect, and we thank the women with whom we have shared so much time for their insights, commentaries, and stories.

These New Orleans women who lived in public housing during the flooding after Hurricane Katrina have taught us, first, that fewer resources and less access to them extend the emergency phase of a disaster and sustain its harmful effects. Preparation that anticipates the intersectionality of gendered, racial, and class inequalities will not prevent the next flooding of New Orleans (Liu and Plyer 2009) but could mitigate these effects. Second, planning should address differences in needs and circumstances, not only for disaster preparedness but also as an ongoing effort. This requirement for a broader infrastructure is supported by extensive research being conducted with women displaced twice from their homes: by flooding and by urban planning.

Background

When IWPR began research with women along the Gulf Coast in 2005, we observed expanding socioeconomic and racial divisions among household and neighborhood resources and in rebuilding, both in New Orleans and between the city and other Gulf Coast regions (Gault et al. 2005). Discrimination and indifference had produced inadequate housing stock for low-income African Americans in New Orleans before 2005 (Cook, Bruin, and Crull 2000), and segregation increased steadily during the 1990s (Brookings Institution 2005). Disaster appeared to worsen these divisions.

In part, this negative trend had to do with the forms of the responses to disaster. As recently as 2007, former renters in private apartments and in New Orleans public housing, who together account for the majority of the city's residents, continued to receive confusing information about their homes. In addition, segregation increased as a result of the disaster itself: people of color of every socioeconomic class inhabited 80 percent of the part of the metropolitan statistical area that flooded (Brookings Institution 2005).

Racial segregation intersects with gender and class both before and after Katrina. At the time of the disaster, all "women in New Orleans faced significantly higher poverty rates than their male counterparts. . . . Both men and women in New Orleans had poverty rates that were almost double the national average" (Gault et al. 2005, 3). As the expanding literature about women and Katrina observes, a greater percentage of older women, female heads of households, and women of color were among those living below the U.S. poverty line average in New Orleans in 2005, whether they had jobs or not (Gault et al. 2005). In other words, many New Orleans women and their families lived in poverty even before flooding forced them to leave their city.

Spatial constraints were linked to racial and socioeconomic divisions in New Orleans before Katrina, but families had adapted to their circumstances, particularly through extended networks and multigenerational families in the area. But since their displacement by the flooding, public housing residents have had to deal with city planners' successful elimination of their homes; not all families have found or formed new networks, and many continue to struggle to get by.

Families formerly residing in New Orleans Big Four public housing complexes were told that most of their apartments would be demolished rather than repaired, and that the housing vouchers for that city and the others where some families remained after the evacuation were contingent upon new criteria. This demolition took place in the context of trauma, heightened rents, and diminished available housing, even though inspectors found the public housing to be structurally sound.

The Big Four

The public housing apartments where the respondents for this study once lived have come to be known collectively as the Big Four: the St. Bernard, B. W. Cooper, Lafitte, and C. J. Peete housing developments. The history of these developments, like that of any such developments in any major urban area of the United States, reflect economic and political cycles and attitudes toward socioeconomic class, race relations, and social theory (Bratt 2008; Bratt, Stone, and Hartman 2006; Cisneros and Engdahl 2009; Feldman and Stall 2004; Goetz 2003; Greenbaum 2002; Greenbaum et al. 2008; *Harvard Law Review* 2003; McClure 2008; Miranne 2000; Turner, Popkin, and Rawlings 2008; Williams 2004). Now that the Big Four buildings are almost entirely demolished, we rely on the memories of those we interview along with academic, popular, and school projects to depict these places (cf. Nelson 2005), including a television series entitled *Treme*.

The Big Four, like other New Orleans developments, provided shelter to thousands of families for decades (Colten 2005; Germany 2007; Lewis 2003). When the levees broke and New Orleans flooded, the percent of female-headed households was high among family households in poverty. Most of the residents of the Big Four neighborhoods were African American, many of them women and their children, and many others were either older or disabled (GNOCDC 2006a, 2006b, 2006c, 2006d).

The Big Four were completed between 1937 and 1941, with newer sections added over the next fifteen years (Germany 2007). By 2005, the Big Four developments varied in acreage and style, but all covered city blocks with multiple rows of two- to four-story buildings in sturdy brick and decorated with lacy iron on their balconies. Many of the apartment interiors and building surfaces were deteriorated and in need of repair before Katrina. Nevertheless, the general belief among the poor in New Orleans over the decades that the developments stood was that whether you lived in them or not, if there were a hurricane, you should "get to the bricks" for safety; now that the buildings are gone, that clearly is no longer an option. In fact, Hurricane Katrina left people in the Big Four housing apartments by and large without injury and, had it not been for the flooding that followed the breaking of the levees, residents say they would not have had to leave the city.

By the 1990s, city planners apparently saw the neighborhoods as better off without the apartments at all and began multiple attempts to obtain federal permission and funding to tear the developments down. Federal housing policy had changed in the mid-1990s to provide dollars for demolition rather than for construction, but the Housing Authority of New Orleans (HANO) received funding for the destruction of only two of the Big Four complexes: C. J. Peete in 1998 and B. W. Cooper in 2002 (HUD 2004). As of 2007, HANO had received a revitalization grant for only one of the two, C. J. Peete (HUD 2008).

The situation with respect to these demolition attempts might have been expected to alter after Hurricane Katrina passed through New Orleans, since homes were few and costly to maintain and most of the buildings across the Big Four remained sound, if in need of cleaning because of the flood. Nevertheless, and despite protests and lawsuits as well as demolition difficulties when the bulldozers were confronted by the high quality of the brick construction, New Orleans administrators had the preponderance of the Big Four torn down.

New Orleans is changing again as it rebuilds (Willinger and Gerson 2008); its newer demographics create opportunities not just for post-disaster greed but also for creative and progressive options. Both possibilities nevertheless follow from the elimination of a large segment of those who did much of the hard labor to build and operate the city in the past. However New Orleans might carry on without that population, it will be a different city (Miller and Rivera 2008; Penner and Ferdinand 2009). Gentrification, privatization, and out-pricing old families with new homes have taken place neither slowly nor with concern for either architectural history or building safety (Arena 2007; Crowley 2006; GNOFHAC 2009; Lipsitz 2006; Luft and Griffin 2008; PolicyLink 2007). Instead, thousands of poorer women of color and their families were forced to leave their homes because the levees failed, but actually lost their homes to city planning.

Methods

To date, we have completed approximately 200 ethnographic interviews of the 240 planned for this four-year project. In each city, respondents generously participated in the semi-structured and open-ended interviews that lasted roughly an hour and usually (whenever possible) took place where they lived.

We have conducted follow-up interviews with a portion of those with whom we spoke initially and are conducting longer in-depth interviews with a small subset for a final report to be published in 2011. The ongoing and longitudinal character of the study has been critical and will make the final analysis more dimensional. First, the women with whom we are speaking and their families remain in volatile circumstances, and many of them do not keep the same telephone number or address within even a short period of time, much less the four years over which this project takes place. Second, typical of ethnographic interviews, the narratives are usually nonsequential; not so typical, they are often very difficult to relate, and completing one interview has occasionally taken more than one meeting. Third, part of our interest is in how networks of relatives and friends might have been involved in the ability to return to New Orleans or remain elsewhere, and we find that we learn more about that as we hear how lives go on and changes take place. Our follow-up telephone conversations help us gather new details and stay in touch. We learn about other hurricanes and other difficulties the women and their children experience, and about new jobs or businesses and new babies.

We present this stage of our analysis in part because we want to continue to contribute to the fortunately expanding scholarship on the gendered aspect of the Katrina disasters. In addition, we regard it as of importance that our findings seem in keeping with most gender and disaster research, even though that scholarship predominates outside the United States in nations presumed to have worse conditions for women.

Living "in Limbo": Survival Needs and Concerns

Beyond their double displacement, former residents of New Orleans public housing tell us that they remain "in limbo." They have received assistance in various cities but sometimes through the wrong voucher programs and often in ways that leave the women and their families much worse off than before. Although the women with whom we conducted interviews were part of a vulnerable population before their displacement, we find that by and large those renting apartments in New Orleans public housing in 2005 were adapted in their daily lives to what feminist geographer Melissa Gilbert (2000) calls a "spatial boundedness," using social networks to deal with relatively limited circumstances while keeping up with their responsibilities as mothers, employees, partners, volunteers, and providers. Five years later, their circumstances are simultaneously more circumscribed and wide open and, for many, their resources are more expensive and farther away.

The constraint that respondents describe includes inadequate access to housing, transportation, and organizations and resources where they are living now (see map of respondents' locations before and after Katrina). The women from New Orleans public housing now must pay higher rents and utilities in markets where companies take advantage of evacuee payments, find jobs in competition with locals who know how to drive and who own cars, deal with being isolated on city peripheries and in neighborhoods of violence, and find ways to stay connected to their families. Some of those we have interviewed are now homeless and going hungry; they are learning that, as apartments become available in the smaller publicly subsidized buildings constructed during urban redevelopment to replace their demolished apartments, former residents of the Big Four are not among the first chosen to return. Although there are exceptions to this set of circumstances—women supporting their families and living in solid houses, completing high school and college, with children going to schools the family likes—in general, the situation for former residents of the Big Four with whom we have spoken is one of relative limitations and extreme frustration.

Information Gaps

The sense of having been targeted by city and federal administrators' plans for redevelopment varies among residents of different housing developments, but most women tell of anxiety about traveling to housing agencies across the city multiple times to obtain and use correct information. While some say they miss the community quality and supports of the former public developments and wish they could return, other women express less a preference for returning to the old developments than outrage that so many former tenants have been left out of the discussion and reconstruction process, despite federal requirements with respect to development demolitions (see Kleit and Page 2008). Even their involvement with protests against the demolitions has been restricted by boundedness, in the form of the absence of affordable transportation.

Women describe varying concerns regarding their circumstances with voucher-subsidized housing in New Orleans, Baton Rouge, and Houston. Previously, women paid a relatively small portion of their wages and other income for rent, and utilities were provided; Section 8 vouchers, if accepted by a landlord or apartment manager, now demand both rent and utilities at escalated rates along with a proven credit history, which many families had never had to create. Compounding this is the confusion that arose outside New Orleans, where women were unaware that they had been assigned temporary emergency vouchers designed for renters who were not in public housing; as these short-term emergency vouchers expire, unlike the long-term public housing vouchers intended for low-income individuals and families, they can not be renewed.

Indeed, the restrictions of their new spatial boundedness can go beyond a sense of disconnection to one of rejection: when one woman was told to check into a homeless shelter after her Section 8 housing voucher was stolen and the city authority would not replace it, she asked what then as a disabled and retired person she was to do during the daytime and received the answer, "We have some beautiful parks." Mocking her experiences with bureaucrats and policies, as well as incompetency and theft, she says: "I feel like a bag of snacks at a Super Bowl party—I just get passed round and round." The uncertainty and inconsistency of support within this new form of boundedness keeps many of the women and their families feeling both vulnerable and victimized long after the trauma they endured as New Orleans flooded.

Immobility

Access to reliable and affordable transportation appears to play a critical role in respondents' continued efforts to locate sustaining jobs, dependable child care, affordable stores, and trauma-sensitive health care. These ongoing survival needs are compounded by their costs and by housing built without adequate transportation access. For women in all three cities, new safety and transportation issues arise and spatial boundedness has taken a new form, since resources do not cluster nearby or connect, even when there is transportation to the places where family members (many still scattered) go to school, reside, and work. When asked why she would like to return to New Orleans, one woman in Houston stated simply, "The buses," and when asked whether there might be any additional reason, said no.

Women contrast their lives before evacuation with their current circumstances in terms of proximity to or transportation access to doctors, stores, work, school, and day care. When asked about her primary mode of transportation before the evacuation of New Orleans, one woman now living in Baton Rouge responded:

> Walk. I walk[ed] a lot. Walk, walk, walk walk walk. Walk, or the bus. . . . Out here I can't get around easily. It's so long, I can't walk. And I'm walking and I'm on the bus. I don't have no car, no transportation to get around out here. Out there, I could get around out there because the bus is, like, so close there. My sister's there, you know, my momma's there, you know, my friends, you know. I had people, you know, with cars. Out here, you know, I just can't get around. No transportation at all. That's what I liked most out there; I could get around out there in New Orleans. Out here I can't.

Respondents who returned to New Orleans appear to be relatively better off in terms of transportation than those who live in Houston or Baton Rouge although in New Orleans the buses still are not back to pre-Katrina standards (see GAO 2009, 15). Most commonly, complaints about buses in New Orleans reference unreliable and infrequent scheduled stops. A woman who returned to New Orleans discusses the impact of the changed bus schedule on her working life, contrasting what used to be a fifteen-minute wait between buses with the current typical hour-long wait: "Well, I was working; that was the reason why I couldn't finish work because of the bus transportation. It was kind of making me late for work; I'd get up like two hours in advance and still be late for work. They were kind of laying me off because of that."

Meanwhile, former tenants of public housing who have relocated to Baton Rouge and Houston experience isolation in geospatial locations women describe as wide and far and spread out. In Baton Rouge especially, women and their adolescent children seem to be isolated without individual cars, and the adults state that this is their greatest need and one that is compounded by the dependence on others it creates. One woman says: "Most jobs, they want you to have your own car here. In New Orleans, I like riding the bus, the streetcar, I love riding. But here, that's why it's so hard for me to find a job. No car." Another says: "They put that in the ads and applications—do you have your own transportation? And when I first got here, I noticed you really do need your own transportation. . . . I don't drive. I've never wanted to drive, but I would like to now." In Houston, an emphasis on car ownership is evident as well, but more of those with whom we spoke during our first round of interviews there had been able to find employment and bus rides to it than in Baton Rouge. However, as one woman puts it: "Why every time we [have to go to HUD], we've got to go so far out? Everybody don't have no car, you know. . . . This is too hard. I tried to catch the bus one time, out here. Well, twice. Um, and I got lost. Houston is big. New Orleans fit right in the middle. I mean, New Orleans still can't compare to Houston."

No New Networks

One major issue for women in all three cities is the lack of a positive and supportive aspect to their boundedness. As in many poorer cities where family members tend to remain across generations (Sánchez-Jankowski 2008), New Orleans's schools once formed a core around which neighborhood residents linked, but new schools have yet to create such a bond; meanwhile, in Houston and Baton Rouge, New Orleanian families do not feel connected to children's schools or to the areas where they live, and other institutions have yet to take a linking role. In addition, for many women and their families, no new social networks have replaced those that permitted relatively limited circumstances to suffice before the storm, enabled survival during the disaster, and helped provide dignity during its aftermath (see David 2008; Litt 2008).

Although former residents did recall their concerns with safety and violence in their former neighborhoods, one respondent links her memory of feeling safe within the Lafitte neighborhood to its population by cousins, aunts, uncles, and other family members. Now in most contexts, regardless of the city, families face new surroundings and neighbors with whom they have little in common other than a geographic and socioeconomic distance from the cities' major employers, administrators, and financial activities.

Age as well as race and gender seem to matter: often, younger women seem less bounded by their new circumstances, but not necessarily in a well-supported way. A new mother, eighteen when we spoke, remains determinedly optimistic: "I want it to work out, but I don't know how it's going to work out." In contrast, other young women report little or no expectations for their future and a bewildered sadness over the loss of their adolescence brought on by the flooding and diaspora. Reports from some of the older women about their daughters' experiences during the disasters and since may signal compounding future problems (see Klein, n.d.). For their part, many younger women are worried about finding permanent or long-term housing they can afford and about their need to pay for gas, as well as about the lack of secure housing and transportation for their often ailing or disabled mothers and older sisters.

A cyclical issue is the difficulty of getting information about organizational support services that could help with adaptation to new networks. One woman currently living in Houston says: "Well, they say they have a lot of food banks. I don't know where it's at. They have a lot of people to help you as far as counseling. I don't know where that's at. They say they have a lot of people that will help you with gas, uh, uh, try to get your car fixed. I don't know where that's at. . . . I don't know where half of that stuff at, and then not only that, when you do find out about it, it'll be over with."

Conclusion

Women of color in particular and all women in general must be part of planning for both disasters and the everyday, while such planning must acknowledge articulations with race and class rather than merely with markets (Bratt, Stone, and Hartman 2006; Brenner, Marcuse, and Mayer 2009; Mann 2006). Women's needs, and their access to resources, must become elements in design and allocation (Meyer 2006); these should include but not be limited to housing and transit systems that help daily, as well as anticipate disasters (Bratt 2008; Comerio 1998). Women often hold multiple roles within a household: for women who are the sole caregivers and bread winners, trying to tighten the connections between work and home can lead to spatial boundedness, while the use of social networks within that configuration can expand but sometimes constrict opportunities (Gilbert 2000; Silbaugh 2008; Weisman 1994). If we refine policy to require a focus on women and their families as these intersect with race and class within planning, then we might produce and perhaps surpass what Dolores Hayden (1980) called "a non-sexist city." We are eager to learn from the next steps in our research whether changes to the former residents' lives and consequent updates to our data will challenge what we observe at this juncture, and we owe the attempt to the women who resided in New Orleans public housing at the time of the flooding in August 2005. Our goal is to continue to learn from them, so that our standards and expectations of planning reach theirs (Check 2007).

Doubly Displaced: Respondent Locations Before and After Katrina

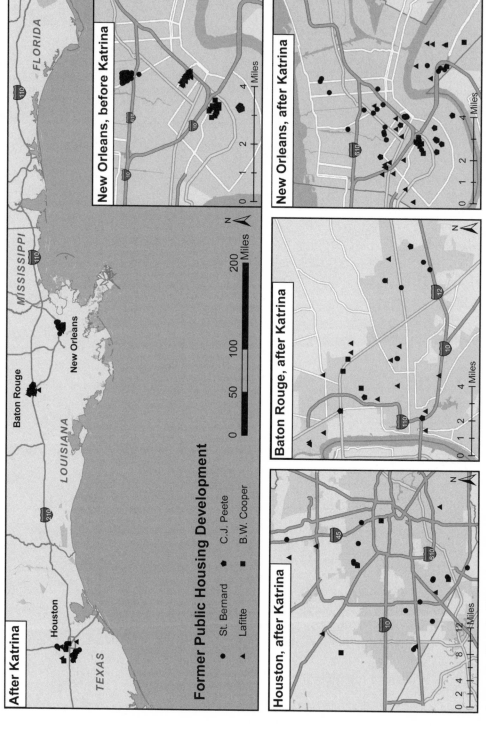

Source: Institute for Women's Policy Research 2011

Jane M. Henrici is study director at the Institute for Women's Policy Research. She is coauthor of *Poor Families in America's Health Care Crisis: How the Other Half Pays* (2006) and editor of *Doing Without: Women and Work after Welfare Reform* (2006). In 2006, she was a Fulbright Scholar in Peru.

Allison Suppan Helmuth is a graduate student in sociology at George Washington University and a former research analyst and Mariam K. Chamberlain fellow at the Institute for Women's Policy Research. She previously studied gender and development at the University of the West Indies and used her Fulbright award to study urban backyard chicken rearing in Kingston's underserved communities.

Angela Carlberg is a graduate student in American politics with a focus on race, gender, and ethnicity at Ohio State University and an affiliated scholar with the Institute for Women's Policy Research.

ACKNOWLEDGMENTS

The Institute for Women's Policy Research sought and received funding for a multiyear project from the Bill and Melinda Gates Foundation as part of a working group of the Social Science Research Council Katrina Task Force. This chapter, based on material midway through the study, was written with a great deal of help, most of all from the women who kindly agree to give us their time and let us interview them. In addition, we have had intensive assistance with interviewing, data management, coding, and brainstorming from Shirley Adelstein, Jackie Braun, Jessica Chow, Ariana Curtis, Laura Dean-Shapiro, Rhea Fernandes, Helene Hurrey, Lakshmi Kannan, Monica Martinez, Sarah Michelsen, Amanda Milstein, Paulina Montañez-Montes, D'Ann Penner, Niara Phillips, Morganne Rosenhaus, Cristina Sainati, Sovini Tan, Kennedy Turner, Shannon Williams, and Natalie Young. We would like to acknowledge the contribution all have made to this project. Correspondence to *henrici@iwpr.org*.

REFERENCES

Arena, J. (2007). Whose city is it? Public housing, public sociology, and the struggle for social justice in New Orleans before and after Katrina. In K. A. Bates and R. S. Swan (Eds.), *Through the eye of Katrina: Social justice in the United States* (pp. 367–383). Durham, NC: Carolina Academic Press.

Bratt, R. G. (2008). Viewing housing holistically: The resident-focused component of the housing-plus agenda. *Journal of the American Planning Association, 74*(1), 100–110.

Bratt, R. G., Stone, M. E., and Hartman, C. (2006). *A right to housing: Foundation for a new social agenda.* Philadelphia: Temple University Press.

Brenner, N., Marcuse, P., and Mayer, M. (2009). Cities for people, not for profit. *City, 13*(2–3), 176–184.

Brookings Institution. (2005). *New Orleans after the storm: Lessons from the past, a plan for the future.* Washington, DC: Brookings Institution.

Button, G., and Oliver-Smith, A. (2008). Disaster, displacement, and employment: Distortion of labor markets during post-Katrina reconstruction. In N. Gunewardena and M. Schuller (Eds.), *Capitalizing on catastrophe* (pp. 123–146). Lanham, MD: AltaMira Press.

Check, T. (2007). The voices of Katrina: Ethos, race, and congressional testimonials. In K. A. Bates and R. S. Swan (Eds.), *Through the eye of Katrina: Social justice in the United States* (pp. 239–257). Durham, NC: Carolina Academic Press.

Cisneros, H. G., and Engdahl, L. (2009). *From despair to hope: HOPE VI and the new promise of public housing in America's cities.* Washington, DC: Brookings Institution.

Colten, C. E. (2005). *An unnatural metropolis: Wrestling New Orleans from nature.* Baton Rouge: Louisiana State University Press.

Comerio, M. (1998). *Disaster hits home: New policy for urban housing recovery.* Berkeley: University of California Press.

Cook, C., Bruin, M., and Crull, S. (2000). Manipulating constraints: Women's housing and the "metropolitan context." In K. B. Miranne and A. H. Young (Eds.), *Gendering the city: Women, boundaries, and visions of urban life* (pp. 183–207). Lanham, MD: Rowman and Littlefield.

Crowley, S. (2006). Where is home? Housing for low-income people after the 2005 hurricanes. In C. Hartman and G. D. Squires (Eds.), *There is no such thing as a natural disaster: Race, class, and Hurricane Katrina* (pp. 121–166). New York: Routledge.

David, E. (2008). Cultural trauma, memory, and gendered collective action: The case of *Women of the Storm* following Hurricane Katrina. *NWSA Journal, 20*(3), 138–162.

Feldman, R. M., and Stall, S. (2004). *The dignity of resistance: Women residents' activism in Chicago public housing.* New York: Cambridge University Press.

GAO (U.S. Government Accountability Office). (2009). *Hurricane Katrina: Barriers to mental health services persist in greater New Orleans, although federal grants are helping to address them.* Washington, DC: U.S. Government Accountability Office.

Gault, B., Hartmann, H., Jones-DeWeever, A., Werschkul, M., and Williams, E. (2005). *The women of New Orleans and the Gulf Coast: Multiple disadvantages and key assets for recovery. Part 1: Poverty, race, gender, and class.* Washington, DC: Institute for Women's Policy Research.

Germany, K. B. (2007). *New Orleans after the promises: Poverty, citizenship, and the search for the great society.* Athens: University of Georgia Press.

Gilbert, M. R. (2000). Identity, difference, and the geographies of working poor women's survival strategies. In K. B. Miranne and A. H. Young (Eds.), *Gendering the city: Women, boundaries, and visions of urban life* (pp. 65–88). Lanham, MD: Rowman and Littlefield.

GNOCDC (Greater New Orleans Community Data Center). (2006a). B. W. Cooper Apts neighborhood: People and household characteristics. Retrieved from *gnocdc.org/orleans/4/60/people.html.*

———. (2006b). Central City neighborhood: People and household characteristics. Retrieved from *gnocdc.org/orleans/2/61/people.html.*

———. (2006c). St. Bernard area neighborhood: People and household characteristics. Retrieved from *gnocdc.org/orleans/4/26/people.html.*

———. (2006d). Tremé/Lafitte neighborhood: People and household characteristics. Retrieved from gnocdc.org/orleans/4/42/people.html.

———. (2009). Ten-minute briefing on New Orleans' recovery. Retrieved from *www.gnocdc.org/NewOrleansIndex/video.html.*

GNOFHAC (Greater New Orleans Fair Housing Action Center). (2009). *Housing choice in crisis: An audit report on discrimination against Housing Choice Voucher holders in the greater New Orleans rental housing market.* New Orleans: Greater New Orleans Fair Housing Action Center.

Goetz, E. G. (2003). *Clearing the way: Deconcentrating the poor in urban America*. Washington, DC: Urban Institute Press.

Greenbaum, S. (2002). Report from the field: Social capital and deconcentration; Theoretical paradoxes of the HOPE VI program. *North American Dialogue, 5* (September), 9–13.

Greenbaum, S., Hathaway, W., Rodriguez, C., Spalding, A., and Ward, B. (2008). Deconcentration and social capital: Contradictions of poverty alleviation policy. *Journal of Poverty, 12*(2), 1–16.

Gunewardena, N. (2008). Human security versus neoliberal approaches to disaster recovery. In N. Gunewardena and M. Schuller (Eds.), *Capitalizing on catastrophe* (pp. 3–16). Lanham, MD: AltaMira Press.

Harvard Law Review. (2003). When hope falls short: HOPE VI, accountability, and privatization of public housing. *Harvard Law Review, 116*(5), 1477–1498.

Hayden, D. (1980). What would a non-sexist city be like? Speculations on housing, urban design, and human work. *Signs, 5*(3), 5170–5187.

HUD (U.S. Department of Housing and Urban Development). (2004). HOPE VI demolition grants: FY 1996–2003. Retrieved from *www.hud.gov/offices/pih/programs/ph/hope6/grants/demolition/*.

———. (2008). HOPE VI revitalization grants. Retrieved from *www.hud.gov/offices/pih/programs/ph/hope6/grants/revitalization/*.

Jones-DeWeever, A. (2008). *Women in the wake of the storm: Examining the post-Katrina realities of the women of New Orleans and the Gulf Coast*. Washington, DC: Institute for Women's Policy Research.

Jones-DeWeever, A., and Hartmann, H. (2007). Abandoned before the storm: The glaring disaster of gender, race, and class disparities in the Gulf. In C. Hartman and G. Squires (Eds.), *There's no such thing as a natural disaster: Race, class, and Hurricane Katrina* (pp. 85–102). New York: Routledge.

Klein, A. (n.d.). *Sexual violence in disasters: A planning guide for prevention and response*. Hammond, LA: Louisiana Foundation Against Sexual Assault and National Sexual Violence Center.

Klein, N. (2007). *The shock doctrine: The rise of disaster capitalism*. New York: Metropolitan Books/Henry Holt.

Kleit, R. G., and Page, S. B. (2008). Public housing authorities under devolution. *Journal of the American Planning Association, 74*(1), 34–44.

Lewis, P. F. (2003). *New Orleans: The making of an urban landscape*. Santa Fe, NM: Center for American Places.

Lipsitz, G. (2006). Learning from New Orleans: The social warrant of hostile privatism and competitive consumer citizenship. *Cultural Anthropology, 21*(3), 451–468.

Litt, J. (2008). Getting out or staying put: An African American women's network in evacuation from Katrina. *NWSA Journal, 20*(3), 32–48.

Liu, A., and Plyer, A. (2009). *The New Orleans index: Tracking the recovery of New Orleans and the metro area*. New Orleans: Brookings Institution and Greater New Orleans Community Data Center.

Lubiano, W. (2008). Race, class, and the politics of death: Critical responses to Hurricane Katrina. In N. Gunewardena and M. Schuller (Eds.), *Capitalizing on catastrophe* (pp. 117–122). Lanham, MD: AltaMira Press.

Luft, R. E., and Griffin, S. (2008). A status report on housing in New Orleans after Katrina: An intersectional analysis. In B. Willinger (Ed.), *Katrina and the women of New Orleans: Executive report and summary of findings* (pp. 50–53). Newcomb College Center for Research on Women. New Orleans: Tulane University.

Mann, E. (2008). Race and the high ground in New Orleans. *World Watch, 19*(5), 40–42.

McClure, K. (2008). Deconcentrating poverty with housing programs. *Journal of the American Planning Association, 74*(1), 90–99.

Meyer, M. D. (2006). Women's issues in transportation: Policy and planning. *Research on Proceedings, 1*(35), 51–58.

Miller, D. S., and Rivera, J. D. (2008). *Hurricane Katrina and the redefinition of landscape.* Lanham, MD: Lexington Books.

Miranne, K. B. (2000). Women "embounded": Intersections of welfare reform and public housing policy. In K. B. Miranne and A. H. Young (Eds.), *Gendering the city: Women, boundaries, and visions of urban life* (pp. 119–136). Lanham, MD: Rowman and Littlefield.

Neighborhood Story Project. (n.d.). Retrieved from *www.neighborhoodstoryproject.org/.*

Nelson, A. (2005). *The combination.* New York: Soft Skull.

Penner, D. R., and Ferdinand, K. C. (2009). *Overcoming Katrina: African American voices from the Crescent City and beyond.* New York: Palgrave Macmillan.

PolicyLink. (2007). *Fewer homes for Katrina's poorest victims: An analysis of subsidized homes in post-Katrina New Orleans.* New Orleans: PolicyLink.

Reed, A., Jr. (2008). Class inequality, liberal bad faith, and neoliberalism: The true disaster of Katrina. In N. Gunewardena and M. Schuller (Eds.), *Capitalizing on catastrophe* (pp. 147–156). Lanham, MD: AltaMira Press.

Sánchez-Jankowski, M. (2008). *Cracks in the pavement: Social change and resilience in poor neighborhoods.* Berkeley: University of California Press.

Schuller, M. (2008). Deconstructing the disaster after the disaster: Conceptualizing disaster capitalism. In N. Gunewardena and M. Schuller (Eds.), *Capitalizing on catastrophe* (pp. 17–28). Lanham, MD: AltaMira Press.

Silbaugh, K. B. (2008). Women's place: Urban planning, housing design, and work-family balance. *Fordham Law Review, 76,* 1797–1852.

Turner, M. A., Popkin, S. J., and Rawlings, L. (2008). *Public housing and the legacy of segregation.* Washington, DC: Urban Institute Press.

Weisman, L. K. (1994). *Discrimination by design: A feminist critique of the man-made environment.* Urbana: University of Illinois Press.

Williams, E., Sorokina O., Jones-DeWeever, A., and Hartmann, H. (2006). *The women of New Orleans and the Gulf Coast: Multiple disadvantages and key assets for recovery.* Part 2: *Gender, race, and class in the labor market.* Washington, DC: Institute for Women's Policy Research.

Williams, R. Y. (2004). *The politics of public housing: Black women's struggles against urban inequality.* New York: Oxford University Press.

Willinger, B., and Gerson, J. (2008). Demographic and socio-economic change in relation to gender and Hurricane Katrina. In B. Willinger (Ed.), *Katrina and the women of New Orleans: Executive report and summary of findings* (pp. 25–31). Newcomb College Center for Research on Women. New Orleans: Tulane University.

PART IV

Against the Tide
Resisting, Reclaiming, and Reimagining

The final series of empirical chapters in this book investigates how women along the Gulf Coast have resisted the social forces that threaten their lives and livelihoods and how they have collectively organized for a better future for themselves and their loved ones after Hurricane Katrina. Grounded in a range of compelling issues, from the politics of place and the environment to struggles over collective identity, religion, and culture, the chapters demonstrate that after disaster, women rise to the challenge to rebuild and strengthen social ties.

As tragic as they may be, disasters can be windows of opportunity to rebuild better, stronger, and more resilient communities, reweaving the fabric of everyday life in ways that are more just and more equitable. Indeed, many women were active in social change efforts after Katrina through their work in communities, nonprofits, politics, and policy arenas. While some received praise for their efforts, the work of most went unnoticed—yet it mattered tremendously. Women resisted rebuilding practices that did not serve their communities or that put women and their families at increased risk of violence or of negative health effects. They reclaimed a sense of identity and culture through their individual and collective activities. They began to reimagine a world transformed through care, connectedness, and concern for others. Not unlike women's work in noncrisis times, these efforts were anchored in women's families, neighborhoods, cultural practices, and memories, and their activism attests to women's agency in the face of crisis and their ability to radiate hope in the midst of destruction.

CHAPTER 19

Gender, Race, and Place Attachment

The Recovery of a Historic Neighborhood in Coastal Mississippi

Mia Charlene White

An hour's drive east of New Orleans along the Gulf of Mexico, there thrives the largely unknown historic black settlement of North Gulfport and Turkey Creek, Mississippi, established in 1866. Despite Interstate 49, which separates North Gulfport from Turkey Creek, these two historically connected communities still organize as one and together advocate against gentrification, environmental racism, and the unsustainable infill development of the Turkey Creek watershed, which community leaders insist makes their historic enclave of kinfolk dramatically flood prone. Given the floodplain location and development-related watershed threats, it is no surprise that Hurricane Katrina raised the waters of Turkey Creek. Heavy winds and rainfall, no municipal storm-water management plan, and poor related infrastructure combined to ensure the flooding of the North Gulfport and Turkey Creek neighborhoods. Many homes were destroyed or significantly compromised. Some families who had very little to begin with found themselves with even less; others, particularly renters, found the gates to their public housing complexes chained shut despite little to no sustained damage.

Places in the Black Belt of the South, such as the site of this chapter, are characterized by, among other things, a history of ownership of the best land by a comparatively small group of white families, with landlessness and embedded poverty widespread. Yet a closer look within the Black Belt reveals many historic towns and places that survive this time of gentrification, environmental degradation, and disinvestment. Established after the U.S. Civil War, these pockets of communities proudly dot the Black Belt in rural, semi-urban, and urbanized areas. This chapter examines the work of an advocate leader, Ms. Rose, in one of these places—the Turkey Creek and North Gulfport community.

The story of North Gulfport and Turkey Creek has come to be more widely known in community development circles since Katrina through the work of a diaspora of advocacy organizations partnering with the founder of the North Gulfport Community Land Trust, Ms. Rose Johnson. For years, Ms. Rose has largely been the de facto spokeswoman for the North Gulfport community. Born and raised in the community, she is a tireless organizer and advocate, her foremost concern securing this historic community, the land and the wetlands, because as she has said, "keeping the creek and keeping our community" are the same thing. In her widely heard advocacy narratives about the North Gulfport community, the land, and its history, she has often said that keeping the community is natural for her, that "it's what our ancestors did and it's what we must do now." Ms. Rose extends ideas of home to the community through an advocacy and narrative discourse, which she presents as rules and logic that frame the establishment of a land trust. She believes that the land trust will provide a lasting testament to the heritage and survival of the people of Turkey Creek.

Here, the evolution of Ms. Rose's life story in North Gulfport and her related community work helps guide the illustration of the diachronic connection between gender, race, and struggles about the meaning of place. This chapter examines the knowledge practices Ms. Rose uses, which are defined by racialized histories that create the unique sociospatial dialectic of Turkey Creek and convey a sense of the "social" as a spatial phenomenon. Understanding that some may dismiss Ms. Rose as an atypical community leader unrepresentative of similar places and people, I posit that establishing typicality is not this chapter's goal. Rather, I work from a different premise: exploring the intricacies of this particular story and its author allows us to examine a place most urban theorists ignore—the Deep South—and provides an opportunity to register the ways gendered histories and memories are critical platforms for understanding race and for engaging in spatial action.

Gender, race, or place attachment alone cannot sufficiently explain why a land trust model came to prominence in this historic black community. In particular, I am interested in the path-dependent factors that led Ms. Rose to legitimize this particular community strategy, factors found in the rules she presents that motivate her community action. These are founded on a historically racialized and insecure relationship to citizenship; on the way gender frames advocacy partnerships with white women; and on the gendered nature of church "telling" and "visiting," roles or repertoires of action that become mechanisms for maintaining the different scales of black space. These repertoires are narrative representations of place that reproduce rules and norms informed by a strong gendered regime.

Methods

This chapter interrogates a case study of place-maker Ms. Rose and her community development work in Turkey Creek and North Gulfport, Mississippi, in order to elaborate on the ways in which gender, race, and place reassemble the social (Latour 2005) and give meaning to black spaces.[1] I explore the idea that places are ideas maintained by people, and women in particular, through the use of local histories. These histories provide ways of knowing and repertoires of action, and these place repertoires can reflect informal (and gendered) community rules and norms for planning. To better understand redevelopment planning, we must understand how individuals develop identification and attachment to both social and physical places, the context under which their attachments are translated outward, and whether these identification processes themselves are structured by broader dominating narratives/narrators.

I have pursued the case study approach as an empirical inquiry that "investigates a contemporary phenomenon within its real-life context" (Yin 2003, 13), particularly because the boundaries between phenomenon and context are not clearly and immediately evident in this instance. I used an open coding method, creating labels to classify and assign meaning to pieces of information Ms. Rose shared with me, which helped me make sense of the data. Codes answer the questions, What do I see going on here? and How do I categorize the information? I eventually developed race, gender, place attachment, history, land, religion, and justice as my main codes (code names are abbreviated here).

Participant observation and informal, open-ended interviews occurred between November 2005 and July 2007, during which time I was a program officer leading the Katrina Women's Response Fund of the Ms. Foundation for Women, a national grant-making organization located in New York City. I developed relationships with many individuals in Turkey Creek and North Gulfport, and with Ms. Rose especially, and spent time working alongside community members in a variety of efforts As a mixed-race woman of color with African American, Korean, and Oneida heritage who at the time resided in New York, I carried certain privileges and ways of knowing that impacted how I understood events and practices. My perspectives were influenced by several factors, including feeling a level of familiarity with the Turkey Creek community because of my own African American roots in the South. As well, previous work on a 9/11 redevelopment portfolio at the Robin Hood Foundation had organized my thought models about redevelopment and disaster in the context of marginalized communities, and I was specifically in search of understanding what role, if any, women play in local recovery processes.

Materials I rely on from my participant observation and open-ended interviews include travel notebooks I kept in order to report back to my team in New York, documents Ms. Rose shared with me, informal memos and reports I created for the Ms. Foundation based on time spent with Ms. Rose, as well as recordings from a community radio project in the community that I helped organize in 2006. I also rely on analysis of the Turkey Creek and North Gulfport Neighborhoods Community Plan, a review of website material related to the land trust, and news reports, literature reviews, and personal reflections.

This research is based on narrative understanding, because the rationale and legitimization of the land trust occurred through a coherent system of practices, narratives, and tools. Ms. Rose's narratives tell us about the logic and ideologies she uses to develop and talk about the land trust; an ideology is defined as "an articulated and self-conscious belief and ritual system aspiring to offer a unified answer to problems of social action" (Swidler 2001, 96), and narration as a process of production that involves an agent who produces a story or text. Listening to narratives about people's lives helps the researcher figure out what a particular place meant or means, how the actor understands the world, and how the actor perceives causality for the unfolding of life.

There is broad agreement on the dualistic nature of narrative, that it has a "what" and a "way." The "what" of narrative can be viewed in terms of content about events, actors, time, and location. The "way" has to do with how the narrative is told: arrangement of stories, emphasis/deemphasis, or magnification/diminution of any of the elements of the content. The "what" therefore is the story, while the "way" is the discourse. Discourse has a strong relationship to the "glue" that Latour describes as signifying the social: "the social is not some glue that could fix everything including what the other glues cannot fix; it is what is glued together by the types of connections made" (2005, 5).

History as Context

In 1866, former slaves settled on a few hundred acres along Mississippi's Gulf Coast, most of which was undesirable swampland. Over time the area became a community place of related neighbors, or kinfolk, made up of farms and the first African American school in the Gulfport region; it became a safe place for African Americans after the Civil War. The brutality of this period and the struggle for citizenship and human rights in Mississippi have been well documented (Bond 2003; Dittmer 1995; Erenrich 1999; Payne 1995).

The late nineteenth and early twentieth centuries saw the Mississippi coast as the site both of a resort economy and of sawmill, turpentine, boat, and brickyard industries. Men from Turkey Creek and nearby districts sorted, shaved, trimmed, and treated longleaf pine to be used as railroad ties and utility poles. Women worked largely as domestics, traveling back and forth between large plantation and beachfront homes that by this time had resumed antebellum prominence as weekend and summer retreats for well-off southern whites (D. Evans, personal communication, May 2006). Land was security, passed informally from one generation to the next in shared models of inheritance often referred to as "heir property." Important community fixtures like the Mount Pleasant United Methodist Church and the Turkey Creek ball diamond, as well as several jukes, stores, and other small businesses preserved the settlements' distinct local fabric.

Today, the communities of Turkey Creek and North Gulfport are incorporated neighborhoods within Harrison County and the City of Gulfport, the second-largest city in the state of Mississippi. Military bases and casinos largely shape the local economy. From a planning perspective, major circulation routes are jeopardizing neighborhood sustainability, forcing residents to act on their concerns of being "priced and flooded out" (ibid.). In Gulfport, African American community leaders have formed a steering committee for community-based planning modeled on the Dudley Square Neighborhood Initiative in Roxbury, Massachusetts. They have formed relationships with out-of-town organizing entities and political and legal organizations, increasing their networks and framing capacities. In particular, the North Gulfport Community Land Trust and Turkey Creek Community Initiatives (led by the brilliant and strategic Derrick Evans) have taken the lead on planning the future of the area, focusing on community self-determination and on ecological and historic preservation, which together provide the basis for organizing since Katrina.

Resistance through Narrative

Ms. Rose Johnson is a retired middle-class black woman in her midsixties who stayed in her North Gulfport home during Hurricane Katrina along with her daughter, grandkids, friends, and neighbors. Born and raised in North Gulfport, Ms. Rose has very deep knowledge and place attachment to the community she has organized for so many years. It would be very difficult to find a single person in this community who does not know Ms. Rose or who does not claim some measure of relation to her. At one of my first meetings with Ms. Rose, in her home soon after the hurricane, I noticed that all her furniture was very clean despite the water damage to the floors and ceiling. I was pregnant, and we sat drinking tea, breaching the initial distance between us through talk of our experiences with pregnancy and the pains and joys I was yet to know. Afterward she showed me where she had used a sharp umbrella point to pop holes into the ceiling plaster to let some of the water out during Katrina. On countless later visits with her as she called on others, or as we enjoyed a church service or a fish fry, I saw the deference paid to Ms. Rose by every kind of resident (including Derrick Evans), as well as the consistency of her narrative throughout the visits. She tells the hurricane story like this:

> My daughter's van's brakes were bad and needed work; I couldn't leave my daughter and grandkids. When I realized it would be bad, we knew we were too late, we were there to stay. I wasn't afraid because I had been there when Camille hit. The only thing that frightened me was that it hovered for eight hours. We took the hit of the hurricane. But people forgot about us because New Orleans is so damaged.

Given the damage sustained by her community at large, Ms. Rose feels lucky.

> I was blessed. Our house was built out of cinderblock. My dad built it, fifty years ago. We lost all our shingles; water started to come in, maybe six hours into the hurricane. There were fourteen of us in the house, and you could hear the roof almost coming off.

Ms. Rose told me that the day after Katrina, she went to the Good Deeds Community Center to begin fulfilling her promise to God to preserve her community should she and her kin survive. She worked for twelve days straight, feeding the hungry, organizing care, and giving comfort. Ms. Rose says:

> We had no water. Every day, I would go home and bathe in a bucket. Despite having no running water, I would go to sleep and think, "I can't go again." Then I would be wide awake at 6 a.m. The people who came to eat were so thankful—just the look on their faces kept me going. God saved me and my entire family. I'm so grateful. My promise to him is that I will work the rest of my life to help others. It was just like Jesus on the water, when he said, "Be still." All of the sudden, everything was still. It was a spiritual thing I went through; it transformed me. I decided then, . . . the land trust will be my vehicle.

Over the course of two years and many visits to the region, I and others I brought with me listened to Ms. Rose talk about her memories of life in Turkey Creek and North Gulfport—asserting a specific history of place and people that she had readily available to her. Younger advocates such as Derrick Evans would defer to her, as would other men in our company, often as we sat outside or walked the neighborhood. As we walked, as we visited people, as we got groceries, as we gave other people rides to places, or as we sat outside, Ms. Rose shared vivid memories of what life was like when she was a child—fishing, picking blackberries, playing softball—all on the Turkey Creek. She often talked about the current state of things—children with no safe places to play, abandoned lots owned by speculative developers taken over by drug dealers. Ms. Rose is clear about the social reasons that the physical place of Turkey Creek provided safe haven to African Americans. She said that blacks were not permitted to swim in the Gulf of Mexico, so "we played in the Turkey Creek" and

> we also used it for baptizing and fishing. We didn't have to worry about white people driving by and yelling, "Niggers go home!" and throwing stuff at us. Nobody else wanted this area, so our parents and grandparents created these little neighborhoods and churches. We must save the Turkey Creek. It saved us.

Ms. Rose is instructive on how the now diminished wetlands used to absorb water and filter out the pollutants after a strong rain, when flooding was not as bad as it has been in her later years. She refers to the creek and the wetlands as the "the greatest filter in the world," saying "we were safer with the wetlands," both environmentally and socially.

It was a neck injury that conspired with fate to enlist Ms. Rose, a former employee of the Mississippi Department of Highway Patrol and Safety, into her current role of community and environmental activist. Her physical therapy program required that she walk every day in order to heal, and as she walked, Ms. Rose began to take in very deeply how her neighborhood was changing for the worse. No longer working outside the neighborhood full-time, she noticed, for example, that a wooden pallet company had moved into town and had become an eyesore, so she decided to fight to have it removed. With the backing of her church, as well as many signatures, she won that fight. Ms. Rose learned the intricacies of local bureaucratic policies and she tapped into the leadership of other mature black women leaders such as the locally elected House representative.

Eventually, her activism led Ms. Rose to the Sierra Club, or rather, led the Sierra Club to her. They wanted to know "what the black community thought" about what was happening to the watershed and needed an African American chair for the local chapter, and Ms. Rose says she needed the Sierra Club. She tells me that they sent her to chapter chair trainings, where she learned how to frame development issues in the context of environmental justice. Already armed with a historical narrative unique to her voice and moral ethic, Ms. Rose was soon seamlessly connecting environmental justice, unsustainable development, and gentrification, invoking history through her memories of North Gulfport. She turned to the question of real estate at the urging of a friend who pointed out that "there's white people buying up all our property and selling it back [to us]." Hearing this sentiment echoed through her church visits with others in the community, Ms. Rose felt she was on to something. Through her connections with longtime racial justice advocates like Gus Newport, as well as growing advocacy relationships from a sewer lines fight, Ms. Rose heard about the concept of land trusts and decided such a trust would be a perfect solution for her community. She often invoked God and said that the way to fight the temporary was to invoke the eternal. Forever practical, Ms. Rose theorized that any planning solution for her community needed to incorporate both affordable housing and environmental protection. With her authority as a longtime resident, Ms. Rose developed steadily into a sophisticated and aggressive public figure.

Such work by Ms. Rose finds confirmation in other studies by social movement scholars who have long observed that, on a global scale, women are consistently the first to both become aware of *and* to take action on environmental problems in their communities (Di Chiro 1992; Merchant 1996; Seager 1993; Stein 2004; Sturgeon 1997). Ms. Rose's analysis, intuition, and narrative also reflect what the disaster literature has established—that without proper collective or private tenure systems in place, overexploitation of resources and environmental degradation are thought to increase a community's vulnerability to disaster (Brown and Crawford 2006). With lived experience in mind, Ms. Rose began to organize and handpicked nine people to help her develop a vision for a local land trust:

> I picked people I knew I could work with and we created a mission "to protect the culture, historic character, and environment of the community." It honors our parents and our grandparents who worked so hard to raise us, to care for our families and the land, and they weren't treated well. This land is so sacred and deserves to be protected. It is my vision, my dream, to give people an affordable home on this land, so that they can have a part of the American dream, so they can raise their kids in a home, so they are here to protect the land.

In 2004, Ms. Rose went to her first land sale. She caught on to how it worked and bought five parcels of land with money "cobbled together from too many people to count." Eventually, the original black owners of those parcels, who had been unable to pay the back taxes, were able to buy their land back from her. Not long afterward, however, Katrina hit the Gulf Coast—turning the black community, once again, into what Ms. Rose calls an "invisible race":

> With a disaster, they reach to the top and start helping people at the top and nothing is left for the poor. African Americans are one of the most discriminated groups of people in the world. Katrina put a light on race, class, and indifference. People were treated like we live in the third world, and this is the richest country in the world. We were so disappointed in our federal government. They didn't show up in our community until October. It showed us what we knew: they don't value us; we have to do for ourselves.

After tending to the immediate needs of her community, Ms. Rose turned to the larger picture. To her, it was clear that developers were buying up land, taking advantage of the chaos brought by the storm. "There are a lot of greedy people," Ms. Rose says. "A lot of money is being made off Katrina." Her organization had developed a plan before the storm, but after the storm implementation became more urgent because of fears of an accelerated land grab. She had initially decided to start small: they were going to raise money through block parties to try to stop the prospectors, buy up the property, and then build affordable homes. Suddenly, however, after Katrina they found they had media attention, support, and partners they hadn't expected; they filed for 501(C)3 status and funders came forward, Ms. Rose says:

> People wanted to help. The nuns at Mercy Housing Corps, Healthy Builders, Youth Build, the Ms. Foundation for Women, and the Enterprise Corporation of the Delta—all were helping. In fact, I remember when you called us—right out of the blue. I thought, I remember when Gloria Steinem gave a shout-out to Mississippi women in something I read. I knew that you would understand this *whole place* is our home.

Now, several years after the storms and facing increasing health challenges, Ms. Rose remains committed to her goal of protecting African American communities and increasing their access to home ownership.

> I believe if you own a home, you take care of it and the place around it. But I'm also bringing my people together and fighting the vision people have of us. I want to make the community safe and attractive. I want to see my grandchildren living here . . . and I want your grandchildren to be comfortable visiting mine.

When you have lost everything, says Ms. Rose, you know how truly "home is where the heart is":

> Home is for spiritual things to happen, for storytelling about who did what back in the day, a place to be secure. After Katrina, people were not secure, people were lost in so many ways. I saw how important home is. You know, not just your four walls. This is a place for black people to protect themselves.

These reflections illuminate the relationship between people and place attachment, the ideal of home, which is always gendered, as it is separate from work, and its amorphous boundaries ("this whole place is our home") that shape community and we-ness. Here, home means a dwelling but it also represents relational space—a means for recognized space.

Place Attachment and the Church

To further contextualize Ms. Rose's story, I turned to some of the literature on place attachment. I found that much of it focuses on individual feelings and experience and has not placed these bonds in the larger sociopolitical or historical context in which planners and scholars should operate. In another dimension exist the community development and planning literatures, which while emphasizing the importance of community participation, voice, and empowerment, overlook the emotional and cognitive connection to place. Yet Ms. Rose's narrative illuminates how emotional connections and bonds can form the basis and motivation for community action. Despite the limited gender theorization, there exists interesting research on psychological adaptation and adjustment to extreme and unusual environments. Scholars have found that rewards from challenges met and overcome play a strong role in passion for place, a finding that clearly resonates with my observations.

Other aspects of the literature on place attachment focus on attachments that facilitate a sense of security and well-being through the definition of group boundaries and the stabilization of memories against the passage of time. A theory of place develops where place is shaped by centuries of symbolic investment in local qualities. De-Filippis (1999) elaborates "locality" (nexus of community, household, and workplace) as the scale of experience where "common sense" is formed by arguing that the state, as a codification of power relations, is one of the central structures in people's daily lives and that it is one of the primary arenas in which contests over which people's "common sense" get played out. A gendered lens may be interpreted from his nexus of locality, when, for example, we see that Ms. Rose engages the "state" historically through postemancipation narrative and connects a historically mediated relationship between state, people *in* place. This literature establishes place attachment, place character/identity, and sense of community (common sense) as resources for neighborhoods that require cultivation to withstand the social and economic forces that can lead to displacement through natural disaster, gentrification, segregation, or a combination of these.

The Church

The Mount Pleasant United Methodist Church operates as one of the loci of the Turkey Creek community. Ms. Rose describes the feeling of being in church after Katrina, when members—women in particular—characteristically used the community medium as an opportunity to report on who was where and on what was needed, information gathered through women's neighboring and visiting in the community:

> I'm guided by the divine spirit of God. I'm close to my minister and to praying. My minister knows that women are the backbone of the community. Praying and knowing God as I do, this work guides me. The greatest resource in the African American community is hope and our faith in God.

On almost every Sunday, the importance of protecting the environment and fighting gentrification is brought up sometime during service. This practice correlates with studies which show that church attendance strongly influences place attachment, encouraging membership in local organizations by enhancing personal leadership skills, creating social contacts, providing organizational resources for collective action, and strengthening solidarity (Barnes 2003; Harris 1999). Religion is understood as a mobilizer of African American political activism, reflecting a trend in the evolution of black churches in the U.S. South, where the 1950s saw a transformation of church missionary services into social service work—work done largely by women (Gilmore 1996).

Women's role of carrying this social gospel via pedestrian neighboring is a significant method for creating belonging and for being the dominant place planners. In fact, Ms. Rose's walking confirmed for her that despite her perception of neighborhood disorder, this was her "place," her home and community. Fenster finds a parallel in her work in Jerusalem: "Belonging and attachment are built on the basis of walking. A sense of belonging changes with time as these everyday experiences grow and their effects accumulate" (2005, 243). Fenster frames informal acts of belonging as springing from the casual daily encounters between people. Space is claimed through everyday acts of exchange of information about the spatial environment—"narratives of belonging." Women claim this space in their neighboring and visiting, transferring historiographies, narratives, and repertoires of place, memory, and belonging. Historical research in the South illuminates belonging through "home" as a political centerpiece of African American life: "While white political leaders kept their eyes on black men's electoral political presence and absence, black women organized and plotted an attack just outside their field of vision, . . . transforming church missionary societies into social service organizations" (Gilmore 1996, 226).

Conclusion

The land trust is Ms. Rose's way of institutionalizing and memorializing the histories of her community. Memory and place are gendered because of the process through which place making and attachment are created. Sandercock spatializes belonging and memory for us: "Memory, both individual and collective, is deeply important to us. It locates us as parts of something bigger than our individual existences. . . . Memory locates us, as part of family history, as part of a tribe or community, as part of city building and nation making" (1998, 207).

In the South and in this coastal Mississippi community, issues of representation have also been issues of citizenship and the struggle for power over space and place. This chapter offers an ecological model for understanding community development, diffusing cultural concepts across disciplines to contribute to debates on the impacts of gender, race, place, and history. Although research is needed to better illuminate the relationship between citizenship and the processes of place making, as well as what might be the community ramifications of using place- or heritage-based strategies for redevelopment planning, the struggle for black space cannot, I believe, be won without women.

Mia Charlene White is a doctoral student in the Department of Urban Studies and Planning at the Massachusetts Institute of Technology. Formerly, she was program officer at the Ms. Foundation for Women and the Robin Hood Foundation, and program associate at the Ford Foundation, focusing on nonprofit community development programs for women, communities of color, Indian country, and the immigrant diaspora. Her dissertation builds on this chapter's ideas about space and investigates collective approaches to housing tenure and spatial citizenship, with an interest in the political, racialized, and gendered social forces that shape it.

NOTE

1.   Latour provides a performative definition in which the social exists through the "group-making" efforts, ways, and manners. In other words, if the "dancer stops dancing, the dance is finished. No inertia will carry the show forward" (2005, 35).

REFERENCES

Barnes, S. L. (2003). Determinants of individual neighborhood ties and social resources in poor urban neighborhoods. *Sociological Spectrum, 23*(4), 463–497.

Bond, B. G. (2003). *Mississippi: A documentary history.* Jackson: University Press of Mississippi.

Brown, O., and Crawford, A. (2006). *Addressing land ownership after natural disasters—an agency survey.* Winnipeg: International Institute for Sustainable Development.

Buthe, T. (2002). Taking temporality seriously: Modeling history and the use of narratives as evidence. *American Political Science Review, 96*(2), 481–494.

Chatman, S. (1978). *Story and discourse: Narrative structure in fiction and film.* Ithaca, NY: Cornell University Press.

DeFilippis, J. (1999). Alternatives to the "new urban politics": Finding locality and autonomy in local economic development. *Political Geography, 18*(8), 973–990.

Di Chiro, G. (1992). Defining environmental justice: Women's voices and grassroots politics. *Socialist Review, 22*(4), 93–130.

Dittmer, J. (1995). *Local people: The struggle for civil rights in Mississippi.* Urbana: University of Illinois Press.

Erenrich, S. (1999). *Freedom is a constant struggle: An anthology of the Mississippi civil rights movement.* Washington, DC: Cultural Center for Social Change.

Fenster, T. (2005). Gender and the city: The different formations of belonging. In L. Nelson and J. Seager (Eds.), *A companion to feminist geography* (pp. 242–256). London: Blackwell.

Garber, J. A., and Turner, R. S. (1995). *Gender in urban research.* Thousand Oaks, CA: Sage.

Gilmore, G. E. (1996). *Gender and Jim Crow: Women and the politics of White supremacy in North Carolina, 1896–1920.* Chapel Hill: University of North Carolina Press.

———. (2002). *Who were the progressives?* New York: Palgrave.

Harris, F. C. (1999). *Something within: Religion as a mobilizer of African-American political activism.* Oxford: Oxford University Press.

Kundera, M. (1980). *The book of laughter and forgetting,* Michael Henry Heim, trans. New York: Harper Perennial Modern Classics.

Latour, B. (2005). *Reassembling the social: An introduction to actor-network-theory.* New York: Oxford University Press.

Merchant, C. (Ed.). (1996). *Earthcare: Women and the environment.* New York: Routledge.

Nelson, L., and Seager, J. (Eds.). 2005. *A companion to feminist geography.* London: Blackwell.

Payne, C. M. (1995). *I've got the light of freedom: The organizing tradition and the Mississippi freedom struggle.* Berkeley: University of California Press.

Rose, D. (1993). *Feminism and geography: The limits of geographical knowledge.* Minneapolis: University of Minnesota Press.

Sandercock, L. (1998). *Towards Cosmopolis: Planning for multicultural cities.* Chichester, UK: Wiley.

Sandercock, L., and Forsyth, A. (1992). Feminist theory and planning theory: The epistemological linkages. *Planning Theory, 7/8,* 45–49.

Seager, J. (1993). *Earth follies: Coming to feminist terms with the global environmental crisis.* New York: Routledge.

Steel, G. D. (2000). Polar bonds: Environmental relationships in the polar regions. *Environment and Behavior, 32*(6), 796–816.

Stein, R. (Ed.). (2004). *New perspectives on environmental justice: Gender, sexuality, and activism.* New Brunswick, NJ: Rutgers University Press.

Sturgeon, N. (1997). *Ecofeminist natures: Race, gender, feminist theory, and political action.* New York: Routledge.

Swidler, A. (1986). Culture in action: Symbols and strategies. *American Sociological Review, 51,* 273–286.

———. (2001). "Cultural repertoires and cultural logics: Can they be reconciled?" Paper presented at the American Sociological Association, Anaheim, CA.

Yin, R. K. (2003). *Case study research: Design and methods.* 3rd ed. London: Sage.

CHAPTER 20

Gender and the Landscape of Community Work before and after Katrina

Pamela Jenkins

It has been more than five years since the waters of Katrina receded. In that time, some of us from the diaspora have found our way home. It is bittersweet, our homecoming, filled with the loss of our old lives and hope for the community's return. Our voices sound the same, but the tenor is different. Across the country, we, as displaced persons, were making decisions about what to do, both as family and community members and as academics. None of the decisions were easy. We could not find our friends; some of us could not find our families. We began to contact each other and to think about what we could do in both our lives and our work.

This chapter is based on a set of conversations with women I have known for more than two decades. We worked with each other before Katrina on very successful projects and projects that were much more challenging. So, in a way, this is my story as well. Like many here, I lost my house and belongings in the flood. I was a nomad, living here and there, for nearly two years before coming back to my rebuilt home.

In this chapter, women from New Orleans reflect on their lives, Katrina, and their work. It does not describe the people who came in from the outside to organize and help but is the story of people who had been on the ground here for a very long time. Several years before Katrina, in 2002, a colleague (Alice Kemp) and I interviewed a diverse set of community activists. The goal of that project was to document how they thought about themselves in the community through both a gendered and racial lens. Then, after the storm, I began a series of observations, conversations, and interviews with community activists, most of whom had been part of the original research. Two of the women first interviewed have since died. Most of this group of women fled to higher ground; one did not. She stayed in an apartment building with her family for four days and then was evacuated to I-10, where she stayed until the bus took her to another part of the country.

I include the voices of these women from before the storm to add depth and understanding of the post-Katrina world. In these earlier interviews, they spoke most often of children, even though not all of them were involved in children's issues. Most of these women activists, ranging in age from their late forties to midsixties, have been in the field for all their adult lives. The shift in their understanding about their work after Katrina was not drastic, but a subtle linking of old work and new (Culley and Angelique 2003).

This chapter places their experience in concepts of motherwork and transformative work. Collins (1994) offers a conceptualization of women's work that includes motherwork. Deeply connected to their self-definition as women and mothers, women of color have always been "other mothers," functioning as an extended family. These women work for the survival of family life in communities where their family solidarity is constantly challenged by racism. Collins places motherwork at the "boundaries of the artificial dualities of public and private, family and work, the individual and the collective, and identity as individual autonomy and identity growing from the collective self-determination of one's group." Motherwork "recognizes that individual survival, empowerment, and identity require group survival, empowerment and identity. 'Work for the day to come' is motherwork, whether it is on behalf of one's own biological children, children of one's racial ethnic community, or children who are yet unborn" (Collins 1994, 59).

Collins's concept of the relationship between individual survival and group survival became an important aspect of how these women defined their work after the storm. As they framed their work before the storm about "work for the day to come"—for children to have better schools, health care, and safety—they began after the storm to add to that list and reshape their community. As Hurricane Katrina rushed to the Gulf Coast, other mothers were already at work figuring out how to get their families out. These communities of embedded networks, although fractured and spread across the country (Litt, forthcoming) struggle now to survive. In another sense, Mullings describes transformative work as the work that women do "to construct a space in which they can ensure continuity for themselves, their children and their communities" (1995, 133). Before the storm, this work in New Orleans was difficult; after the storm, the ability of women to construct a space or spaces to care for their families and their communities is an everyday struggle.

The Context of Disaster and Women's Work

In the face of the federal and state governments' inability and lack of will to respond in the days and now years after Katrina, nongovernmental and faith-based agencies still attempt to fill the void. These nongovernmental organizations were a critical part of New Orleans before the flooding. Church congregations and service organizations represented sources of community, neighborhood strength, and employment. New Orleans was home to a variety of secular and faith-based social service and grassroots organizations. Since the early 1980s, when significant federal funding for social programs slowed in New Orleans, there was a sense that the government wasn't to be counted on. Before Katrina, small nonprofits dotted the neighborhoods. The corner church might run an after-school program or an elderly activity center, often without much of an operating budget and dependent upon donated space and volunteer staff. After Katrina, many of these neighborhood and community places were not able to return.

Since the storm, I have documented the rebuilding work of local nonprofits and organizations. These organizations include local foundations, multifaceted organizations, battered women programs, day-care centers for children or adults, after-school programs, literacy programs, homeless organizations, a small neighborhood development organization, and a variety of congregations, from those of small neighborhood churches to those of megachurches. I have been in contact with a wide variety of women working in these organizations. Here, I discuss my conversations with fourteen women from foundations, general multilevel organizations, day-care centers, and small developmental organizations; eight are black women, and six are white. All hold professional positions at a variety of levels in the city; all but two had their homes flooded.

Faith-based and nonprofit organizations played a critical role in the immediate response and recovery after the flood. Initially, their work seemed connected with the dual concepts of "chronic corrosive processes" and "therapeutic interventions and processes" (Picou and Marshall 2007) in postdisaster New Orleans. After a disaster, factors are in place that can further tear apart a community (corrosive processes), while other factors aid a community in recovery (therapeutic processes). These organizations were trying to prevent further damage while healing the victims of the continuing disaster. Because this event was outside the normal disaster experience, the frame for understanding the role of nonprofits and faith-based groups shifted as well: understanding the work of the city after Katrina is to understand women's work.

The Work of Women

Women activists, black and white, in many ways dominated the caretaking work of the city before Katrina; there was so much work to be done, from organizing day-care centers to dealing with issues of domestic violence. Women involved in community work here faced many of the problems of any very poor urban area. What came up repeatedly in the original interviews was that they did not separate their personal lives from their work in the community, that is, they all linked their activism to their own lives. As well, White (2005) suggests that, especially for African American women, ties to family create opportunities and a climate for activism. While issues of class and race often divided communities of women, the need to be part of something larger was central to their lives, as the director of a small philanthropic project reveals:

> I think that always was the interest in the trite phrase of "giving something back." Well, I think that is very important because this community needs so much and I think there are a number of different knowledge bases that I have and so I can work on those and really give something back. If you see that you're in a place where you're going to live for some period of time, then I think it's important to have input into what that community is or can be.

This commitment to what the community can be is another way to say "work for the day to come." Another white woman who was in charge of an advocacy agency talks about her work before the storm: "I'm driven to hook up with like-minded people. I'm always looking for like-minded people. And if like-minded people get together, we can accomplish a lot. And so there's a sense of mission there of hooking up."

The view of giving back or finding like-minded people altered drastically in the storm. Many of us working in neighborhoods before the storm were concerned with racism, violence, and youth. It seemed to us, when we looked over the landscape of what was New Orleans, that the high level of violence and the threats to youth were underscored by racism. But we were hopeful: we thought if we just worked on prevention, on schools, on being inclusive at the table, that we might at least change the frame from despair to hope. A white woman reflects on her experience:

> The issue of violence is something that is just striking in terms [of] what you read in the paper about something and you think, What about the kids? Who is going to take are of who is left behind when a parent is killed, or a neighbor is host, or a kid at school is stabbed or something? We really tried to look at this from a whole breadth of the issues.

This woman's commitment to antiviolence work resulted in a collaboration to work on violence funded with both local and national money. This collaborative attempted to connect the local community and national funders to define the issue, strategize solutions, and implement the program.

A few national funders had historically been involved in New Orleans before Katrina, but millions of dollars were sent to the Gulf Coast through a myriad of sources after the storm. Katrina captured the imagination of national and international funding that led, for some organizations, to attention and monies never before possible. Some of the women became actively involved in connecting or even becoming gatekeepers of these new lines of funding. There was great variation in national funding. To one woman, the influx of national funding and her connection to these sources changed how she viewed her work; she became an integral part of many of the funding initiatives: "I was able to connect and represent New Orleans to a number of funders who were very receptive to New Orleans."

An African American director of a small nonprofit had a very different take on this outside funding. While she received some funds, they were never enough to support more than day-to-day existence. For her, the outside funding became too difficult to navigate, so she had to rely on older sources of funding. Over the years since Katrina, her conversations about these sources reflected a frustration that somehow she had been kept out of the larger loop of major funding. She describes a process of being at the table, thinking that she was part of something that would result in funding, only to be shut out of the process. Finally, in her latest efforts, she has connected with a supportive national funder.

Along with the money, people came to the Coast. The outpouring of people to help and advise threatened to overwhelm the tenuous return of residents. All of us were eventually contacted by outside individuals and organizations. Many of the groups came with financial and personnel assets. One African American organizer said that it took a while to figure out how to evaluate the help. Some of the organizations and individuals knew how to listen, she thought, but "others thought they had the solution and we [the locals] should sit back and listen." This relationship with national funders, both with monies and people, continues to be part of the new landscape of post-Katrina New Orleans.

The Work Transformed

This influx of funds and people transformed the community, including these women. Even before locals returned after the storm, the issues had changed irrevocably. For the first several weeks, most of us were stunned. We were trying to figure out where everyone was, what had survived, where our accounts were, what programs existed. The uncertainty of those first few weeks caused us to figure out ways to communicate. We began texting, finding each other on the Internet, and meeting in Lafayette, Shreveport, and Baton Rouge. The weeks turned into months while we still lived in suitcases, still trying to figure out how best to connect.

One of the women found a way back into the city to get her agency's checkbook so she could write checks. She met up with a family friend, a police officer who met her at the parish line and drove her to her office. She said that she felt obligated to pay her grantees even though no one yet had returned to the city: "I knew these small agencies were counting on this money when other sources were drying up."

After the storm, the big question for nearly everyone was, What is the work now? A white woman organizer with national connections captures it best for many of us: "The first thing I thought about immediately—what is going to happen to all these people that are strewn across the country?" The answer to this question haunts us to this day.

Subjects and Objects of the Recovery

The women interviewed are both subjects and objects of the recovery, a fragile position under which the ground continually shifts. Because 80 percent of the city flooded, few organizations or individuals were not directly impacted. This impact ranged from staff who lost their homes to agency buildings that were damaged or destroyed. The time frame of rebuilding homes and work stretched into days, weeks, and years. The earlier interviews with women who had grassroots connections foreshadow all of our experience with seeking assistance. A woman who advocated for public housing residents referred to applying for welfare in the earlier interview.

> So we all sit down and we coach them and we let them know. And there's one thing that we use all the time is you're going to them for help. No matter how demeaning the questions are, you need the help. So we say, take a deep breath, go in, answer the questions as honestly as you can, and get it over with. Once you leave it, if you need to scream or hit something, do it after you leave.

In her statement, we can imagine people standing in the welfare line and also all of us standing in FEMA (Federal Emergency Management Agency) and Red Cross lines after the storm. During the weeks and months following Katrina, we became, for the first time in our lives, advocates for ourselves (Fothergill 2003). We had to fight to get our FEMA rent monies, our insurance, and Road Home funds (monies given to homeowners to make up the difference between insurance payouts and actual damage costs). Many of the women interviewed were temporarily homeless and out thousands of dollars.

Another example of this foreshadowing of the Katrina experience comes from a woman, a former welfare recipient, speaking before the storm about those who wanted welfare reform:

> It's like society has developed this system that cripples you and now they're tired. So [society says] we're tired of feeding them now, we're tired of handing them stuff now, they're the ones that created this system.

Her description of attitudes about welfare reform could aptly illustrate the "Katrina fatigue" that communities and organizations reported almost immediately after the disaster. We heard people say: "Shouldn't they be okay by now?" What these women recognize is that the problems that came to the surface after Katrina had long roots in the community. While violence, schools, and poverty dominated the discourse before Katrina, these issues were exacerbated by the growing current problems of homelessness and the ongoing issue of mental health.

Homelessness and mental health certainly were integral in my conversations with these long-term activists. The organizations they work with are concerned globally with two groups—those who have come back to New Orleans and those who are trying to return. They are attempting to ensure that the infrastructure is rebuilt. For example, two of the women interviewed were part of the collaboration that created a website for information on rebuilding. Another aspect of their work is to bring back day-care centers for the working poor and working-class families. The storm altered many family ties, so the need for day-care centers increased. Others are rebuilding after-school programs, children's advocacy programs, and other educational programs.

The work of all the women and organizations contacted had altered in the last five years. After Katrina, work took place where it could. For example, one woman who funds mental health providers talked about how clinicians met with clients in coffee shops, at the mall, or under a tree. Beyond place, people, and funding, women tried to reconnect with the community in ways that match the changing landscape. While collaboration was often the preferred way of getting things done before the storm, it is now the *only* way in which things get done.

Concern for children and community are salient in the voices of these women, pre- and poststorm. This is a group of other mothers, black and white, who are recreating their networks in different ways. In the construction of space that will be safe for their families, these women relied on their old strategies, created new ones, and transformed their work. They are engaged, in Nancy Naples's (1991, 1992) terms, in their own civic lives.

Additionally, all these women are politically outspoken. Unlike the isolated groups that Putnam (2000) and others describe, these women are involved in their community at a variety of levels. Everyone in these conversations worked for the Obama campaign in some fashion. The link between civic participation and political activism is direct (Hays 2007) in their post-Katrina environment.

After the storm, the women changed. Their commitment grew deeper, now tinged with an understanding of how the tragedy unfolded. As one African American women stated: "In many ways, I am more cynical, a little bit bolder. Kind of what the hell. The worse has happened. . . . I might as well be stronger in some of the stances that I take in regards to work."

Mediated by Class and Race

Race and class issues were vividly demonstrated immediately after Katrina as we watched our friends and neighbors on television at the Superdome and Convention Center (Anderson 2006). Discourse around social class, especially after Katrina, was often framed as a contradictory set of thoughts and feelings. Many of the women lost their homes, and they rebuilt their home lives, as one said, "simultaneously as I did the community work." But no matter how difficult this was—deciding to tear down your home, moving seven or eight times, talking to insurance agents, the myriad of life's seemingly endless tasks of recovery—the women think of themselves as standing in privilege. To a person, they understood that their life circumstances did not stop their work of rebuilding the community.

As well, the lived experiences of race and racism have been central to the work of this group of women leaders in New Orleans. A college professor and activist who spoke of the difficult role of being black and teaching black and white students describes the dilemma not only in the classroom, but in community work:

> And added to this dilemma that I am black. And so you can tell that they're [white students] trying to say all they might say and yet what comes out is so loaded. And then black students, they're hesitant too because they are not sure if it's going to divide the other relationships they've had or they wonder why I'm not as conservative as they are because I should know better. One black student told me, she said, "You persist on these issues and I take aspirin before I come to your class because I know we're going to be in for it."

A white woman activist in child-care advocacy echoes the difficulty: "And then the other area of concern that I'm strongly attached to in the community is racism. And that—it's something that people don't want to talk about but it's so much there and it's so much of what is put on the necks of children and families."

Race was much discussed in New Orleans before Katrina; various groups met to talk about race relations, and a national organization is based here that trains on the issue of race. But Katrina brought the unresolved issues of race into stark relief. A male leader of one the most progressive groups in the city put it simply in public meetings: "Katrina is the new slavery." Others are not so outspoken, but one of the Africa American women said: "Part of the way that I can live in this city and do the work I do is not to think about it [racism]. If I allowed myself to think about it, I would have to leave." The racial discourse in this city has grown more complex since the storm and remains a constant, unresolved part of the city's landscape.

Final Reflections

Five year after Katrina, the women we originally interviewed are not the same. Their organizations, for the most part, are bigger and their work is harder. The floodwaters opened up a world of possibility in every aspect of their lives. The essential elements of all our work—funding, developing, and implementing programs—have changed. For example, instead of developing programs to create quality child care, many of these women first had to create a way to rebuild day-care centers. This meant funding for bricks and mortar, architects, and contractors.

Motherwork for the day to come has also taken on different dimensions. One of the women stated: "We have to learn to live our lives differently. We know we will have a normal life for nine months, but then through hurricane season, it will be chaotic. We have to think differently about the space and pace of our lives." Even in terms of disaster preparedness, she offers a new way to think about how to live in New Orleans.

The storm passed that morning and the floodwaters came. We have not resolved many of the issues raised here and race, class, gender, and displacement loom large. The closing and reformation of public housing, public schools, and the public hospital are not resolved. All those who speak here were displaced, all the agencies and businesses shut down for a period of time. To all appearances, the lives of these committed community "othermothers" stopped short. What did they do? They stood back up. This is our story—not yet fully written.

Practical Implications

As each of the women returned, she had to make decisions about what her life would be like in the New Orleans reshaped by Katrina. These women have been part of some of the major changes in New Orleans. The lessons learned from their experience might focus on how national funders discover and engage local leadership in a disaster. Some of these women connected with national leaders and funders, while others were never reached. As national groups discovered New Orleans, the effect of their funding and interest was uneven, partly because the city and much of is surroundings were empty after the storm. Few of the women profiled here went to centers of national decision making in Washington, D.C., or New York, but evacuated instead to places such as Monroe, Shreveport, or Amite, Louisiana.

The links between national leadership and people on the ground need to be strengthened and built long before a disaster or catastrophe occurs. Planning for future disasters should involve development of ongoing relationships and communication between national philanthropic leadership, national disaster leadership, and diverse local leadership. National funders need to recognize that their information about a community may not be complete either before or after an event; they will know about some groups, but they may discover other individuals and groups only by drilling deeper into community networks. The local community can build on already existing self-assessments to identify mechanisms to reach different parts of the community.

New Orleans is, in many ways, a small town; the activists involved in this study all know each other and will continue to work together in many ways. They can be catalysts for engaging the nation in a long-term discussion of how to organize around the needs of a community in chronic crisis as it shifts to a community in acute crisis. They have learned much about the possibility of recovery and betterment with and for women. What they know now about how their world changed is worth preserving.

———

Pamela Jenkins is professor of sociology and a faculty member in the Women's Studies Program at the University of New Orleans and a founding member of UNO's Center for Hazard Assessment, Response, and Technology. Her publications have focused on community responses to domestic violence, responses of Louisiana coastal communities to coastal erosion, first responders, faith-based communities, and the elderly in Hurricane Katrina.

ACKNOWLEDGMENTS

More than 1,400 people died as the storm surge battered the Gulf Coast and the floodwaters rose. Many died because the levees failed and, more insidiously, because no one came. As they waited for help, they died in attics, on bridges, and on patches of high ground. This chapter is dedicated to honoring those who died, many of whom were elderly and poor.

REFERENCES

Anderson, E. (2006). Inadequate responses, limited expectations. In E. Birch and S. Watcher (Eds.), *Rebuilding urban places after disaster* (pp. 193–201). Philadelphia: University of Pennsylvania Press.

Collins, P. H. (1994). Shifting the center: Race, class, and feminist theorizing about motherhood. In D. Basin, M. Honey, and M. Kaplan (Eds.), *Representations of motherhood* (pp. 56–74). New Haven, CT: Yale University Press.

Culley, M., and Angelique, H. (2003). Women's gendered experiences as long-term Three Mile Island activists. *Gender and Society, 17*, 445–461.

Fothergill, A. (2003). The stigma of charity: Gender, class, and disaster assistance. *Sociological Quarterly, 44*, 659–680.

GNOCDC (Greater New Orleans Community Data Center). (2009). New Orleans: Nonprofit Knowledge Works. Retrieved from *www.gnocdc.org/*.

Hays, R. A. (2007). Community activists' perceptions of citizenship roles in an urban community: A case study of attitudes that affect community engagement. *Journal of Urban Affairs, 29*, 401–424.

Litt, J. (Forthcoming). "We need to get together with each other": Women's narratives of "help" in Katrina's displacement. In L. Weber and L. Peek (Eds.), *Displaced: Life in the Katrina diaspora*. Austin: University of Texas Press.

Mullings, L. (1995). Households headed by women: The politics of race, class, and gender. In F. Ginsburg and R. Rapp (Eds.), *Conceiving the new world order: The global politics of reproduction* (pp. 122–140). Berkeley: University of California Press.

Naples, N. (1991). Just what needed to be done: The political practice of women community workers in low-income neighborhoods. *Gender and Society, 5*, 478–494.

———. (1992). Activist mothering: Cross generational continuity in the community work of women from low-income urban neighborhoods. *Gender and Society, 6*, 441–463.

Picou, S., and Marshall, B. (2007). Katrina as paradigm shift: Reflections on disaster research in the twenty-first century. In D. Bursma, S. Picou, and D. Overfelt (Eds.), *The sociology of Katrina: Perspectives on a modern catastrophe* (pp. 1–22). Lanham, MD: Rowman and Littlefield.

Putnam, R. D. (2000). *Bowling alone: The collapse and revival of American community.* New York: Simon and Schuster.

White, M. (2005). Familial influence in the autobiographies of Black South African and African American women activists. *Michigan Family Review, 10,* 27–44.

CHAPTER 21

Battered Women's Shelters in New Orleans

Recovery and Transformation

Bethany L. Brown

Two weeks before Hurricane Katrina, the director of the New Orleans Battered Women's Shelter was pondering the restructuring of its organization. She asked herself, "What would we do if the slate were wiped clean?" Soon after, Katrina did wipe the slate clean when dozens of businesses, organizations, homes, and institutions were inundated with water and/or burned. Among them was New Orleans Battered Women's Shelter (NOBWS), a residential shelter for survivors of abuse, which burned to the ground two days after Hurricane Katrina made landfall. The entire facility, and everything in it, was lost. Despite an almost complete lack of resources, three staff members who did not evacuate from the city and remained at their jobs sustained the organization with a deep sense of purpose and attachment to a mission to stop violence against women.

With the shelter reduced to a pile of ashes, these antiviolence advocates had to consider what rebuilding meant after the storm, for themselves and for the mission they cared for so deeply. They found that skills they had developed and strengthened through their everyday experiences helping survivors of violence were priceless after the storm. For example, one staff member who drew upon her crisis intervention skills observed: "We deal with hurricane victims every day under the guise of abused kids." Such skills, along with funding, staff and social networks, and a prestorm vision for change allowed NOBWS to take advantage of the "clean slate" to realize its vision of organizational transformation from a traditional residential shelter model to a Family Justice Center model, a place where a multidisciplinary team of service providers are all in one building to help expedite services.

The magnitude of Hurricane Katrina qualifies it as a catastrophe, something categorically worse than a disaster. Beyond all the numbers, though, Katrina resonates because it challenged our notions of what it means to be a so-called developed nation. Was this level of suffering really happening in the United States? Katrina also forced race and class to the center of discussions about emergency preparedness and response. Shortly after Katrina hit, Enarson (2006; see also David 2008; Jenkins and Phillips 2008) reminded us that it is women who rebuild; it is women who mend the social fabric of the communities disaster events so indiscriminately tear apart.

Drawn from a larger project examining response and recovery trajectories of three battered women's shelters in Louisiana after Hurricanes Katrina and Rita, this chapter captures a snapshot of the lived experience of one battered women's shelter in New Orleans and the innovation of the shelter as a driver of disaster recovery (Muhammad and Chaya-Chen 2009). Emergency planning for battered women's shelters is especially difficult because residents cannot join the exodus of disaster evacuees. Survivors of abuse are especially vulnerable during evacuation to losing the anonymity and protection a battered women's shelter provides; a woman could end up at a disaster shelter with her abuser. One of the biggest obstacles for battered women after a disaster is finding housing, because affordable housing is scarce. Federal Emergency Management Agency (FEMA) issues only one trailer per household, so there is no mechanism for a battered woman to leave an abusive household that has already received FEMA assistance to acquire her own housing.

Previous literature on disaster and violence against women shows that women are exceptionally vulnerable to violence after the disaster event (Enarson 1999). Thus, it is especially important for a battered women's shelter to recover and to continue offering services during a time when demands on organizations increase. Finally, understanding the recovery trajectory of a battered women's shelter leads to better thinking about how to restore the public service infrastructure for people beginning the long road of recovery.

When we look more closely at resources, beyond money and other tangible items, we learn that NOBWS has strengths and capacities that helped it survive the storm. To understand how NOBWS continued with its organizational mission while contending with a community-wide crisis, I use resource dependency theory as manifest in physical, economic, social, and human capital to highlight the resources of NOBWS that could be useful in planning for, responding to, and recovering from future events.

Gender, Disaster, and Battered Women Shelters

Marginalized groups are more vulnerable to disaster events because they lack access to resources such as transportation and are less able to anticipate, cope with, resist, and recover from disasters (Blaikie et al. 2004; Fothergill et al. 1999). Traditional gender roles, such as disproportionately serving as the primary caregiver for children and elderly parents, and unequal access to resources make women vulnerable to disaster in ways that differ from men (Enarson 1999; Enarson and Morrow 1998; Fothergill 1996).

The threat and incidence of domestic violence increase women's gendered vulnerability during disaster (Enarson 1999). Power and control are central features in the cycle of violence, and battered women often have few social networks, restricted transportation and employment opportunities, and controlled household resources (Dobash and Dobash 1998; Schecter 1998; Walker 1979). A disaster situation, which can have a severe impact on the survivor's social networks, transportation and employment opportunities, and household resources, can aggravate an already hazardous household environment (Enarson 1998, 1999; Honeycombe 1993; Jenkins and Phillips 2008). Survivors of abuse, then, are in crisis before a disaster strikes. Battered women's shelters were created to aid the most vulnerable while they were in a personal crisis, but not necessarily during a crisis such as a communitywide disaster.

The gender scholarship in social science research notes that organizational structures and practices are gendered (Acker 1994). Social justice advocacy jobs at non-government organizations (NGOs) are an occupational niche women most often dominate; these caregiving jobs are seen as women's work (Lorber 1994). Violence against women is often seen as a women's issue; because it affects only women, it is not perceived as a legitimate public health issue. In fact, the concept of violence against women entered public consciousness only in the late 1970s after centuries of belittlement (Walker 1979). Battered women's shelters were formed as collective, egalitarian, feminist organizations, a contrast to traditional bureaucratic, male-dominated workplaces. In bureaucratic, for-profit organizations, perceived as more credible, often the most powerful organizational positions are occupied by men (Acker 1994). A marginalized organization already under significant stress faces particular challenges not experienced by male-dominated occupational niches, such as difficulty securing funding, little inclusion in community planning, and limitations on the types of social networks the organization is able to build. NOBWS is an example of a marginalized organization because all the advocates working at the shelter at the time of Katrina were women. As a result, the resources of these battered women's agencies, such as experience and social networks, are largely unacknowledged.

Little in the literature focuses on how NGOs may understand a rapid onset crisis. Research using the Disaster Research Center (DRC) Typology has examined organizational response to disaster events, identifying different types of organizations in terms of tasks performed and structural arrangement (Dynes 1970). The typology cross-tabulates two dimensions (tasks and structure) to produce a fourfold typology of organizational involvement in disaster events in terms of tasks performed and structured arrangement (ibid.). Type 1, an established organization, performs the same tasks it usually carries out. Type 2, an expanding organization, undergoes change in structure during the emergency period while performing tasks similar to the ones it normally does. Type 3, an extending organization, retains its pre-event structure but engages in disaster-related tasks that are new. Type 4, an emergent organization, is a newly formed organization.

The DRC Typology is useful but oversimplified: organizational structures and tasks do not fall neatly into the identified categories. Each disaster produces a unique blend of organizational tasks and structure. NOBWS became an extending organization, because advocates extended their crisis intervention skills to the disaster-stricken community. Simply naming NOBWS an extending organization, though, does not fully capture the lived experience of the organization and its unique repertoire of resources.

Given the varying sizes of NGOs, insight can be drawn from the business preparedness and vulnerability literature on organizational process. What is known from this research is that disasters have different effects depending on the type, size, age, and location of a business, whether or not management owns or leases the property, and level of engagement in disaster preparedness activity (Alesch et al. 2001; Dahlhammer and D'Souza 1995; Tierney 1997; Tierney and Dahlhammer 1995; Tierney and Nigg 1995). A smaller organization is less likely to remain open following a disaster (Alesch et al. 2001; Webb, Tierney, and Dahlhammer 2002). Dahlhammer and Tierney (1998) also describe business size, financial standing, lifeline disruption, and size and scope of disaster event as significant predictors of disaster recovery. This research would predict that battered women's shelters, as small, nonprofit, feminist organizations, would be highly vulnerable and therefore significantly impacted by a catastrophic event. Recognizing the capacities at the organizational level that battered women's shelters carry, such as crisis intervention skills and extensive social networks, challenges conceptions that women-gendered and marginalized organizations are just vulnerable, helpless, and passive victims desperate to be rescued (Enarson and Morrow 1998).

Methodology

In this study of a battered women's shelter in New Orleans, Louisiana, after Hurricane Katrina, I relied on several information sources to explore the shelter's response to and recovery from the storm, including semi-structured interviews, document analysis, and direct observation.

For a pre- and postevent comparison, I examined documents that detailed general information about the shelter, other nonprofit organizations, and community outreach, as well as organizational charts, disaster plans for local and state levels, violence statistics, and minutes from the Domestic Violence Advisory Committee (DVAC). More than thirty hours of direct observation of staff members' activities shed light on the organizational culture.

Twenty respondents, six of whom were employed before the storm, participated in this study—all women, ranging in age from twenty-two to fifty-five years old. Most were black. Almost all had a background in social service or nonprofit work; the director and assistant director worked in the for-profit sector before shifting to nonprofit work. Academics at local universities, policy makers, and legal and public health advocates were also interviewed. Again, all respondents outside the shelter were women, pointing to the gendered character of social service work.

The Organizational Context

For a survivor of abuse, evacuating the shelter and the impacted zone after disaster might provide a window of opportunity for escape from her abuser (Enarson 1999). At the organizational level, Hurricane Katrina may have provided a window of opportunity for New Orleans Battered Women's Shelter to implement organizational change. Previous research has shown that organizational changes are more likely to occur when changes were considered before a disaster event (Nigg and Tierney 1993). In other words, the adoption of a disaster recovery strategy that incorporates change may reflect a change that was on the cusp of occurring before the disaster.

Data revealed that there was a vision for organizational change at the New Orleans Battered Women's Shelter before Katrina struck. Staff thought that the services they were delivering were incomplete. One of the advocates who stayed behind was familiar with the history of the battered women's movement in the United States and felt NOBWS was falling prey to the conflicts and structural evolution many shelters were experiencing. As the number of battered women's shelters had grown, questions about organizational structure had arisen; some shelters worked collectively, congruent with the movement's goals, while others organized themselves hierarchically (Schecter 1999). As more shelters and programs received government monies and social work became more professionalized, shelter workers slowly started to call survivors of abuse "clients." More attention was given to individual counseling for women and less to peer support. Simultaneously, a growing number of women living with crises other than violence had sought refuge at battered women's shelters. The director at NOBWS felt the agency had moved away from what a battered women's shelter was supposed to be and do, which led her to question the organizational model:

> Part of the problem was that the residential shelter was very institutional, which is what I think happens and I think part of what—Coming from a social work background (I have a business and social work degrees, I have both), what I perceived happened from the battered women's movement is that we all opened up these shelters and trying to do all this work for survivors and what happens is—and this is the population that we had prior to Katrina—you end up serving . . . chronic, very needy populations of women who have chronic histories of homelessness, histories of substance abuse, and histories of mental illness, and our shelters are not equipped.

NOBWS staff thought that they were not reaching battered women because other social problems such as homelessness and substance abuse were, as one noted, "stealing the show." The social context of New Orleans, with a large homeless population and a mental health system already in crisis, contributed to the organizational assessment before Katrina. This growing population of women living with multiple crises made NOBWS question whether it was really reaching survivors and victims of abuse. The battered women's movement embraced the ideology that violence against women affected all women, while the practical response—battered women's shelters—reached only a specific segment of women (Murray 1988). The literature shows that violence against women cuts across all social barriers (Dobash and Dobash 1998; Schecter 1980; Walker 1979). Yet NOBWS was seeing more women who required extensive case management in the traditional service provision model rather than in the empowerment model of battered women's shelters. Thus, shelter advocates felt that they needed to question what was and what had been happening organizationally at NOBWS over the years.

In New Orleans, service delivery for survivors of domestic violence was historically fragmented, much as the criminal justice system was. In a foreshadowing of the post-Katrina reality, just two weeks before the storm the director of NOBWS in collaboration with a private foundation brought together local domestic violence experts to reframe how to provide service to these survivors.

When Katrina Hit

Battered women's shelters often have to implement an evacuation plan during non-disaster times because a survivor may suddenly be in a lethal situation if her batterer discovers the location of the shelter. Upon intake, a survivor devises a safety plan with advocates at the shelter, identifying someone (usually family or friends) or a sister shelter with whom she can stay if she has to evacuate the shelter. If evacuation is necessary, the shelter has a stock of bus tickets—or money to purchase a bus ticket—for the survivor, and one of the advocates transports her to the bus station.

However, after Katrina hit, the bus station had closed by the time advocates were able to get survivors at NOBWS there. The director then commandeered a yellow school bus to drive the twenty-four women north to a sister shelter where they could stay or catch another bus to get to family. After Katrina's landfall, three staff members remained in New Orleans at the shelter to try and make sense of the catastrophe that took everything. Despite the devastation, a deep sense of purpose and attachment to the organizational mission allowed them to help the disaster-stricken community. These women demonstrated their accumulated crisis skills by debriefing survivors of Katrina. Their experience with routine crises was an intangible and invaluable resource that withstood the destruction of the storm. As the director explained: "You look into the faces of the other two staff people who are there with you. Shell-shocked, these women are. And you are too. But you see traces of determination, lines that seems to say, 'We came back because we are survivors and we believe in survivors. We came back to reclaim our work and our lives.'"

Without such dedication and leadership, NOBWS as an organization might not have survived the storm. Yet, the staff who stayed with their city and shelter found the people who needed them. NOBWS advocates went to the FEMA disaster relief center, community centers, and mental health centers to hand out cards informing people that NOBWS was there to help. They partnered with congregations and synagogues. In other words, they found alternative ways to reach victims (Jenkins and Phillips 2008). When NOBWS advocates learned that a local organization was functioning as a disaster relief center, they set up a card table there with pamphlets and contact information to let the community know that services were available.

Meanwhile, NOBWS had to change its methods of reaching survivors in the moment while it was so drastically transforming to the Family Justice Center model. Immediately after the storm, NOBWS began offering outreach services from a house across the street from the charred remains of the residential shelter. At this point, weeks and months after the storm, NOBWS was using outreach strategies reminiscent of the early movement activities. Immediately after the hurricane and still to some degree, the traditional mechanisms for referral were diminished. The domestic violence detectives in the New Orleans Police Department were reduced from eight prestorm to three. The municipal, state, and civil courts were not in their prestorm buildings and not conducting trials for a long period of time. Nearly one-half the hospitals were closed and other public health facilities were barely open.

During this time, the shelter had to rethink how to provide services and what type of services to provide. The ability to shelter battered women in the traditional way no longer existed, so the staff created alternative methods to provide services. For example, through trial and error, the shelter implemented a three-tier system for housing that included hotels, temporary housing, and more permanent apartments. Each stage of this housing represented a step away from the top-down supervision and individual focus of traditional sheltering.

The losses NOBWS suffered were glaringly evident for many months after the storm; the transitional house out of which they were operating needed major structural work, and space was extremely limited. The ideological closeness of the staff was mirrored in their newfound but necessary physical proximity as multiple staff members shared what had been bedrooms in an old house. Interviews revealed that needs were dynamic. Countless obstacles prevented them from securing funding. Yet NOBWS leadership was committed to restoring some semblance of normalcy. Immediately following the storm, funding increased because of an influx in disaster monies. However, preexisting lines of funding were disconnected and, as one advocate explained, "lots of our contracts were up for grabs." The State of Louisiana halted funding for social service organizations because in order to be eligible, an organization had to demonstrate provision of services. Given that the mass exodus from New Orleans meant a lack of survivors seeking services, NOBWS was technically ineligible for state funding.

During the organizational transformation, others in the local antiviolence community ideologically resisted the change. The director of NOBWS explained: "Other [battered women's shelters] feel this paradigm shift is threatening because it challenges what people fought for during the women's and battered women's movements." Suddenly, friends and colleagues who were once intimately part of a social network, who shared the mission of helping survivors of abuse, were in conflict. During this early period, NOBWS, now calling itself New Orleans Shelter Healing Center, functioned as a walk-in antiviolence service center. From the perspective of New Orleans Women's Shelter, this model more closely matched battered women's shelters that were based on self-help and empowerment, which staff members perceived was more successful in supporting feminist ideologies.

Because the Healing Center techniques departed so drastically from traditional methods of reaching survivors of abuse, the program became of interest to the federal Office of Violence Against Women (OVW). The director of the center, on an unrelated trip to Washington, D.C., was able to meet with the then head of OVW and make the case for organizational transformation. Not only her ability to convey the struggle and the triumph of this organization but also her vision for organizational change to better reach survivors of abuse led OVW officers to travel to New Orleans and engage in the process of building a unique Family Justice Center (FJC) model—an all-inclusive antiviolence support center that houses a multidisciplinary team of antiviolence experts representing many segments of the social and criminal justice system. Services that were once scattered become proximate to each other, reducing the number of visits survivors must make and the number of places they must go to access and receive support. The result can be a better-served and more empowered survivor of abuse.

The philosophy of Family Justice Centers across the country is based on the assumption that in colocating agencies, service provision for battered women increases. National best practice points to the need for multi-institutional collaboration, as women who are victims of domestic violence may ask for help in various places, such as neighborhood clinics and hospitals, and welfare and child protection offices (Schecter 1999). Once the key players were identified, the New Orleans Family Justice Steering Committee opened the local FJC on August 29, 2007—in six months rather than the usual year and half it takes most FJCs to open.

New Orleans Battered Women's Shelter Resources

Among the intangible resources of NOBWS as a collective were the skills of each advocate. Using theories of human capital, we can better understand the effectiveness of the skills and experience of each battered women's organization as useful both in a disaster situation and in routine community capacity building. The knowledge and skills belong to the individual, but an organization may be wealthy in human capital as a whole through its employees (Becker 1975). Human capital here refers to training, formal and informal education, and experience. A critical resource in a nonprofit organization is its staff and their experience with routine crisis.

With the potential for a crisis every day, staff and the shelter need to be ready for anything. As one staff member explained: "We all have to put on different hats at any given time because you never know what's going to walk through that door. We're dealing with crisis all the time." Therefore, advocates are prepared to improvise, or to react quickly and in the moment (Mendonca 2001). The shelter staff, along with those of other nonprofit organizations working with crisis situations, improvises daily, which allows them to do so in a crisis like Katrina.

Experience with crisis situations and familiarity with a lot of people involved with nonprofit organizations were critical resources the shelter used in response to the storm. Knowing a lot of people in a specific sector or having extensive networks is known as social capital (Bourdieu 1985; Putnam 2001). The people in nonprofit organizations are profoundly involved in the community, and community involvement is an indicator of social capital. Before the storm, the shelter had cultivated rich community involvement over many years by working to help survivors of intimate partner violence. Often, survivors of abuse also need help from other nonprofit organizations. Over time, this group effort and interaction creates the kind of social networks on which the shelter was able to capitalize during and after the storm. As one staff member explained: "We interact with all types of social service organizations." Social capital encapsulates the notion of "it's who you know," and for the battered women's shelter, "who you know" enables the collective organization to help save women's lives. For example, one staffer explained that because she knew an employee at a local hospital, she could—in an emergency—send a survivor of abuse to the hospital to stay for a short time.

Yet NOBWS lacked vertical, or bridging, social capital with organizations outside the human and social service network, arguably the result of an organizational-level glass ceiling (Morrison, White, and Van Velson 1994). These organizations may perceive women's organizations as less credible and domestic violence as not a legitimate public health issue. Some research indicates that this credibility gap makes it difficult for women's organizations to build vertical links (Foster and Meinhard 2005). The organizational exclusion of NOBWS was evident during Hurricane Katrina: the shelter's local expertise and crisis experience went unacknowledged and untapped by organizations not associated with human and social services.

Yet NOBWS held key information about the local population that could be useful in both disaster and nondisaster times. As one staff member who had been working in the social service sector for decades noted: "It is impossible to work with women from abusive situations and not deal with mental illness issues, or substance abuse issues, or even issues of homelessness, because it goes hand in hand." As Schecter (1999) notes, many survivors come to shelters with more issues than exposure to violence. National and local experts agree that some survivors of violence also deal with serious mental health issues, substance abuse problems, or chronic homelessness. This was certainly the case at the shelter before Katrina, when NOBWS staff provided services to a diverse population with a wide-ranging set of complex needs.

Conclusion

NOBWS staff members' experience with antiviolence advocacy, as well as their widely applicable skill sets and social networks, were invaluable resources that helped shape the recovery path of the organization. Yet women's work of this kind is systematically excluded from emergency planning and policy. NOBWS is excluded from formal disaster planning because their resources are not identified as valuable. In the disaster context, the formal emergency-response organizations are not the only stakeholders. These battered women's agencies, too, are resource stakeholders. Other established organizations can benefit from the resources these battered women's organizations possess, such as knowledge of the local area and population. The skills and knowledge base these organizations employ for the everyday crisis of abuse may in fact be useful to groups and organizations that are traditionally involved in disaster issues (Wilson 1999).

One staff member who lived through Katrina explains: "Recovery is another disaster." As we move through the five-year anniversary of Hurricane Katrina, New Orleans is living through this recovery. The lack of available social services, in addition to the fact that severely impacted citizens—not only battered women—are still working through the recovery, has created the need for need for long-term case management. Policies should enable advocates to follow survivors of both the storm and abuse through the long road of recovery. In addition to long-term case management, organizations in impacted areas should be working to build alliances with other agencies in the community, which would increase knowledge and awareness about the resources available to battered women (Schecter 1999). As more constituents become aware and involved, there will be greater commitment to addressing the public health crisis of abuse and serving individuals who suffer from other social problems. This may help shatter the organizational glass ceiling that battered women's organizations experience and may also foster an integrated community response (Schecter 1999).

Bethany Brown is an assistant professor in the Department of Criminal Justice at Loyola University, New Orleans. She was selected a Public Entity Risk Institute national fellow and received the Samuel H. Prince dissertation award. Her areas of expertise are social vulnerability and disasters, and organizational perspectives involving community-based groups in disaster planning, response, and recovery

ACKNOWLEDGMENTS

I gratefully acknowledge my coauthors, Pamela Jenkins and Tricia Wachtendorf, and their contributions to an earlier version of this chapter, which appeared in the *International Journal of Mass Emergencies and Disasters* under the title "Shelter in the Storm: A Battered Women's Shelter and Catastrophe" (August 2010).

REFERENCES

Acker, J. (1994). Gendered institutions: From sex roles to gendered institutions. *Contemporary Sociology, 21*, 565–569.

Alesch, D., Holly, J., Mittler, E., and Nagy, N. (2001). *Organizations at risk: What happens when small businesses and not-for-profits encounter natural disasters.* Fairfax, VA: Public Entity Risk Institute.

Astley, W. G., and Van de Ven, A. (1983). Central perspectives and debate in organizational theory. *Administrative Science Quarterly, 28*, 245–273.

Becker, G. (1975). *Human capital.* New York: Columbia University Press.

Berg, B. (2004). *Qualitative research methods for the social sciences.* Boston: Allyn and Bacon.

Blaikie, P., Cannon, T., Davis, I., and Wisner, B. (Eds.). (2004). *At risk: Natural hazards, people's vulnerability, and disaster.* 2nd ed. New York: Routledge.

Bourdieu, Pierre. 1985. The forms of capital. In J. G. Richardson (Ed.), *Handbook of theory and research for the sociology of education* (pp. 241–258).

New York: Greenwood.

Bureau of Justice Statistics. (2003). *Crime data brief, intimate partner violence*, 1993–2001. Data file. Retrieved from *bjs.ojp.usdoj.gov/content/intimate/ipv.cfm*.

Coleman, J. (1990). *Foundations of social theory.* Cambridge, MA: Belknap Press of Harvard University Press.

Dahlhammer, J., and D'Souza, M. (1995). Determinants of business disaster preparedness in two U.S. metropolitan areas. Preliminary paper no. 224. Newark: University of Delaware Disaster Research Center.

Dahlhammer, J., and Reshaur, L. (1996). Business and the 1994 Northridge earthquake: An analysis of pre- and post-disaster preparedness. Preliminary paper no. 240. Newark: University of Delaware Disaster Research Center.

Dahlhammer, J., and Tierney, K. (1998). Winners and losers: Predicting business disaster recovery outcomes following the Northridge earthquake. Preliminary paper no. 243. Newark: University of Delaware Disaster Research Center.

David, E. (2008). Cultural trauma, memory, and gendered collective action: The case of *Women of the Storm* following Hurricane Katrina. *NWSA Journal, 20*(3), 138–162.

Dobash, R., and Dobash, R. (1979). *Violence against wives.* New York: Free Press.

————. (Eds.). (1998). *Rethinking violence against women.* London: Sage.

Dynes, R. 1970. *Organized behavior in disaster.* Lexington, MA: D. C. Heath.

Enarson, E. (1998). Through women's eyes: A gendered research agenda for disaster social science. *Disasters, 22*, 157–173.

————. (1999). Violence against women in disasters: A study of domestic violence programs in the U.S. and Canada. *Violence against Women, 5*, 742–768.

————. (2006). Women and girls last? Averting the second post-Katrina disaster. Understanding Katrina: Perspectives from the Social Sciences (Social Science Research Council website). Retrieved from *www.understandingkatrina.ssrc.org*.

Enarson, E., and Morrow, B. H. (Eds.). (1998). *The gendered terrain of disaster: Through women's eyes.* Westport, CT: Greenwood.

Foster, M., and Meinhard, A. (2005). Women's voluntary organizations in Canada: Bridgers, bonders, or both? *Voluntas, 16*(2), 143–159.

Fothergill, A. (1996.) Gender, risk, and disaster. *International Journal of Mass Emergencies and Disasters, 14,* 33–56.

Honeycombe, B. (1993). Special needs of women in emergency situations. *Symposium: Women in Emergencies and Disasters.* Queensland Bureau of Emergency Services. Brisbane: Queensland.

Jenkins, P., and Phillips, B. (2008). Battered women, catastrophe, and the context of safety after Hurricane Katrina. *NWSA Journal, 20*(3), 49–69.

Leonard, R., and Onyx, J. (2003). Networking through loose and strong ties: An Australian qualitative study. *Voluntas, 14*(2), 189–203.

Lorber, J. (1994). *Paradoxes of gender.* New Haven, CT: Yale University Press.

Mendonca, D. (2001). Improvisation in emergency response organizations: A cognitive approach. PhD diss., Rensselaer Polytechnic Institute.

Morrison, A., White, R., and Van Velson, E. (1994). *Breaking the glass ceiling: Can women reach the top of America's largest corporations?* New York: Basic Books.

Muhammad, H.-Y., and Chaya-Chen, H. (2009). On the lived experience of battered women residing in shelters. *Journal of Family Violence, 24,* 95–109.

Murray, S. (1988). The unhappy marriage of theory and practice: An analysis of a battered women's shelter. *NWSA Journal, 1*(1), 75–92.

Nigg, J., and Tierney, K. (1993). Disaster and social change: Consequences for community construct and affect. Preliminary paper no. 195. Newark: University of Delaware Disaster Research Center.

Patton, M. (2001). *Qualitative research and evaluation methods.* 3rd ed. Thousand Oaks, CA: Sage.

Putnam, R. D. (2001). *Bowling alone: The collapse and revival of American community.* London: Simon and Schuster.

Quarantelli, E. L. (1998). Disaster recovery: Observation on what it means, success and failure, those assisted, and those assisting. Preliminary paper no. 263. Newark: University of Delaware, Disaster Research Center.

Schecter, S. (1980). Women and male violence: The visions and struggles of the battered women's movement. Boston: South End Press.

———. (1999). New challenges for the battered women's movement: Building collaborations and improving public policy for poor women. National Resource Center on Domestic Violence. Retrieved from *www.NRCDVPublications/BCSDV/Papers/BCS1_col.pdf.*

Tierney, K. (1997). Business impacts of the Northridge earthquake. *Journal of Contingencies and Crisis Management, 5*(2), 87–97.

Tierney, K., and Dahlhammer, J. (1995). Earthquake vulnerability and emergency preparedness among businesses in Memphis/Shelby County Tennessee. Preliminary paper no. 233. Newark: University of Delaware Disaster Research Center.

Tierney, K. and Nigg, J. (1995). Business vulnerability to disaster related lifeline disruption. Preliminary paper no. 223. Newark: University of Delaware Disaster Research Center.

Wachtendorf, T., and Kendra, J. (2004). Considering convergence, coordination, and social capital in disasters. Preliminary paper no. 342. Newark: University of Delaware Disaster Research Center.

Walker, L. (1979). *The battered woman.* New York: Harper and Row.

Webb, G., Tierney, K., and Dahlhammer, J. (2002). Predicting long-term business recovery from disaster: A comparison of the Loma-Prieta earthquake. Preliminary paper no. 328. Newark: University of Delaware Disaster Research Center.

Wilson, J. (1999). Professionalization and gender in local emergency management. *International Journal of Mass Emergencies and Disasters, 17*(1), 111–122.

CHAPTER 22

Listening for Gender in Katrina's Jewish Voices

Judith Rosenbaum

In communities and households around the globe, Jewish women play central roles in creating, expressing, preserving, and transmitting Jewish identity and Jewish history. Oral histories and family narratives capture these roles, helping Jewish women speak for themselves and to future generations about their work and contributions, which often go publicly unrecognized. The aging of the Holocaust generation has brought particular urgency to oral history and memoir projects. Women's historians and scholars of the Holocaust have documented through survivor narratives and other memoirs how gender norms and women's life experiences created unique vulnerabilities but also helped women during the Holocaust cope in ways that were not available to men (Goldenberg 1996; Gurewitsch 1998; Tec 2003). Striving to build and sustain a sense of family under duress, they sometimes made survival possible. Though one cannot compare the scale of suffering, Jewish women's Holocaust experiences have parallels in their refugee experiences in the wake of the Katrina disaster, in the passionate commitment women made to their family and community, all the more precious when jeopardized by catastrophe—man-made, natural, or both.

After the Gulf Coast storms, the American Jewish Women's Foundation was among the first to reach out to affected communities, both through Jewish women's networks and through partner organizations such as Oxfam America, the MS Foundation, and GROOTS (Grassroots Organizations Operating Together in Sisterhood). To understand this history and capture its lessons, Jewish experiences of Katrina and its aftermath were sought out and archived in *Katrina's Jewish Voices* (*katrina.jwa.org*), an online collection of the Jewish Women's Archive, a national nonprofit organization devoted to chronicling the stories, struggles, and achievements of Jewish women in North America, and an oral history project of the Jewish Women's Archive and the Goldring/Woldenberg Institute for Southern Jewish Life (*www.isjl.org*) (Jewish Women's Archive 2011).

A Calamity of Place and People

When Hurricane Katrina struck New Orleans and the Gulf Coast, it brought in its wake physical devastation on an unprecedented scale and a massive dislocation of residents of all races and socioeconomic levels. It also brought about the devastation of a Jewish community that had been nearly 250 years in the making.

On the eve of Hurricane Katrina, the Jewish community of the greater New Orleans metropolitan area included ten thousand residents (many of whom had several generations of local family roots), 1,300 students at Tulane University, and an additional 250 individuals scattered across the Mississippi Gulf Coast. Members of the New Orleans Jewish community were important contributors to the cultural, economic, and philanthropic life of the city and were served by a broad range of Jewish communal organizations, including eight synagogues, two day schools, two vibrant Jewish community centers, and an active Federation. Jewish women played central roles in community leadership, serving, for example, as presidents of five synagogues (C. Wise, personal correspondence, June 16, 2007; Goldring/Woldenberg Institute 2006).

Much of the attention paid to the Katrina catastrophe has rightly focused on the woefully inadequate local, national, and federal response, and the current need for support to restore the physical infrastructure of the communities (and especially the African American community) dislocated or destroyed by the storm. But a secondary casualty of the catastrophe is the loss of community history and documentation of the diverse experiences and responses of those who lived through these historic events.

The Jewish Women's Archive, in partnership with the Goldring/Woldenberg Institute of Southern Jewish Life, conducted eighty-five in-depth oral history interviews with members of the Jewish communities of New Orleans, Baton Rouge, and the Gulf Coast. This oral history project captures the rich and complex stories of the Jewish communities of New Orleans and the Gulf Coast, documenting a wide cross-section of these communities, with particular attention to gender, generation, affiliations, and Jewish identities. The collection presents a unique opportunity to analyze the gender dynamics at play in the communities' varied experiences of Katrina and its aftermath.

This chapter examines the oral histories and their stories of evacuation, migration, resettlement, and communal rebuilding, with particular attention to how gender roles and expectations shaped women's areas of concern and responsibility within their families and their communities during experiences of relocation and return. I analyze women's roles in the community during the course of the disaster and recovery efforts, and how men and women, in narrating their stories, reflect on their experiences and the meaning of these traumatic historical events.

Gender Themes in Jewish Women's Hurricane Stories

The experience of Katrina began with loss of control, as people tracked the hurricane's approach to New Orleans and later watched as the city filled with water that destroyed homes, businesses, and community institutions. This loss of control was further exacerbated by the dislocation of evacuation and the breakdown of most usual means of communication with friends and family. While the difficulty of dealing with loss of control was a nearly universal theme in the oral histories, the men and women interviewed described their approaches to managing this experience in different terms. The female interviewees focused on how they used their social networks and mobilized their networking skills to track down friends and family members, and to find shelter and other basic needs. They created e-mail lists, used text messaging, and when local technology failed them, called friends and relatives in other cities to ask them to use their cell phones and Internet connections to help locate people.

At first, they explain, these activities were primarily focused on emergency response, and the picture they paint is one of anxious but efficient activity. Roselle Ungar, who became the interim director of the Jewish Federation of New Orleans after Katrina, evacuated to Houston with her husband and son. On Tuesday, one day after the storm, she went into high gear, tracking the New Orleans Jewish community from the Federation office in Houston as well as arranging for the evacuation of her mother's nursing home in New Orleans and finding an apartment for her family. She recalls that

> starting that Tuesday morning, I started working sixteen-, twenty-hour days, just doing search and rescue with the Federation staff that were with us in Houston. It was very stressful, but very helpful, because I felt productive. I felt I was doing something. I wasn't just sitting or obsessing on the news, which was heart wrenching enough. . . . My husband and son kept reminding me that first week, because I would come back, exhausted and strained and stressed, and I'd talk about everything I did that day, and they looked at me and said: "You don't get it. We don't have that. We don't know what to do. We're watching television. We're sitting here and we're looking."[1]

Ungar experienced her gendered organizing instincts as a form of salvation. Lainie Breaux had given birth the week before Katrina and had to evacuate without her newborn, who remained in the hospital because of a breathing problem. When the levees broke, she lost touch with the hospital and did not know where her son had been taken. She explains:

> I am an active person, I am hands-on. So we got the phonebook out. We called Red Cross. That didn't help. We called everybody. . . . We were calling every hospital in the five states we could dream up. . . . I just need a course of action, and I'm going to go that direction, and if I get stuck I'm just going to change my direction and have as much control over it as I can, because I can't sit here and not do anything about it.[2]

The women interviewed detail how, even when the immediate emergencies had resolved, they continued to rely on their networks to recreate social support structures. The daughter-in-law of Bluma Rivkin, wife of the Chabad rabbi at Tulane, had evacuated with a large e-mail list, which came in handy in the early days after the storm to track people down and make sure everyone in their community was safe. In the following months, the women of the community reconnected in other virtual ways, maintaining a monthly study group by phone, for example, and creating a Yahoo group to stay in touch.[3]

This is not to say that Jewish men did not rely on their social networks. They most certainly did, but the networking they describe is primarily in service of their businesses—locating and reconnecting with business colleagues and employees. When describing their immediate coping strategies, the men interviewed were also likely to mention making early return trips to the city to check on their homes and businesses. Most of the men who returned permanently to New Orleans did so earlier than the other members of their families so that they could throw themselves completely into the work of reconstituting their business lives and begin the reconstruction of their homes.[4]

While men focused on rebuilding their businesses, women described investing equal amounts of energy in the rebuilding effort, turning to community activism in both volunteer and professional capacities. Madalyn Schenk, president of the board of the New Orleans Center for Creative Arts and board member of the New Orleans Center for Science and Math Education, captured these parallel gender roles in explaining the reason she and her husband returned to the city: "We're here because we have a role to play; . . . my husband is in a construction business and I'm in the business of helping get these, getting the fund-raising done, helping these schools get on their feet."[5] Each was essential to the rebuilding of the city.

This gendered distinction between business work and community work in part reflects traditional roles that label business as a male domain and communal activities (often volunteer) as women's work. But it is also important to note that Jewish women's leadership after Katrina took place not only in the more traditional context of women's organizations, but also in the mainstream (Jewish and non-Jewish) communal institutions. Additionally, these female lay leaders played crucial roles in encouraging and supporting the male professionals of these institutions to return to their jobs, often urging male professional leadership to return to New Orleans from their evacuation locations so that they could get back to work in earnest.

Ruth Kullman, the president of Touro Synagogue, became the central source of support for her congregation and for her rabbi, who remained in Houston through the end of November 2005. Immediately after the storm, she reports, she was "primarily dealing with the synagogue issues, where was everybody, was everybody safe, trying to start making a list and identifying locations where congregants were. And then getting executive committee members together, trying to get phone numbers, trying to bring people together on the phone to see what we were going to do about the synagogue, was the synagogue okay." Part of this work involved supporting Rabbi Andy Busch, who was new to town. Ruth says: "I really felt that it was my responsibility to try and take care of him; . . . let's make decisions together, you don't have to take all the responsibility, . . . who do I know in Houston who could be helpful to you, just to be somebody to bounce things off and ask. . . . So that I felt was really what I needed to do, to be there for the synagogue."[6] Rabbi Busch reported that the "added comfort in this is frankly the way Ruth Kullman dealt with all of this as our president. . . . Ruth as president really carried a fair amount of this load . . . in terms of hand-in-hand really having to make sure the finances were there and make some decisions and deal with some things and just reassure us."[7] At the time of the interview, more than one year post-Katrina (November 2006), Ruth still felt "my main responsibility beyond my family is to make sure that Touro is as healthy and prosperous and thriving as possible while I'm president through this transition period."[8]

In Baton Rouge, where the Jewish community devoted its resources to rescuing and supporting its New Orleans counterpart, Jewish professionals and volunteers came together two weeks after the storm and formed what they called the Kitchen

Cabinet. The kitchen in question belonged to Donna Sternberg, a lay leader in the Baton Rouge community who knew right away that "I didn't need to be taking care of a stranger in my home, it was more important for me to be where the meetings were taking place, to be part of the brain trust that was organizing and making decisions and raising money and whatever it took to put this together." While some of the male federation professionals and volunteers went to New Orleans to rescue Torah scrolls from flooded synagogues and schools, Sternberg joined forces with Sandy Levy, director of the Jewish Endowment Foundation of New Orleans (and president of Temple Sinai), as well as Allan Bissinger of the Jewish Welfare Federation of New Orleans and Howard Feinberg of United Jewish Communities, to develop a partnership between the New Orleans and Baton Rouge Federations and the Endowment Foundation. Sternberg recalls that

> we sat in the kitchen for, I'd say, from eight o'clock to probably six o'clock at night. . . . And by the end of the day we had put together a plan for office, for staff, for all manner of computers and copiers and fax machines, for activities that would be needed, for apartments, for funding for Hillel, for the youth, for—as I said, for staff, for programming for the elderly. All kinds of aspects of organizing a community, which would be managed jointly by a board or a committee selected from the three agencies. And we asked for $1 million and by the middle of the next week that had been approved.

She explains their success very frankly: "I'm a good listener and I have a lot of contacts and I realized very quickly that without a plan it wasn't going to happen. And so we sat down and we made a plan." Donna also organized and chaired the Disaster Relief Fund, raising almost $400,000 in a matter of days through her broad network of contacts.[9]

The roles Jewish women played in their communities drew on their organizing skills and contacts, but in narrating their experiences they also referred to their sense of family and nurturance. Sandy Levy captured both these impulses in describing how her work during the aftermath of Katrina solidified her professional position and amplified her sense of family connection to the community: "I feel like a mom there trying to take care of my staff, to take care of the community to the extent that I can. I certainly feel as though I'm a senior member of the professional Jewish community in New Orleans . . . and now I feel like I'm the mom, so to speak."[10] Jackie Gothard, first female president of the Orthodox Beth Israel congregation, explained that her commitment to her role was in part "standing up for the capacity of women to do this job, of the capability of women to do this job," but also declared that "my drive is more family rooted."[11]

The sense of community as family was heightened by the overwhelming response of the national Jewish community to the Katrina crisis. Within hours of the storm's devastation, national and local Jewish institutions across the country began to organize and collect money and supplies for New Orleans residents, and communities that received evacuees mobilized their resources to welcome New Orleans Jews, providing free housing, furniture, clothing, and school tuition. (Jewish communities around the country also offered their physical labor, coming in groups throughout the months—and years—that followed to help in the city's rebuilding efforts.)

While this communal response provided much work for Jewish women who took leadership roles in managing the outpouring of support, it also put many who were used to being on the giving end in the position of accepting community help, rather than offering it. A striking theme in these oral histories is the discomfort Jewish women felt when forced by circumstances to be on the receiving end of *tzedakah*, charitable giving.

Roselle Ungar recounted her experience collecting her check from the Red Cross:

> They had this long line. And they had this woman, this Red Cross volunteer. And she was working the line. She was entertaining. She was visiting with people while they were waiting in line to fill out their forms. . . . This volunteer comes up to me and she goes, "How are you doing?" And I looked at her, and I burst into tears, and I said: "No, no, no. This is wrong. I'm supposed to be you. I'm always the one who works the line. I'm the volunteer that always talks to people, keeps them company, makes them feel good." And I just burst into tears, and I said: "I'm not supposed to be standing here. I'm supposed to be you. There's something wrong with this picture." And she put her arm around me, and she said: "It's really okay. It's okay." I said: "You know, I'm the one who writes the check to the Red Cross. I'm the one who—I've never been on this side." And it was very, very uncomfortable.[12]

Bluma Rivkin captured her feelings about accepting help in one simple phrase: "It was torture."[13] Her discomfort with this role was so strong that she did not elaborate but immediately moved on to explain how they very quickly mobilized to help others. The prevalence of this discourse within the interviews likely stems from women's direct experience as providers of assistance, as well as their role within their families as the ones who directly received storm-related aid—they were more likely to be waiting in the Red Cross line, for example.

Legacies

This project raises the question, Do people at moments of crisis transcend their socialization or rely more heavily on the skills they have cultivated? The answer here is both: they draw on their socialized skills but put them to work in some new contexts—for example, women drew on their skills as communal leaders in mainstream organizations to help in the storm recovery.

There is much still to be determined about how Jewish women's roles in the aftermath of Katrina will impact their place in their (much smaller but, by their reporting, tighter) communities going forward. One example—that of Roselle Ungar, who served as interim executive director of the Jewish Federation of New Orleans when the male executive director chose to remain in Houston after the storm, but who was not hired to fill this position permanently—suggests that their essential work has not been fully appreciated or fully integrated into the fabric of the reconstituted, post-Katrina community. But the relationships forged among women who worked together during and after the storm—for example, the female presidents of the three Reform synagogues in New Orleans, who overcame the traditional rivalries of their institutions and have continued to collaborate with one another as they rebuild their communities—may yet provide models that will change the shape of the New Orleans Jewish community and the City of New Orleans itself.

Judith Rosenbaum is director of public history at the Jewish Women's Archive. She received her PhD in American civilization from Brown University. The recipient of a Fulbright fellowship to Israel, she has taught women's studies and Jewish studies at Brown, Boston University, and the Center for Adult Jewish Learning at Hebrew College. She is currently editing an anthology on contemporary redefinitions of the "Jewish mother."

ACKNOWLEDGMENTS

This chapter would not have been possible without *Katrina's Jewish Voices*, an oral history project of the Jewish Women's Archive and the Goldring/Woldenberg Institute of Southern Jewish Life. Thanks also to Jayne K. Guberman, who led the *Katrina's Jewish Voices* project and helped me think through many of the ideas in the chapter.

NOTES

1. Oral history of Roselle Ungar by Rosalind Hinton, August 30, 2006, Metairie, LA, 79. All oral histories cited in this chapter are drawn from the *Katrina's Jewish Voices* collection of the Jewish Women's Archive and the Goldring/Woldenberg Institute of Southern Jewish Life.
2. Oral history of Lainie Breaux by Rosalind Hinton, September 27, 2006, New Orleans, LA, 30.
3. Oral history of Bluma Rivkin by Rosalind Hinton, October 12, 2006, New Orleans, LA.
4. Oral history of Allan Bissinger by Rosalind Hinton, August 3, 2006, Metairie, LA; oral history of Joel Brown by Rosalind Hinton, October 23, 2006, Metairie, LA; oral history of Michael Ferrand by Rosalind Hinton, November 1, 2006, New Orleans, LA; oral history of Steve Kupperman by Rosalind Hinton, September 8, 2006, New Orleans, LA.
5. Oral history of Madalyn Schenk by Rosalind Hinton, July 25, 2006, New Orleans, LA, 56.
6. Oral history of Ruth Kullman by Rosalind Hinton, November 8, 2006, New Orleans, LA, 14–15.
7. Oral history of Andrew Busch by Rosalind Hinton, August 2, 2006, New Orleans, LA, 38–39.
8. Oral history of Ruth Kullman, 34–35.
9. Oral history of Donna Sternberg by Rosalind Hinton, November 28, 2006, Baton Rouge, LA, 16, 24; oral history of Sandy Levy by Rosalind Hinton, October 3, 2006, New Orleans, LA; oral history of Allan Bissinger.
10. Oral history of Sandy Levy, 91.
11. Oral history of Jackie Gothard by Rosalind Hinton, September 20, 2006, Metairie, LA, 78.
12. Oral history of Roselle Ungar, 29–30.
13. Oral history of Bluma Rivkin, 42–44.

REFERENCES

Goldenberg, M. (1996). Lessons learned from gentle heroism: Women's Holocaust narratives. *Annals of the American Academy of Political and Social Science*, 548, 78–93.

Goldring/Woldenberg Institute for Southern Jewish Life. (2006). New Orleans, Louisiana. In *Encyclopedia of Southern Jewish Communities*. Retrieved from *www.isjl.org/history/archive/la/new_orleans.htm*.

Gurewitsch, B. (Ed.). (1998). *Mothers, sisters, resisters: Oral histories of women who survived the Holocaust*. Tuscaloosa: University of Alabama Press.

Jewish Women's Archive. (2011). *jwa.org*.

Katrina's Jewish Voices. (2011). *katrina.jwa.org/*.

Tec, N. (2003). *Resilience and courage: Women, men, and the Holocaust*. New Haven, CT: Yale University Press.

CHAPTER 23

Building Coalitions and Rebuilding Versailles

Vietnamese American Women's Environmental Work after Hurricane Katrina

Gennie Thi Nguyen

During coverage of Hurricane Katrina's dramatic devastation, the media helped shape the story of racial inequality between blacks and whites but ignored the sizable Latino population, various Native American tribes, the oldest Filipino community in North America, and others (Bond 2007). Vietnamese Americans were among the ethnic groups whose experiences during and after the storm the media did not initially cover. During the disaster, members of the Vietnamese American community in New Orleans relied largely upon other Vietnamese Americans in the region and across the nation, and they returned to their homes more quickly than members of surrounding communities did. In summer 2007, nearly two years after the storm, Versailles, a Vietnamese American enclave of seven thousand in New Orleans East, had a 95 percent return rate but faced different and at times additional challenges compared to surrounding communities. I want to caution, however, that higher and earlier rates of return do not reflect a simple success story for this Vietnamese American community. Its members still struggle with language access, cultural competency, low income, access to adequate health care and education, a high murder rate, absence of working street and traffic lights, and a nearly nonexistent levee system that would protect them from future storms.

The Vietnamese American community faced additional challenges in the post-disaster recovery when the massive Chef Menteur landfill, a site expected to hold one-third of storm debris from the city of New Orleans, opened soon after the storm and in close proximity to their homes. Both women and men of this community actively struggled to close the Chef Menteur landfill, but Vietnamese American women operated quite differently from the men by strategically using their gender and ethnicity (e.g., their identities as women of color and Asian American women) to build coalitions. The women sought to find commonality in multiple points of oppression with others dealing with similar environmental and social issues during the recovery efforts. It is important to note that the women working on these issues spanned generations. This chapter addresses the role of second-generation Vietnamese American women in organizing their community to close the Chef Menteur landfill following Hurricane Katrina, specifically how and why the coalitions built in part by these women worked across class, gender, and racial lines.

Methodology

I used participant observation, which requires the researcher to be immersed in the research setting—and many cultural anthropologists live in the communities they study for extended periods of time, observing and participating in the local customs and rituals. Born and raised in the Versailles community, I returned after Hurricane Katrina and spent eight months participating in and observing the community's recovery. In addition, I conducted nine in-depth interviews and countless informal conversations with Vietnamese American women living in Versailles during summer 2008. All the women I interviewed share the political identity of Viet Kieu, that is, Vietnamese living overseas. This identity implies that they or their family fled Viet Nam after its reunification after 1975 for various reasons, which include opposing the rule of the North Communist government, fear of persecution due to involvement with the U.S. government, and fear of religious persecution. Four of the women interviewed represent the first generation, born between 1940 and 1965 in Viet Nam. Five of the women interviewed represent the second generation, born between 1965 and 1990 in the United States or very young when they first moved to the States.

Generational comparisons help guard against a linear view of history by not comparing periods or historical events but instead recognizing that each historical era has its own problems, issues, and actors (Werner 2004). Additionally, this method situates actors and cultural factors within historical eras and does not assume a timeless culture. It helps measure and observe how culture changes over time, especially when two historical eras vary widely (ibid.). Therefore, the category "Vietnamese women" here needs an intergenerational analysis that considers the differences between women who came of age during and after the Vietnamese Civil War, the American war in Viet Nam. This conflict is one of many suffered by the Vietnamese people, including the Japanese wars, Viet Nam's revolutionary war, the First Indochina War (with the French), the Second Indochina War (involving the United States), and the Third Indochina War (with the Chinese).

Background of the Vietnamese American Versailles Community

The Vietnamese American community of Versailles is part of a broader migration of Vietnamese people who left their homeland in response to specific political-economic realities and politics. Hurricane Katrina was a tragic experience for everyone who endured it, but for Vietnamese Americans, the storm also raised memories of past experiences of suffering, loss, and dislocation. For some generations in this group, the separation of North and South Viet Nam in 1954 forced them to migrate as a community for the first time from North to South Viet Nam. The fall of Saigon in 1975 uprooted them again, forcing a second migration from South Viet Nam to the United States, where many eventually settled in New Orleans. Hurricane Katrina threatened to become a third major experience of uprooting, community displacement, trauma, and extensive material loss for this group of people.

As a result, their beliefs and values—shaped by historical events—affected the kinds of communities they established and some of their collective ideas about the role of government in their lives. In interviews with journalists after Katrina, many Vietnamese Americans recalled devastating memories of the Viet Nam War, which was a vital presence that shaped the Versailles community's responses to Katrina. Trieu Giang, a Vietnamese American woman stated: "They came here with empty hands. Suddenly they lost everything they worked so hard for. And then that puts them in a really tragic shock" (Tang 2005). Referring to the history of Versailles as a community, Father Vien, a priest of Mary Queen of Viet Nam Church [Maria Nu Vuong Viet Nam] in Versailles, stated: "For many of our people, they have been displaced twice in their life prior to this—from North to South Viet Nam, South Viet Nam to here. They are well experienced in it" (Chen 2007). Before they arrived to New Orleans, many Versailles residents were connected through Catholic villages in North Viet Nam; in the early 1990s, for example, approximately 60 percent of Versailles's adult residents originated from the North Vietnamese bishoprics of Bui Chu and Phat Diem (Airriess 2002). Similar religious connections bind the community in New Orleans East. About seven thousand Vietnamese Americans live within a one-mile radius of the Mary Queen of Viet Nam Church.

Before Katrina, 31 percent of Versailles residents lived in poverty, compared to 18 percent of the larger New Orleans area and 12 percent of the U.S. population. The median household income for Versailles residents was about $31,000, compared to approximately $35,000 for New Orleans residents and almost $42,000 for the larger population of Americans. Furthermore, only 52 percent owned their homes, compared to approximately 62 percent of residents in New Orleans and 66 percent of people in the United States. Lastly, only 12 percent of Versailles residents twenty-five years old and older had earned a bachelor's degree, compared to 19 percent of the New Orleans population and 26 percent of Americans (Airriess 2008).

Thirty years after Viet Nam's reunification in 1975, Hurricane Katrina devastated the Versailles community and its surrounding areas. In just a few days, thirty years of work at rebuilding their lives were lost, as destructive winds and floodwaters destroyed their material belongings. The extent of the destruction varied in Versailles—many businesses along the higher ground near Chef Menteur Highway had minimal flooding, but many houses stood in up to nine feet of floodwater. At least one elderly woman died because she lived alone, was not fluent in English, and was not told to evacuate. Vietnamese Americans who immediately returned to their homes after the storm came in small boats.

Many fled to Houston and Dallas, where other Vietnamese Americans were waiting with help and supplies. While many New Orleans residents waited out the storm at the Superdome in New Orleans or the Astrodome in Houston, many Vietnamese Americans relied on the community's regional and national social networks. A number took refuge in Houston's Hong Kong mall, owned by a Vietnamese American man. A handful of Vietnamese Americans people were in the Superdome, as indicated by some of my interviews, but they stayed together and did not allow anyone to go anywhere alone in the Superdome. Others, like my family, relied on nearby relatives in the surrounding areas. Thus, cohesion rooted in ethnic identity and past experiences of disaster kept the Vietnamese American community afloat during this disastrous time.

By the first week of October 2005, Father Vien, head of the Vietnamese American Catholic church in Versailles, returned with three hundred parishioners. By mid-October, five hundred Versailles residents signed a petition asking Entergy, the local electric provider, to provide power to the community (Strange 2006). Nearly one-fourth of the residents had returned to Versailles by late January 2006 (Hill 2006). About ten months after the storm, in June 2006, 90 percent of Versailles residents had returned and 25 percent of Vietnamese American businesses had reopened (Airriess et al. 2008). Meanwhile, only 10 percent of pre-Katrina businesses in New Orleans had reopened (ibid.). In fall 2006, a year after the storm, only 44 percent of New Orleans's prestorm population had returned (Vu et al. 2009). The data show that the residents of the Versailles community were returning sooner and at higher rates than residents of surrounding communities.

After Hurricane Katrina, the City of New Orleans created the Bring New Orleans Back Commission, which had the daunting task of beginning to plan for the rebuilding of the city. In one of the first city council meetings after the storm, the Vietnamese American population packed the room. As city officials explained the rebuilding process, the residents of Versailles realized that their community was not even represented on the map that was provided for the presentation. In fact, from the recommendations of the Urban Land Institute, the city had proposed to make their community into green space, without prior discussion with the community. This was just one of the struggles the community faced when residents returned. Another threat, one almost in their backyards, proved equally threatening.

The Race of Gender and the Gender of Race in Environmentalism

Hurricane Katrina has been called one of the worst environmental disasters in U.S. history, producing 20 million cubic yards of debris across ninety thousand square miles in Louisiana, Mississippi, and Alabama (Luther 2006). An estimated 96 percent of the debris, or 17.8 million cubic yards, was found in Orleans, St. Bernard, St. Tammany, Washington, and Plaquemines Parishes (Bullard and Wright 2009). In the midst of the recovery, questions soon arose about the location of debris dump sites. According to Robert Bullard and Beverly Wright: "What has been cleaned up, what gets left behind, and where the water is disposed of appear to be linked to more political science and sociology than to toxicology, epidemiology, and hydrology" (2009, 26). This statement proves true for New Orleans East neighborhoods, including the Versailles community, because of the controversy surrounding the proposed Chef Menteur landfill.

Environmental racism is key to the larger analysis of Katrina because of the question of returning home, but additionally, of returning home to a safe and sustainable environment. African Americans in the Lower Ninth Ward are among the best known of the communities that faced environmental racism before and after the storm, but the story of environmental racism—and the resistance to it—goes well beyond the Lower Ninth Ward to include the struggles of Versailles residents in New Orleans East.

Environmental racism manifests in at least two ways in the Katrina recovery efforts: first, where recovery efforts were and were not prioritized, and second, where authorities dumped or did not dump storm debris. More specifically, Benjamin Chavis Muhammad defines environmental racism as the "racial discrimination in the de-liberated targeting of ethnic and minority communities for exposure to toxic and haz-ardous waste sites and facilities, coupled with the systematic exclusion of minorities in environmental policy making, enforcement, and remediation" (Bullard 1993, 15). Environmental racism goes beyond the poisoning of air, water, and soil: it is embed-ded in discriminatory practices, policies, and procedures; it accumulates over many years, and links pollution, toxic waste, and race (Checker 2005). Addressing these matters is known as environmental justice, which combines environmentalism and social justice (Bullard 1993).

To understand the fuller picture of environmental racism and environmental justice, we must look at how gender and race are linked in environmental concern. Research shows that women and minorities have a similar pattern of concern for the environment (Bord and O'Connor 1997; Flynn, Slovic, and Mertz 1994; Kalof, Dietz, and Guagnano 2002; Mohai and Bryant 1998; Taylor 1989). In addition, the perceived gender differences in environmental concern are modified by race. For ex-ample, Krauss examined the different perceptions of white, African American, and Native American women involved in toxic waste protests. White women defined en-vironmental justice as rooted in socioeconomic class issues; women of color linked environmental justice to race instead of class. While African American women con-nected environmental justice to jobs, crime, and other social justice issues, Native American women found that environmental justice was "bound up with the sover-eignty of the indigenous peoples" (Krauss 1993, 260). As these examples show, race and gender cannot be separated when addressing issues of environmental racism.

The Chef Menteur Highway Landfill: Vietnamese American Women Organizing in Their Communities

As the Versailles community returned and began to rebuild after the storm, residents began to notice dump trucks filled with hurricane debris regularly entering the com-munity. An executive order by Mayor C. Ray Nagin, the Louisiana Department of Environmental Quality, and the U.S. Army Corps of Engineers had granted initial permits to Waste Management, Inc., to reopen and operate the Chef Menteur High-way landfill in April 2006; the landfill had been open before Katrina and was then reopened. Soon after, the government and private companies began dumping toxic debris into the unlined landfill. To the surprise of Versailles residents, the landfill, which was to hold more than one-third of the Hurricane Katrina debris from New Orleans, was located less than a mile from the community.

Although government officials insisted that the debris was harmless, geological analysis proved that toxins from the landfill were already contaminating the ground-water that flowed into the canal (Kemp 2006; Pardue 2006) that many residents used to irrigate their gardens. These gardens produce vegetables, which residents sell in the local market (Do 2007). Toxins such as arsenic, chromium, and copper can leach from treated lumber, and hydrogen sulfide gas is emitted from deteriorating gypsum drywall; furthermore, household chemicals, paint, batteries, and other toxic debris were dumped into the unlined landfill (Lydersen 2009; Pardue 2006). Government officials made several claims about the safety of the Chef Menteur site. First, they asserted that the risk of toxic materials at the site was insignificant and that the materials were sorted to keep hazardous waste from entering the landfill. Second, they insisted that protective liners were not needed for construction and demolition (C&D) materials because they are cleaner than other rubbish (Eaton 2006). Federal laws do not require C&D landfills to have protective liners; however, federal laws do require municipal landfills to be lined, since they are expected to contain hazardous household waste (Bullard and Wright 2009).

Despite governmental claims that the landfill was safe, a report to Congress shows that disaster debris from the storm were mixed, because the separation of harmful materials such as oil, pesticides, paints, and cleaning agents is difficult or nearly impossible (Luther 2006). In extensively flooded areas, containers holding household hazardous waste may have leaked and contaminated the surrounding debris that would otherwise usually be safe for unlined landfills.

Women Take a Stand to Close the Landfill

The local Vietnamese American nonprofit, Co Quan Phat Trien Cong Dong—Mary Queen of Viet Nam Community Development Corporation (MQVN CDC)—organized the Vietnamese American community after Hurricane Katrina. The majority of staff members and volunteers who work at MQVN CDC are second-generation Vietnamese American women. Their role in informing community members about the landfill and its potential negative health effects required both cultural competency and Vietnamese language fluency. They organized transportation for community members to go to city hall to protest the landfill. The Bring Back New Orleans Commission met nearly every week after Katrina, and every week, only about ten people showed up at the public meetings. In one of the meetings, however, four hundred Vietnamese Americans packed the room in an attempt make their existence visible to government officials. Organizers had to provide transportation and language interpreters for community members to voice their opinions at the meeting, since many of the older community members do not drive or speak English. This is especially true for first-generation women of the community. Many do not earn income and rely on their husbands' and children's income; therefore, they often are not encouraged to learn English. Although not as fluent as second-generation women in English, it is common for first-generation women who run businesses to be more fluent in English than those who work at home. The Versailles community was politically invisible before the storm; therefore, creating visibility for the community was an important task.

Second-generation Vietnamese Americans provided high levels of organization that shocked both elected officials and protestors. Unlike first-generation Vietnamese American women, second-generation women have fluent English language skills, are generally more educated, and are acculturated into Vietnamese and American culture. Second-generation women played a significant part in the landfill protests by negotiating with various political and community actors involved. MQVN CDC staff members, who were mostly women, began networking with local politicians and policy makers. They began to make politicians more accountable by deliberately attracting media attention to the struggles in New Orleans East, Versailles, and the Vietnamese American population.

Members of MQVN CDC and other nonprofits in the community also went door to door and visited local businesses to rally support for the landfill campaign. They organized transportation and language access, and convinced individual community members to participate in political action such as marches at the state capital, protests, and visits to city hall. Such political action included being involved in the effort to close the Chef Menteur landfill. The women had knowledge and access to informal networks in the community, which they used to spread information and to organize community members. Such actions were important in making the community more politically visible. Community members I spoke to speculated that the politicians that had approved opening the Chef Menteur landfill did not expect Vietnamese American community members to object. When asked why she thought the city put the landfill near the Versailles community, a Vietnamese American woman, who was a MQVN CDC community organizer involved in the landfill protest, stated: "It's because we are a minority community. The city did not expect the community to protest because we had always been quiet before. Also, [the city] didn't think we cared about the environment."

Eric Tang points out: "For all the news of returnees scraping by without basic resources, the residents who took to City Hall that day somehow managed to arrive with sleekly printed signs and T-shirts denouncing the landfill. Nobody—neither the elected officials nor the protestors' supporters outside—was prepared to see this level of organization" (2008, 8).

Community members, including women, fearing the negative health effects of the landfill for current and future generations, organized with determination to close the landfill and remove the toxic debris. The campaign did not make direct connections between the landfill and reproductive health, but rather focused on the overall health of the community. However, older women in the community did speak to me about the lack of gynecologists in the area after Katrina, so they are well aware of women's health, but they never directly connected it to the landfill campaign. They went to the city council, seeking political support to pressure Mayor Nagin to close the landfill. The city council unanimously supported the community, but Nagin refused. Mimi Nguyen, the first Vietnamese American and Asian American to work for a city council member in New Orleans, was hired to conduct legislative and policy research for the office of Councilwoman Cynthia Willard-Lewis. She commented on the landfill: "All the environmental groups came in and said, 'Oh, this is wrong. You don't put that in Uptown. You don't put that in French Quarter.' Why did you put it in, you know, the Vietnamese American community, where people don't speak the language? So you don't think the people can protest. You don't think they know the law or their rights?" (Chiang 2009).

In the weeks that followed the opening of the landfill, Vietnamese American community members, including women, organized a major protest. Before Katrina, leaders in the community often held libertarian attitudes toward government that implied, "If you don't bother us, we won't bother you." Community leaders, women among them, clearly began to understand that Katrina changed everything and decided to become more involved in government, particularly the decisions affecting the health and lives of their community. This formerly politically quiet community organized protests, participated in city hall meetings, and attended rallies and marches to Baton Rouge, Louisiana's state capital.

The most organized protest took place on the day the landfill permit was up for renewal, August 23, 2006. The Vietnamese Americans in New Orleans East of all ages involved themselves in closing the landfill. That day, youth and elderly members, men, women, and children stood side by side outside the landfill gates, determined to stop dump trucks from entering their community. Several of the elderly who had lived through numerous political turmoils in Viet Nam prepared for civil disobedience by bringing additional clothes and medicine in case they were arrested. One older male member of the community boldly stated in Vietnamese during the protest: "All of us young and old have to stick together so we can fight. It doesn't matter what the price is. Even if I get arrested, get the death penalty, or starve to death in jail, we are prepared to accept that death or imprisonment, so we can succeed and remain happy and healthy" (Chiang 2009). That day, the trucks never came (Tang 2008), and the next day, Mayor Nagin allowed the landfill permit to expire, essentially closing down the landfill. While this is one positive outcome that resulted from the action, the community still waits for the landfill to be cleaned up. Mimi Nguyen states: "The experience with the landfill, it gives people back their voice" (Chiang 2009).

Although the trucks have stopped coming to the Chef Menteur landfill since that day, the debris has not been removed. When asked about the current state of the neighborhood, Ms. Tran, a nineteen-year-old high school student who protested the landfill, answered: "A lot of houses are not up. They have a lot of houses that are still vacant. They have not been gutted. They have mold in it, and it's really bad for the environment. In the East we have the landfill, [and] even though it's closed down, they still have, um, all that toxic and all that trash and it's not good for the future of the neighborhood." This statement illustrates that although community members were successful in closing the landfill, they are well aware that its toxic debris continues to threaten the health and living environment of the community.

Generational Differences, Border Crossing, and Coalition Politics

To understand the generational differences within the Vietnamese American community and the way these differences played out in women's responses to the landfill issue, one must understand how identities are changed and transformed during border crossing. I use "border crossing" instead of "transnational migration" because, according to Lynn Stephen (forthcoming), the term "transnational" overemphasizes the nation. Overemphasizing the nation is problematic because the nation does not encompass a single coherent identity. Viet Nam, for example, has many regional and local cultural differences that result in varied experiences of being Vietnamese. "Border crossing," in addition, refers not only to the physical crossing of borders, but also to migrants' and refugees' crossing cultural borders, including racial/ethnic and gendered borders (Stephen, forthcoming). This means that when Vietnamese people migrated from Viet Nam to the United States, being Vietnamese changed from being a national identity to an ethnic identity. Additionally, gendered meanings change in the context of migration. The meanings, values, and norms associated with Vietnamese gender roles also change and become transformed during border crossings (Levitt and Glick Schiller 2004; Stephen, forthcoming).

The first generation of Vietnamese Americans came of age in Viet Nam. Most from the first generation, such as my parents, identify themselves ethnically only as Vietnamese, with a smaller number identifying themselves as Vietnamese Americans. The second generation encompasses a range of ethnic, racial, and political identities that the previous generation does not. Such identities include American, Vietnamese American, Southeast Asian, Asian, Asian American, minority, and person of color. These additional identities are the result of border crossing to the United States. For Vietnamese American females, all such identities are also modified by gender. They learn to encompass not only the multiple identities just stated, but also their gendered roles within these categories (e.g., Vietnamese American woman, woman of color, Asian American woman, etc.), because race, ethnicity, and gender are inextricably connected.

The additional identities of the second generation are important because they helped the community build coalitions with surrounding communities to close the Chef Menteur Highway landfill. They not only recognized the potential cultural capital that resulted from these additional identities, but also recognized the perceived differences between communities of color such as the model minority myth. Cognizant of the potential use of the model minority myth to separate the Vietnamese American from other minority groups in the area, community leaders pointed out that the landfill campaign was a multiracial collaboration (Tang 2008).

Why did the coalition building of these women work across gender, class, and racial lines? Understanding coalition politics will help answer this question. Di Chiro uses Reagon's work, which describes coalition politics as "transcommunal alliances and communities of practice forged in the knowledge that survival depends not on the retreat to the comfort of 'home' (what some refer to as identity politics), but on the worldly and laborious engagements with the fleshly realities of socio-ecological interdependence" (Di Chiro 2008, 279). In addition, Di Chiro points out that coalitions result from the "strategic assemblage of 'uncomfortable' but necessary social, economic, environmental, and cultural practices implemented by different communities joining together in mutual recognition that 'I ain't gonna let you live unless you let me live.'" Di Chiro claims that coalition politics is also about articulation—"the practices of interconnection, alliance building, and 'joined up thinking'"—which is "produced by diverse social actors through engaging 'situated knowledges' about the world and creating new collective eco-political entities in the hopes of 'surviving together.'" Coalition building is temporary, according to Di Chiro, and the hard work lies in reframing and sustaining social, political, and economic issues to find common ground, linking diverse movements and common ideas and creating the conditions for "joining knowledge-producing and world-building practices" (2008, 280).

As minorities and people of color fighting for the survival and protection of a community of color, second-generation Vietnamese American women were able to build trust and partnerships with various local and regional multiracial and women's organizations that played a vital part in closing the landfill. Addressing environmental concerns, they worked with organizations such as Citizens for a Stronger New

Orleans East, Louisiana Environmental Action Network, and Advocates for Environmental Human Rights, "a nonprofit organization that for years prior to Katrina had defended residents of black New Orleans East from environmental hazards, including previous attempts at dumping city waste into wetlands" (Tang 2008, 10). On regional and national scales, the Versailles community also collaborated with the Sierra Club, a nationally recognized environmental justice organization, and National Alliance of Vietnamese American Service Agencies, which provided necessary cultural resources to assess community needs.

Women were better able to build these coalitions by finding commonalities in multiple points of oppression. For instance, they were able to connect not only as people of color but also as women of color. Their multiple identities, all modified by gender, allowed them to connect with diverse movements. In coalition politics, multiple identities and subjectivities become advantageous because they gives social actors more opportunities to reframe their issues to realign, connect, and work with others with diverse issues.

Another important question is how these women themselves imagine coalition building and politics. I am a former MQVN CDC volunteer, and in my interviews, conversations, and time with my female coworkers, we often discussed racial and gender politics in relation to the civil rights and women's movements in the United States. This suggests that these women recognize and identify with the historical racial and gender oppression in the United States. However, we also often discussed the struggles and sacrifices of the previous generation during the civil war in Viet Nam and their potentially perilous migration to the United States. This suggests that the Vietnamese national identity is still present among many second-generation Vietnamese American women. For these women, being more educated than the first generation, bilingual, and multicultural allows them to move between their multiple identities, including those modified by gender. Coalition politics allows them to practice border crossing in more than one direction.

Conclusion

Because disasters and environmental degradation challenge people in culturally and historically specific ways, scholars, activists, and environmentalists need to recognize that gender, race, ethnicity, and class shape the ways in which different groups organize to meet those challenges. The Vietnamese American communities in New Orleans examined here have a history of loss, displacement, and recovery, which affected their responses to both Hurricane Katrina and the Chef Menteur landfill. This case study demonstrated that women were central to the ethnic cohesion and environmental activism that made the Vietnamese American community members successful in returning home and in closing the Chef Menteur landfill. Studying the responses of minority groups such as Vietnamese Americans helps us discern the complexities of environmental racism, including their gender dimension. Women of different generations brought to the struggle against the proposed landfill different sets of skills and life experiences, all of which proved useful in eventually protecting their community. For second-generation Vietnamese American women in Versailles, engaging in environmental activism after Hurricane Katrina involved recognizing the struggles and sacrifices of the previous generations and moving in and out of different gender, ethnic, racial, and national identities in order to build effective coalitions.

———

Gennie Thi Nguyen is completing doctoral studies in cultural anthropology at the University of Oregon. Her research focuses on environmental justice, race and racism, gender, overseas Vietnamese culture, and intergenerational trauma.

REFERENCES

Airriess, C. (2002). Creating Vietnamese landscapes and place in New Orleans. In K. L. Berry and M. L. Henderson (Eds.), *Geographical identities of ethnic America: Race, space, and place* (pp. 228–254). Las Vegas: University of Nevada Press.

———. (2006). Scaling central place of an ethnic-Vietnamese commercial enclave in New Orleans, Louisiana. In D. H. Kaplan and W. Li (Eds.), *Landscapes of the ethnic economy* (pp. 17–33). Lanham, MD: Rowman and Littlefield.

———. (2008). Spaces and places of adaptation in an ethnic Vietnamese cluster in New Orleans, Lousiana. In R. C. Jones (Ed.), *Immigrants outside megalopolis: Ethnic transformation in the heartland* (pp. 163–188). Lanham, MD: Lexington Books.

Airriess, C., and Clawson, D. L. (1991). Versailles: A Vietnamese enclave in New Orleans, Lousiana. *Journal of Cultural Geography*, *12*(1), 1–15.

———. (1994). Vietnamese market gardens in New Orleans, Louisiana. *Geographical Review*, *84*(1), 16–31.

Airriess, C., Li, W., Leong, K. J., Chen, A. C., and Keith, V. M. (2008). Church-based social capital, networks, and geographical scale: Katrina evacuation, relocation, and recovery in a New Orleans Vietnamese American community. *Geoforum*, *39*(3), 1333–1346.

Bond, J. (2007). In Katrina's wake: Racial implications of the New Orleans disaster. *Journal of Race and Policy*, *3*(2), 15–32.

Bord, R., and O'Conner, R. (1997). The gender gap in environmetnal attitudes: The case of perceived vulnerabiltiy to risk. *Social Science Quarterly*, *78*, 830–840.

Bullard, R. (1993). *Confronting environmental racism: Voices from the grassroots*. Boston, MA: Southview Press.

Bullard, R., and Wright, B. (2009). *Race, place, and environmental justice after Hurricane Katrina*. Boulder, CO: Westview Press.

Butterbaugh, L. (2005). Why did Hurricane Katrina hit women so hard? *Off Our Backs*, *35*(9/10), 17–19.

Checker, M. (2005). *Polluted promises: Environmental racism and the search for justice in a Southern town*. New York: New York University Press.

Chen, M. (2007). Do-it-yourself disaster relief snubs New Orleans planners. *NewStandard*, April 27. Retrieved from *newstandardnews.net/content/index.cfm/items/2753*.

Chiang, L. (Director). (2009). *New Orleans: A village called Versailles*. Motion picture.

Davidson, D. J., and Freudenburg, W. R. (1998). Toward a theory of choice: Socially embedded preference construction. *Journal of Socio-Economics*, *24*(2), 261–279.

Di Chiro, G. (2008). Living environmentalisms: Coalition politics, social reproduction, and environmental justice. *Environmental Politics*, *17*(2), 276–298.

Do, S. (2007). *Village de l'Est: Landfill battle reveals a new generation of community leaders*. Retrieved from *www.youthradio.org/oldsite/environmental/pri070413_village.shtml*.

Eaton, L. (2006). A new landfill in New Orleans sets off a battle. *New York Times*, May 8. Retrieved from *www.nytimes.com/2006/05/08/us/08landfill.html?pagewanted=1&_r=1*.

Flynn, J., Slovic, P., and Mertz, C. K. (1994). Gender, race, and perception of environmental health risks. *Risk Analysis, 14*, 1101–1108.

Hill, L. (2006). The miracle of Versailles: New Orleans Vietnamese community rebuilds. *Louisiana Weekly*, January 17. Retrieved from *www.southerninstitute.info/commentaries/?p=8*.

Kalof, L., Dietz, T., and Guagnano, G. (2002). Race, gender, and environmentalism: The atypical values and beliefs of white men. *Race, Gender, and Class, 9*(2), 1–19.

Kemp, G. P. (2006). *Geological analysis of Chef Menteur landfill site, Orleans Parish, Louisiana.* Baton Rouge: School of the Coast and Environment, Louisiana State University.

Krauss, C. (1994). Women of color on the frontline. In R. Bullard (Ed.), *Unequal protection: Environmental justice and communities of color* (pp. 256–271). San Francisco: Sierra Club Books.

Levitt, P., and Glick Schiller, N. (2004). Conceptualizing simultaneity: A transnational social field perspective on society. *International Migration Review, 38*(3), 1002–1039.

Luther, L. (2006). *Disaster debris removal after Hurricane Katrina.* Washington, DC: Congressional Research Service.

Lydersen, K. (2009). Landfill worries cloud hope for New Orleans gardens. *Washington Post*, July 4. Retrieved from *www.washingtonpost.com/wp-dyn/content/article/2009/07/03/AR2009070302436.html?hpid=moreheadlines*.

Mohai, P., and Bryant, B. (1998). Is there a "race" effect on concern for environmental quality? *Public Opinion Quarterly, 62*, 475–505.

Nguyen, T. (2007). Armed with my first-grade Vietnamese and digital video camera. MSNBC.com, June 15. Retrieved from *insidedateline.msnbc.msn.com/archive/2007/06/15/226703.aspx*.

Nguyen, V. T. (2002). *Race and resistance: Literature and politics in Asian America.* New York: Oxford University Press.

Pardue, J. H. (2006). *Anticipating environmental problems facing hurricane debris landfills in New Orleans East.* Baton Rouge: Louisiana Water Resources Research Institute, Louisiana State University.

Reagon, B. J. (1983). Coalition politics: Turning the century. In B. Smith (Ed.), *Home girls: A Black feminist anthology* (pp. 356–368). New York: Kitchen Table Press.

Stephen, L. (Forthcoming). Conceptualizing transborder communities. In R. Marc and D. Tichenor (Eds.), *The Handbook of International Migration.* New York: Oxford University Press.

Strange, P. (2006). Strength to lead the charge. *Nola.com*, August 29. Retrieved from *www.nola.com/katrina/stories/east_church.html*.

Tang, E. (2008). The Vietnamese Americans of black New Orleans East. Typescript.

Tang, I. (2005). Hurricane Katrina victims recover from "tragic shock." *AsianWeek*, September 16. Retrieved from *www.huongduong.org/giaoxu/tintuc/asianweek%20091905.htm*.

Taylor, D. E. (1989). Blacks and the environment: Toward an explanation of the concern and action gap between blacks and whites. *Environmental Behavior, 21*, 175–205.

Vu, L., VanLandingham, M., Do, M., and Bankston, C. (2009). Evacuation and return of Vietnamese New Orleanians affected by Hurricane Katrina. *Organization and Environment, 22*(4), 422–436.

Werner, J. (2004). Managing womanhoods in the family: Gendered subjectivities and the state in the Red River Delta in Vietnam. In L. Drummond and H. Rydstrom (Eds.), *Gender practices in contemporary Vietnam* (pp. 26–46). Singapore: Singapore University Press.

CHAPTER 24

Cultural Trauma, Memory, and Gendered Collective Action

The Case of Women of the Storm
Following Hurricane Katrina

Emmanuel David

On January 10, 2006, an emergent group of women conversed at kitchen tables in Uptown New Orleans and began a grassroots endeavor to bring the members of Congress to the city to witness the storm and flood damage firsthand. They began by calling women throughout the city, seeking to create a diverse group of women to travel to Washington, D.C., to extend hand-delivered invitations to lawmakers. By late January 2006, they had taken the name Women of the Storm and become a formal social movement organization, extending a long tradition of women-centered advocacy, volunteerism, and reform in New Orleans (Tyler 1996). Aware that the survival, rebirth, and cultural memory of an American city were at stake, the women mobilized around the goal of inviting every member of Congress to tour Katrina's devastation.

On January 30, 2006, Women of the Storm assembled 130 Louisiana women, some of whom had lost their homes in the flood, and took a chartered flight to Washington. The plane was filled with women from diverse class and race backgrounds and life experiences—ranging from philanthropists to florists, from attorneys and small-business owners to former debutantes and Mardi Gras royalty, from housewives and mothers to bankers, writers, and two Catholic nuns. The women recognized the urgent need to bring decision makers to the city and claimed that "nothing is more powerful than witnessing the devastation first-hand and experiencing the hardship and triumph that accompany recovery and rebirth of the state" (Women of the Storm 2006a). At a press conference that morning, they unfurled in unison bright blue umbrellas, symbolically representing the tarps of the same shade of blue that covered thousands of homes across the region. Afterward, the women split into pairs intended to represent the racial diversity of New Orleans and set out two by two to hand deliver formal invitations to every member of Congress to tour the destruction.[1]

At the time of Women of the Storm's January 2006 trip, while lights remained out across the desolate and depopulated city in neighborhoods such as Lakeview, Gentilly, Mid-City, the Upper Ninth Ward, and the Lower Ninth Ward, only fifty-five U.S. representatives and thirty U.S. senators had visited post-Katrina New Orleans (Alpert 2006b). As Women of the Storm founder Anne Milling put it: "It was a storm that was felt around the world. . . . Yet, who would dream that 87 percent of the House of Representatives and 70 percent of the Senate haven't found time to visit the site of the largest catastrophe in the history of America?" (ibid.; for a discussion of the differences between emergencies, disasters, and catastrophes, see Quarantelli 2006). Seemingly, the region had been forgotten by national lawmakers as thousands of (still displaced) residents tried to rebuild their lives. The women mobilized behind Milling's persuasive call to action: "Our elected officials need to see for themselves—block by block, mile by mile—the immense devastation and the pressing challenges faced by so many people in this region" (Women of the Storm 2006b).

Armed with personal invitations, the group offered lawmakers an all-expense-paid, thirty-six-hour trip to New Orleans with an itinerary that included meetings with civic and business leaders, land tours of the abandoned neighborhoods, visits to the major levee breaches, and flyovers of the storm-damaged region and eroding coastal wetlands in Blackhawk helicopters, assisted by Brigadier General Hunt Downer of the Louisiana National Guard (Williams 2006). In addition to the invitations, the women presented lawmakers with the book *America's Wetlands*, on the erosion of Louisiana's coast, and shared haunting photographs of the flooded homes of some of their members. Perhaps most importantly, the women communicated personal and collective stories of loss, trauma, and resilience.

One Women of the Storm participant in her early fifties explained:

> People brought whatever they wanted to, but what we really brought were stories. The stories of [*long pause*]—. . . my two [adult] children lost everything. And when I say everything, I literally mean everything. And to a congressional person, looking at someone probably like myself, they don't understand how anybody like me could lose everything. Well, my children did and now they live with me. Until they find . . . they'll be fine, they both have good jobs, you know. But, so we really brought stories to the people in Congress and their aides.

In addition to providing organized tours for congressional leaders who accepted the women's invitations, the group partnered with America's Wetlands, an organization that frames itself as an environmental group, to encourage federal support for a sustainable revenue source drawn from offshore oil and gas royalties to help protect and restore Louisiana's coastal wetlands. In March 2006, lawmakers began visiting New Orleans, including a thirty-two-member bipartisan congressional delegation led by Speaker of the House Dennis Hastert and House Minority Leader Nancy Pelosi (Alpert 2006a). Shortly thereafter, Women of the Storm partnered with four national women's groups—the Association of Junior Leagues International; the National Women's Leadership Council, United Way of America; the Links Incorporated; and the National Council of Jewish Women—thereby extending its base beyond Louisiana (Women of the Storm 2006c). In September 2006, Women of the Storm made a second trip to Washington, continuing to invite members of Congress and link the Katrina catastrophe to broader environmental concerns. The group has kept an ongoing count of congressional visits to post-Katrina New Orleans (specifying name, state, and political party affiliation) on the Women of the Storm website (*womenofthestorm.net*), and more recently expanded its efforts to other spheres of U.S.

politics through the (ultimately unsuccessful) bid to the Commission on Presidential Debates site selection committee to hold the 2008 presidential debates in New Orleans, which was endorsed by seven presidential candidates.[2]

Don't Forget Us: Remembrance Work as Postdisaster Activism

I first became interested in Women of the Storm while conducting fieldwork in post-Katrina New Orleans. Given that elite groups are often inaccessible to social science researchers (Marcus 1983), the opportunity to study an elite women-organized social movement has relevance beyond a particular historic event; "studying up" has democratic significance for understanding relations of power and inequality (Nader 1972). While Women of the Storm represents itself (on its website, in press releases, and in organized political actions) as a diverse organization, with participants from different cultural, racial, and class backgrounds, the core organizers who maintained the group between the major collective actions are arguably part of the city's social and economic elite. Continuity and survival of women's movements over time have often depended upon the stewardship of elite women, as demonstrated by Taylor (1994) in her work on the twentieth-century women's movements.

The focus of this chapter is on the methods used by Women of the Storm, particularly remembrance practices and cultural memory, to activate a political response to the many crises plaguing New Orleans in the aftermath of Katrina. Ethnographic research provides the tools to study the dynamics and processes of memory (Prus 2007; see also the special issue of *Symbolic Interaction* [Fine and Beim 2007] on interactionist approaches to collective memory). Accordingly, I conducted ethnographic field research in New Orleans between October 2005 and September 2006, conducting in-depth interviews with women activists in the New Orleans area, attending weekly meetings, observing collective actions, and collecting documents.

Women of the Storm, made up of women from New Orleans and south Louisiana, played a pivotal role in the region's ongoing recovery following Hurricane Katrina.[3] Here, I propose that the group accomplished this largely through performative actions, some of which were patterned after traditional gender norms, remembrance practices, and place-based rituals. These actions were designed to pressure Congress to pass federal legislation related to Hurricane Katrina recovery efforts. While the group did not frame its actions as political and in fact explicitly describes itself as nonpolitical, this research indicates that the actions of the group politicize remembrance and forgetting through their claims and requests for material and symbolic resources.

On Women of the Storm's first trip to Washington, the group collectively unfurled what would become its signature symbol: blue-tarp umbrellas. Created by Women of the Storm specifically for this debut, the umbrellas unfurled at the morning press conference were the same distinctive shade of blue as the tarps that covered thousands of tattered homes across the region. This reference to a particular blue pointed to the fact that the hue had entered the region's postdisaster cultural syntax through the FEMA (Federal Emergency Management Agency) relief effort. In the hands of Women of the Storm, the umbrellas were strategically and symbolically used in gendered performance, remembrance practices, and collective actions. Absorbed into the visual nomenclature of postdisaster New Orleans, Women of the Storm's collective raising of blue-tarp umbrellas synthesized symbols associated with protection from storms and widespread government failures.

This symbolism took on particular significance for the women participants. Overflowing with excitement during our in-depth interview, a woman in her mid-fifties explained to me the symbolic power of the reference to blue tarps:

> It was blue tarp. I mean it's [the color of] a blue roof. But it was very—three buses of women and we all opened our umbrellas as soon as we got off of the bus. It was very visual because you see these, we walked for about a block and a half I guess, and I was on the third bus, and you see these blue umbrellas going up and then you see them coming up the [Capitol] Hill. And I think it was very impressive, . . . and I know one person told me that she thought that Senator Landrieu, when she turned around and saw that—people including her mom, Verna, was on the plane—that the cavalry had come. You know, it was like she had been holding the fort virtually alone, she and the delegation, but here is the support, here is the cavalry, in this visible way, heading up the Hill. (February 5, 2006)

Another interviewee, a woman in her early sixties, suggested that the blue-tarp umbrellas not only referenced the actual tarps that covered homes, but also symbolized the human dimensions of the Katrina catastrophe:

> It was unbelievable, those umbrellas, the impact. Just simply because it's blue tarps. That's what it represents, the people that are still struggling to get their lives together and their houses, everything. (March 14, 2006)

The double reference speaks to the materiality of patching damaged homes as well as of those who suffered direct loss. Describing how the blue tarps affected her emotionally, a woman in her early sixties spoke about how the symbols invoked a "stinging" sense of loss:

> It's still stinging when you go into an area where there's an unusual number of blue roofs. It just—I'm in an area where I don't see a lot of it, but then I go into other areas, and it's a stinging feeling, because you realize that we are three months from hurricane season, and we still have so many houses that are not up and running. (March 16, 2006)

As her narrative suggests, the symbols did not just reference the past; these were also poignant reminders about disaster vulnerabilities in the near future. At the same time, they came to symbolize women's solidarity, as she went on to note:

> I think that the experience that was most warming and satisfying and exciting to me was marching up the Hill. We got off the buses at the bottom of the Hill, and all of the women were together and we opened our umbrellas, and marching up the Hill, I was near the front, and when I looked back down the Hill to see all those little umbrellas, I thought, "God, this is just so incredible, that we are women of—we're not young women, and we are together, marching up the Hill, marching on the

Hill." The thing about—one of the things I think is so significant about the Women of the Storm is that, first of all, our blue umbrellas say to people that we're gentle. We're not here to hurt you or hurt your feelings or anything like that. We're just trying to represent New Orleans in the best possible way. (March 16, 2006)

The actions of Women of the Storm were performative, and they were gendered. Accordingly, the use of the umbrellas invoked a gentle, nonthreatening symbol of collective action, instead of, for example, accusatory statements on placards or oppositional activities that shut down organizational or institutional operations.

While these narratives speak to how the use of umbrellas garnered attention through performance and invocations of emphasized femininity (Connell 1987), some participants also recognized how this particular symbol might not have been understood by intended audiences and the general public outside of New Orleans and the Gulf Coast. Another woman in her early sixties spoke of the performative dimensions of the collective deployment of the storm symbol in just this way:

They were blue, so they had the "blue tarps," although I'm not sure a lot of them in Washington understood that part. But it was very effective, because immediately we were spotted. We got off the buses and popped those umbrellas. People driving by asked, "What is this?" One of the cops in front of the Rayburn Building stopped and said, "What is this?" and [name of Women of the Storm partner] talked to him and said, "I've lost my home and I'm up here because I want things changed." So the cop was even—he took notice of us. (March 21, 2006)

In this regard, gaining attention through performance does not always involve comprehension of symbolic codes. While umbrellas are a powerful, place-based symbol tied to New Orleans culture, it is understandable that the icon may not be immediately legible to lawmakers in Washington or to readers of this chapter.[4]

The currency of Women of the Storm's performances derives from the broader sociocultural context of memory traditions in New Orleans. The use of symbolism in rituals surrounding death and rebirth is a visible aspect of the culture of New Orleans, where the umbrella, among other objects, has served as an important prop in mourning and remembrance practices. For instance, ritual spectacles involving umbrellas are part of a long tradition of jazz funerals in New Orleans, which themselves have origins in West African ritual traditions. The traditional jazz funeral often includes a solemn procession from the church service to the cemetery, which is followed by a moment referred to as "cutting the body loose" whereby "the deceased parts company with the procession in his honor" (Roach 1996, 278) and the mourners turn back as uplifting music, joyous shouts, and laughter fill the air. This transitional moment in the mourning ritual gives rise to what is known in local vernacular as the "second line," a type of parading that consists of celebratory elements like brass bands, upbeat music, unfurled umbrellas that are popped and twirled, improvised dancing, and gendered ritual performance and attire, including, for some women, baby-doll outfits (Coclanis and Coclanis 2005; Roach 1996, 2001). This highly stylized, place-specific script for mourning and celebration is rooted in the history of the city's working-class African American community. After the Civil War, such symbolic rituals became more visible throughout the region as they were appropriated by the tourism industry and other segments of society, including the city's elites (Regis 1999, 2001).

In this cultural context, the women drew upon the religious symbol of mourning and celebration unique to the city and transformed these rituals tied to death and rebirth into secular and aesthetic rituals. Through the performative unfurling of the blue-tarp umbrellas, this reconfigured place-based ritual is itself a form of rebirth in Katrina's wake. To be sure, the use of acts of remembrance could point in a troubling way to racial and class-based disparities in people's ability to return to the city, as well as to the cultural appropriation of memorial practices. In this regard, displaced residents who could not return to New Orleans used the second-line tradition in consideration of their relationship to New Orleans as home (Breunlin and Regis 2006).

It could be argued that the group's modification of cultural practices tied historically to communities of color is less a cultural appropriation of ritual remembrance practices by elite women than an attempt to establish a coherent narrative of collective mourning grounded in the politics of place and the preservation of the city's cultural memory. Thus, in addition to the struggle over material resources, Women of the Storm was also engaged in a larger symbolic struggle over the meaning of a place, the moral challenges and contradictions of speaking on behalf of the displaced, and the gendered responsibility of repairing a sense of home and community.

In focusing on the redirected course of political action and attempts to define new forms of moral responsibility by Women of the Storm, my intent is to call attention to the ways in which the cultural trauma of Katrina was constructed. My aim is not to depoliticize the catastrophe, which some may argue occurs when one draws on and deploys psychological discourses that might suggest that trauma inevitably and uniformly results from extreme events themselves. As Alexander (2004) points out, this would be a naturalistic fallacy that erases the political complexity of processes that produce cultural trauma. Instead, I want to direct attention to some of the ways in which the cultural trauma of Katrina was constructed and made visible, especially through the concerted efforts of a group of women guided by a sense of collective and moral responsibility. In this regard, the women displayed agency, innovation, and resiliency in times of extreme uncertainty. My approach to cultural trauma, informed by social constructionist research on the topic, helps move our understandings of suffering, violence, and loss out of the recesses of the individual psyche and into the body politic.

The transformation of cultural symbols and the practice of representing the displaced were ultimately a struggle over being remembered, as one member in her mid-forties reflected:

> It was a phenomenal day for me, one that I will never forget as long as I live. Just the fact that we felt like the American process was in action. We had the ability to go to Washington, meet with our congressmen, voice our concerns, meet with the White House, that this is part of being an American. In that respect, I think it was very worthwhile and fulfilling for us. We were actually doing something, we were

working with the government to open up some communication lines and begin the process of the federal government assisting our state. Because I think we all felt that there was a strong possibility that things would just move on and we would be forgotten. (April 7, 2006)

A woman in her midfifties spoke in a similar way about reminding the nation not to forget New Orleans:

The rest of the nation can't close their eyes and forget it. We have to constantly remind them. This is day-to-day stuff. (March 20, 2006)

For many Women of the Storm participants, memory work as political activism was characterized by its repetition and persistence. A woman in her midthirties described how persistence over time defines the group's efforts:

So you just have to keep at it. But I am not naïve . . . to think, "Oh, that is fine, they are all going to come down and they are going to sign off on $240 billion to New Orleans and it is all going to be saved." And I think pretty much everybody else feels the same way, that we did our part but it is a long, long, long road that won't have been solved by one one-day trip to Washington. So [I feel] both. Excitement, but also realization cracking in a little bit. That it is so much bigger than you are. (February 4, 2006)

This work was also saturated with elements of gendered cultural practices. After returning from Washington, Women of the Storm sent handwritten thank-you notes to elected officials reminding them of the group's invitation to visit. The thank-you notes served to keep the memory of post-Katrina New Orleans alive while simultaneously pressuring elected officials on the point that local and regional disaster recovery necessitated federal support through congressional appropriations. These handwritten correspondences were a gendered form of communication connected to what many view as women's traditional role of building and maintaining familial relationships and other social ties (di Leonardo 1987), and they correspond to notions of refined, polished, and cultured femininities. One interviewee, a woman in her early fifties, explained the gendered cultural practice in this way:

Southern women write thank-you notes—that's what we do. That is part of our makeup. We have to get our thank-you notes out to every single person that we saw. Whether it be an aide or a congressman or whatever. And we have to do it now. So all of them are due today. (February 3, 2006)

Despite uncertainty about the outcomes, the women's performances were publicly validated through widespread media attention. The collective performance demanded that the public and the state pay attention to issues the group defined as important, which included responding to Katrina as a serious issue in need of immediate attention. Describing the first trip to Washington, another woman in her early fifties stated:

So we all put on our pins and we all had an umbrella. And, um, the only props that we had, and we wanted to make sure that no one thought that this was not a serious trip. This wasn't Mardi Gras. This wasn't Bourbon Street. This wasn't second lining in Washington, D.C. This was women saying, "Pay attention to us." (February 3, 2006)

While the blue-tarp umbrellas undoubtedly conjure imagery of traditional jazz funerals, the interviewee's words make clear that the women's actions should not be mistaken for the moment of "cutting the body loose," which would emblematically signal a transition to the second-line celebration of New Orleans's own passing. Instead, the symbolic crossover to celebration had yet to occur, and the mournful tone extended onward, reflecting the urgency and despair of a nearly forgotten city. In these ways, Women of the Storm, on its first trip to Washington, used performance "in the transmission of traumatic memory, drawing from and transforming a shared archive and repertoire of cultural images" (Taylor 2003, 187). That is, the women highlighted cultural traditions and the symbolic meaning of a particular shade of blue that continues to conjure memories of "the storm." The widespread recognition by elected officials and media agencies in turn encouraged social cohesion among the Louisiana women, a recharging of group sentiments that set the stage for collective actions over the subsequent months in multiple place-based locations of loss and suffering.

Emmanuel David is an assistant professor in the Department of Sociology and Criminal Justice at Villanova University.

An earlier version of this chapter, "Cultural Trauma, Memory, and Gendered Collective Action: The Case of 'Women of the Storm' following Hurricane Katrina," was first published in 2008 in *NWSA Journal*, *20*(3): 138–162. © 2008 by Johns Hopkins University Press. Reprinted by permission.

NOTES

1. Complete with RSVP card and return envelope, the presentation of the invitation is significant because it reveals how the women drew upon traditionally feminine forms of communication and social practices akin to correspondence that would be sent out for a formal luncheon, tea, or dinner party.
2. These include endorsements by Joe Biden, Sam Brownback, Hillary Clinton, Chris Dodd, John Edwards, John McCain, and Barack Obama.
3. The group included several women from southwestern Louisiana, the area of the state hit by Hurricane Rita. This helped the group frame themselves as Louisiana women rather than just New Orleans women. However, most participants were from the Greater New Orleans Metropolitan area.
4. The iconography of the umbrella also resonates in popular images of the Southern Belle. I am grateful to Elissa Auther, who pointed out that the umbrella in these images connects to intersecting discourses of gender, race, and class, since historically many women have tried to shield their skin from the sun so as not to suggest they labored outdoors. This resonates

with Joseph Roach's interpretive reading of John Ogilby's folio atlases and his conclusion that the "umbrella seems to represent an icon in the atlas of cultural difference" (2003, 95) and that the parasol is "evocative of prestige, luxury, and pampered excess" (2003, 105), especially when held overhead by others.

REFERENCES

Alexander, J. (2004). Toward a theory of cultural trauma. In J. C. Alexander, R. Eyerman, B. Giesen, N. J. Smelser, and P. Sztompka (Eds.), *Cultural trauma and collective identity* (pp. 1–30). Berkeley: University of California Press.

Alpert, B. (2006a). Bipartisan tour brings 32 congressmen to N.O.: Leaders to tour devastated areas. *Times-Picayune*, March 2.

———. (2006b). Louisiana women storm Washington. *Times-Picayune*, January 31.

Breunlin, R., and Regis, H. (2006). Putting the Ninth Ward on the map: Race, place, and the transformation of Desire, New Orleans. *American Anthropologist, 108*(4), 744–764.

Coclanis, A., and Coclanis, P. (2005). Jazz funeral: A living tradition. *Southern Cultures, 11*(2), 86–92.

Connell, R. W. (1987). *Gender and power: Society, the person, and sexual politics.* Stanford: Stanford University Press.

di Leonardo, M. (1987). The female world of cards and holidays: Women, families, and the work of kinship. *Signs, 12*(3), 440–453.

Fine, G. A., and Beim, A. (2007). Introduction: Interactionist approaches to collective memory. *Symbolic Interaction, 30*(1), 1–5.

Marcus, G. (Ed.). (1983). *Elites: Ethnographic issues.* Albuquerque: School of American Research, University of New Mexico Press.

Nader, L. (1972). Up the anthropologist: Perspectives gained from studying up. In D. Hymes (Ed.), *Reinventing anthropology* (pp. 284–311). New York: Pantheon Books.

Prus, R. (2007). Human memory, social process, and the pragmatist metamorphosis: Ethnological foundations, ethnographic contributions, and conceptual challenges. *Journal of Contemporary Ethnography, 36*(4), 378–437.

Quarantelli, E. L. (2006). Catastrophes are different from disasters: Some implications for crisis planning and managing drawn from Katrina. Retrieved from *understandingkatrina.ssrc.org/Quarantelli/*.

Regis, H. (1999). Second lines, minstrelsy, and the contested landscapes of New Orleans Afro-Creole festivals. *Cultural Anthropology, 14*(4), 472–504.

———. (2001). Blackness and the politics of memory in the New Orleans second line. *American Ethnologist, 28*(4), 752–777.

Roach, J. (1996). *Cities of the dead: Circum-Atlantic performance.* New York: Columbia University Press.

———. (2001). Cutting loose: Burying the "first man of jazz." In R. Harvey (Ed.), *Joyous wakes, dignified deaths: Issues in death and dying* (pp. 3–14). Stony Brook, NY: Humanities Institute.

———. (2003). The global parasol: Accessorizing the four corners of the world. In F. A. Nussbaum (Ed.), *The global eighteenth century* (pp. 93–106). Baltimore: Johns Hopkins University Press.

Taylor, D. (2003). *The archive and the repertoire: Performing cultural memory in the Americas.* Durham, NC: Duke University Press.

Taylor, V. (1994). An elite-sustained movement: Women's rights in the post–World War II decades. In R. R. Dynes and K. J. Tierney (Eds.), *Disaster, collective behavior, and social organization* (pp. 281–305). Newark: University of Delaware Press.

Tyler, P. (1996). *Silk stockings and ballot boxes: Women and politics in New Orleans, 1920–1963*. Athens: University of Georgia Press.

Williams, L. (2006). "Women" to personally invite congressmen to tour the city. *Times-Picayune*, January 25.

Women of the Storm. (2006a). Invitation to members of U.S. Congress. Author files.

———. (2006b). Louisiana women storm Capitol Hill, urge leaders to visit New Orleans and America's wetland: More than 150 "Women of the Storm" deliver personal invitations on Capitol Hill. Press release. January 30.

———. (2006c). National women's groups join Women of the Storm, urge Congress to visit New Orleans and South Louisiana. Press release. March 29.

CHAPTER 25

Grounded in Faith, Inspired to Action

Bayou Women Own Their Own Recovery

Kristina J. Peterson and Richard Krajeski

> We evacuate our people as a whole, as a community. We were
> not splintered, like others who go here, or go there, or go your
> way. No, we evacuated as a whole, as one unit. And when
> we came back, if the houses were in need of repair then we
> worked together on those repairs and helped each other. We are
> community.
>
> —A woman of the Louisiana bayous

Organizations based in faith commitments are extremely important in the recovery process, often inspiring spontaneous and reflective action vital to repairing homes and addressing the needs of those who otherwise fall through the cracks of federal, state, and local assistance programs (Jenkins and Phillips 2008). Faith-based organizations active in disasters also tend to focus on people who suffer from human rights abuses, on social and economic justice, and on exploited and oppressed populations. "Faith" here is not to be construed as religious affiliation, though most of the women of faith reflected in this work have strong roots in traditional formal religions, indigenous practices, or both. Faith is conceptualized instead as embodied, manifested in relational and reflective care (Hamington 2006; Held 2006).

Women of faith have historically been advocates, caretakers, prophets, and catalysts for change. Since the earliest days of documentation, stories from the Christian Bible and Jewish Torah tell us of women who stood up against the power regimes of the day to declare human rights and environmental justice. Jewish and Christian narratives describe models of resistance, protest, and advocacy that have informed the work of many activist women. Esther, as a historical figure, used every means within her resources to save her kinfolk from racial genocide when confronting the precarious situation of a minority people in a hostile, dominant culture. She has been a narrative source of courage and action for many women within many traditions (Smith-Christopher 1989). The women of the bayous regularly mention Esther's story as a relevant historical narrative that validates, calls, and affirms today's women to act boldly in times of crisis and disaster. In this sisterhood of history, from past to present, women's stories give women authority in crisis to serve a God of love and justice. Women know and tell these stories, living by them, surviving with them, and growing from them (Kearney 2002; Ricoeur 1995). These are often nonpublic stories shared when a bond of trust and kindred spirit is present (Scott 1990). The stories are profoundly personal and are not generally shared with people outside the community or habitus. "We have lived a past with discriminations of all sorts; we have learned and gained strength from our mothers and sisters for fighting the biggest discrimination of our time—our extinction."[1]

Strategies for Understanding Women of Faith in the Louisiana Bayous

This chapter is situated by historical events in the context of women acting in faith within this Judeo-Christian context following the storms that shattered coastal communities in southeast Louisiana. It is a qualitative narrative based on the stories of culturally and ethnically diverse women who were affected by hurricanes Katrina and Rita in 2005, by Gustav and Ike in 2008, and now by the oil spill of 2010. The indigenous and historied communities of the bayous navigated through adversity with respect for and through the strength of community, in accordance with the gemeinschaft form of organization described by Tönnies (1988). The bayou communities and the women who knit them together are resilient because of their habitus, which includes faith, place, and community.

When a seasoned sociologist experienced this type of community for the first time in her fieldwork, it was with awe and curiosity.

A participatory model made the project that of the community, and thus it is the community that owns and guides this collaborative work. The process of this body of knowledge is best understood as participatory problem solving, solution innovation, and co–knowledge creation. Informed by the work of Paulo Freire (1996), Peter Park (1993), Orlando Fals-Borda (1998), and Tuhiwai Smith (1999), we are pleased if our co–problem solving and co–knowledge creation proves valuable to others beyond the context of our work. Feminist and postcolonial methodologies encourage the lived experiences of those involved to arise (Smith 1999). Often described as an indigenous or fourth-world approach to creating knowledge, the central characteristic of this method is the egalitarian nature of problem solving. Thus, this chapter is best read as "testimonio" (Beverly 2005), or as a narrative of narratives. With Tuhiwai Smith, we feel the greatest gift of knowledge is for a people to share their story (Denzin, Lincoln, and Smith 2008). We strive to honor the voices of those embedded in the situation—not only their storm response but also their deep commitment to addressing entrenched and resistant socioeconomic justice issues ever present in communities along the Gulf Coast (Mitchem 2002).

To hear and understand these women's narratives of faith, the authors participated in numerous disaster recovery meetings, problem-solving sessions, workshops, and other activities related to community rebuilding. Learning emerged from dwelling with, working with, and advocating with the women in group activities and in settings mostly in their place and habitus and on their time. This kind of participation can present challenges, among them the possibility for subjective bias and the potential to influence the process and outcomes. To address these concerns, our data were triangulated among communities and groups of women. Themes were summarized and provided to the women for their review, discussion, and discourse that enhanced the trustworthiness of the data. The interactions and participation include approximately 130 women of faith from five communities recovering from disasters, including the Gulf storms of 2005 and now the oil in the bayous of Southeast Louisiana.

The lead author-facilitator was at the time serving as pastor of a Louisiana bayou congregation and had to evacuate for Katrina-Rita and Gustav-Ike, as did her parishioners. Her history as a disaster consultant in the region dates back to Hurricane Andrew in 1992, enabling her to quickly respond with resources after Katrina. This role also afforded her entrée and allowed her to facilitate community meetings among women of faith. Notes and recollections, meeting agendas, minutes, posters, handouts, sermons, bulletins, newsletters, and related materials served as secondary data sources. The women were asked if they would like to contribute to a paper or document that would describe their current situation and how they are dealing with it. The following discussion describes the prevailing lifeworlds of bayou women of faith and their struggle with the loss of place-commons and community, which we believe is the critical context for understanding disaster recovery and resilience. Before turning to the participatory research, we sketch the critical contexts of place and faith.

Place and Faith

Place matters (Malpas 1999; Massey 1994). The Louisiana coast is a network of old deltaic formations that weave their way through time and culture. Shell middens and mounds that date back thousands of years offer remnants of the people who have gone before. The waters and the lands provide a physical location for living and for telling a unique narrative.

These bayous, marshes, and cypress forests of the Mississippi Delta worlds, once thought to be never ending, are now precarious, disappearing or endangered. Predators of all types, including development, industry, levees, oil extraction, invasive species, and global climate change, aggressively threaten this intricate network of estuaries, avian flyways, and people. The commons are disappearing. Predictions for the region are brutally harsh, and the people of this place experience their tangible link to history and culture physically disappearing. Communities have succumbed and cultures have vanished. The angst of the people and their lifeworld increases exponentially with each new prediction of increasing storm intensity and storm surges. Social and ecological adaptation cannot keep pace with the rapidity of the challenge. "This is our life—we can no longer tolerate policies that exploit us and colonize us," they respond. Coming out of historical patterns of colonization and commoditization of the commons, the bayou women have known how to adapt to and create strong habitus between self, family, neighbor, land, and place, and their faith. "God placed us here for this time and our ancestors gave us strength to stand and witness to the effects of climate change—misuse of land and land practices." All intermingle to share a narrative of past that invites a self-definition of future that is not dependent on external colonizers.

Commons provide the place for community, the space for relationships, the limits and controls, as well as opportunities, capabilities, well-being (Nussbaum 2000; Nussbaum and Sen 1993), and freedoms of a people. Lifeworld is the setting for everyday life (Habermas 1987), the dwelling place or dwelling in place (Heidegger 1971) and the world people may take for granted but also love and care for deeply

(Seamon 1979; Seamon and Mugerauer 1989). In the language of the bayou women, lifeworld is "home." This lifeworld gives and shapes identity.

Women of faith came to the forefront of leadership and activism after Hurricanes Katrina and Rita, often leaving other jobs or occupations to address human and ecological injustices. "I see the land of my ancestors washing away. Don't they know that when this is gone, everyone in the world will be hurt? Not just for the loss of their beauty but what they provide for the birds and the waterways and for all God's creatures. What God made is good and we are responsible for keeping it good. We haven't done a very good job." Women of faith, both within and outside the affected region, committed resources and long-term support rooted in their theological understanding of the situation. Women came to serve as temporary pastors, community activists, construction volunteers, healers, and advocates. The Jewish Fund for Justice, for instance, sent their rabbi in residence, and Payne Seminary sent their president. Both women exemplify an understanding, as outsiders, of those who responded to the region and were moved by the faith and witness of local women. The women of the delta, who historically have not been active in local and regional government, could no longer be silent bystanders as they saw their land, their culture, their people, and their precious lifeworld split apart by politics, policies, and a disappearing coast. Many now raise their voice in settings such as the United Nations, and in ways that would have been unimaginable only a short time ago, such as interviews and filming sessions with the media.

The Lifeworlds of Bayou Women

During our eight years of work with women in the bayous at the extreme southern end of the deltas reaching into the Gulf of Mexico, four themes emerged that are the context for their survival and recovery work. First, it is understood that faith is a primary motivator for deciding what to do and how to do it. The women's faith is rooted both in traditional religious communities and in the extended family and place. Many, perhaps most, of the women articulate their faith in vocabulary that can be understood only in the context of the bayou region. The reappropriation of religious vocabulary for local usage has historical roots, in that French, Creole, and indigenous languages blend easily into English idioms; religious terminology, too, picks up local language. The local electrical cooperative sponsors monthly gospel sings, mostly in French. Many of the women belong to a local congregation yet have other ties that extend beyond their faith affiliation. Their collaborative recovery work in the region is based on faith but not necessarily on an institutional structure or affiliation.

Second, it is understood that an ethic and culture of care is ever present. Care ethics, in the tradition of Gilligan (1982), are based on "relational" knowledge rather than "representational" knowledge (Park 1993). Care work predominates in the lives of these women, expressing "who I am" and "who we are" as people. "We need to care for our common land and heritage so that we can give our children and their children their inheritance." To take responsibility for the other, even to hostage oneself to the other, is the vocation of true selfhood (Levinas 1969). This is a radical and perhaps uncomfortable view for those raised with an ethic of individual autonomy and individual rights. The ethic expressed by Levinas can be viewed as oppressive, but as one of the women we know said: "Just because we are caregivers does not mean we cannot be hell-raisers." Perhaps an important question to pursue is how men, too, can be freed to act from an ethic of care and why the idea of caring has become an oppressive concept in our time.

Third, it is understood that bayou women work in an egalitarian way. As women gathered to share work or chores after these storms, there was no designated leader; almost without exception, each could stand alone in leadership if need be. Women and children did what they normally did in the extended family setting, including cooking, speaking, community organizing, tending cattle, shrimping, and caring for family members. The disaster event did not stop the bayou women from community making but altered how they kept community, such as in extended-family dwellings, gardens, and specific recovery projects. Neither they nor the men in their lives waited for government or external agencies to come serve them—they took action.

Fourth, it is understood that bayou women are not volunteers but fully engaged citizens of their communities. Since the women see themselves as active participants in the work and survival of the community, their contribution is whatever they are called to do as family member, neighbor, and citizen, and thus not an oppressive duty or burden. It is their very life and necessary to maintain habitus and the lifeworld. After a tragic accident of a community member, people came to the emergency room and intensive care unit to be with neighbor, coworkers, friends, or family, to stand with and be with their community member in need. They did not even consider not taking time off from routine activities to be there. The presence of community enables these women to endure long months and years of postdisaster recovery. There is anger about the systems of agency and governmental recovery services and the delays of formal decisions regarding recovery, sadness about the loss of place, anger about unnecessary suffering, and fear about an uncertain future. All these emotions were felt to be natural and bearable when addressed in community. Thus, the women did not feel they had to leave after Katrina because "the experience was too intense," as some outsiders recommended, not understanding this community.

Disaster Recovery Grounded in Women's Faith

"When one's life or their family's well-being is at stake, you have to speak up." A thread woven through the women's stories is their urgency to protect their land and community from both sudden-onset disasters such as hurricanes and the creeping disaster of losing protective wetlands. It is often thought by academics or agencies that local folks do not know or understand the complexities of pending socioecological land-loss and community-displacement issues. The great majority of the bayou women readily voiced their concern about these issues, albeit in their own way or their own idioms, relying on sources ranging from BBC radio reports, articles in the local paper on environmental issues, and local ecological knowledge shared through common activities and conversations. As one woman noted about her grandkids: "Our kids won't be fishing the bayou, there's fish kills and the water is running brackish—guess they'll go to [church camp] instead. What will happen to our drinking water?" As stories and narratives of everyday life are shared in worship, in Bible study groups, and in fellowship, the women do a sophisticated critical analysis (Brookfield

1987, 2005) of the socioenvironmental impact on the community. The Habermasian search for the public sphere is alive and well in these gatherings (Calhoun 1992; Habermas 1991; Hill and Montag 2000).

Many of the women said they are strengthened and encouraged by other women in their neighborhood, church, or synagogue taking what the women would call brave or courageous action. Some took stranded Katrina families into their own homes, set up shelters, emptied their pantries, or even gave their homes, trailers, or possessions to strangers, extended family, or friends. One family had as many as thirty-eight people living with them for almost a year. Another procured tents and other forms of shelter and set up an extended family colony on their own yard. Homes became communications headquarters (sharing phones, computers, and Internet); shelters for family, pets, and farm animals; and distribution sites of multiple levels of support and resources.

At one women's faith gathering, the women were asked about their own extraordinary generosity, hospitality, and advocacy. They claimed that they did not do anything out of the ordinary but simply what the situation called for to make the community whole. "When growing up, these were things that happened all the time. This is our community; we do for our community." The question about the commitment to community caregiving was raised at a women's group meeting during a time of extreme cold in the northern states, with news reports of several people freezing to death. The women wondered: "How could anyone freeze to death? Didn't their family or neighbors know that they didn't have enough to keep them warm?" It was beyond their comprehension that someone would be left alone in a crisis.

Local women spoke as one as they worked to retain their homes and their community and to forestall additional damage to their lifeworld. Some women have had to slow down or drop out for various time periods due to change of employment, family situations, health, death, and storm-related displacement, but working collaboratively through these ebbs and flows of the women's recovery work helps them weather change. The faith and voice of local women were also enhanced by the presence of people of faith who came from outside the region. It is both the people of faith (embodied care) and the coming that makes embodied care so powerful.

As thousands of volunteers came, the bayou women who have prided themselves on self-sufficiency and subsistence living were moved to new levels of action, this time by the actions of others. The women felt empowerment and solidarity, without the sense of shame, failure, or disempowerment about accepting help that has been expressed by others, such as the Grand Forks flood survivors interviewed in North Dakota by Alice Fothergill (2003). We speculate that this is because the women of the bayous share a lifeworld of care, solidarity, and reciprocity, and because so many outside volunteers were people of faith who came to care as colleagues and equals, as sisters of faith. Strong relationships were built between bayou women and work teams of outside volunteers. Beyond the recovery work in which they were already engaged, bayou women offered hospitality (family care) in a multitude of ways to the visiting volunteer work teams, no matter who they were. The more the local women responded to the outsiders, the more confident and active the locals became in their advocacy.

The energy that was brought by women from outside the region helped create synergy with the women in the region, each strengthening the other's work and vision. "How can we stand by and do nothing when all these folks keep coming in to help us?" This interactive outsider-insider relationship was strongest where there were volunteer villages, sites developed to house people from outside of the region for short-term work assignments. Where these villages were found, there were religious groups that provided food, entertainment, and conversation.

One congregation hosted volunteers from the Good Earth Village (sponsored by the Presbyterian Church USA) in Houma at their weekly worship service. The congregation showered each group with tokens of their affection, gratitude, and appreciation in the form of mugs, pins, poetry, prayers, hugs, and tears. Long-term friendships emerged and have been maintained through the exchange of letters, photos, calls, and visits and financial contributions to the work of recovery. Each week a different volunteer work group was present at the hosting congregation. The congregation invited the groups not only to their weekly worship service but also to a midweek home-cooked Cajun bayou meal. Afterward, the congregation helped interpret coastal life and wetland issues to the visiting work teams. The volunteers also experienced Cajun dancing and music, a major part of the local culture. Thousands of volunteers from communities, churches, synagogues, mosques, and colleges have enjoyed the hospitality of the bayou women who say, in turn: "We never had so much fun." Most of the women are not wealthy by outside standards; many are pensioners and live very simply—yet they share abundantly and with joy what they have.

The passion of bayou women inspired in outsiders who came to the area after these storms a new desire for study groups in their home communities on the subject of coastal erosion and wetland loss. The continual return of groups and their sustained interest, inspired by the bayou women's own passion, is far from the norm in disaster relief volunteerism. The bayou women have become agents of change this way, too, through collaboration forged through their faith networks with others in and outside the region.

Concluding Observations

Hurricanes and oil disasters represent only the latest threats to the vital communities and commons embedded in the bayous. To recover from disaster requires attention to faith, social and cultural networks, and related ties to physical places, to the commons, and to lifeworlds. For the bayou community and environment, the ecosystem is at a tipping point and will soon not be able to sustain the livelihoods of the traditional fishing communities. It is widely recognized that the region has only a few more years to exist (among others, see Schielfstein 2009) if no counteractions are taken.

Hurricanes Katrina and Rita (and most recently the BP oil disaster) brought a groundswell of national attention, volunteers, and resources to the bayou region. But, the media often neglected the active response network of women described here, highlighting the actions of a few individuals instead. Even after three long, arduous years of creative and difficult work after these hurricanes, when smaller ones came (Gustav and Ike), the bayou women were not deterred from advocating policy change, offering hospitality, taking leadership, and stepping out of their everyday roles to address the crisis at hand.

The networks for women of faith that are created through grassroots networks, e-mails, calls, and word of mouth sustain the activities that are essential to collective rebuilding in a way that t reduces risk and protects the values of local communities.

Grounded in faith, the bayou women carry on, doing all it takes to save their home, community, and lifeworld from cultural and ecological genocide. This spirit is precious:

> I was frequently kicked out of school for fighting back—I was not going to be called names because I am Native American. I am still kicking and fighting for those workers who have been brought here by corporations cashing in on disaster contracts. . . . Now these women and children are suffering both here and those who were left behind elsewhere in the world.

The women of the bayou call for a different standard of recovery and response based on justice and equity for all of creation, speaking truth to power and standing firmly for principles that may be neither understood nor wanted by the larger society. This means taking risks—even working outside the structures of religious and other institutions when they find those institutions restrictive. In the wake of the storms and now the oil disaster, they continue to give their voice and time to a broader vision of recovery—the prevention of the impending extinction of their culture, community, and place.

Rev. Kristina J. Peterson received her doctorate in urban studies from the University of New Orleans. A senior researcher at UNO's Center for Hazards Assessment, Response, and Technology, she presents and writes on collaborative justice, resilience, and mitigation from a grassroots and participatory perspective.

Rev. Richard L. Krajeski has served the ecumenical community and the disaster response community for thirty years. He is a fellow in the International Society for Applied Anthropology and engaged in policy analysis with the Center for Hazards Assessment, Response, and Technology, University of New Orleans.

ACKNOWLEDGMENTS

The authors thank Professor Brenda Phillips of Oklahoma State University for comments and ideas relevant to this chapter, and the women of Bayou Blue Presbyterian Church, local unit of Church Women United, Pointe au Chien, Grand Bayou, and Jean Lafitte, Louisiana.

NOTE

1.   All first-person quotations are taken from the women of the bayou with whom we work.

REFERENCES

Beverly, J. (2005). Testimonio, subalternity, and narrative authority. In N. Denzin and Y. Lincoln (Eds.). *The Sage handbook of qualitative research.* 3rd ed. London: Sage.

Brookfield, S. (1987). *Developing critical thinkers: Challenging adults to explore alternative ways of thinking and acting.* San Francisco: Jossey-Bass.

———. (2005). *The power of critical theory: Liberating adult learning and teaching.* San Francisco: Jossey-Bass.

Calhoun, C. (1992). *Habermas and the public sphere.* Cambridge, MA: MIT Press.

Denzin, N., Lincoln, Y., and Smith, L. T. (2008). *Handbook of critical and indigenous methodologies.* London: Sage.

Fals-Borda, O. (Ed.). (1998). *People's participation: Challenges ahead.* London: Apex Press.

Fals-Borda, O., and Rahman, M. A. (1991). *Action and knowledge: Breaking the monopoly with participatory action-research.* New York: Intermediate Technology Press.

Fothergill, A. (2004). *Heads above water: Gender, class, and family in the Grand Forks flood.* New York: State University of New York Press.

Freire, P. (1996). *Pedagogy of the oppressed.* New York: Continuum Press.

Gilligan, C. (1982). *In a different voice: Psychological theory and women's development.* Boston: Harvard University Press.

Habermas, J. (1987). *Lifeworld and system: A critique of functionalist reason.* Boston: Beacon Press.

———. (1991). *The structural transformation of the public sphere: An inquiry into a category of bourgeois society.* Cambridge, MA: MIT Press

Hamington, M. (2006). *Socializing care: Feminist ethics and public issues.* Lanham, MD: Rowman and Littlefield.

Heidegger, M. (1971). *Poetry, language, and thought.* New York: Harper.

Held, V. (2006). *The ethics of care: Personal, political, and global.* Oxford: Oxford University Press.

Hill, M., and Montag, W. (Eds.). (2000). *Masses, classes, and the public sphere.* London: Verso.

Jenkins, P., and Phillips, B. (2008). Battered women, catastrophe, and the context of safety after Hurricane Katrina. *NWSA Journal, 20*(3), 49–68.

Kearney, R. (2002). *On stories.* London; Routledge.

Levinas, E. (1969). *Totality and infinity: An essay on exteriority.* Pittsburgh: Duquesne University Press.

Malpas, J. E. (1999). *Place and experience: A philosophical topography.* Cambridge: Cambridge University Press.

Massey, D. (1994). *Space, place, and gender.* Minneapolis: University of Minnesota Press.

Mitchem. S. (2002). *Introducing womanist theology.* Maryknoll, NY: Orbis Press.

Nussbaum, M. (2000). *Women and human development: The capabilities approach.* Cambridge: Cambridge University Press.

Nussbaum, M., and Sen, A. (Eds.). (1993). *The quality of life.* New York: Oxford University Press.

Park, P. (1993). *Voices of change: Participatory research in the United States and Canada.* Westport, CT: Bergin and Garvey.

Ricoeur, P. (1995). *Figuring the sacred: Religion, narrative, and imagination.* Minneapolis: Fortress Press.

Schielfstein, M. (2009). State wants to keep corps on fast tract. *Times Picayune*, August 5. Retrieved from *www.nola.com/news/t-p/frontpage/index.ssf?/base/news-13/1249450301171190 .xml&coll=1.*

Scott, J. C. (1990). *Domination and the arts of resistance*. New Haven, CT: Yale University Press.

Seamon, D. (1979). *A geography of the lifeworld: Movement, rest, and encounter*. London: Croom Helm.

Seamon, D., and Mugerauer, R. (1989). *Dwelling, place, and environment: Towards a phenomenology of person and world*. New York: Columbia University Press.

Smith, L. T. (1999). *Decolonizing methodologies: Research and indigenous peoples*. London: Zed.

Smith-Christopher, D. (1989) *The religion of the landless: The sociology of the Babylonian exile*. Bloomington, IN: Meyer-Stone.

Tönnies, F. (1988). *Community and society (Gemeinschaft und Gesellschaft)*. New Brunswick: Transactions Publishers.

PART V

Gender in Disaster Theory, Practice, and Research

In the preceding parts of this book, we examined the gendered dimensions of Hurricane Katrina through protest pieces and compelling first-person testimonials before moving to rigorous empirical studies grounded in statistical data, interviews, and ethnographic field research. This final section offers two synthesizing pieces by leading scholars in disaster social science, both speaking about the volume as a whole, first in terms of disaster policy, practice, and research, and second on the significance of this repertoire of work for theoretical development. Both scholars offer pathways to a future in which women's experiences and strengths will be credited as valuable resources in disaster preparedness, response, recovery, and reconstruction, and in which the inequalities they endure today will not be repeated. The chapters make real the notion that women and gender relations mattered greatly in this great American tragedy and can move the nation toward a more resilient future.

CHAPTER 26

Gendered Disaster Practice and Policy

Brenda D. Phillips

> Out of chaos, hope.
> —motto of Presbyterian Disaster Assistance

Emergency managers need practical, sound advice that can transform their communities into safer locations for those at risk. This collection offers that advice, based on good science and direct experience from both the research and practitioner sectors. In moving toward a goal of disaster-resilient communities, we must work in concert. Emergency managers must pick up good volumes such as this book and apply the content. In this chapter, I write from my own lived experience as a disaster and gender scholar, a professor of emergency management, and simultaneously as a post-Katrina volunteer, researcher, and consultant. From those multiple roles, and the content of the preceding chapters, I pull together and integrate themes that apply to emergency management practice and policy.

The days since Hurricane Katrina have clearly revealed problems with how we manage the gendered vulnerabilities embedded in our communities. Progress has been made with general response and recovery, but often in a generic manner that is assumed to leverage resources for the vast majority of those at risk. The problem is that historically entrenched vulnerabilities—as we see reflected in this volume—are not so easily modified in a presumably cost-saving and expedient across-the-board approach. To foster disaster resilience, to reduce the need for response resources, and to shorten expensive recoveries means that we must attend to social vulnerabilities as they appear, exist, and linger within our communities.

Ultimately, that means that emergency managers must recognize and address social problems—including salary disparities that require women to spend higher proportions of their incomes for mitigation, evacuation, and recovery efforts; housing affordability issues that necessitate help from faith-based organizations so elderly widows can return home; issues of accessibility so that women with disabilities can travel to work from home and to access critical health care and social services (National Council on Disability 2009); and the exposure of both women and men to violence, especially girls with cognitive disabilities and elders at risk of financial exploitation (Phillips, Jenkins and Enarson 2010).

Emergency managers must accept that tackling the thorny, entrenched issues of social problems ultimately reduces the impact of disasters—and that they must work in concert with those in their communities targeting issues of housing, poverty, equity, accessibility, violence, child care, employment, health care, and more.

Social problems, particularly those associated with gender, compound disaster consequences. We cannot afford to move emergency management forward without acknowledgment of and action on gender issues.

We must therefore be proactive, not reactive, if we are to invoke meaningful change and promote safety. Doing so requires reading, understanding, and applying lessons learned from both experience and careful research. This chapter examines many of those key lessons and connects them with the necessary practical and policy work that must be undertaken. This volume also follows on more than two decades of dedicated work by researchers and practitioners concerned with reducing vulnerabilities tied to gender. In short, materials and insights exist to reach the goals of life safety for women and girls in harm's way. The failure to integrate these lessons into the daily practices and policies that guide emergency management suggests a callous disregard for human life.

The voices and perspectives of women and girls also come from and represent our own families, colleagues, faith community members, and neighbors. By listening to the lessons of this volume, we gain fresh viewpoints into the gendered experiences faced by our elderly parents, a sister parenting alone after divorce, our daughters and nieces who face renewed risk of violence, or a displaced colleague now seeking gainful employment. If in our roles as emergency managers we do not pay attention to their voices and needs, then we will have to do so as part of the broader community, responding through our volunteer time, agency donations, and taxpayer dollars.

The lessons from this volume also follow in another tradition from those concerned with gender and disaster issues. The gender and disaster community firmly believes that we need to be involved and connected with those at risk. Women know best what works for them—and failure to hire them as emergency managers, first responders, contractors, and specialists, or to include them in participating in response and recovery planning shortchanges the social capital that they can bring to disaster management. Women are not just victims; they are players and partners in the process of vulnerability reduction. Significant untapped resources exist within our communities, particularly among minority women, women with disabilities, and older women. We need what they know; we need insights from their lived experiences. They have a lifetime of identifying practical solutions to the realities in which they live. Building a bridge between emergency management and women in our communities simply makes sense.

The Starting Place

Those in positions of power expect dissidence, nay-saying, and even outright protest. For those working in the field of emergency management, such conflict, dissension, or disagreement should represent a potential point of insight. Social protest often erupts around issues of unmet needs, areas of concern, and locations where true need, pain, and suffering exist. Voices raised in outcry speak meaningfully of human conditions, of problems that require redress so that people can return to their home, to work, and to supportive social relationships they experienced prior to the onset of disaster.

In this volume there are multiple examples of women effectively pushing for a place at the table and consequently making considerable contributions because of the perspectives, connections, and resources they bring. In Biloxi, Mississippi, Coastal Women for Change transformed perspectives to incorporate concerns about child care, elder care, public housing, mental health needs, and more. Their seat at the table came after local women realized the powerful ways that developers and casino owners were influencing the post-Katrina recovery (see Hanshaw in this volume). Comprehensive recovery planning recognizes and integrates the full community (Phillips 2010).

For the emergency management community, this set of testimonials and firsthand accounts represents the voices of our partners, daughters, granddaughters, sisters, mothers, grandmothers, neighbors, colleagues, and faith family members. The women in our lives make a difference in a disaster. They are the ones who stand in line or go online for aid while simultaneously caring for elderly family members and neighbors, raising children, and working second jobs. We need to be partners in building their capacity to resist disaster by tapping into their usable knowledge and facilitating their safety and recovery.

Gendered Disaster Practice: Lessons Learned from This Volume

This extraordinary and unique volume instructs us through the voices of women and girls who experienced Katrina firsthand as survivors, caregivers, mothers, pregnant women, girls, elderly women, first responders, organization directors, advocates, and more. Women's roles after Katrina were as diverse as the ways in which the lives of women and girls were shattered, reshaped, and recovered. Throughout the volume, we gain a more clear understanding of how understanding gender alone is insufficient. Robichaux (in this volume), for instance, asks us a question from Houma women: "How much can people endure?" These Native American women, unrecognized yet as a federal tribe, felt distanced from and forgotten by a government they experienced as incompetent and unfeeling. Yet, as this volume also reveals, excruciatingly marginalized women stepped up and into roles to rebuild their communities, helping to provide the resources and support necessary to endure and survive. Women's survival and contributions after Katrina are noteworthy, particularly in the context of dislocation, unemployment, and stresses that resulted in debilitating mental health conditions, profound exhaustion, and grief. The story told here is one of tragedy and triumph, agony and survival, commitment, grit, and perseverance.

In reading through this volume it is clear that emergency managers can and must build a more gender-sensitive practice. Though it is essential that preparedness and mitigation be undertaken well in advance of a disaster in order to reduce injuries, life loss, and property damage, it is also clear that for many women in poverty such preparedness and mitigation is impossible. Some older women, many female-headed households, marginalized minority women, women with disabilities, and lesbians may require assistance and support to financially and physically reduce their risks. Becoming involved in disaster preparedness also clearly requires additional supports, such as holding training sessions where women work, live, and socialize; incorporating preparedness into school lessons so that parents benefit from reverse socialization; offering educational materials on public transportation to be read while commuting; holding sessions or posting material (in multiple literacy levels and languages) in laundry rooms, public housing lobbies, community centers, and senior centers—in short, it must be offered in the context of real women's lives. The lives of women who are caregivers for children or the elderly are particularly complex, and efforts to reach them through child care, maternal health care providers, domestic violence providers, and home health care must be considered.

When disasters loom, emergency managers must leverage the resources available to them to motivate compliance with evacuation and protective action directions. Social networks provide crucial conduits to deliver information, as research and first-hand accounts document here (e.g., see Litt, Skinner, and Robinson and Davis and Rouba in this volume). It is not enough, though, to think that a gender-specific message may reach the intended audience, given the diversity of women in our communities. Message specificity must consider the contexts and conditions in which women live. Pregnant women, for example, may face challenging choices regarding evacuation (see Zotti et al. in this volume). Poverty, disability, and multiple caregiver roles may compromise women's evacuation even more; it is clear since Katrina that those with caregiver roles for seniors and people with disabilities faced daunting transportation challenges. As they experienced Katrina, the evacuation became as problematic as staying. Mary Gehman's firsthand account of personal survival (in this volume) as she watched beloved neighbors face death speaks compellingly of our need to organize well in advance to provide for those in need of transportation.

For those who do evacuate, concerns linger about their shelter experience; after Katrina, women and girls in shelters experienced personal violence, harassment, and assaults. Pregnant women dealt with poor living conditions in shelters and other locations, including overcrowding, difficulty with breastfeeding, disrupted health care, and high-risk pregnancies (Zotti et al. in this volume). Loretta J. Ross (this volume) describes the hidden emotional work that women needed to do, especially those heading their own households. First responders, mental health providers, and shelter workers watched as mental health conditions deteriorated, especially for women bearing the burden of caring for others (see chapters in this volume by Marquis, by Berggren, and by Reid). Yet little was done to provide for the care of those who came to care for those displaced by Katrina. Few emergency management courses teach about a need for lactation support.

Moving out of temporary shelter into trailers or to permanent housing, in the unlikely event it was secured, was fraught with problems. Women with disabilities could not find affordable housing or accessible FEMA (Federal Emergency Management Agency) trailers. Older women lacked the income or sufficient insurance to rebuild. Formerly well-connected neighborhoods of people who took care of each other, shared resources, and made daily survival possible were gone. Resources needed to survive, such as battered women's shelters, had been destroyed (see Brown in this volume), as were critical prestorm social relationships (see Sterett in this volume). Health care services for people with disabilities could not be restored, and those in need of health care had to establish services with new providers (see Taylor in this volume). It became nearly impossible to find public housing, particularly in Louisiana, leaving public housing residents "stuck in limbo" for years (Henrici, Helmuth, and Carlberg, this volume).

Displacement profoundly affected women and girls all along the coast, in large part because of preexisting vulnerabilities, including reduced incomes that particularly compromised women of color (see Willinger and Knight in this volume). Women's status worsened further after the storm, resulting in lower wages and an elongated search for housing. Post-Katrina economic recovery also revealed insidious treatment of immigrant and migratory women, prone before and after the storm to dangerous debris and unhealthy work conditions, violence, and harassment; nonpayment for work rendered; and unhealthy living conditions (see "Antonia" in this volume). Because of the widespread displacement of people from the coast, their voices have not been present in critical places to raise concerns about public housing, schools, and hospitals. Those able to return must not only challenge these conditions, but also bravely face their own recoveries as well, in discourses complicated by gender, income, and racial disparities (see Jenkins in this volume). Though emergency managers typically focus on disaster situations, a recovery plan must clearly think comprehensively about economic needs specific to woman-owned businesses, women working part-time without benefits or insurance, workers in hazardous conditions, and those displaced from home-based employment (Enarson 2001).

Emergency managers must realize that these complex realities exist and plan for them accordingly. This volume speaks to that need as well by presenting good case studies of people, organizations, and agencies who stepped up. It is clear that, while Katrina undermined the lives of women and girls, there was also resiliency and determination to overcome. The concluding chapters present compelling instances of women building internal and cross-coalition efforts to deal with gender-specific issues. The messages are clear here: emergency managers can find partners to build effective emergency preparedness, response, and recovery efforts. By integrating women of color, a more culturally relevant approach can be generated (see Nguyen in this volume). Groups that historically have not been invited to planning tables, including the lesbian, gay, bisexual, and transgender communities, should be (Eads 2002). When disaster strikes, people set aside differences and collaborate to organize, fund, and help (see Rosenbaum in this volume). The networks that women rely on to gain information, initiate evacuation, survive dislocation, and launch recoveries become the vehicles through which emergency managers can act (see Peterson and Krajeski in this volume). Those networks, both formal and informal, offer linkages, resources, energy, and insights to fuel even the most catastrophic context. From this volume, it is clear that emergency managers must tap into that social capital well in advance of disaster (Passerini 2010).

A Roadmap for Further and Future Transformation

Disasters are frequently referred to as windows of opportunity. Transformative moments occur, particularly in the aftermath of the big ones such as Hurricane Andrew, the Northridge earthquake, and the Indian Ocean tsunami. When major events occur, funding is released, policies are reviewed and revised, and new advocates step up for those affected. Perhaps the model for transformative change in gendered practice and policy stems from what the disability community brought about after September 11 and Hurricane Katrina. Several lead organizations pushed for change, understanding that a return to normalcy postdisaster ultimately meant that risk remained. In this section, I review some of the key efforts that—while not necessarily coordinated—resulted in significant progress, with more to come. These endeavors suggest that a decentralized effort, a common model for women's activism, can foment significant change. (In the sections that follow, URLs are provided so that readers may look at the examples pointed out. All URLs were last accessed April 20, 2011.)

After September 11, the National Organization for Disability (NOD) established an Emergency Preparedness Initiative (EPI) that resulted in several model efforts. The first EPI director, Elizabeth Davis, wrote *Guide on the Special Needs of People with Disabilities for Emergency Managers, Planners, and Responders* (a revised edition is available at *www.nod.org/resources/PDFs/epiguide2005.pdf*). NOD sent the guide to emergency managers in every state, an effort that should be replicated for gender issues. NOD extended their work by creating a series of disability-specific brochures usable at the household and organizational levels (*www.nod.org/index.cfm?fuseaction=Feature .showFeature&FeatureID=1539*). While the Gender and Disaster Network offers similar types of usable materials at their website (*www.gdnonline.org*), the full range of possible materials suitable for diverse contexts and diverse populations has not yet been developed.

A good example of converging social forces occurred with the signing of Presidential Executive Order 13347 (*www.fema.gov/pdf/nims/nims_executive_order_13347 .pdf*). The National Organization on Disabilities and its EPI effort offered suggestions to the Department of Homeland Security (DHS) Office of Civil Rights and Civil Liberties (OCRCL). Daniel Sutherland, an officer in the OCRCL, worked with then-DHS secretary Tom Ridge to push forward a presidential executive order that mandated the inclusion of people with disabilities in all phases of emergency management activity, particularly preparedness and planning. More recently, the Obama administration is reworking the executive order for reissuing. This national-level policy paved the way for important new coordinating and leadership opportunities in the area of disabilities and disasters.

Section 2 of EO 13347 authorized the creation of the Interagency Coordinating Council on Emergency Preparedness and Individuals with Disabilities (ICC). The ICC serves as a means to coordinate and communicate among more than twenty federal agencies, as well as invited members such as the U.S. Access Board, the Equal Employment Opportunity Commission, and the Federal Communications Commission. Nine focus areas, linked to specific lead agencies, include emergency communications, workplace preparedness, emergency transportation, health and human services, housing, tribal outreach, nongovernmental outreach, policy, and research (U.S. Department of Homeland Security 2008). The ICC development has fostered critical exchanges at the federal level and allowed disability organizations to offer reviews, input, and suggestions to guides, legislation, and policies as they are under development. One policy that exhibits that influence is Public Law 109-295, which passed on October 4, 2006. The act made appropriations for the Department of Homeland Security and included Katrina funding and disability-specific content.

As noted by Mary Troupe, executive director of the Mississippi Coalition for Citizens with Disabilities, PL 109-295 served to launch a number of proactive initiatives, particularly the position of disability coordinator. In particular, Troupe (2009) notes that the position was to "be appointed by . . . [and] . . . report directly to the FEMA administrator," which created a communication channel to expedite issue-specific concerns directly to the top of FEMA. Section 513 of the law outlined the position of disability coordinator, to be hired after "consultation with organizations representing individuals with disabilities, the National Council on Disabilities, and the Interagency Coordinating Council on Preparedness and Individuals with Disabilities, established under Executive Order No. 13347" (U.S. Congress 2006). The section outlined ten key responsibilities, ranging from providing guidance to developing training materials to ensuring that emergency broadcasts reached their intended audience. Section 648 mandated the DHS director to work with the National Council on Disability and others to "carry out a national training program to implement the national preparedness goal" and related activities. In Section 649, the DHS administrator tasked the National Council on Disability and others to "establish a comprehensive system to assess, on an ongoing basis, the Nation's prevention capabilities and overall preparedness." Section 683 directed DHS, the National Advisory Council, and the National Council on Disability to develop a National Disaster Housing Strategy, which was released by FEMA and DHS in January 2009. Section 689a mandated nondiscrimination in disaster assistance by adding the term "disability."

In contrast, a search of Public Law 109–295 uncovered three gender-specific segments. Section 697 guided the DHS administrator to "establish and maintain a registry of contractors who are willing to perform debris removal, distribution of supplies, reconstruction, and other disaster or emergency relief activities," and insured that the registry would include woman-owned businesses. Section 845 directed that "the Administrator shall take reasonable steps to ensure that the student body represents racial, gender and ethnic diversity" in its Homeland Security Education Program. Obviously, an opportunity to transform disaster practice relevant to disaster concerns was lost.

Clearly, a federal agency tasked with responsibility for those at risk can make a difference, as indicated in how the National Council on Disability was integrated into Public Law 109–265. In 2005 (before Katrina) and 2009 (as a result of Katrina), the National Council on Disability published documents that described, explained, and promoted change across the four phases common to emergency management practice: preparedness and planning, response, recovery, and mitigation. Between publications, the National Council on Disability held quarterly meetings in which emergency managers, social workers, medical professionals, community advocates, and others described efforts under way in their communities. By providing a national traveling forum, this independent federal agency gave a formal voice to the disability community. Additional work resulted in a 2009 document titled *Effective Emergency Management: Making Improvements for Communities and People with Disabilities* (*www.ncd.gov/newsroom/publications/2009/pdf/NCD_EmergencyManagement.pdf*). NCD presented the document to the U.S. Congress and published it as a downloadable, accessible document on their website at *www.ncd.gov* and is now translating the empirically based document into materials usable for emergency managers and first responders.

Beyond federal initiatives, advocates within the disability community took up the call for change. Their efforts ranged from supporting displaced people with disabilities to filing lawsuits. The best known of the lawsuits, *Brou (et al.) v. FEMA (and DHS)*, stemmed from efforts by the Welfare Law Center, the Advocacy Center of Louisiana, the Mississippi Center for Justice, and the Public Interest Law Project. The class action lawsuit, which was filed on February 27, 2006, focused on a lack of available and accessible temporary trailers after Hurricane Katrina. Lengthy delays in securing accessible units resulted in protracted stays in shelters and other marginal accommodations. Those who moved into nonaccessible trailers faced difficulties with basic activities, including bathing, cooking, and moving about (National Center for Law and Economic Justice 2006a). The settlement, reached on September 26, 2006, resulted in creating a system with a toll-free number, staffing and a process for providing accessible trailers or modifications (National Center for Law and Economic Justice 2006b). According to the Advocacy Center of Louisiana, 2,553 people with disabilities contacted FEMA for help after the settlement. By March 28, 2007, FEMA had provided 1,400 accessible trailers and 256 modifications.

Assisting people in disasters often required not only advocacy but also professional case management. Until Hurricane Katrina, there was no case management process in place for use by any long-term recovery committee. The United Methodist Committee on Relief, along with support from FEMA, created case management materials that guided a caseworker through planning a recovery with a client. The National Disability Rights Network (NDRN) and its affiliates participated in this Katrina Aid Today process by helping to locate housing, child care, and other resources; making referrals for employment, job training, and medical benefits; and finding needed equipment for clients with disabilities (National Disability Rights Network, n.d.). To their credit, the NDRN subsequently assessed their efforts, finding that helping clients required considerable advocacy work. Case managers reported that they often had to convince FEMA and others that the client's needs were real and not an attempt to manipulate the system. Further, case managers indicated they had difficulty procuring needed resources specific to a client's needs (Stough and Sharp 2008).

Within the Department of Homeland Security (DHS), the Office for Civil Rights and Civil Liberties (OCRCL) supports disability and other such initiatives through four main ways: providing advice, investigating and resolving complaints from the public, providing leadership to the DHS equal employment opportunity program, and serving as a means through which information can pass. According to the DHS website and published materials (U.S. Department of Homeland Security, n.d.), the OCRCL "has helped advance civil rights and civil liberties by leading an energetic, government-wide effort to integrate people with disabilities into all aspects of emergency preparedness, response and recovery."

More broadly, Congress's failure to pass an Equal Rights Amendment has meant a protracted series of court battles. Conversely, the Americans with Disabilities Act (ADA) has prompted federal attention to disability issues. To illustrate, the U.S. Department of Justice has created emergency sheltering guidelines based on compliance with ADA. The guidance includes both narrative and checklist guidance that is both legal and practical (*www.ada.gov/pcatoolkit/chap7shelterchk.htm*). Individual lawsuits, such as *Savage v. City Place Limited Partnership*, have also challenged specific emergency planning and evacuation procedures for people with disabilities in malls and other public places (EAD and Associates 2004). Federal agencies such as the Federal Communications Commission continue to monitor and push for compliance with policies that require emergency messaging. There are no such parallels for gender issues.

Most recently, FEMA has created draft guidance documents for special needs. Comprehensive Planning Guide (CPG) 301, titled *Interim Emergency Management Planning Guide for Special Needs Populations* (*www.fema.gov/pdf/media/2008/301.pdf*), centers on disability issues; CPG 302 (in noncitation draft status as of December 2, 2009) will include guidelines for assisting service animals after disaster. CPG 301 is presently organized around functional needs areas such as communication, evacuation, transportation, medical needs, and shelter, while also recognizing phase-specific needs, including recovery (for further information on a functional approach, see Kailes and Enders 2006). Besides the value of a topical guide, what the participation of a federal agency demonstrates is the importance of addressing specialized needs—imagine what a federal guidance document on gender issues might do to increase safety and help emergency managers feel more competent in both functional and phase-specific needs related to gender!

Additional federal and national efforts demonstrate this potential. For example, after the *FEMA v. Brou* lawsuit, the U.S. Access Board, an independent federal agency, established the Emergency Transportable Housing Advisory Board and issued recommendations (*www.access-board.gov/eth/*). The U.S. Federal Highway Administration published an extensive primer, *Evacuating Populations with Special Needs*. Imagine if a similar primer could be created that, with the support of a federal agency, as a start organizes and expedites the safe relocation of women and children living in domestic violence shelters (Jenkins and Phillips 2008)!

Gendered Disaster Policy: A New Vision

To summarize, a wide range of disability initiatives has emerged and promoted the needs of a specific group within a fairly short period of time, most of which have occurred since September 11, 2001. Katrina served as a means to further institutionalize the organizations and initiatives in progress. Though much work remains to be done in the disability arena, it is equally clear that a national-level framework exists within which additional change can be made. What if that framework could be used to further gender issues?

Imagine the transformative value that would occur if we could accomplish the following:

- Convene federal agencies and advocacy organizations in a national conference to set a policy-making agenda that addresses the full range of gender concerns across the full spectrum of emergency management: mitigation, response, recovery, and preparedness.
- Craft and pass a presidential executive order that requires the integration and participation of women in all facets of emergency management and tasks a federal agency with creating a full set of materials to guide emergency managers in their local work.

- Appoint a national gender and disaster coordinator and use legislative opportunities after a disaster to delineate key responsibilities.
- Invite women's organizations, offices, and agencies to participate in an Interagency Coordinating Council on Gender and Disasters.
- Conduct cross-training between emergency management agencies and women's advocacy organizations.
- Task existing members of the ICC, FCC, and similar organizations to identify and address gender concerns. For example, challenge the National Council on Disability to research and address recommendations for gendered disability concerns or the Administration on Aging to specify the gendered issues of older women.
- Include funding in all disaster legislation to address gender-specific concerns.
- Fund a qualified set of researchers and/or advocacy organizations or federal agencies with developing a gender and disaster guide that would be sent out to all emergency managers.
- Require *www.ready.gov* to create and post gender-specific material.
- Conduct outreach to a diverse set of women and provide diverse means to involve them in planning efforts.
- Go to the places where women and girls live, work, recreate, and attend school—a variety of settings that could include individual homes, public housing, nursing homes, assisted living, group homes, and domestic violence survivor locations—and seek input, offer training, seek training, and plan together.
- Require that a domestic violence policy be present in the National Disaster Housing Strategy.
- Launch lawsuits to challenge exclusionary acts, the absence of policies that are gender-specific, or locations that fail to address gender concerns.
- Embed a means to evaluate the extent to which contracts are offered to woman-owned businesses.
- Create a National Council on Gender.
- Develop gender-friendly case management materials for use after a disaster.
- Research and craft a comprehensive national examination of gender and disaster issues similar to the work conducted by the National Council on Disability.
- Issue a comprehensive planning guide on gender issues through FEMA and integrate gender issues into existing CPG series guides.
- Incorporate those most marginalized into efforts that plan for all elements of disaster, including before, during, and after impact. Those living in areas of risk often understand what threatens them all too well, as they have probably experienced it previously. They also have strategies they use to mitigate, respond to, and recover from disaster—because they have done it before. Further, their experiences with the daily challenges of life outside disaster events have afforded insights and strategies that can be used in a disaster context.

Ultimately, though, addressing gendered disaster concerns will result only in reducing disaster impacts. To truly redress the impacts of disasters, it is absolutely necessary to tackle the entrenched and resistant social problems that foster unequal outcomes in the first place. Toward that end, emergency managers must work locally in their communities and support national efforts to accomplish the following ends:

- Pass equal rights laws.
- Afford access to health care, including reproductive rights.
- Increase affordable housing.
- Eliminate issues of accessibility.
- Protect older women from financial exploitation.
- Stop domestic violence, including that directed at women and girls with cognitive disabilities.
- Provide affordable child care.
- Correct salary disparities and job discrimination.
- Redress racial and ethnic discrimination and prejudice in the community, workplaces, and organizations.

In short, it is not enough to just do emergency management. It is necessary to also do justice work to make the world outside of disasters safer for our daughters, mothers, siblings, nieces, grandmothers, friends, colleagues, and neighbors.

Brenda D. Phillips is a professor in the Fire and Emergency Management Program at Oklahoma State University, where she teaches in the Gender and Women's Studies and International Studies Programs. She is also a senior researcher at the Center for the Study of Disasters and Extreme Events.

REFERENCES

Advocacy Center. (2007). Update on FEMA lawsuit. Retrieved from *www.advocacyla.org/news/fema.php*.

EAD and Associates. (2004). Landmark decision requires accessible evacuation procedures at all Marshall's stores nationwide. Retrieved from *www.eadassociates.com/marshalls.html*.

Eads, M. (2002). Marginalized groups in times of disaster. Quick response report no. 152. Boulder: Natural Hazards Research and Applications Information Center, University of Colorado.

Enarson, E. (2001). What women do: Gendered labor in the Red River Valley flood. *Environmental Hazards, 3*, 1–18.

Jenkins, P., and Phillips, B. (2008). Battered women, catastrophe, and the context of safety after Hurricane Katrina. *NWSA Journal, 20*(3), 49–68.

Kailes, J., and Enders, A. (2006). Moving beyond special needs: A function-based framework for emergency management and planning. *Journal of Disability Policy Studies, 17*(4), 230–237.

National Center for Law and Economic Justice. (2006). *Brou v. FEMA.* Press release. Retrieved from *www.nclej.org/pdf/FEMA_description.pdf*.

National Council on Disability. (2009). *Effective emergency management: Making improvements for communities and people with disabilities.* Washington, DC: National Council on Disability.

National Disability Rights Network. (n.d.). Katrina Aid Today fact sheet. Retrieved from *www.napas.org/emerg/FS_KAT0606.pdf*.

Passerini, E. (2010). The nature of human communities. In B. Phillips, D. Thomas, A. Fothergill, and L. Blinn-Pike (Eds.), *Social vulnerability to disasters* (pp. 307–322). Boca Raton, FL: CRC Press.

Phillips, B. (2010). *Disaster recovery*. Boca Raton, FL: CRC Press.

Phillips, B., Jenkins, P., and Enarson, E. (2010). Violence and disaster vulnerability. In B. Phillips, D. Thomas, A. Fothergill, and L. Blinn-Pike (Eds.), *Social vulnerability to disasters* (pp. 279–306). Boca Raton, FL: CRC Press.

Stough, L., and Sharp, A. (2008). An evaluation of the National Disability Rights Network participation in the Katrina Aid Today project. Washington, DC: National Disability Rights Network.

Troupe, M. (2009). Testimony before the Committee on Homeland Security, House of Representatives, hearing on PKEMRA implementation: An examination of FEMA's preparedness and response mission.

U.S. Congress. (2006). Public Law 109–295. Retrieved from *frwebgate.access.gpo.gov/cgibin/getdoc .cgi?dbname=109_cong_public_laws&docid=f:publ295.109.pdf*.

U.S. Department of Homeland Security. (2008). About the Interagency Coordinating Council on Emergency Preparedness and Individuals with Disabilities. Retrieved from *www.dhs.gov/files/ committees/editorial_0592.shtm*.

———. (n.d.). Brochure. Washington, DC: U.S. Department of Homeland Security Office for Civil Rights and Civil Liberties. Retrieved from *www.dhs.gov/xlibrary/assets/CRCL_Brochure_ May05.pdf*.

U.S. Federal Highway Administration. (2009). *Evacuating populations with special needs*. Washington, DC: U.S. Federal Highway Administration. Retrieved from *ops.fhwa.dot.gov/ publications/fhwahop09022/index.htm*.

CHAPTER 27

Critical Disjunctures

Disaster Research, Social Inequality,
Gender, and Hurricane Katrina

Kathleen Tierney

Throughout its history, the field of disaster research has been characterized by a series of "critical disjunctures," a term I use here to refer to discontinuities in research, the systematic neglect of some research topics and a preference for others, and an apparent collective resistance to the introduction of new ideas. Critical disjunctures, which are problematic for any discipline, may actually be more common in disaster research than in other fields, for reasons I discuss here. I highlight several examples of disjunctures, looking at the field historically and with a particular emphasis on its neglect of issues related to social inequality, including in particular gender inequality, and its lack of attention to the lived experiences of disaster survivors.

Early Research on Disasters: Seeing Yet Not Seeing

Some critical disjunctures are linked to the origins and early years of the field itself. First, classic studies did almost nothing to address disparities in disaster impacts or the varied experiences of populations exposed to disasters. Instead, to satisfy the needs of early funders, research emphasized typical or modal patterns in disaster response, such as the expansion of altruistic behavior, the emergence of therapeutic communities, mass convergence, and forms of organizational adaptation, including in particular group emergence (Brouillette and Quarantelli 1969; Dynes 1970; Fritz 1961; Stallings and Quarantelli 1985). Information on group behavior was used to debunk popular (and elite) myths about public behavior under conditions of extreme stress, such as myths surrounding panic and antisocial behavior.

Second, in studying group and organizational behavior, researchers generally obtained data from organizational informants who played major roles in responding to disasters, not from community residents themselves. When disaster researchers did begin to collect data from residents of affected communities (such as information on how victims assessed support received from the disaster assistance system and information on service needs and mental health problems), those data were obtained through surveys and analyzed quantitatively. In contrast with most of the research in this volume, early studies paid scant attention to the actual experiences of disaster survivors as they passed—or failed to pass—through various stages of the disaster cycle.

Third, for at least the first three decades of its existence, the field of disaster re-search remained largely impervious to influences from the broader field of sociology and from general scholarship in other social science fields. Notwithstanding some efforts to connect the field with other subdisciplines, such as the study of organiza-tions and collective behavior (Dynes 1970; Haas and Drabek 1970; Mileti, Drabek, and Haas 1975; Wenger 1987), disaster researchers appeared more concerned with de-veloping a body of evidence specific to disasters and other crisis situations than with linking the study of disasters with broader sociological and social science concerns.

Most important for the discussions that follow, for many years the field was largely unaffected by the rise of the study of women and gender as a topic for socio-logical research. This may be in part because in many respects classic disaster research was itself a strongly gendered enterprise. The topics studied were largely those that were of interest to the military. The organizational managers and personnel who were interviewed—now termed "first responders," even though the first responders in all disasters are community residents—were by and large men. Most of the organiza-tions studied were gendered (Acker 1990). Field researchers, including the pioneer-ing researchers who established the field, were also men. Women did not begin to play key roles in disaster fieldwork until the 1970s, and even when they did, their research activities were undertaken within the already-established classic disaster re-search frame (Tierney 2002). The field thus developed in a way that privileged male-oriented perspectives on disasters and their management. Put another way, from their positions of privilege, early researchers did not "see gender" in the same way whites in the United States do not "see color." Indeed, Joseph Scanlon argues that the bias toward masculinist portrayals of disaster responses began with the work of Samuel Henry Prince himself: "His [Prince's] most-quoted source was an unpublished manu-script by Dwight Johnstone (circa 1919), which, in spite of the examples of women staying on the job despite the risk, women taking part in the postimpact response, and examples of both men *and* women fleeing when there were rumors of a second explosion, Prince omits all the positive references to women, as well as the negative references to men" (1998, 47).

A Growing Emphasis on Diversity and Inequality: The 1970s and 1980s

Over time, the field evolved. Beginning in the late 1970s and early 1980s, studies on topics such as evacuation and emergency sheltering brought to light patterns that were related to axes of inequality and diversity such as race, ethnicity, social class, and household composition. Other studies pointed to race and ethnicity as factors that affected disaster recovery processes and outcomes (Bolin 1982; Bolin and Bolton 1986) and looked at other dimensions of diversity, such as age (Kilijanek and Drabek 1979) and disability (Tierney, Petak, and Hahn 1986), as factors that affected disaster vulnerability and victims' experiences. In the 1970s, studies on societal responses to the earthquake threat in Southern California (Turner, Nigg, and Heller Paz 1986) also emphasized the role of class, race, gender, and other social factors in predicting risk perception, preparedness behaviors, and other disaster-related behaviors. Other research pointed to the significance of axes of inequality and diversity for psychosocial and mental health outcomes following disasters (for meta-analyses incorporating both earlier and more recent work, see Norris et al. 2002). However, despite its value, the body of knowledge that developed around race, class, gender, and related concepts in the 1980s was mainly survey oriented. Very much in line with the mechanistic "race as a variable/class as a variable" approach that dominated sociological research during the period, research on populations affected by disasters revealed important general patterns but did little to illuminate the lived experiences of those who were touched by disaster or to take advantage of insights from emerging disciplines such as gender, race, or ethnic studies. Regarding the treatment of gender in both classic and contemporary disaster research, Bolin, Jackson, and Crist observed that

> because of generally conservative theoretical approaches, the U.S. literature has failed to engage issues of socially produced gender inequality and vulnerability in disasters; . . . neither gender nor other factors are adequately theorized or analyzed as complex historically situated phenomena. . . . Discussions that simply compare differences in disaster responses between men and women routinely avoid any in-depth analysis of the social-structural inequalities (economic, political, legal, occupational, familial, ideological, cultural) underlying and variously producing observed gender differences. As a consequence, important questions about the social dynamics of gendered experiences are left unasked. (1998, 29)

Despite the advances in research reviewed in the sections that follow, as the editors of this volume note in their introduction, these statements remain largely true today.

U.S. Urban Disasters and the Rise of New Theoretical Frameworks

Disaster events and broader disciplinary trends brought about a further evolution of disaster scholarship in the 1990s. In many respects, the 1989 Loma Prieta earthquake was a watershed for the field. Loma Prieta was a large earthquake that created disastrous impacts in many parts of the San Francisco Bay Region, affecting highly diverse populations. Because of the scope and severity of the earthquake's impacts, agencies such as the National Science Foundation and the U.S. Geological Survey made special funds available for social science research in the affected region—funding that enabled social science researchers to conduct in-depth studies.

Loma Prieta vividly demonstrated the ways in which disasters affect large heterogeneous urban regions and interact with ongoing problems such as homelessness and the lack of affordable housing in large urban areas to disproportionately affect vulnerable groups. In many respects, the communities affected by Loma Prieta were natural laboratories that enabled researchers to examine the influence of predisaster vulnerability, social diversity, and community context, both in terms of the distinctiveness of place as experienced by groups within the impact region and in terms of the importance of historical trends affecting people and places. Researchers documented the ways in which Loma Prieta affected Latino workers in Santa Cruz County and immigrants in general, and they also noted the ways in which the official disaster assistance system failed vulnerable populations in the aftermath of the disaster (Phillips 1998). Like all disasters, Loma Prieta resulted in an outpouring of altruistic behavior. However, it also was accompanied by contentious collective action, including protests by and the establishment of an alternative disaster shelter by Latinos in Santa Cruz County; lawsuits against FEMA (Federal Emergency Management Agency) for its failure to assist equitably all disaster victims; and demands that money raised by the Red Cross, ostensibly for victims of the earthquake, actually be spent in the Bay region. With this particular disaster event, sociological disaster researchers grappled with issues of race, class, ethnicity, and disaster-related conflict, even as gender issues remained largely overlooked (but see Phillips 1990 for an exception).

Despite the fact that the Los Angeles urban unrest of 1992 was a federally declared disaster, few disaster sociologists conducted research on that event. To vastly oversimplify a complex series of events, those who attacked people and property in the 1992 unrest (but mostly property, since the loss of life was not large relative to other U.S. riot episodes) tended to be African Americans and Latinos, and those who suffered disproportionate losses tended to be Korean and other Asian business owners whose businesses happened to be located in neighborhoods with high concentrations of African Americans and Latinos (Abelmann and Lie 1995). Like Loma Prieta, the 1992 rebellion revealed the significance of race, class, and ethnicity in large-scale community crisis events and again highlighted issues associated with delivering disaster services to diverse populations (for discussions, see Baldassare 1994; Gooding-Williams 1993). However, here again, while some scholars chronicled women's experiences in the Los Angeles insurrection, gender issues were eclipsed by those associated with race, class, and ethnicity.

That disjuncture was addressed to some degree in research conducted following Hurricane Andrew later in 1992. Like Loma Prieta and the Los Angeles rebellion, Andrew struck a highly diverse group of communities and brought to the fore issues of differential vulnerability associated with race, class, and ethnicity. However, in contrast with those events, Andrew helped inspire researchers like Betty Hearn Morrow and Elaine Enarson, themselves victims of the hurricane, to probe seriously the significance of gender in disasters. Research on the Andrew disaster also signaled a small but significant shift in disaster research from positivistic and objective research to more interpretive forms of research centered on the lived experiences of disaster victims. The impact of these changes is best exemplified in the edited volumes *Hurricane Andrew: Ethnicity, Gender, and the Sociology of Disaster* (Peacock, Morrow, and Gladwin 1997) and especially *The Gendered Terrain of Disaster: Through Women's Eyes* (Enarson and Morrow 1998).

Studies on women's experiences in Hurricane Andrew reflect both the incorporation into disaster research of a distinctly gendered voice and the interpretive turn that was gaining momentum in the broader field of sociology. Like other disciplines, sociology and disaster research were becoming increasingly open to the less positivistic and more subject-centered approaches associated with qualitative, interpretive, ethnographic, and narrative methods of data collection and analysis. This new focus on documenting the lived experiences of disaster survivors in their complexity yielded many important insights, although such insights continue to be underappreciated within the field.

The second assessment of research on natural hazards, coordinated by Dennis Mileti of the University of Colorado during the 1990s (see Mileti 1999 for a summary of assessment findings), also addressed a number of disjunctures in the disaster literature, including those associated with gender. Under the auspices of the second assessment, Alice Fothergill developed comprehensive literature reviews on the role of gender across all phases of the hazards cycle, along with critiques of the ways in which the larger field ignored gender issues (Fothergill 1996, 1998). Fothergill later went on to write *Heads above Water: Gender, Class, and Family in the Grand Forks Flood* (2004) and other publications on gender and disasters. Lori Peek, who also worked on the second assessment, now specializes in the study of gender, age, ethnicity, and religion in disasters (Enarson, Fothergill, and Peek 2006; Peek 2008; Peek and Stough 2010).

While the disjunctures that had characterized earlier work had by no means been addressed by the end of the last century, they had at least been made more evident. Equally important, the 1990s saw the development of a small but very active cadre of researchers who were determined to ensure that previously ignored topics would receive increased attention.

September 11, Katrina, and Beyond

The first five years of the new millennium were marked by the occurrence of two of the most significant disaster events in U.S. history: the terrorist attacks of September 11 and Hurricane Katrina. At a historical distance of ten years and after the occurrence of Katrina, it is perhaps understandable that memories of 9/11 and the research it inspired have faded. However, at the time they took place, the attacks generated enormous interest on the part of both funding agencies and the research community. Large amounts of funding were again made available by the National Science Foundation and other agencies, and both quick response and longer-term studies were launched. The New York–based Social Science Research Council began collecting research essays on 9/11 for an online archive (as it later did more extensively following Hurricane Katrina), leading to the publication of *Understanding September 11* (Calhoun, Price, and Timmer 2002), a volume that focused mainly on global violence and terrorism, as opposed to the impacts of the 9/11 attacks in New York.

Gender was addressed to some extent following the terrorist attacks, but in varying ways. Survey-based studies revealed gender-related differences in mental health symptoms, fear of terrorism, and views on national security (see Chu et al. 2006; Neria et al. 2006). Gender was also discussed in connection with the oppressed status and life experiences of women in the Muslim world (see Caiazza 2001; Reed 2002), as well as in connection with U.S. Muslim students' coping efforts—including efforts to deal with backlash against Muslims—in the wake of 9/11 (Peek 2004). However, to the extent that gender-based narratives developed following 9/11, those narratives tended to center on global themes related to masculine violence and the oppression and silencing of women worldwide, as opposed to the lived experiences of men and women who survived and coped with the attacks' aftermath.

For some researchers, 9/11 represented a return to the study of more longstanding research concerns, such as disaster convergence and interorganizational coordination and collaboration (Kendra and Wachtendorf 2003a, 2003b) The attacks also generated important new insights into common but little-studied disaster-related processes, such as organizational improvisation in the face of surprise (Wachtendorf 2004). September 11 did result in significant advances in disaster research, but not necessarily in areas related to social diversity and inequality.

In addition to their troubling policy outcomes, the 9/11 attacks signaled a return to classic masculine social constructions of disasters: the elevation of first responders as the heroes of 9/11; a focus on the work of crisis relevant organizations, which are themselves highly gendered; an emphasis on the value of effective postdisaster responses, as opposed to the less visible work of mitigation, preparedness, and recovery; and a preoccupation with the state as the ultimate provider of public security, accompanied by a downplaying of the role of civil society. Women's activities were not entirely ignored following 9/11. Important to the 9/11 story were emergent groups like the women-led Skyscraper Safety Campaign; the Family Steering Committee, some of whose members became known as the Jersey Widows, or the Jersey Girls (a group that was derided by Ann Coulter, the siren of the far right); and the "bubble girls" who staffed the respite center at Ground Zero. The founders of the Skyscraper Safety campaign were Sally Regenhard, whose son, a firefighter, died at Ground Zero, and Monica Gabrielle, whose husband died in the World Trade Center attacks. The group pushed for investigations of the events of 9/11 and also campaigned for stricter safety codes in high-rise buildings. The Family Steering Committee was instrumental in the establishment of the 9/11 Commission. Several members, including some of the Jersey Widows, are featured in the 2006 documentary *9/11: Press for Truth*, by Ray Nowosielski and John Duffy. The "bubble girls" and their support activities are documented in the film *9/12: From Chaos to Community*, by Susanna Styron. But by and large the gender narratives that emerged after 9/11 centered on men—particularly first responders—and valorized their experiences (e.g., see Langewiesche 2002; Monahan 2006, 2010).

Equally important, the hypermasculinized response to 9/11 foreshadowed patterns that would more fully unfold in the aftermath of Katrina. As both an act of international terrorism and an attack that was framed by the Bush administration as an act of war, 9/11 was accompanied by a then-unprecedented mobilization on the part of military, security, and law enforcement agencies. There was of course reason to fear follow-on acts of terrorism, particularly in New York, but the convergence of public safety, investigative, and military personnel on that city can also be interpreted as a symbolic response to the attacks, similar to security theater performances at airports, that was meant to reassure the public and the media that the terrorist threat was under control. September 11 also provided an early glimpse of the official reactions Katrina would engender. The difference was that in Katrina, it was the victims who were socially constructed as the enemy (Tierney and Bevc 2007; Tierney, Bevc, and Kuligowski 2006).

U.S. disaster research became increasingly globalized in the new millennium—a positive trend that was reinforced by the occurrence of the Great Sumatra earthquake and Indian Ocean tsunamis of December 2004. Gender issues came to the fore to some degree in that catastrophic event, which took the lives of more than 230,000 people in twelve nations in the Indian Ocean region. Women were more likely than men to die in the tsunamis. In Tamil Nadu state in India, the death rate for women was triple that of men. In early research, Aryiabandu (2006) highlighted disparities in women's treatment in Sri Lanka following the tsunamis. Among the many depredations they suffered, women were denied direct access to government funds under male "head of household" rules; rape and violence against women increased; women's need for privacy was not recognized in short-term housing arrangements; and women were given little voice in reconstruction and recovery. Research conducted in Tamil Nadu revealed gender disparities in assistance given to women, even though in that state the Indian government took the unusual steps of requiring that replacement housing be deeded to women (sometimes to both men and women) and stipulating that home ownership could not be transferred to men, in contravention of customs of male ownership. Even with such assurances, women were disadvantaged in access to postdisaster assistance and marginalized as the result of their status as widows or unmarried women, and many coped with food shortages by eating less so that their children could be fed.

Men also suffered as a result of losing their livelihoods, and many began to drink heavily. Because so many women died, men were required to take on new household and parenting duties. Young girls and boys who had lost parents and family members in the tsunamis experienced various hardships, such as being forced into marriage (for an extended discussion of gender issues in the Indian Ocean tsunamis, see Pincha 2008; see also Wachtendorf et al. 2006). Pincha also discusses the post-tsunami experiences of the *aravani*, or "third sex," who are men or transsexual persons who live as women and are ostracized in Indian society.

Katrina Research: Continuities and Contributions

After Katrina, a broad base of academia and to a lesser extent the general public became aware of societal patterns that the tiny community of disaster scholars had gradually come to understand over decades, although imperfectly: that the damage and disruption disasters cause offer direct insights into how societies function during nondisaster times; that far from being acts of God that strike victims randomly, disasters are the products of human decisions and processes of social triage that condense into short time frames patterns of oppression that normally play out over time; and that activities undertaken to respond and recover from disasters—if there is such a thing as recovery—serve primarily to reproduce predisaster inequities.

Just as other groups emerged in the aftermath of the Katrina catastrophe, a large cadre of new disaster scholars has also emerged. This is not a new phenomenon; disasters invariably attract new researchers into the field, typically scholars from higher-education institutions in areas affected by disasters, whose studies of those local events often constitute their only ventures into disaster research. Various disasters have attracted a second group of repeat offenders, but generally prior to Katrina the study of hazards and disasters had remained a small and esoteric specialty (for discussions on various levels of involvement by researchers, see National Research Council 2006). But Katrina was different. As one of a handful of true catastrophes to strike the United States, and as an event that brought into sharp relief both the astounding ineptitude of governmental systems and the systemic violence of a society characterized by equally astounding patterns of inequality and injustice, Katrina shocked the conscience and stirred the curiosity both of seasoned disaster researchers and of the broader academic community in ways no other U.S. disaster has. Massive in its scale and scope and multifarious in its effects, Katrina became, in the words of disaster scholar Shirley Laska (2008), "the Mother of all Rorschachs," a dark crystal whose every facet yields important insights for a wide array of academic disciplines, as well as for multidisciplinary, interdisciplinary, and transdisciplinary research. Indeed, Katrina is among the most-studied disasters in history. The still-emerging body of social science research on the Katrina catastrophe, of which the chapters in this volume are an example, will add immeasurably to social scientific knowledge on the root causes, processes, and outcomes of disasters. It will also make major strides in addressing critical disjunctures in earlier research.

Many contributors to this volume provide the kinds of contextual analysis the field of disaster research needs. New Orleans is a unique American city. Katrina was a uniquely catastrophic event, and much of what occurred during the Katrina catastrophe, such as the involuntary movement of tens of thousands of victims who were given no choice in where they were moved, was also unique in modern U.S. history. However, even as there are unique disasters and distinctive contexts, there are patterns that continually appear in disasters of all kinds. The task of disaster research is both to document what is distinctive about particular disasters and to highlight commonalities that exist across different disaster events. This volume captures the uniqueness of the setting and the event, but at the same time, it connects women's experiences to their positions in community and social hierarchies, as well as to women's experiences in other disasters.

Much of the work contained here emphasizes the notion that women and men organize their lives and cope with life's vicissitudes within specific places and spaces. For the women of New Orleans, that meant living close to relatives who could provide material and social support, relying on public transportation or on cars available through network ties, and finding ways of making do on low incomes derived from working in purportedly women's jobs. As Litt, Skinner, and Robinson point out, survival in New Orleans also meant finding ways of compensating for deficiencies in the city's ability to provide for basic life needs such as physical safety, housing, jobs, and health care. Writing about the plight of women of the Houma nation, Robichaux observes that after Katrina, "they were made dependent and then given nothing to depend on." This was true for many victims after the hurricane—but it was also true for many groups before the hurricane, not only in the impact region but across the nation. As Litt, Skinner, and Robinson observe, Katrina and its aftermath represent the products, first, of a predisaster nationwide "destruction of public provision" and, second, of a postdisaster destruction of the social networks that made life possible for the most vulnerable.

The poor and vulnerable nonetheless find ways of coping, as these narratives show. Even the worst off were able to build a "vibrant, collective, and interdependent life" (Litt, Skinner, and Robinson, this volume). However, as chapter authors also emphasize, coping strategies are typically locally based. Henrici, Helmuth, and Carlberg, for example, discuss the experiences of public housing residents after Katrina. Residents were able to cope during regular times, but their coping capacities were "spatially bounded"—adapted to the particular ecology of their New Orleans neighborhoods. Coping strategies like these are not portable. One consequence of Katrina was the massive destruction the hurricane and levee failures wrought—a level of destruction that ensured a difficult path to recovery for all victimized groups. Another consequence, which the governmental response itself helped create, was the way in which the disaster ripped women and men away from what was left of their local networks and indigenous resources, leaving them unmoored when they most needed those ties—the way it "made them dependent but gave them nothing to depend on." Indeed, Katrina in New Orleans captures the imagination of researchers like those whose work is compiled here in part because it represents a logical extension of the project of the neoliberal state: a largely African American population made vulnerable through both government neglect of cities and the welfare of their residents and the machinations of economic profiteers; hollowed-out public institutions that were barely functioning even during nondisaster times; the profit-driven destruction of the protections offered by the natural environment; and then, when the catastrophe struck, a governmental response that failed victims in their time of greatest need.

For those struggling to cope in the aftermath of Katrina, broken and even intact social networks offered little comfort. Because of the unique history of New Orleans, networks were especially local and tight-knit. As research in this volume indicates, those who were displaced did their best to maintain and reestablish ties social network ties, but that was extremely difficult. Moreover, the process of returning to New Orleans was racialized and gendered, with African American women returning to the city at lower rates than their white, Hispanic, and Asian counterparts. The decision to demolish low-income housing made that process all the more difficult.

Chapters in this collection reveal both the distinctiveness of the lives of the women of Katrina and the ways in which they resemble the lives of women across the nation and around the globe. The women of Katrina were heads of households, providing for their children without the help of men. They were the ones who did the networking and emotional work that sustained their families. They toiled in low-wage jobs and came home to work the second shift. They were afraid for the safety, well-being, and education of their children. At the same time, the authors in this volume present a much more nuanced portrait of the women of Katrina—women whose identities were constructed out of their experiences as African Americans, people of color, immigrants, Jews, Asian Americans, Native Americans, women of the bayous, people of faith, and poor and working women. Observations by Nguyen and other authors on the significance of intersectionality and of multiple identities and subjectivities provide an important corrective to overly general treatments of women's experiences in both daily life and in disasters. This approach shows how those who are socially constructed as victims of disaster can become agents in their own lives and the lives of their communities. The recognition by the women of Versailles of one kind of environmental injustice—differential vulnerability and unequal treatment in the Katrina disaster—accompanied by their growing sense of empowerment, led to collective action to address another environmental injustice, a toxic landfill in their own backyard.

Like the chapter by Mia Charlene White, who writes eloquently in this volume about the sense of attachment African American residents feel for Turkey Creek and North Gulfport, Peterson and Krajeski's chapter shows women of faith constructing communities that play important roles in responding and advocating for the rights of victims in disasters. They remind us that just as place matters, faith also matters, and the sense of identity and community derived both from place and faith matter even more.

Women may suffer disproportionately in disasters, but suffering does not rob them of their agency; indeed, to the extent that disasters create the potential for collective action, they can even strengthen it. The empirical record contains many examples of women's active involvement in disaster response and recovery in the United States, such as the work of Women Will Rebuild after Hurricane Andrew (Enarson and Morrow 1998) and the activities of Women of the Storm, discussed by Emmanuel David in this volume, after Hurricane Katrina (and see Yonder, Akcar, and Gopalan for the case of India and Turkey [2005]).

Like the work in this volume, new studies must continually aim to reconcile disjunctures, fill gaps, and give voice to the lived experiences of the victims of disaster: the poor and marginalized, as well as the better-off; those with political power and those without; and women as well as men. On this last point, gender researchers have a responsibility to ensure that the study of gender in disasters focuses not only on women but also on men. As neglected as women have been in disaster studies, and as important as the contributions in this volume are in redressing that imbalance, researchers cannot lose sight of the fact that gendering disaster research requires studying the social forces that affect the experiences of men as well as women. This volume has appropriately brought to the fore the importance of history, community, intersectionality, and identity, social and family networks, race, ethnicity, disability, religion, and other factors in understanding the experiences of the women of Katrina. However, the same kinds of factors also affected and continue to affect the men of Katrina—men whose stories also need to be told. The men of Katrina experienced the pain of losing loved ones, jobs, and longstanding community ties. Like the women whose stories are told here, many of their experiences were structured by gender—although of course not by gender alone. For example, Dave Eggars (2009) documents the story of Abdulrahman Zeitoun, a Syrian-born painting contractor who stayed behind in New Orleans in order to help those in need when his American wife and children evacuated, but who was arrested as a suspected terrorist and held incommunicado for weeks, first in the infamous Camp Greyhound and later in a special Department of Homeland Security–operated section of the Elayn Hunt Correctional Center in St. Gabriel, Louisiana.

Part of the gendered story of Katrina is that the hurricane and the devastation it caused provided for some men an occasion in which to exercise their need for dominance. After Katrina, New Orleans became a city populated by the military, defense contractors, and various other security agencies. Guns were ubiquitous, and a macho, Wild West climate developed. In the most egregious cases, men were shot and some were murdered for no reason other than the color of their skins and the fact that they were in the wrong place at the wrong time when other men felt the urge to kill (Solnit 2010). Soldiers who had fought in Iraq were redeployed to New Orleans, where they took part in the largest military mobilization for any disaster in U.S. history, which was framed by the media and public officials alike as a war-zone operation (Tierney and Bevc 2010; Tierney, Bevc, and Kuligowski 2006). Katrina reminds us that although they often actively oppress or are complicit in the oppression of women, many men are also victims of oppression and, when disasters strike, are themselves vulnerable by virtue of social class, race, ethnicity, and other axes of inequality and diversity.

The field of disaster research continues to learn from Katrina, even as it turns its attention to disasters around the world, including the 2008 earthquake in China and most recently the 2010 Haiti earthquake catastrophe and the devastating earthquake, tsunami, and nuclear power plant accident that struck Japan in 2011. As this volume shows, many researchers are committed to addressing disjunctures and conceptual and theoretical blind spots that have long been part of the history of the field. This work is important and merits greater support, both for what it tells us about disasters and, equally important, for what it reveals about the societies in which they occur.

Kathleen Tierney is professor of sociology and director of the Natural Hazards Center at the University of Colorado at Boulder. She is the coauthor of *Facing the Unexpected: Disaster Preparedness and Response in the United States* (2001), and her numerous publications on disaster theory and research appear in leading journals and books.

REFERENCES

Abelman, N., and Lie, J. (1995). *Blue dreams: Korean Americans and the Los Angeles riots.* Cambridge, MA: Harvard University Press.

Acker, J. (1990). Hierarchies, jobs, bodies: A theory of gendered organizations. *Gender and Society, 4,* 139–158.

Ariyabandu, M. M. (2006). Gender issues in recovery from the December 2004 Indian Ocean tsunami: The case of Sri Lanka. *Earthquake Spectra, 22,* S759–S775.

Baldassare M. (Ed.). (1994). *The Los Angeles riots: Lessons for the urban future.* Boulder, CO: Westview Press.

Bolin, R. C. (1982). Long-term family recovery from disaster. Boulder: Natural Hazards Center, Institute of Behavioral Science, University of Colorado.

Bolin, R. C., and Bolton, P. (1986). *Race, religion, and ethnicity in disaster recovery.* Monograph no. 42. Boulder: Natural Hazards Center, University of Colorado.

Bolin, R. C., Jackson, M., and Christ, A. (1998). Gender inequality, vulnerability, and disaster: Issues in theory and research. In E. Enarson and B. H. Morrow (Eds.), *The gendered terrain of disaster: Through women's eyes* (pp. 27–44). Westport, CT: Greenwood.

Brouillette, J. R., and Quarantelli, E. L. (1969). Types of patterned variation in bureaucratic adaptations to organizational stress. Working paper no. 18. Newark: Disaster Research Center, University of Delaware.

Caiazza, A. (2001). Why gender matters in understanding September 11: Women, militarism, and violence. Washington, DC: Institute for Women's Policy Research.

Calhoun, C. C., Price, P., and Timmer, A. (Eds.). (2002). *Understanding September 11.* New York: New Press.

Chu, T. Q., Holman, E. A., Poulin, D. J., Gil-Rivas, V., and Pizarro, J. (2006). Ethnicity and gender in the face of a terrorist attack: A national longitudinal study of immediate responses and outcomes two years after September 11. *Basic and Applied Social Psychology, 28,* 291–301.

Dynes, R. R. (1970). *Organized behavior in disaster.* Lexington, MA: D. C. Heath.

Eggers, D. (2009). *Zeitoun.* San Francisco: McSweeney's Books.

Enarson, E., Fothergill, A., and Peek, L. (2006). Gender and disaster: Foundations and directions. In H. Rodriguez, E. L. Quarantelli, and R. R. Dynes (Eds.), *Handbook of disaster research* (pp. 130–146). New York: Springer.

Enarson, E., and Morrow, B. H. (Eds.). (1998). *The gendered terrain of disaster: Through women's eyes.* Westport, CT: Greenwood.

Fothergill, A. (1996). Gender, risk, and disaster. *International Journal of Mass Emergencies and Disasters, 14*, 33–56.

———. (1998). The neglect of gender in disaster work: An overview of the literature. In E. Enarson and B. H. Morrow (Eds.), *The gendered terrain of disaster: Through women's eyes* (pp. 11–25). Westport, CT: Greenwood.

———. (2004). *Heads above water: Gender, class, and family in the Grand Forks flood.* Albany: State University of New York Press.

Fritz, C. E. (1961). Disasters. In R. K. Merton and R. A. Nisbet (Eds.), *Social problems* (pp. 651–694). New York: Harcourt.

Gooding-Williams, R. (Ed.). (1993). *Reading Rodney King/Reading urban uprising.* New York: Routledge.

Haas, J. E., and Drabek, T. E. (1970). Community disaster and system stress: A sociological perspective. In J. McGrath (Ed.), *Social and psychological factors in stress* (pp. 264–286). Austin, TX: Holt, Rinehart and Winston.

Hines. R. (2007). Natural disaster and gender inequality: The 2004 tsunami and the case of India. *Race, Gender, and Class, 14*, 60–68.

Kendra, J. M., and Wachtendorf, T. (2003a). Creativity in emergency response after the World Trade Center attack. In *Beyond September 11: An account of post-disaster research* (pp. 121–146). Special publication no. 39. Boulder: Natural Hazards Center, University of Colorado.

———. (2003b). Reconsidering convergence and converger legitimacy in response to the World Trade Center disaster. In L. Clarke (Ed.), *Terrorism and disaster: New threats, new ideas* (pp. 97–122). Research in Social Problems and Public Policy, vol. 11. New York: Elsevier.

Kilijanek, T. S., and Drabek, T. E. (1979). Assessing long-term impacts of a natural disaster: A focus on the elderly. *Gerontologist, 19*, 555–566.

Langewiesche, W. (2002). *American ground: Unbuilding the World Trade Center.* New York: North Point Press.

Laska, S. (2008). The "Mother of all Rorschachs": Katrina recovery in New Orleans. *Sociological Inquiry, 78*, 580–591.

Mileti, D. S. (1999). *Disasters by design: A reassessment of natural hazards in the United States.* Washington, DC: Joseph Henry Press.

Mileti, D. S., Drabek, T. E., and Haas, J. E. (1975). *Human systems in extreme environments: A sociological perspective.* Monograph no. 21. Boulder: Natural Hazards Center, University of Colorado.

Monahan, B. A. (2006). Media, September 11, and the collective valorization of the FDNY: Exploring the status implications of mediated representations. Paper presented at the annual meeting of the American Sociological Association, Montreal, August 11.

———. (2010). *The shock of the news: Media coverage and the making of 9/11.* New York: New York University Press.

National Research Council. (2006). *Facing hazards and disasters: Understanding human dimensions.* Washington, DC: National Academies Press.

Neria, Y., Gross, R., Marshall, R., and Susser, E. (Eds.). (2006). *9/11: Mental health in the wake of the terrorist attacks.* New York: Cambridge University Press.

Norris, F. H., Friedman, M. J., Watson, P. J., Byrne, C. M., Diaz, E., and Kaniasty, K. (2002). 60,000 disaster victims speak. Part 1: An empirical review of the empirical literature, 1981–2001. *Psychiatry, 65*, 207–239.

Peacock, W. G., Morrow, B. H., and Gladwin, H. (1997). *Hurricane Andrew: Ethnicity, gender, and the sociology of disasters.* New York: Routledge.

Peek, L. (2004). Backlash mitigation plan: Protecting ethnic and religious minorities following a terrorist attack. *Journal of the American Society of Professional Emergency Planners, 11*(1), 115–122.

———. (2008). Children and disasters: Understanding vulnerability, developing capacities, and promoting resilience—an introduction. *Children, Youth, and Environments, 18*(1), 1–29.

Peek, L., and Stough, L. (2010). Children with disabilities in the context of disaster: A social vulnerability perspective. *Child Development, 81*(4), 1260–1270.

Phillips, B. (1990). Gender as a variable in emergency response. In R. Bolin (Ed.), *The Loma Prieta earthquake: Studies of short-term impacts* (pp. 84–90). Monograph no. 50. Boulder: Natural Hazards Center, University of Colorado.

———. (1998). Sheltering and housing of low-income and minority groups in Santa Cruz County after the Loma Prieta earthquake. In J. M. Nigg (Ed.), *The Loma Prieta, California, Earthquake of October 17, 1989: Recovery, mitigation, and reconstruction.* U.S. Geological Survey professional paper 1553-d. Washington, DC: U.S. Department of the Interior.

Phillips, B., Thomas, D., Fothergill, A., and Blinn-Pike, L. (2009). *Social vulnerability to disasters.* Boca Raton, FL: CRC Press.

Pincha, C. (2008). *Indian Ocean tsunami through the gender lens: Insights from Tamil Nadu, India.* Mumbai: Earthworm Books for Oxfam America.

Reed, B. (Ed.). (2002). *Nothing sacred: Women respond to religious fundamentalism and terror.* New York: Nation Books.

Rodriguez, H., Wachtendorf, T., Kendra, J., and Trainor, J. (2006). A snapshot of the 2004 Indian Ocean tsunami: Societal impacts and consequences. *Disaster Prevention and Management, 15*, 163–177.

Scanlon, J. (1998). The perspective of gender: A missing element in disaster response. In E. Enarson and B. H. Morrow (Eds.), *The gendered terrain of disaster: Through women's eyes* (pp. 45–51). Westport, CT: Greenwood.

Solnit, R. (2010). Reconstructing the story of the storm: Hurricane Katrina at five. *Nation,* September 15. Available at *www.thenation.com.*

Stallings, R. A., and Quarantelli, E. L. (1985). Emergent citizen groups in emergency management. *Public Administration Review, 45*, 93–100.

Tierney, K. J. (2002). The field turns fifty: Social change and the practice of disaster field work. In R. A. Stallings (Ed.), *Methods of disaster research* (pp. 349–374). Philadelphia: Xlibris.

Tierney, K. J., and Bevc, C. (2010). Disaster as war: Militarism and the social construction of disaster in New Orleans. In D. Brunsma, S. Overfelt, and S. Picou (Eds.), *The sociology of Katrina: Perspectives on a modern catastrophe* (pp. 37–54). 2nd ed. Lanham, MD: Rowman and Littlefield.

Tierney, K. J., Bevc, C., and Kuligowski, E. (2006). Metaphors matter: Disaster myths, media frames, and their consequences in Hurricane Katrina. *Annals of the American Academy of Political and Social Science, 604* (March), 57–81.

Tierney, K. J., Petak, W., and Hahn, H. (1986). *Disabled persons and earthquake hazards.* Monograph no. 46. Boulder: Natural Hazards Center, University of Colorado.

Turner, R., Nigg, J. M., and Heller Paz, D. (1986). *Waiting for disaster: Earthquake watch in California.* Berkeley: University of California Press.

Wachtendorf, T. (2004). Improvising 9/11: Organizational improvisation in the World Trade Center disaster. PhD diss., University of Delaware.

Wachtendorf, T., Kendra, J. M., Rodriguez, H., and Trainor, J. (2006). The social impacts and consequences of the December 2004 Indian Ocean tsunamis: Observations from India and Sri Lanka. *Earthquake Spectra, 2*(S3), 693–714.

Wenger, D. E. (1987). Collective behavior and disaster research. In R. R. Dynes, B. DeMarchi, and C. Pelanda (Eds.), *Sociology of disasters: Contribution of sociology to disaster research* (pp. 213–237). Milan: Franco Angeli.

Yonder, A., Akcar, S., and Gopalan, P. (2005). Women's participation in disaster relief and recovery. SEEDS. Pamphlet no. 22. New York: Population Council.

Zahran, S., Peek, L., and Brody, S. D. (2008). Youth mortality by forces of nature. *Children, Youth, and Environments, 18*(1), 371–388.

Index

The letter t *after a page number refers to a table.*